GOOD FAITH AND RELATIONAL CONTRACTS

This book explores the use of the doctrine of good faith in the common law when interpreting contracts and resolving disputes. This doctrine is well-accepted in civil law, is reflected in international commercial law, and is a fundamental aspect of private law in the USA. However, its use in the UK is extremely limited. Inconsistent application has given rise to confusion and uncertainty. This apparent antipathy is somewhat hard to fathom, given its previous widespread acceptance in English law.

The book explains in depth the history of good faith in English law, and clarifies its current status in English, Australian and international law. It explores the relationship between good faith within contractual relations and the neighbour principle in tort law, and notes the workability of good faith in the commercial context of insurance. This will be welcomed by contract lawyers in both common law and civil law jurisdictions. A subsequent volume will explore how acceptance of good faith in the law might lead to a re-interpretation of existing contract law doctrine.

Volume 48 in the series Hart Studies in Private Law

Good Faith and Relational Contracts

Theory, Practice and Future Developments

Anthony Gray

•HART•
OXFORD • LONDON • NEW YORK • NEW DELHI • SYDNEY

HART PUBLISHING

Bloomsbury Publishing Plc

Kemp House, Chawley Park, Cumnor Hill, Oxford, OX2 9PH, UK

1385 Broadway, New York, NY 10018, USA

29 Earlsfort Terrace, Dublin 2, Ireland

HART PUBLISHING, the Hart/Stag logo, BLOOMSBURY and the Diana logo are trademarks of Bloomsbury Publishing Plc

First published in Great Britain 2024

A catalogue record for this book is available from the British Library.

A catalogue record for this book is available from the Library of Congress.

Library of Congress Control Number: 2024940182

ISBN: HB: 978-1-50997-305-7
ePDF: 978-1-50997-307-1
ePub: 978-1-50997-306-4

Typeset by Compuscript Ltd, Shannon

ACKNOWLEDGEMENTS

This book is dedicated to my mother, who passed away during the period in which the book was written. She in particular lived her life in a selfless manner, putting others first. She lived by the motto of 'do unto others as you would have them do to you'. Typically, her very last words to my family and me reflected her concern with us, not with herself and her situation. She had no legal training, but she inculcated in me this fundamental principle. I have learned the value of applying this principle to a much broader canvas, the law that regulates the relations between contracting parties. Though the canvas differs, the principle of having due regard to others holds. It is a good way to live one's life. This book argues it is a good basis for our contract law.

CONTENTS

TABLE OF CASES

Introduction

In a 1993 Masters' class, I first heard about a recent development where an Australian court in the *Renard Constructions* case had found that contractual powers were subject to a doctrine of good faith. I have had an interest in good faith since that time. I flirted with doing my PhD on the subject. I am very pleased that now, finally, 30 years after my initial interest, I have been able to give my full attention to the subject, as it deserves.

There were numerous questions in my mind when I considered good faith as it applied to contract. I had read about the English 'hostility' towards the doctrine, and wondered why. I resolved to find out the history of this. Chapter one of the book traces the history of good faith back to early Roman law, and its initial transplant to England through various channels. I then wanted to understand whether English acceptance and adoption of good faith was widespread. Thus I did a search through the English Reports of all express references to good faith. I was particularly interested in the contractual context, of course, but references elsewhere would also assist in developing the picture regarding the extent to which the doctrine was applied in English law. I read hundreds of cases. I found that it was accepted and applied to many disparate areas of English law, for many years. The fruits of that exercise form the basis of chapter two.

I then wanted to understand how we got from this picture of widespread apparent acceptance of good faith to a situation of 'hostility' towards the doctrine. Thus, chapter three is devoted to understanding the significance of freedom of contract during the nineteenth century in particular, and how it led the law away from notions of good faith, with the promise of certainty and predictability. The lessons from Roman times might have taught that, one way or the other, the law has a need for flexibility in order to do justice. The Romans had moved away from rigid contracting rules, because they did not permit justice in particular cases. However, this learning was apparently lost in the industrial revolution and economic theories of capitalism that reified supposed certainty over all else, even if the certainty it promised would prove illusory. Chapter four charts the inevitable movement to provide more flexibility.

I thought it important to document the important debate regarding whether good faith is really 'foreign' to English law, as some claim, to support an argument it should not be imported. A different, potentially inconsistent, argument, against good faith is that it is not necessary because the law already reflects it. Hopefully the documented history scotches the first argument; the second argument has more force, but can be met with an argument based on transparency. Further, there is evidence that in order to get to results which good faith would suggest and support, courts are twisting the law, twisting the facts, or both. This is not desirable. The remainder of chapter five then documents how good faith has developed in a piecemeal manner in the courts. Though the decision in Yam Seng showed promise, progress has been slow. English courts continue to deny that good faith is a general organising principle in the common law. They limit it to conditioning of contractual discretion, and in particular classes of contract that are 'relational'. Neither limit is particularly defensible on intellectual grounds; it appears courts are very wary of the principle and limit its development to a case by case basis. Again, the court is seduced by arguments it would create intolerable uncertainty. Chapter six documents developments elsewhere. Canadian contract law has accepted good faith as a general organising principle of the common law. United States has recognised the doctrine for many years, as have international contract law instruments. Sub-national courts in Australia recognise and apply the doctrine. At the time of writing, Australia's highest court refuses to place its cards on the table. This is regrettable.

Chapters seven and eight provide the intellectual basis for recognition of a generalised good faith doctrine. Scholars such as Ian Macneil and Stewart Macaulay argue that the assumptions typically made by the law of contract, regarding individuals being rational utility maximisers who can negotiate a deal most advantageous to them, and that the written contract is taken to reflect the parties' entire agreement, are not typically accurate. They argue that traditional contract law unacceptably ignores the importance of the relationship between the parties. Acceptance of this theory potentially has very significant implications for the law of contract. These chapters seek to draw some of these out. Of all areas of the law, commercial law typically hems closely to commercial practice. An allegation that contract law does not gel with the realities of how contracts typically run has a pungency that would not exist in other areas of the law.

Chapter nine considers how our approach to contractual interpretation might change if a relational view of contract were accepted. One specific issue is the question of the relevance of actual performance in terms of contract interpretation. Traditionally this was ignored, based on the parol evidence rule, though English courts have modified their position. The chapter demonstrates that acceptance of relational contract theory would enable courts to look at contractual relationships in a more holistic manner, not expecting that all of the parties' agreement is reflected in the written terms, being prepared to consider actual performance, and evidence of pre-contractual discussions.

Chapter ten considers the interplay between good faith in contract generally, and principles of negligence. There is a long history of the connection between these principles. The essential idea is that if the law of negligence requires individuals to be other-regarding and to have others (mostly strangers) in our contemplation when considering activity, it should not be such a stretch to require contract law to require contracting parties to be other-regarding when deciding how to act in relation to a contract. The lengthy history and overlap between liability in contract and tort is considered here, to encourage use of 'neighbour'-type analysis to further support a rule that contracting parties have due regard to the interests of the other contracting party. And good faith in insurance is briefly considered to demonstrate that such a doctrine is entirely feasible in a commercial contracting environment.

The book is considered to be a blend of the historical, the practical and the theoretical. History should teach us that, one way or the other, the law will find ways to escape the rigidities of rules promising 'certainty'. The desire for justice is innate and too strong. It is reflected in Roman law, and it will be reflected in our law. Shutting out good faith to keep uncertainty at bay will not work. The practicalities of contracting are reflected in numerous practical studies that demonstrate a serious mismatch between contracting rules and contracting practice. This must be addressed. The book has provided a theoretical model that has most potential to justify and support recognition of good faith in contracting. Adopting this doctrine would be a step towards aligning the contract law with contract expectations. It is time to end the 'hostility' to good faith.

1

Good Faith in Roman Law and its Transplant to England

I. Earliest Times

There is evidence of fairness in contractual dealings from the earliest times. Herodotus (484–425BC) recounts an early form of barter. The Carthagians were reported to visit a particular place in modern day Libya. They unloaded their wares upon the beach. After returning to their ship, they created a great smoke. Those with whom they wished to trade would see the smoke and enter upon the beach to inspect the wares. They lay out the quantity of gold they are prepared to pay for the wares. The Carthagians return to the beach. If they believe the deposited gold is sufficient, they take it; if not, they return to their ship. Those with the gold then return and add more until the quantity is sufficient for the Carthagians. The Carthagians do not touch the gold until the offer is sufficient, and the others do not touch the wares until the Carthagians have indicated they are satisfied with the quantity proferred.[1] This example is taken to reflect that traditionally, individuals engaged in contractual relations with scrupulous fairness, reflecting ancient customs and norms of behaviour.[2]

Classic Greek philosophy recognised the idea of the 'good'. Aristotle emphasised the link between the good and actions. Actions are aimed at achieving the good.[3] The end of these actions is happiness. Happiness includes honour.[4] These ideas, and the business customs which exemplify them, became reflected in Greek law.[5] The idea of the good is related to good faith.[6]

[1] FRB Godolphin (ed) and George Rawlinson (trans), 1 *The Greek Historians* (New York, Random House, 1942) 292.

[2] N Palmieri, 'Good Faith Disclosures Required During Precontractual Negotiations' (1993) 24 *Seton Hall Law Review* 70, 80.

[3] *Nichomachean Ethics* Book 1, 1094a.

[4] ibid, 1097b.

[5] 'The Greeks … saw good faith as a universal social force that governed their social interrelationships – that is, each citizen had an obligation to act in good faith towards all citizens': E Holmes, 'A Contextual Study of Commercial Good Faith: Good Faith Disclosure in Contract Formation' (1978) 39 *University of Pittsburgh Law Review* 381, 402.

[6] S Corcoran, 'Good Faith as a Principle of Interpretation: What is the Positive Content of Good Faith?' (2012) 36 *Australian Bar Review* 1, 3.

II. Good Faith in Roman Law

The Romans adapted these ideas. Cicero's *The Good Life* also recognises the link between integrity and happiness. In *On Duties*, Cicero called good faith the foundation of justice.[7] Scaevola said that it 'permeate(d) throughout' the Roman legal system.[8] There are links between good faith and natural law.[9] It is suggested that good faith (bona fides) appeared in Roman law by the second century BC.[10] These ideas were also reflected in the Institutes of Gaius (second century AD) and Corpus Iuris of Justinian (533 AD).[11] The latter states that 'it cannot be provided by agreement that a person shall not be responsible for bad faith'.[12] Good faith was broader than an absence of bad faith.[13]

Roman law originated with a series of strict rules (*ius civile*) which included forms of civil action (*legis actiones*). Early forms in the area we would now recognise as contract include the *nexum*, *mancipatio* and *mutuum*.[14] The first two of these were particularly formal, involving a required five witnesses and a ritual ceremony. *Mutuum* was more informal. These suited conflicts that involved something definite and express (*re*). This limited their scope, and appeal. They could not apply to many typical transactions in Roman society which lacked the required strictness in scope.[15] An example of the strictness of this rule is that the *ius civile* provided no remedy to one who only entered into a contract through being compelled by fear, or one who only did so under duress.[16] They were considered legally bound by their bargains.

However their harshness and inflexibility were ameliorated by the praetor's yearly edicts (*ius honorarium*), which supplemented the *ius civile*. The praetor distinguished obligations as being either *stricti juris*, to which the *ius civile* would apply, or *bonae fidei*, where a more flexible approach would apply.[17] In turn, judges

[7] JF O'Connor, *Good Faith in English Law* (Aldershot, Dartmouth, 1991) 22. He refers to an obligation of disclosure as inherent in a good faith requirement: *On Obligations* (PG Walsh trans) (Oxford, Oxford University Press, 2000) Book 3, 54, 57; G McMeel, 'Foucault's Pendulum: Text, Context and Good Faith in Contract Law' (2017) 70(1) *Current Legal Problems* 365, 387–88.

[8] F Pastori, *Gli Istituti Romanistici Come Storia E Vita Del. Diritto* 3rd edn (Milan, Cisalpino, 1992) 740–41.

[9] HA Rommen, *The Natural Law: A Study in Legal and Social History and Philosophy* 4 (St Louis, B Herder Book Co, 1947); Hugo Grotius (a natural law scholar) noted: 'a person who is making a contract with anyone ought to point out to him the faults of the thing concerned in the transaction which are known to himself': *De Jure Belli ac Pacis* (1625) reprinted in 2 *Classics of International Law* (London, Clarendon Press, 1925) Ch XII, ix.

[10] B Nicholas, *An Introduction to Roman Law* (Oxford, Clarendon Press, 1962) 163.

[11] Corcoran (n 6) 3–4.

[12] Justinian's *Digest*, II.XIV.27.3.

[13] Palmieri (n 2) 81.

[14] W Burdick, *The Principles of Roman Law and their Relation to Modern Law* (Rochester, Lawyers Cooperative Publishing, 1938) 432–33.

[15] R Powell, 'Good Faith in Contracts' (1956) 9(1) *Current Legal Problems* 16, 19.

[16] Burdick (n 14) 395–97.

[17] ibid 391.

would later exercise this discretion in resolving disputes, applying good faith to achieve just results that may not have occurred if the fixed rules had applied.[18] The praetor refused to enforce contracts tainted by threats or duress. It is suggested that good faith entered Roman law through the *ius honorarium*.[19] Good faith seems to have reflected the practice of merchants in these times. It did not, at least originally, have a moral basis.

In Gaius's time Roman law recognised four types of contract. One of these was the strict *iuris* (formal) contract such as the *stipulatio*, where all terms had to be expressed. The contract here was only created through a particular process involving the use of certain binding words. The stipulation encompassed most of the range of formal-type contracts that previously existed, but permitted contracts to be made verbally rather than in writing. This trend, away from the focus on the written and towards acceptance of verbal agreements, was linked to the increased use of the discretion granted to judges through the *ius honorarium* just discussed.[20]

Another one of these was the consensual contract, which was most commonly used for standard commercial contracting, including sales transactions, leases, employment contracts and partnerships. Consensual contracts were all subject to a requirement of good faith.[21] Consignment sales were also so subject.[22] It was recognised that for these contracts the other types of contract, *re* (based on a specific thing) and *stipulatio* (verbal) may not be suitable. There was a practical need to create a binding contractual arrangement that was not ritual based. Thus the praetor effectively created a different class of contracts.[23] This contract did not require every single promise or expected norm of behaviour to be spelled out expressly in the contract, as the earlier contracts had. It was sufficient that basic promises were agreed between the parties.[24] It was recognised that consensual contracts required a meeting of the minds, and that defects in the contract could mean that such a meeting did not exist. One such defect was *dolus*, which included fraud or bad faith. If the decision maker determined that a contract was affected by *dolus*, they might refuse to enforce it.[25] Or alternatively they might determine

[18] MJ Schermaier, 'Bona Fides in Roman Contract Law' in R Zimmermann and S Whittaker (ed), *Good Faith in European Contract Law* (Cambridge, Cambridge University Press, 2000) 76; WT Tete, 'Tort Roots and Ramifications of the Obligations Revision' (1986) 32 *Loyola Law Review* 47, 58.

[19] Schermaier (n 18) 74: 'in the course of the second century BC … bona fides had ceased to be a merely ethical yardstick of contractual liability and had been incorporated into the praetorian law'. There are obvious parallels with English law here, with the sometimes harsh rules of the common law being supplemented by the more flexible rules of equity, as will be discussed later in the chapter. It should be noted, though, that Roman law also developed the principle of *aequitas* (equity) and *bonum et aequum* (doing what is right).

[20] S Litvinoff, 'Good Faith' (1997) 71 *Tulane Law Review* 1645, 1652.

[21] DJ Ibbetson, *A Historical Introduction to the Law of Obligations* (Oxford, Oxford University Press, 1999) 8.

[22] R Zimmermann, *The Law of Obligations Roman Foundations of the Civilian Tradition* (Oxford, Oxford University Press, 1990) 536.

[23] Burdick (n 14) 442.

[24] Litvinoff (n 20) 1652.

[25] Corcoran (n 6) 4.

that the plaintiff was entitled to compensation for the failure of the other to act in good faith, or that the plaintiff's compensation might be reduced due to their lack of good faith.[26] Good faith also applied to agency-type situations.[27]

The requirement of good faith in Roman law primarily related to good faith in performance of the contract.[28] It included taking care of the thing agreed to be sold until it was delivered to the purchaser.[29] Recognition of this principle mitigated previous acceptance of a caveat emptor rule. One of the claimed advantages of the principle of good faith at this time was the flexibility it provided, given that it was unrealistic to expect the parties to be able to reduce all of the details of their agreement to writing:

> Even where the promise was uncertain, the obligation that resulted was not precisely defined in its details. The parties were bound to perform what could be required fairly and reasonably under the circumstances of the case, and certain duties were imposed upon them by the very nature of the transaction, whether expressly undertaken or not.[30]

Pound also noted the Roman notion of good faith as 'the idea that justice demands one should not disappoint well founded expectations which he has created; the idea that it is not so important that rules should be certain as that men's conduct should be certain'.[31] As Pound recognises, from Roman days the reality was recognised that contracts would not expressly specify every expectation the parties had of the other, there was an expectation of reasonable and fair behaviour by the other, the fact that contractual obligations might exist which were not expressly stated, that the fact of the contract having been made could create reasonable expectations in the minds of both parties and a response to the criticism that such rules make contracts certain, by arguing that a requirement that parties act reasonably in itself serves to create some certainty.

As Zimmermann summarises it:

> It was with the consensual contracts that the wider and more liberal manner of interpretation gained ground. Here one did not necessarily have to stick to the meaning that was typically associated with the words contained in formal declarations, but one could freely take into consideration, and was on account of the 'ex bona fide' clause even encouraged to do so, the individual circumstances of each case.[32]

[26] W Tetley, Good Faith in Contract: Particularly in the Contracts of Arbitration and Chartering (2004) 35 *Journal of Maritime Law and Commerce* 561, 566.

[27] Zimmermann (n 22) 437.

[28] A Farnsworth, 'Good Faith Performance and Commercial Reasonableness under the Uniform Commercial Code' (1962–63) 30 *University of Chicago Law Review* 666, 670. Farnsworth distinguishes between 'good faith performance', relating to fairness and reasonableness in contractual performance or enforcement, and 'good faith purchase', referring to lack of notice of wrongdoing (668).

[29] Burdick (n 14) 444.

[30] R Pound, *Jurisprudence Volume 1* (St Paul, West Publishing, 1959) 414; Zimmermann (n 22) 385: 'the contents of the contract and all details of the parties' obligations were determined by the agreement of the parties; failing that, by the standard of (good faith)'.

[31] Pound (n 30) 413.

[32] Zimmermann (n 22) 627.

In Roman times good faith meant trustworthiness, conscientious behaviour and honourable conduct.[33] It also provided a remedy for duress-type behaviour in relation to the formation of a contract.[34] It was utilised against a contracting party, in a situation where the effective performance of the contract was subject to a condition, who did something to prevent the fulfilment of that condition.[35]

It seemed to emanate more from a wish to have ordinary business practice reflected in the legal principles applied to resolve business disputes, rather than the conscious insertion of ethical principles to business.[36] It was based on reasonable expectation – both parties were expected to act with honour and probity, and the law enforced this expectation by imposing a good faith requirement. This was not merely a tool of interpretation of the written terms.[37]

Cicero provides numerous examples of the good faith enshrined in aspects of Roman law. This includes a merchant who arrives with a ship full of grain when there is a famine, who does not disclose that other merchants are on their way; a person selling a house with known defects; and a person acting in a situation of a conflict of interest.[38] The examples relate to non-disclosure and taking advantage of a vulnerable individual. He defined good faith broadly, stating the words

> express all the honest sentiments of a good conscience, without requiring a scrupulousness which would turn selflessness into sacrifice; the law banishes from contracts ruses and clever manoeuvres, dishonest dealings, fraudulent calculations, dissimulations and perfidious simulations and malice, which under the guise of prudence and skill, takes advantage of credulity, simplicity and ignorance.[39]

We learn more about the nature of good faith in these times because of the recognition of *dolus*. Effectively *dolus* was the opposite of good faith. *Dolus* was something of an exception where the courts would refuse assistance to someone found to have committed it. Zimmermann notes that *dolus* was broader than deceit or trickery. It includes plaintiffs who might 'turn a situation to his advantage against the precepts of natural equity'.[40] It meant conduct in which a good Roman would not have engaged.[41] Zimmermann notes that the Romans determined good faith in accordance with generally accepted standards of business decency, not abstract moral philosophy.[42]

Zimmermann uses an example of a sales contract where the purchaser agrees to pay a fixed sum for the number of fish caught by fishers during the season. Good faith applied to such a contract, and would require them to 'cast their net and to

[33] O'Connor (n 7) 117.
[34] Zimmermann (n 22) 652.
[35] ibid 730.
[36] Powell (n 15) 20–21.
[37] Litvinoff (n 20) 1652.
[38] P Thomas, 'Late Republican (R)evolutions in Roman Law' (2020) 65 *SUBBiur* 992. The non-disclosure case is discussed in Schermaier (n 18) 66–68.
[39] Cicero, *De Officiis* 3.17.
[40] Zimmermann (n 22) 668.
[41] ibid 669.
[42] ibid.

make a reasonable effort to procure a good haul'.[43] It included that the purchaser of something would have a continuing right to enjoy it.[44] If a person took a lease of agricultural land, good faith would require they did not permit the land to lay fallow.[45] A guarantor would act without good faith if they paid the debtor's debt, but did not tell the debtor, leading them to pay again.[46]

Good faith also seemed to involve a kind of enlarged duty of care. For example, if a party had contracted to sell property to another, they were required to take special care of the thing until it was transferred to the purchaser. Zimmermann notes the link between good faith and gross negligence: 'even grossly negligent behaviour can hardly be regarded as reconcilable … with … Roman good faith'.[47]

There was also a kind of implied warranty regarding the quality of what the seller was selling associated with the good faith requirement. Similar rules applied to lease arrangements as applied to conveyances. For example, if the lessor leased premises to the lessee for a particular purpose, there was an implied promise by the lessor that the land could lawfully or suitably be used for such a purpose.[48] A vendor was held to have acted with a lack of good faith where they sold something with a defect known to them, without disclosing it, or assured the purchaser during negotiations that the thing the subject of the contract was free from particular defects or possessed particular qualities, where this was not true.[49]

Different views were expressed as to the kinds of contracts that were subject to the requirement of good faith. Cicero indicated such a requirement applied to contracts of sale, contracts for work, lease, agency, fiduciary relationships and guardianship.[50] Later Gaius expanded the list to include cases where a person takes over the affairs of another, banking, partnerships, family law. Later Justinian increased the list to include pledges, property division claims, succession disputes and the contractual action *praecriptis uerbis*.[51] Eventually, the consensual contracts became dominant in Roman law. Thus, contracts in general became subject to good faith.[52] Obviously, principles of good faith were translated to domestic laws in other parts of Europe.[53]

It is interesting that in an 1800 decision, reflecting on the practice of exchanging prisoners during wartime, the court considered the good faith of the masters of the vessels transporting the prisoners, and the governments that had engaged their services. The court noted that good faith was long-running and

[43] ibid 247–48.
[44] ibid 297.
[45] ibid 375.
[46] ibid 428.
[47] ibid 463.
[48] Burdick (n 14) 444–49.
[49] Zimmermann (n 22) 309 (good faith and reliance were relevant here).
[50] Schermaier (n 18) 70.
[51] A Triggiano, *Holistic Analysis of Law, Connecting Theory and Practice: Universal Solutions to Global Problems* (Newcastle, Cambridge Scholars Publishing, 2023) 51–53.
[52] Zimmermann (n 22) 548.
[53] For example, s157 BGB (Germany) requires courts to interpret contracts according to good faith and consistently with common usage.

well-established within Europe: 'the most scrupulous attention to good faith has always been observed by the old governments of Europe', and that this was a principle upon which the public affairs of Europe had always been managed.[54] And a judge in 1803 noted the good faith 'which has always marked the proceedings of the British Government' in relation to a British licence held by a foreign citizen, at a time of war.[55]

III. Influence of Roman Contract Law Elsewhere

The ceremonial aspect of agreement making originally featured in Roman law was adapted in other jurisdictions. Pollock and Maitland noted the use by the Franks and Lombards of a binding contractual ceremony known as the *fides facta*.[56] The ceremony would typically occur in court, with parties 'making faith' with the other. Ecclesiastical courts were developed in England, and these embraced the *fides facta*. Those engaged in contractual dealings put their salvation up as security for their performance.[57] Sometimes, a third party (*fideiussor*) is involved in this ceremony. They are often a person with coercive power over the promisor, such as a bishop or sheriff. The *fideiussor*'s role was to encourage the promisor to fulfil their promise/s. The ecclesiastic courts were heavily influenced by Roman law.[58]

There is evidence of the use of Roman law in England from a very early stage in its history. Ethelbert, King of Kent, compiled laws of his kingdom circa 600 AD. His wife was French, and in making his compilation, he acknowledged he did so 'according to the example of the Romans'.[59] William the Conqueror introduced a feudal system of land ownership to England based on the Roman model.[60] His prime minister and chief adviser was an Italian scholar steeped in Roman law.

The reign of Henry II is well-known for its substantive reform of the administration and structure of the English legal system. The legal system was centralised and staffed with professional, full-time judges, and what we would now recognise to be the jury system introduced. Henry II was born in France. During his reign, what is believed to be the first book on English law, *A Treatise on the Laws and Customs of the Kingdom of England*,[61] was published. It was probably authored by

[54] *The "Daifjie"* (1800) 3 C. Rob. 139, 146; 165 ER 414, 417 (Sir W Scott).

[55] *The "Planter's Wensch"* (1803) 5 C. Rob. 22, 26–27; 165 ER 683, 685 (Sir W Scott).

[56] F Pollock and F Wiliam Maitland, *The History of English Law Vol 2 Before the Time of Edward I* (Cambridge, Cambridge University Press, 1895) 184–86.

[57] ibid 196: 'in the earliest years of Henry II's reign, the ecclesiastical tribunals, even the Roman curia, were busy over agreements made by Englishmen with pledge of faith'.

[58] Burdick (n 14) 66: 'the ecclesiastical courts … administered the canon law of the continent. This body of law … was permeated with many principles of (Roman civil law), the procedure being almost entirely derived from Roman law'.

[59] Bede, *Historium Ecclesiastical Gentis Anglorum* (1735) 2, 5.

[60] Burdick (n 14) 64–65.

[61] R de Glanville, *Tractatus de Legibus et Consuetudinibus Regni Angliae* (estimated to be published between 1180–90).

Glanville. The book bears structural similarities to the Justinian Institutes, and it regularly compares English law Roman and Canon law. In relation to contracts, much of the language is similar to that of Roman times.[62]

Further, Bracton's *The Laws and Customs of England* in the mid-thirteenth century is very well known. Though it continues to excite debate as to the extent to which it actually reflects English case law, there is no doubt that in significant respects it reflects Roman law. Spence suggests that Bracton's work reflects mainly English law, and is not simply a copy of Roman law.[63] Burdick notes discovery of a manuscript by Bracton containing marginal notes against approximately 2000 English cases, which leads support to the view that The Laws and Customs of England did substantially reflect actual English law.[64] Roman law was taught at Oxford and Cambridge Universities in the twelfth and thirteenth centuries respectively.

Specialist courts received Roman law. The ecclesiastical courts enforced canon law of the continent. There were significant similarities between canon law and Roman civilian law. As has been shown, good faith was an essential aspect of Roman law. Canon law also regarded good faith as a universal moral norm.[65] Henry II appointed prelates of the church as his justices. Through this channel as well, good faith came to English law.[66] Simpson notes that from the time of Aquinas, Christian moralists argued for high ethical standards in contract bargaining, in response to the growth of trade in the high Middle Ages.[67] The canon lawyers naturally placed good faith within a moral context.[68] Holdsworth notes that canon law

> put into legal form the religious and moral ideas which … coloured the economic thought of all the nations of Europe (and) … contributed to enforce those high standards of good faith and fair dealing which are the very life of the trade.[69]

Maritime courts enforced maritime law, much of which was derived from Roman law, as influenced by the commercial practices of merchants on the Mediterranean Sea and Atlantic Ocean. It is well known that the law merchant became very significant in the development of English commercial law, with Lord Mansfield recognised as playing a leading role in having the law merchant adopted in the English common law. Lord Mansfield was Scottish, and learned in Roman law. The traditionally strong influence of good faith on mercantile law has been noted,[70] and will be explained in more detail later in the book.

[62] Burdick (n 14) 68–71.
[63] 72.
[64] Burdick (n 14) 72.
[65] Holmes (n 5) 402.
[66] O'Connor (n 7) 2 stating that the appointment of prelates as justices 'was the decisive event in the history of the development of good faith in common law because it ensured the institutionalisation of the Roman canon law concept of bona fides in that system. Even the most superficial acquaintance with canon law would include some knowledge of that system's assimilation of the Roman law bona fides with the notion of Christian conscience'; Powell (n 15) 21.
[67] AWB Simpson, 'The Horwitz Thesis and the History of Contracts' (1979) 46(3) *University of Chicago Law Review* 533, 536.
[68] Powell (n 15) 21.
[69] W Holdsworth, *A History of English Law* 2nd edn (London, Sweet and Maxwell, 1937) 79–81.
[70] O'Connor (n 7) 4–5.

The Chancery court was established in the mid-fourteenth century. Edward III ordered that all judicial matters 'of Grace' should be dealt with in this court. The Chancellor who headed this court was a senior member of the Church.[71] It dealt with many matters where the remedy in the ordinary courts was inadequate or non-existent. The Chancellor applied principles of good conscience and fairness in determining matters. In this respect, there was some overlap with the ecclesiastical courts and Chancery law was derived in part from canon law.[72] There is a record of a 1468 proceeding in Chancery court involving breach of an oral promise. The defendant argued that the plaintiff's remedy was (only) in the ecclesiastical court, not Chancery. The Chancellor confirmed that breach of faith actions could attract a remedy in Chancery.[73] Petitions to the Court preyed that the Court decide a dispute as 'truth, good faith and conscience require'. One specific example is *Bellers Case*, where Bellers sought the Chancellor's assistance on the basis that his debtors would act 'against faith and good conscience'.[74] O'Connor calls good faith the principle that lies 'deepest in (the) structure' of the Court of Chancery, its very jurisdiction based upon it.[75] There are obvious parallels here with the practice of the Roman praetor in applying equitable principles to achieve justice in a particular case, thereby altering the law available to resolve future cases. At this time, the equity court was providing remedies that were simply not available in the common law.

Probably the most important example of the acceptance of good faith in the Court of Chancery was its acceptance in the mid-fifteenth century that a breach of a contractual promise was actionable at the hands of the party to whom the promise was made who suffered loss as a result of the breach. This was because the breach of the contractual promise was a breach of good faith. This provided a remedy that was not then recognised in the common law.[76] The common law would subsequently accept this position and the action for breach of contract was established in the legal system with development of the action for assumpsit.[77] Pleadings in equity at this time typically asked the Chancellor to do as good faith required.[78]

[71] Powell (n 15) 22.

[72] Corcoran (n 6) 5.

[73] *Anon.* (1468), Y.B. Pasch. 8 Ed. IV, f. 4, pl. 11: 'you say that for breach of faith he must sue by the Canon Law, but in this case, because he is damaged by the non-performance of the promise, he shall have a remedy here' (quoted in CHS Fifoot, *History and Sources of the Common Law Tort and Contract* (London, Steven & Sons, Limited, 1949) 303.

[74] *Bellers Case* (Cited as After AD 1432), Willard Barbour, *The History of Contract in Early English Equity* (4 Oxford Studies in Social and Legal History, Oxford, Clarendon Press, 1914) 182.

[75] O'Connor (n 7) 2; Holmes (n 5) 422.

[76] Holmes (n 5) 421: 'in the Middle Ages the common law courts, bound to archaic categories of forms of action, had no remedy for breach of a simple contract. In the name of correcting the sinful breach of plighted faith (*fidei laesio*) the Ecclesiastical Courts interposed to enforce simple promises. Every promise was binding on the promisor's conscience, and failure to refuse to fulfil it "was a breach of that person's duty to God"' (quoting CHS Fifoot (n 73) 306).

[77] Fifoot (n 73) 18.

[78] WP Baildon and WT Barbour, 'The History of Contract in Early English Equity' 4 *Oxford Studies in Social and Legal History* (London, Clarendon Press, 1916) 182, 221, 225 and 231.

Works by Cowell[79] and Spelman[80] in the early seventeenth century reflect the strong influence of Roman law on English legal principle. The influence of Roman principle is also evident from the work of Sir Francis Bacon, John Selden and Mathew Hale. Bacon urged Elizabeth I to codify English law, using the model of how this had occurred in Rome.[81] Selden's works show great knowledge of Roman law, and Hale's History of the Common Law acknowledges the influence of Roman law on the common law of England.[82] This includes acceptance of good faith. O'Connor concludes that 'by the close of the Middle Ages in Western Europe, good faith was perceived in philosophical thinking as a universal ethical principle'.[83] It was part of a broader acceptance of equitable principles. Horwitz writes of a 'medieval tradition of substantive justice'.[84]

IV. Conclusion

Some of the earliest legal systems recognised principles of good faith. A lesson from these times is the need for flexibility regarding contractual relations. From the earliest times, the impossibility of parties agreeing on all the terms of their engagement at commencement was recognised. Good faith helped in this regard. It was a proxy for concepts such as fairness and reasonableness, and meeting parties' expectations. It was thought to simply reflect existing business practice, rather than superimpose a concept upon the parties which was unexpected. It did not originally carry moralistic overtones. It had links with concepts of negligence during this time. It originally entered English law through various channels. Key individuals in the development of English law had knowledge of Roman law. It entered through canon law and the ecclesiastical courts, the Chancery courts, charged with policing 'breach of faith', and through commercial practice, particularly in the maritime context and the law merchant more generally. The next chapter will discuss in some detail the ways in which good faith concepts were reflected in English law.

[79] J Cowell, *The Institutes of English Law* (London, 1651).

[80] 'A great part of our Common Law is derived from the Civil … the foundation of our laws … w(as) built upon and polished by material taken from the Canon and Civil laws … (our judges) sought instruction therein when they found no rule at home to guide the judgment by … they in those days judged may (sic) things *ex aequo et bono* (the right or good)': Sir H Spelman, *Of the Law Terms* (1684).

[81] Sir J Macdonnell and E Manson (ed), 2 *Great Jurists of the World* (Boston, Little, Brown and Co, Association of American Law Schools, 1914) 144–45.

[82] M Hale, *History of the Common Law* (Chicago, University of Chicago Press, 1971). I am indebted for these references to Burdick (n 14) ch 3.

[83] O'Connor (n 7) 10.

[84] MJ Horwitz, 'The Historical Foundations of Modern Contract Law' (1974) 87(5) *Harvard Law Review* 917, 917.

2

Acceptance of Good Faith in English Law Until the Mid-Nineteenth Century

I. Introduction

Before discussing the cases in some detail, some explanation is in order regarding the law merchant. This is important in the present context because much of the discussion of good faith below occurs in a commercial context. It should be acknowledged here that the law merchant was influenced and moulded by the practices of those in commerce.[1] As acknowledged in chapter one, this practice had been going on for centuries, including in relation to maritime practice. In turn, the law merchant became assimilated into the general law of commerce.[2] There is a strong argument that commercial law should reflect commercial practice.[3] Thus, these principles of commercial law, of which good faith is an important example,[4] in effect reflect the actual practices of contracting parties. They are not principles simply created or developed by the common law; rather they have a strong basis in commercial (including contractual) practice.

One other point deserves clarification. In finding the cases discussed below, I searched for cases where the words 'good faith' (or their Latin equivalent) were used. I specifically wanted examples where judges had expressly used those words

[1] *Brandao v Barnett* (1846) 3 CB 519, 530; 136 ER 207, 212: 'when a general usage has been judicially ascertained and established, it becomes part of the law merchant, which courts are bound to know and recognise. Such has been the invariable understanding and practice in Westminster Hall for a great many years' (Lord Campbell).

[2] R Davis, 'The Origin of the Duty of Disclosure Under Insurance Law' (1994) 4(1) *Insurance Law Journal* 71, 78: 'since as early as 1543 the common law recognised the usages and customs of merchants as being part of the common law' (citing WS Holdsworth's *A History of English Law* 3rd edn (London, Sweet and Maxwell, 1945)).

[3] P Devlin, 'The Relation Between Commercial Law and Commercial Practice' (1951) 14 *Modern Law Review* 249, 266: 'the law might go further than it does towards meeting the business attitude. In particular, a more generous admission into contract of custom and trade practice would be entirely in keeping with the basic principles of the law merchant and with the traditions which lie at the heart of the common law'.

[4] 'Good faith is not a foreign concept to the common law, the law merchant of businessmen and women. It has been an underlying concept in the law merchant for centuries': *United Group Rail Services Ltd v Rail Corporation New South Wales* (2009) 74 NSWLR 618, 634 (Allsop P).

in the course of their judgment, to explain the basis of their decision. This way, no-one could quibble with my classification of a case as being influenced by good faith considerations, when the courts had not specifically used those words. Now, there are other works which document other cases which the author claims to reflect good faith at work. Examples here include situations where one party to a contract has not been entirely truthful with the other, and where they have not been able to demonstrate good title to the thing they have contracted to sell. These cases are well documented elsewhere in a valuable collection.[5] However, in many of these cases the judges themselves do not *use* the words 'good faith' to describe their decision. Thus, the discussion below focusses on the cases where judges *have* specifically used the words 'good faith' in the course of their decision, describing the parties' conduct and/or the basis of their decision.

II. *Carter v Boehm* – Broad Application of Good Faith

The classic case typically cited for the reception of good faith in English contract law is the insurance case of *Carter v Boehm*.[6] There the insured had failed to disclose to the insurer material facts about the thing insured, including that it was vulnerable to the kind of event against which the insurance related. Lord Mansfield specifically engaged the concept of good faith:

> Good faith forbids either party by concealing what he privately knows, to draw the other into a bargain, from his ignorance of that fact, and his believing the contrary … the governing principle is applicable to all contracts and dealings.[7]

Lord Mansfield explained this on the basis that the failure to disclose meant that the insurer was taking on a risk different from that which they understood and intended. He noted that the relevant facts lay most commonly within the knowledge of the insured.[8] It is fundamental that Lord Mansfield considered good faith to be applicable to all contracts and dealings, and was not limited to the insurance context.

[5] R Harrison, *Good Faith in Sales* (London, Sweet & Maxwell, 1997).

[6] (1766) 3 Burr 1905; 97 ER 1162. Its correctness was accepted in *Haywood v Rodgers* (1804) 4 East 590, 596; 102 ER 957, 959 (Lord Kenyon CJ).

[7] *Carter v Boehm* (n 6) 1910; 1164; see also *Pawson v Watson* (1778) 2 Cowp 786, 788; 98 ER 1361, 1362: 'by the law of merchants, all dealings must be fair and honest' (Lord Mansfield). He also applied it in the context of the transfer of rights under a bill of lading: *Wright v Campbell* (1767) 4 Burr 2046, 2051; 98 ER 66, 69. In *Nabob of the Carnatic v East India Company* (1791) 1 Ves Jun 371, 378; 30 ER 391, 395 it was asserted by the Solicitor-General and Attorney-General that good faith was the foundation of the municipal law of England. In *Harmer v Plane* (1807) 14 Ves Jun 130, 131; 33 ER 470, 471, the plaintiff's submissions include a statement that the principle of good faith 'regulates all other contracts'. This is not controverted by the court.

[8] He applied good faith to apparently deny the need for consideration: 'where a man is under a moral obligation, which no Court of Law or Equity can inforce, and promises, the honesty (good faith) and rectitude of the thing is a consideration … the ties of conscience upon an upright man are a sufficient consideration': *Hawkes v Saunders* 1 Cowp 298; 98 ER 1091 (KB, 1782).

Similarly in a case involving sale of a ship, the court found that the seller had failed to disclose defects of which he had been aware, in circumstances where he had promised the ship was free of defects. Obviously, this was not an insurance context. Lord Kenyon noted:

> In contracts of all kinds, it is of the highest importance that courts of law should compel the observance of honesty and good faith. This was a latent defect which the plaintiffs could not … possibly discover, and which the defendants knowing of, ought to have disclosed to the plaintiffs.[9]

It is clear that Lord Mansfield's sentiments are potentially applicable to a broader range of contracts than those involving insurance. Most, if not all, contracts involve an allocation of risks. Non-disclosure is one example of behaviour that might lead to a party unwittingly taking on risks they did not intend, and perhaps would never have agreed to. It might mean the price is too high, or too low, having regard to the risks that a party is being asked to take on. There are numerous examples of good faith in the context of disclosure in insurance arrangements.[10] However, good faith was not restricted to disclosure aspects of insurance contracts. It was applied beyond that context.[11] It would continue as an expectation of contracts of insurance.[12] It could even serve as a defence where crew on a ship deliberately set fire to it, in order to avoid it falling into the hands of war enemies. The court found the fire insurance policy applied to what occurred, because the crew acted in good faith.[13]

Of course, there are other behaviours that might lead to a party unwittingly taking on risks, and other behaviours that do not involve the allocation of risk that some might view as lacking in good faith.[14] Again, Lord Mansfield's embrace of good faith doctrine was broad – he indicated it was the 'governing principle …

[9] *Mellish v Motteux* (1792) Peake 156; 157; 170 ER 113, 114.

[10] *Clapham v Langton* (1863) 3 F & F 626, 630; 176 ER 286, 288 (Cockburn CJ); *Bates v Hewitt* (1865) 4 F & F 1022, 1029–30; 176 ER 892, 896 (Cockburn CJ, address to the jury).

[11] In *Shawe v Felton* (1801) 2 East 109. 115; 102 ER 310, 312 it was applied to whether the insurer was required to pay the insured the value of the insured vessel at the commencement of the journey, or at the end when it was virtually wrecked (Lord Kenyon CJ); *Kellner v Le Mesurier* (1803) 4 East 396, 403; 102 ER 883, 886 provides a different factual context, again not involving disclosure. And in *Thompson v Hopper* (1858) El Bl & El 1038, 1048–49; 120 ER 796, 800 Willes J considered it was not unlawful for the owner of an unseaworthy vessel to send it to sea; there was no evidence of a lack of good faith, merely a desire to expedite a profitable business. Regarding the failure of a defendant to honour an undertaking regarding the continuity of insurance in a timely manner, the court permitted the plaintiff to proceed against the defendant, noting it was not contrary to good faith because the plaintiffs had not consented to the delay: *Parry v Great Ship Company Limited* (1864) 4 B & S 557; 122 ER 568.

[12] *Everett v Desborough* (1829) 5 Bing 501, 518; 130 ER 1155, 1162 (Park J). In *Wainewright v Bland* (1835) 1 M & Rob 481, 486; 174 ER 165, 168 it was noted in relation to the insured not bringing about the event against which they insured.

[13] *Gordon v Rimmington* (1807) 1 Camp 121, 124; 170 ER 899, 900 (Lord Ellenborough).

[14] J Lowry, 'Redrawing the Parameters of Good Faith in Insurance Contracts' (2007) 60(1) *Current Legal Problems* 338, 343: 'although the disparity in knowledge between the parties has been proffered as the explanation (for imposition of a duty of disclosure as part of uberrimae fidei), this is hardly a satisfactory rationale in itself, given that in other common contracting situations the parties similarly lack equality of information'.

applicable to *all* contracts and dealings' (emphasis added). This requirement would continue to be applied in the context of insurance cases,[15] and those considered to be of analogous nature, such as common carriers.[16]

For a time, Lord Mansfield's intention that the doctrine apply to all contracts and dealings was reflected in the case law.[17] In 1826, in *Snow v Peacock* Best CJ notes that principles of commercial law 'require, in all transactions, good faith and due diligence'.[18] Even in an 1864 decision, there is a reference to good faith that appears to suggest its general application to contracts.[19]

I will now summarise examples where courts referred to good faith in a range of different contractual contexts. The references are typically brief. While I focus mainly on such references in decisions, there are also many occasions in which good faith is referred to in the lawyers' submissions. I will cite these to some extent as well, to show evidence of acceptance and applicability of the doctrine to a wide range of commercial situations. Of course, it is more authoritative when such references appear in judgments rather than submissions, and these references are accorded priority. However, in some cases there is much more detailed evidence of the parties' submissions than there is of the basis of judgment. It will be made clear below when I am citing the case as an example of good faith in the submissions, but most of them reflect discussion of good faith in the judgment/s.

There is recognition of the practical difficulties of reducing all terms of agreement to writing, partly at an executory stage: 'The experience of those who have had to deal with mercantile contracts teaches that they are not uncommonly entered into without an apprehension or foresight of all the circumstances which may result from them'.[20]

Along similar lines are the observations of Knight-Bruce LJ in *Key v Key*:

> In common with all men, I must acknowledge that they are many cases upon the construction of documents, in which the spirit is strong enough to overcome the letter; cases in which it is impossible for a reasonable being, upon a careful perusal of an instrument, not to be satisfied from its contents that a literal, a strict or an ordinary interpretation

[15] *Gibson v Small* (1852–1853) IV HLC 353, 414; 10 ER 499, 523 (Lord Chief Baron Pollock); IV HLC 353, 421; 10 ER 499, 526 (Lord Campbell).

[16] *Belfast and Ballymena Railway Company v Keys* (1861) IX HLC 556; 11 ER 846.

[17] *Salomons v Nissen* (1788) 2 TR 674, 681; 100 ER 363, 366: 'it has been uniformly laid down by this court, as far back as we can remember, that good faith is the basis of all mercantile transactions' (Buller J) and similarly in *Hawkes v Saunders* (1782) 1 Cowp 289, 294; 98 ER 1091, 1093: 'the true rule (regarding enforceability of contracts) is that whenever a defendant is under a moral obligation or is liable in conscience and equity to pay, that is a sufficient consideration' (Buller J). In *Harmer v Plane* (1807) 14 Ves Jun 130, 131; 33 ER 470, 471 counsel refer to the unreported judgment of Lord Chancellor Eldon in *Cartwright v Easer* where he refers to good faith as regulating all contracts. Eldon simply states he adheres to the law he stated in that case (14 Ves Jun 130, 136; 33 ER 470, 472).

[18] (1826) 3 Bing 405, 414; 130 ER 569, 572 (Best CJ).

[19] *Johnson v Helleley* (1864) 34 Beav 63, 65; 55 ER 556, 557 referring to a court selling a property being required 'by that principle of equity to which I have so often had occasion to refer, namely of acting with perfect good faith and of disclosing the whole truth' (Sir John Romilly MR).

[20] *Trefftz v Canelli* (1872) IX Moore NS, 22, 31; 17 ER 422, 425 (Sir Montague Smith, for the Privy Council).

> given to particular passages, would disappoint and defeat the intention with which the instrument, read as a whole, persuades and convinces him that it was framed. A man so convinced is authorized and bound to construe the writing accordingly.[21]

As was noted in chapter one, this was partly the basis of recognition of a good faith obligation in Roman law.

Interestingly, Marshall CJ of the United States Supreme Court also recognised implicit features of contracting in the following passage:

> A great mass of human interactions depends upon implied contracts; upon contracts which are not written, but which grow out of the acts of the parties. In such cases, the parties are supposed to have made those stipulations which as honest, fair and just men, they ought to have made. When the law assumes that they have made these stipulations, it does not vary their contract or introduce new terms into it, but declares that certain acts, unexplained by compact, impose certain duties and that the parties had stipulated for their performance. The difference is obvious between this and the introduction of a new condition into a contract drawn out in writing, in which the parties have expressed everything to be done by either.[22]

Obviously, particularly at this time, statements by the United States Supreme Court regarding the law of contract can be traced to that court's understanding of English law at the time.

From a search of the English Reports, I now document examples where the concept of good faith was (expressly) recognised and applied in the case law. Given the large number of cases, I have attempted to arrange them in their legal context and, where that proves to provide too many cases for a manageable discussion, their factual context.

III. Property and Goods Transactions

Many of the examples are taken from real estate transactions. For example, in *Calcraft v Roebuck*,[23] there was a minor misdescription of land being sold. The defendant advertised 186 acres of freehold land for sale; in fact, about two of the acres were leasehold, not freehold. The plaintiff brought legal action seeking compensation. The Lord Chancellor stated:

> Every consideration, upon which these agreements ought to be executed, must depend upon the bona fides of the transaction; for when the question is upon the selling an

[21] (1853) 4 De G M & G 73, 84–85; 43 ER 435, 439 (Knight Bruce LJ); *Owen v Holman* (1851) 3 Mac & G 378, 403; 42 ER 307, 317: 'at law and in equity every contract is to be construed and effect to be given to it according to the intention of the parties to be collected from every part of the contract, and not according to any particular words or sentences to be found in it which taken independently might import an intention different from that which is to be collected from the whole of the contract', after referring to the question 'whether it is consistent with the intention of the parties and the good faith of the contract' that the contract be interpreted in a particular way (Lord Chancellor Truro).

[22] *Ogden v Saunders* (1827) 25 US 313, 341–42.

[23] (1790) 1 Ves Jun 221; 30 ER 311.

> estate … it is impossible that all the little particulars relative to the quantity, title, situation etc should be so specifically laid down as not to call for some allowance and consideration, when the bargain comes to be executed; therefore the question is where the bona fides is, what is the extent of it, and the conclusion upon it.[24]

Two points may be made. Similar to the comments expressed by Lord Mansfield, the principle was of general application to contracts. Second, the rationale for a good faith doctrine – that flexibility in arrangements is necessary due to the impossibility of reducing everything to writing at an executory stage, is articulated at this early stage. It would find support much later in the case law, as we will see, as well as being a throwback to Roman law.

There were also cases where a lack of good faith was alleged where lessors permitted lessees to make improvements on the leased property, before proceedings to evict the tenants at a time earlier than the tenant expected to be vacating. The possibility of the relevance of good faith in such a context was acknowledged in *Dann v Spurrier*.[25] There the Lord Chancellor (Lord Eldon) noted 'It was upon the plaintiff to prove, not merely to raise a probable conjecture, but to shew upon highly probable grounds a case of bad faith and bad conscience against the defendant. The plaintiff fails in proving that.'[26]

The claim failed there partly because of the lack of evidence that the lessor was aware that the lessee had been making improvements, but the important point is the acknowledgement of the potential viability of a good faith claim in the contract context.[27] The court considered as material whether statements made during precontractual discussions were made in good faith.[28]

In a case with similar facts[29] a tenant argued he had made substantial improvements on the leased property on the understanding that the owner would allow him to stay during the course of the owner's life. Once the improvements had been made, the owner sought to evict the tenant. Sir W Grant (MR) noted:

> If a landlord enters into an arrangement with a tenant relative to improvements, and so completely sanctions them, as himself to agree to advance part of the money, implying that another part is to be in advance by the tenant, I doubt whether that does not fasten an equity upon the landlord, precluding him, when these improvements are made under his authority, from saying there is an end of the lease. Such an arrangement, though without a specific agreement, would imply one; as it would be so contrary to good faith to encourage a tenant in so positive and direct a manner to proceed in

[24] ibid 224; 313.

[25] (1802) 7 Ves Jun 232; 32 ER 94.

[26] ibid 234; 95.

[27] Similarly *Thornton v Ramsden* (1864) 4 Giff 519, 571; 66 ER 812, 834: 'this court has gone very far in many cases to protect the possession of a tenant who has in good faith expended money on land in a reasonable confidence that his possession would not be disturbed'.

[28] *Hopkins v Tanqueray* (1854) 15 CB 130; 139 ER 369; see similarly in relation to statements prior to an auction concerning the vendor's plans to improve the vicinity of the lot to be sold. The improvements were not in fact made. Sir Thomas Plumer asked rhetorically whether this was 'keeping good faith with those who listened to (the) statements': *Beaumont v Dukes* (1821) Jacob, 423, 425; 37 ER 910, 911.

[29] *Pilling v Armitage* (1805) 12 Ves Jun 79; 33 ER 31.

> particular improvements, and then deny him all benefit, that I think equity would interfere; and hold it an implied term that the tenant should have the fair benefit from the improvement, thus made by the concurrence of the landlord.[30]

The case *Lachlan v Reynolds*[31] involved a situation where a vendor offered their property for sale, acknowledging a current lease in place at a particular rental. In fact the person currently living on the premises occupied through adverse possession. The vendor did not tell the purchaser this, or that she could only be lawfully removed by bringing a proceeding of ejectment. When the purchaser discovered the truth, they wished to avoid the contract. The Court found in their favour on the basis of a breach of the vendor's good faith obligation to them. Sir W Page Wood stated:

> If there be one thing which the Court insists upon more than another in dealings between vendor and purchaser it is that there should be perfectly good faith on the part of the vendor in the representations which he makes to the purchaser.[32]

There are many other examples in the contract context.[33] The court found it would be good faith for a purchaser to purchase a property knowing of a charge against it, but then seeking to deny the validity of the charge on technical grounds.[34] A court considered whether a mortgagee was entitled to transfer the security to another, based on whether they had acted in good faith in doing so.[35] A court considered whether an adverse possessor of land had transferred rights to the land to a third party in good faith.[36] Cases often involve the question of the rights of a purchaser of property as against those who claim prior charges or claims over it. The question of the good faith of the purchaser looms large.[37] Courts determined it was contrary to good faith to take advantage of the illegal nature of a contract.[38]

[30] (1805) 12 Ves Jun 79, 88; 33 ER 31, 34. See similarly *Crowder v Tinkler* (1816) 19 Ves Jun 617, 627; 34 ER 645, 648: 'another part of the case is whether such countenance was given to the improvements of the paper mills as makes the erection of the corning-house in this situation a breach of good faith by the defendants' (Lord Chancellor Eldon).

[31] (1853) Kay, 51; 69 ER 23.

[32] (1853) Kay, 51, 54–55; 69 ER 23, 24.

[33] *Gordon v Gordon* (1821) 3 Swans 400, 477; 36 ER 910, 922: 'there must not only be good faith and honest intention, but full disclosure' (Lord Eldon); *Cockrane v Hurrosoondurry Debia* (1857) VI Moore Ind App 494, 506; 19 ER 186, 190 (Knight-Bruce LJ, for the Privy Council).

[34] *Beauce v Muter* (1845) V Moore, 69, 74; 13 ER 416, 418.

[35] *Walker v Jones* (1865) III Moore N.S., 397, 403; 16 ER 151, 153 (appears in the judgment of Chief Justice of the Supreme Court of New South Wales Stephen CJ, from which decision appeal was taken to the Privy Council. The report of the Privy Council decision explains the judgment of Stephen CJ, including his use of good faith).

[36] *Macdonald v Lambe* (1867) IV Moore NS, 486, 503; 16 ER 401, 408 (Lord Cairns).

[37] *Varden Seth Sam v Luckpathy Royjee Lallah and Others* (1862) IX Moore Ind App 307, 326–27; 19 ER 756, 763 (Lord Kingsdown, for the Privy Council); *Sreemanchunder Dey v Gopaulchunder Chuckerbutty and Others* (1866) XI Moore Ind App 28, 44; 20 ER 11, 17 (Lord Westbury, for the Privy Council); *Radanath Ross v Gisborne* (1871) XIV Moore Ind App 1, 21–22; 20 ER 687, 694 (Lord Cairns, for the Privy Council); *Miller v Barlow* (1871) XIV Moore Ind App 209, 218; 20 ER 765, 769 (Peacock CJ of the High Court of Calcutta); *Pilcher v Rawlins* (1872) LR 7 Ch App 250, 269.

[38] *Thomson v Thomson* (1802) 7 Ves Jun 470, 473; 32 ER 190, 191 (Sir William Grant MR). The corollary is that, where a claim is made but not directly upon the illegal contract, it is feasible where the claim is due 'in good faith and justice': *Ex Parte Bulmer* (1807) 13 Ves Jun 313, 318; 33 ER 311, 313 (Lord Chancellor Erskine).

Where courts believe that a party to a contract has taken advantage of the other, who might be suffering distress or from ignorance, or by improperly influencing them, they may find there is a lack of good faith that might justify refusing specific performance of it or setting it aside.[39]

In a case where a court had ordered the sale of a business, the question arose as to the extent of disclosure required to would-be purchasers concerning the right of the vendor to use the business name in another enterprise. Sir John Romilly MR stated that a court, when selling a business, 'must adhere to that principle of equity to which I have so often had occasion to refer, namely of acting with perfect good faith and of disclosing the whole truth'.[40] In *Stevens v Adamson*, a lessee had received notice from their landlord that they would resume possession of the property if repairs were not attended to promptly. The lessee transferred the lease to an innocent third party, without telling them of the notice from the owner. The court report indicates Lord Abbott CJ stated that in such transactions 'good faith was most essential', and the original lessee was required to disclose the fact of the notice to the third party.[41]

A vendor of a property sold it on the basis it had access to certain water rights worth a certain amount per year. This was literally true. He was aware, but did not disclose, that effective exercise of those rights depended on an informal easement whereby the said water travelled across other properties. The court declined to order specific performance of the sales contract, partly on the basis that the vendor had not acted with good faith.[42]

Another vendor sold a property, advertising it on the basis that it had recently been leased at a certain amount per year. This was incorrect, for two reasons. First, that particular tenant possessed the property for one and a quarter years. During one year, they did pay the amount advertised. However, for the other three months, they paid only one pound. Further, in a subsequent lease, the vendor had leased it at a substantially lesser amount. The Court found that the vendor had breached his obligation of good faith to the purchaser in failing to present an accurate picture of the amount for which the property had been leased.[43]

In relation to a purchaser of a property, the court in *Philips v Homfray*[44] determined the purchaser had failed to act in good faith. After expressly confirming that a court of equity required good faith on the part of both parties,[45] it found the purchaser had not met this obligation. They purported to purchase an adjoining coal mine. Unknown to the vendor, the purchaser had already had access to some

[39] *Pickett v Loggon* (1807) 1 Ves Jun Supp 551, 551–52; 34 ER 916, 916–17.

[40] *Johnson v Helleley* (1864) 34 Beav 63, 65; 55 ER 556, 557.

[41] (1818) 2 Stark 422, 423; 171 ER 692, 693.

[42] *Price v Macaulay* (1852) 2 De GM & G.331, 348; 42 ER 903, 907 (Lord Cranworth).

[43] *Dimmock v Hallett* (1866) 2 Ch App 21, 28 (Sir G Turner LJ) and 31 (Sir HM Cairns, LJ).

[44] (1870) 6 Ch App 770.

[45] 'This court requires the utmost good faith between buyer and seller, and will not specifically enforce a contract which is not entirely according to good faith': (1870) 6 Ch App 770, 778 (Lord Hatherley, Lord Chancellor).

of the coal located deep underground on the vendor's property. This gave them awareness of how much coal was there, and what its quality was. The vendor did not have this information. The court refused to grant the purchaser specific performance of the contract in these circumstances.

In *Seton v Slade*[46] the question arose regarding whether time was of the essence of the contract.The parties entered into a contract for the sale of the plaintiff's property to the defendant.The contract was intended to be completed on 12 June, two months after it was executed, the plaintiff being required to demonstrate good title to the property. On 7 June, just before the two months was up, the plaintiff told the defendant they only had title under an agreement, but they were ready to convey, and proposed arrangements. They sent the defendant an abstract. The defendant did not respond until 13 June, demanding a refund of their deposit and interest, claiming that the abstract had been delivered too late to permit the conveyance to occur. The plaintiff sought specific performance of the contract.

In granting the plaintiff's request, the court noted the more flexible attitude of equity towards contractual time deadlines. Unlike at the common law, time was not inevitably of the essence. It took a dim view of the defendant's behaviour:

> The cases before Lord Thurlow proceed upon this: that in the nature of the thing there must be a degree of good faith between the parties, not to turn round the contract upon frivolous objections. As to the contract of the party, the slightest objection is an answer at law. But the title to an estate requires so much clearing and inquiry, that unless substantial objections appear, not merely as to the time, but an alteration of circumstances affecting the value of the thing, or objections arising out of circumstances, not merely as to time, but the conduct of the parties during the time, unless the objection can be so sustained, many of the cases (establish) … that the objection cannot be maintained … no authority would support me in saying that … the defendant can resist a decree (of specific performance) … if a good title can be made.[47]

A slightly different context occurred in relation to the running up of a significant bill by a minor at a licensed premises/café. The owner was aware of the customer's minor status, and that he was of modest means. Yet he allowed him to run up a significant bill, and to place it on credit. When the owner of the academy inquired of the licensed premises what the extent of the bill was, the premises was evasive. The Court found the fact such a large amount of credit was extended to the minor in this situation, together with evasiveness in providing a detailed account of the charges, indicated a lack of good faith on the part of the owner of the premises.[48]

Another context involved a marriage contract. A man to an intended marriage was in possession of valuable property. His mother assured the intended bride's

[46] (1802) 7 Ves Jun 268; 32 ER 108.

[47] (1802) 7 Ves Jun 268, 274–75; 32 ER 108, 111–12 (Lord Chancellor Eldon). Other Chancery cases would treat delay as fatal to the plaintiff's claim: *Harrington v Wheeler* (1799) 4 Ves Jun 86; *Campbell v Graham* (1831) 1 Russ & M 453, 483; 39 ER 175, 186 (Lord Chancellor Brougham).

[48] *Brook and Gally* (1740) Barn C 1, 4; 27 ER 530, 531 (Lord Chancellor).

father that he owned this land, and no debt existed upon it. On that basis, the marriage proceeded. In fact, the mother herself had owned the property. She transferred the property to her son, but took a security over it, which she did not divulge to the intended bride's father. Baron Thompson found that in good faith the mother should not have obtained security over the subject property. It was a fraud of the marriage contract. Further, she aggravated the wrong by wilfully concealing her security.[49]

Another case involved the auction of a property advertised as 'without reserve'. The vendor made bids at the auction to increase the price at which the property was sold. The court refused to enforce the contract of sale against the eventual purchaser. The court found the vendor had not acted in good faith. The advertisement suggested the property would be sold to the highest bidder, without interference by the vendor. This had not occurred.[50]

Hawkes v Eastern Counties Railway Company involved a railway company which had applied to parliament to build a particular railway line. This proposed line went through the plaintiff's property. The plaintiff lodged a formal objection to the proposal. In return for the plaintiff dropping his formal objection, the defendant agreed to buy him out. At the time, the railway company's proposed works being considered by parliament did not include the line over the plaintiff's property. The plaintiffs did not know this. Parliament passed legislation authorising the railway company to do some work, but not to build the line through the plaintiff's property. The defendant then abandoned its plans, and refused to complete the purchase. The court made an order for specific performance in favour of the plaintiff. The court found the defendant had misled the plaintiff as to the status of its plans. It had acted in bad faith.[51]

In *Pope v Lord Duncannon* the plaintiffs owned a wharf. They agreed to sell the wharf to the defendants at a price that would be determined by a panel of three referees. One was to be appointed by the plaintiff, one by the defendant, and a third by the other two referees. After the referees had been appointed, the plaintiffs dismissed them, and notified the defendant they did not wish to proceed with the sale. They argued they were within their contractual rights to dismiss the referees. They sought an injunction to stop the defendants from dismantling existing buildings on site.

The court refused, on the basis of good faith:

> A plaintiff is not at liberty to ask the aid of a Court of Equity in respect of an act done by him against good faith … there is nothing whatever to show that the power which the

[49] *Scott v Scott* (1787) 1 Cox, 367, 381–82; 29 ER 1206, 1212; for another example where one party entered into marriage relying 'in good faith and honesty' on their partner's assurance regarding the effectiveness of a property settlement for her benefit, see *Corley v Lord Stafford* (1857) 1 De G & J 238, 251; 44 ER 714, 719 (Knight Bruce LJ); good faith also mentioned in this context in *Loxley v Heath* (1860) 1 De G F & J 489, 493; 45 ER 451, 452 (Lord Chancellor).

[50] *Robinson v Wall* (1847) 2 Ph 372; 41 ER 986; similarly *Bexwell v Christie* (1776) 1 Cowp 395; 98 ER 1150.

[51] (1852) 1 De G M & G 737, 756; 42 ER 739, 755–56 (Lord Chancellor).

> plaintiffs (gave) to the arbitrators was revoked upon any just or reasonable grounds .. (thus) the revocation was a wanton and capricious exercise of authority on their parts, and consequently the motion (for an injunction) must be refused.[52]

The court noted the plaintiffs did not show evidence of any reasonable grounds for their decision, merely that they considered they had just grounds for making the decision. This was not sufficient to enable the court to determine whether or not the discretion was exercised in a wanton and capricious manner, or fairly and reasonably.

The case *Ormrod v Huth*[53] presents a nice example of the growing acceptance of caveat emptor in the law of contract, though the court still indicates it accepts a good faith requirement. Briefly, the case involved the sale of cotton. A sample of the product was provided to the buyer prior to sale. The buyer argued that the remaining supply of the product was of inferior quality, and sought a remedy. The seller argued he had not been fraudulent and was unaware of the inferior quality of the bulk supplied.

The plaintiffs referred to insurance cases, including *Carter v Boehm*, as examples of contracts that were voidable due to any false representation, even if innocently made. It argued the rule was applicable to insurance applied equally to all contracts. The defendants argued that caveat emptor should apply. The plaintiffs had not sought an express warranty regarding the quality of the bulk supply, and the defendant had not provided one. The defendant was not aware the bulk supply would be of inferior quality. The defendant argued that insurance cases were distinguishable from the present situation; the former were contracts subject to *uberrimae fidei*, other contracts were not.

The court applied caveat emptor and found for the defendant. It embraced the distinction between representations and warranties. Here the defendant had not given a warranty regarding the goods. In so deciding, however, it found that if there were evidence the defendant had acted against good faith, the result would differ.[54]

In *Piggott v Stratton*,[55] a defendant was granted a 999-year lease over adjoining properties B and C. The lease required that the defendant build houses on both plots, with a minimum distance between them of 30 feet. One reason for doing this was to preserve a sea view on property B. Property C had a guaranteed sea view, but if a house were constructed on property C less than 30 feet from Property B, the sea view on Property B would disappear. Rights under the lease were transferred to H, who built houses on Property B which enjoyed a sea view. He then transferred his interest to the plaintiff. Later, the defendant surrendered his long-term lease to the owner, and a new lease was issued. This lease pertained to Property C. The new lease did not contain the previous restrictions on where houses could be built on property C. A sub-lessee took possession of Property C.

[52] (1838) 9 Sim 177, 179–80; 59 ER 326, 327 (Sir L Shadwell, VC).

[53] (1845) 14 M & W 651; 153 ER 636.

[54] (1845) 14 M & W 651, 664; 153 ER 636, 642 (Tindal CJ, for the Court), approved in *Udell v Atherton* (1861) 7 H & N 172, 183; 158 ER 437, 442 (Baron Wilde).

[55] (1859) 1 De G F & J 33; 45 ER 271.

That sub-lessee commenced to build a home upon it that was less than 30 feet from the plaintiff's buildings, and which would restrict the plaintiff's sea views once completed. The plaintiff obtained an injunction against the defendant to prevent the proposed construction on Property C.

The Court was clearly not impressed with the defendant's behaviour. He had not breached any express contractual provision. However, the Court determined it was not 'consistent with equity and good conscience' that the defendant should obtain a windfall profit by effectively building (through the sub-lessee) a house that was contrary to the original lease granted to him, in such a manner as would destroy the sea view of the plaintiff.[56] The Court noted that 'no attempt has been made to defend the good faith or to palliate the perfidy of such a transaction'.

The Court rejected an argument that it was effectively H's fault because he should have been aware that the original lease containing the restrictive covenant could be terminated, and that he should have insisted upon an express term in his lease requiring that the defendant not terminate it, or alternatively an express promise that no buildings would be constructed so as to destroy the sea view. The Court dismissed the argument:

> if (the defendant's) representation had been sincere and faithful, all such precautions were unnecessary, and the business of life could not be conducted if it were required that men should anticipate and expressly guard against the wily devices to which the deceitful may resort.[57]

Good faith often appears in cases of misrepresentation. In *Jorden v Money* the Lord Chancellor noted:

> And then it is said that upon a principle well known in the law, founded upon good faith and equity, a principle equally of law and of equity, if a person makes any false representation to another, and that other acts upon that false representation, the person who has made it shall not afterwards be allowed to set up that what he said was false, and to assert the real truth in place of the falsehood which has so misled the other. This is a principle of universal application.[58]

IV. Contractual Discretion, Discretionary Remedies

In cases where one of the parties has a contractual discretion, the courts would often condition the exercise of that discretion on good faith. For example, in

[56] (1859) 1 De G F & J 33, 49; 45 ER 271, 277 (Lord Chancellor).

[57] (1859) 1 De G F & J 33, 50; 45 ER 271, 278.

[58] (1854) 5 H.LC 185, 210; 10 ER 868, 880. Another example is *Childers v Wooler* (1859) 2 El & El 288; 121 ER 109, where an attorney mistakenly identified a person against whom a writ was to be issued. As a result, the plaintiff's goods were (incorrectly) seized. The court held no action for false representation lay against the attorney, because he had made the indorsement in good faith and without intention to deceive; see also *Shrewsbury v Blount* (1841) 2 Man & G 475, 506–07; 133 ER 836, 848–49 (whether the defendant had good reason to believe the representations he had made relevant to an allegation of lack of good faith in making representations to plaintiff).

Andrews v Belfield,[59] a coachmaker promised to construct the coach to whatever standard the client wished. The finished product did not meet the client's satisfaction, and he rejected it. The court concluded he was entitled to do so. He was acting in good faith and not in a capricious or arbitrary fashion.[60] Good faith was not specifically mentioned but was clearly an operative factor in *Dallman v King*,[61] where a contract obliged a tenant to renovate the leased property to a standard of which the property owner approved. The owner did not approve the renovations. The Court stated the contractual provision should not be interpreted so as to permit the property owner to capriciously refuse their consent.

Good faith considerations are evident when a court of equity is asked to exercise a discretionary remedy, such as an order for specific performance.[62] In a case where the plaintiff sought a special injunction, the court found that the application was judged by the same principles as *uberrimae fidei* in the insurance context. If the party seeking the court order had failed to provide the court with facts material to the application, the court could utilise this fact to deny the remedy.[63]

An order for specific performance was also denied to a vendor who had contracted to sell their property to a purchaser.[64] The vendor insisted that he had obtained the required permission from tenants occupying the premises for the sale to go forward. In fact, he had misunderstood the tenant's response, and they did not consent. The court viewed this as a misrepresentation. It refused to order that the contract be specifically performed, with or without adjustments. It acknowledged that it sometimes did modify parties' agreement to avoid difficulties. However, this only occurred where both parties acted in good faith, which was not the case on the facts.[65]

It was also denied where the vendor did not precisely describe the property interest to be sold. The purchaser mistakenly thought that the contract entitled him to more than it actually did. When they discovered the mistake, they refused to complete the contract. The court rejected the vendor's application for specific performance. The purchaser had made a mistake in good faith as a result of an ambiguous description of the interest to be sold prepared by the vendor.[66]

[59] (1857) 2 CB (NS) 779; 140 ER 622.

[60] (1857) 2 CB (NS) 779, 789; 140 ER 622, 626 (Cresswell LJ). Willes J agreed the purchaser was acting bona fide.

[61] (1837) 4 Bing NC 105; 132 ER 729.

[62] *Vesey v Bodkin* (1830) IV Bligh NS 64, 75; 5 ER 23, 27; *Eastern Counties Railway Co v Hawkes* (1855) V HLC 331, 365; 10 ER 928, 941 (Lord Brougham). In *Calverley v Williams* (1790) 1 Ves Jun 211; 30 ER 306 the Lord Chancellor (Thurlow J) indicated it would be contrary to good faith if both parties to a contract believed a certain quantity of land was being sold, for one of them then to assert that the contract included the sale of a further quantity. This is what we would today regard as a mutual mistake. The Lord Chancellor indicated a claim to have the further quantity conveyed in such a case would be contrary to good faith.

[63] *Dalglish v Jarvie* (1850) 2 Mac & G 231, 243–44; 42 ER 89, 94 (Lord Commissioner Baron Rolfe).

[64] *Viscount Clermont v Tasburgh* (1819) 1 Jac & Walk 112, 120; 37 ER 318, 321 (Sir Thomas Plumer, MR).

[65] (1819) 1 Jac & Walk 112; 37 ER 318.

[66] *Swaisland v Dearsley* (1861) 29 Beav 430, 433; 54 ER 694, 695 (Sir John Romilly, MR).

More generally, the writer of the first major treatise on contract law, Powell, in *Essay Upon the Law of Contracts and Agreements* (Dublin, 1790) notes the well-established rule that in order to engage a court of equity in relation to an agreement, the agreement had to be 'fair, just, reasonable, bona fide, certain in all its parts, mutual, (and) made upon a good or valuable consideration'.[67]

V. Discretionary Powers

It was also considered in relation to the conduct of an election for public office.[68] In *Queen v Rowley*,[69] unsuccessful candidates for political office brought legal action claiming the election was tainted, because it was not made clear which election related to an extraordinary vacancy, and which related to ordinary vacancies. The elections were held at the same time. The court noted the applicants participated in the election and did not then complain about the alleged irregularities of which they now complained, having lost the election. The court dismissed their complaint on the basis it was not made in good faith. In relation to a public official, the court noted no action would lie against them for an exercise of their discretion where it was exercised in good faith.[70] In applying the privilege defence to what would otherwise amount to defamatory claims against a public official, the court noted the claims were made in good faith.[71] The Court noted an expectation that a city council would exercise its power to make by-laws in good faith.[72]

VI. Trustees

It has been applied to judge the behaviour of a trustee.[73] In *Aleyn v Belchier*, Lord Northington stated that 'no point is better established than a person having a power must exercise it bona fide for the end designed, otherwise it is corrupt and void'.[74] In *Portland v Topham*,[75] another case involving a trustee, the Court

[67] (Dublin, Chamberlaine and Rice, 1790) 221. He added it also had to be free from fraud, circumvention and surprise, and be consistent with public policy. In so doing, contracts would 'tend to produce a just end'.

[68] *The King v Mayor, Alderman and Burgesses of the City of Oxford* (1837) 6 Ad & E 349, 353; 112 ER 133 135 (Coleridge J).

[69] (1842) 3 QB 142; 114 ER 461.

[70] *Steel v Schomberg* (1855) 4 El & Bl 620, 630–31; 119 ER 227, 231 (Lord Campbell CJ).

[71] *Harrison v Bush* (1855) 5 El & Bl 344, 348–50; 119 ER 509, 512 (Lord Campbell CJ).

[72] *Hutchins v Player* (1663) Bridgman, O 272, 324; 124 ER 585, 614 (Bridgman CJ).

[73] *McDonnel v White* (1865) XI HLC 569, 587; 11 ER 1454, 1461 (Lord Cranworth); *Morison v Morison* (1855) 7 De G M & G 213, 223–24; 44 ER 84, 88 (Knight Bruce LJ); *Baud v Fardell* (1855) 7 De G M & G 628, 632; 44 ER 245, 246 (Knight-Bruce LJ).

[74] (1758) 1 Eden 132, 138; 28 ER 634, 637, cited with evident approval by a unanimous Supreme Court of Canada in *Bhasin v Hrynew* [2014] 3 SCR 494, [35](Cromwell J, for the Court).

[75] (1864) XI HLC 31; 11 ER 1242.

found against the trustee. They were found to have acted contrary to good faith and sincerity, by seeking to obtain objects beyond that for which they had been engaged.[76] Similar sentiments were expressed in *Mortimer v Picton*.[77] In *Smith v Clay* the Lord Chancellor stated that 'nothing can call forth this court (Chancery) but conscience, good faith and reasonable diligence: where these are wanting, the Court is passive, and does nothing'.[78] The courts also emphasised requirements of 'openness and good faith' in cases involving fiduciary obligations.[79]

VII. General Business Context

They considered arguments about reasonableness and good faith in relation to contractual restraints of trade.[80] In *Wolff v Oxholm* Lord Ellenborough referred to a loan situation where an individual trusted in the good faith of the person with whom they dealt, and applied this to government attempts to appropriate a private loan.[81] In a case where the defendant, entitled to payment on a bond assigned it to another, then forgave the original debt, making the thing assigned virtually worthless, the court found the defendant had acted contrary to good faith, and her actions could be set aside as a result.[82]

In *The 'Nicoline'* the court found that all business people operating under a licence were 'bound to act with the purest good faith'.[83] Because the licensee used their licence for improper purposes (concealing armaments) their licence was cancelled. Similarly in *The 'Cosmopolite'* the Court insisted that the licensee act with 'entire bona fides'. This meant the licensee had to act with 'fair intentions' and within the confines of that for which they obtained a licence.[84] Good faith was also expected of parties involved in a cartel-like agreement.[85]

[76] (1864) XI HLC 31, 54; 11 ER 1242, 1251 (Lord Chancellor): 'The donee, the appointor under the power, shall, at the time of the exercise of that power, and for any purpose for which it is used, act with good faith and sincerity, and with an entire and single view to the real purpose and object of the power, and not for the purpose of accomplishing or carrying into effect any bye or sinister object'.

[77] (1864) 4 De G J & S 166, 178; 46 ER 880, 884 (Lord Chancellor).

[78] *Smith v Clay* (1767) 3 Bro CC 646; 29 ER 743, 744; referred to with evident approval in *Hercy v Dinwoody* (1793) 2 Ves Jun 87, 92; 30 ER 536, 539 (Sir RP Arden, MR) and *Gresley v Mousley* (1859) 4 De G & J 78, 95; 45 ER 31, 37 (Turner LJ) and *Grenfell v Girdlestone* (1837) 2 Y & C Ex 662, 679; 160 ER 560, 567 (Baron Alderson).

[79] *Hesse v Briant* (1856) 6 De G M & G. 621, 629; 43 ER 1375, 1378; see also *Lagunas Nitrate Co v Lagunas Syndicate* [1899] 2 Ch 392, 409 (Romer J) and 435 (Lindley, MR) (CA).

[80] *Shackle v Baker* (1808) 14 Ves Jun 468; 33 ER 600; *Morris v Colman* (1812) 18 Ves 437, 438–39; 43 ER 382, 383.

[81] (1817) 6 M & S 92, 110; 105 ER 1177, 1180.

[82] *Sarah Legh v Frances Legh* (1799) 1 Bos & Ful 447, 448; 126 ER 1002, 1003 (Eyre CJ): 'the court has in many cases refused to allow a party to take his legal advantage where it has appeared to be against good faith'.

[83] (1810) Edw 363; 165 ER 1139.

[84] (1801) 4 C Rob 8, 13; 165 ER 516, 518 (Sir W Scott).

[85] *'La Gloire'* (1804) 5 C Rob 193, 201; 165 ER 745, 748.

VIII. Negotiable Instruments and Finance

Good faith is a common feature of cases involving negotiable instruments. Examples have included transferring a negotiable instrument knowing that the transferor's legal rights over the instrument are in dispute, but failing to tell the transferee,[86] or a financial advisor converting a negotiable instrument to his own use.[87] Another occurred where a party promised not to commence proceedings if a payment were made on a bill of exchange by a certain day. Although the payment was made, the party commenced proceedings. This was argued to be a lack of good faith.[88] Good faith was raised where an adviser was given exchequer bills for investment purposes, but instead applied the raised funds to their own use.[89] In another case, an agent requested a bill of lading, claiming he would return them once he had checked the accuracy of documents. He later declined to do so, thereby seeking to obtain commercial advantage. The Court did not find in his favour.[90] The fact that a debtor was acting in good faith in mistakenly describing a bill of exchange upon which he was liable assisted him in securing the protection of bankruptcy legislation in relation to the bill.[91]

In determining the rights of subsequent holders of a negotiable instrument where there had been a material alteration to it, the court considered whether the current holder had taken the instrument in good faith.[92] It considered whether bankers who cashed a stolen bill had acted in good faith.[93] The court discussed good faith in relation to the fact that third parties could treat the holder as the owner provided they were acting in good faith,[94] and that the holder of a negotiable instrument could pledge it provided they acted in good faith.[95] It confirmed that a person holding a blank bill of exchange can give good title to a third party to whom it is assigned, if they are acting in good faith and gave value, though the assignor lacked good title.[96] Similar issues have arisen in relation to the sale of goods by consignment, where the good faith of a subsequent assignee of bills of lading has been considered.[97]

[86] *Smith v Martin* (1841) Car & M 59; 174 ER 407.

[87] *R v Golde* (1842) 2 M & Rob 423; 174 ER 338.

[88] *Cash v Wells* (1830) 1 B & AD 375; 109 ER 826.

[89] *Rex v White* (1829) 4 Car & P 46; 172 ER 601; similarly *Smith v Braine* (1851) 16 Q B 244; 117 ER 872.

[90] *Hoare v Dresser* (1859) VII HLC 291; 11 ER 116. The Court noted that, by attempting to obtain an unfair advantage, the agent had relinquished a legitimate claim he had possessed. Lord Cranworth noted the outcome, 'for the sake of commercial fairness and good faith', was not to be regretted: (1859) VII. HLC 291, 330; 11 ER 116, 132.

[91] *Booth v Coldman* (1859) 1 El & Bl 414, 417; 120 ER 964, 965 (Lord Campbell CJ).

[92] *Carlon and Haynes v Ireland* (1856) 5 El & Bl 765, 770–71; 119 ER 666, 668; see also *Bramah v E M Roberts* (1835) 1 Bing (NC) 469, 479–80; 131 ER 1198, 1202 (Park J); *Newton v Hunt* (1833) 5 Sim 511, 523; 58 ER 430, 434; *Whistler v Forster* (1863) 14 CB (NS) 248; 143 ER 441.

[93] *Beckwith v Corral and Another* (1826) 3 Bing 445; 130 ER 584.

[94] *Brandao v Barnett* (1846) XII Clark & Finnelly 787, 806; 8 ER 1622, 1629 (Lord Campbell) (as part of the law merchant); *Fancourt v Bull* (1835) 1 Bing (NC) 681, 690; 131 ER 1279, 1283 (Tindal CJ).

[95] *Brandao v Barnett* (1846) XII Clark & Finnelly 787, 802; 8 ER 1622, 1628 (Lord Chancellor).

[96] *Foster v Pearson* (1835) 1 CM & R 849, 855; 149 ER 1324, 1327 (Baron Parke, for the Court).

[97] *Cuming v Brown* (1808) 9 East 506; 103 ER 666; *Lickbarrow v Mason* (1787) 2 TR 64; 100 ER 35; *Wright v Campbell* (1767) 4 Burr 2045; 98 ER 66.

Good faith was raised in relation to a broker who discounted a bill of exchange.[98] The bill had, unknown to the broker, been stolen. The question arose as to the extent to which the broker had made enquiries regarding the person that had brought the bill to them for discounting. Members of the Court indicated it was part of the obligation of good faith for the broker to have asked questions which in the ordinary course of business and trade should have been asked. They were required to exercise due caution and diligence.[99] If they failed to do so, they could not be said to have acted in good faith, and they would not be able to take action on the bill.

In a case where a party otherwise liable on a negotiable instrument sought to argue that a limitation period applied which forbade a remedy for failure to honour it, Lord Brougham noted that at the time of making the agreement, the parties were not contemplating the time at which their obligation to perform would effectively end. He indicated that 'nothing is more contrary to good faith' than such a supposition. If the law did so, it would sanction a 'wrong course of conduct' and effectively encourage and reward evasiveness.[100]

Relatedly, a defendant had provided an annuity to pay the plaintiff. He could not meet his obligations, and re-financed with a new arrangement involving the payment of cash and a new bond. The plaintiff held a security for the payment of the annuity. It sought to enforce this security. The court refused to do so, on the basis the action was in breach of good faith and in contravention of the new agreement which the parties intended to supersede the old, to which the security related.[101]

It was held to be applicable in relation to a surety arrangement. The judgment states:

> When the parties enter into a contract of suretyship, all the parties agree there shall be the utmost good faith between them, that the situation of the creditor and of the principal debtor should be perfectly made known to all the sureties, and therefore the creditor is conceived to have made known to them, whether he does so or not in fact, every security which he possesses, and the existing positions of the parties at the time the contract is entered into.[102]

In relation to loan contracts, and the usury laws, notes to *Jones v Davison* suggest that loan contracts involving risk or contingency are consistent with such laws, provided the risk or contingency is 'real and of good faith'.[103] In *Murray v Harding*,

[98] *Gill v Cubitt* (1824) 3 B & C 466; 107 ER 806.

[99] (1824) 3 B & C 466, 476 (Bayley J) and 477 (Holroyd J); 107 ER 806, 810 (Bayley J) and 810 (Holroyd J); similarly *Miller v Race* (1758) 1 Burr 452, 458; 97 ER 398, 401–02 (Lord Mansfield); cf *Lawson v Weston* (1801) 4 Esp. 56; 170 ER 640 (KB) (honesty only required).

[100] *Don v Lippmann* (1837) V Clark & Finnelly 1, 16; 7 ER 303, 308.

[101] *Sir Harry Goring Bart v Wells* (1799) 1 Bos & Pul 395; 126 ER 972. In *Rex v Walsh* (1812) 4 Taunt 258, 284; 128 ER 328, 338 the court reporter notes passage of legislation making it a criminal offence for brokers, bankers and others to embezzle securities placed with them 'in violation of good faith, and contrary to the special purpose for which they were deposited'.

[102] *Newton v Chorlton* (1853) 2 Drewry 333, 335; 61 ER 748, 749.

[103] (1816) Holt 256, 261 and 267; 171 ER 233, 236 and 239.

the court considered whether financial accommodation made available to a party by another amounted to a loan in breach of then-existing usury laws.[104] The court noted many attempts to evade usury laws. It stated that the essence of a loan was that the lender would be entitled to full repayment. De Grey CJ stated that if this was 'bona fide in hazard', it was not a loan.[105] Blackstone J expressed a similar view.[106]

IX. Bankruptcy

There is evidence of a good faith requirement in a bankruptcy context.[107] Here creditors might make an arrangement to accept a certain part payment, based on a percentage of what is owed. On occasion, a creditor then sought to make another arrangement with the debtor, under which they would be paid a greater amount, or receive priority in payment. The courts often frowned on such arrangements, on the basis of a good faith requirement.[108] Good faith was also raised in relation to whether assignments of property occurred in order to defeat creditors,[109] when an agreement was made between creditor and debtor, the creditor was aware the debtor was technically bankrupt,[110] and the rights of creditors to seize the goods of the bankrupt in payment.[111] Purported transfer of the bankrupt's property to family members in order to defeat creditors have been held to breach good faith requirements.[112]

In a case where a purchaser of goods had become bankrupt after the contract was entered into but prior to delivery, the court found that where the purchaser was no longer capable of performing their obligations under the contract, 'honesty

[104] (1773) 2 Black W 860; 96 ER 507.

[105] (1773) 2 Black W 860, 863; 96 ER 507, 509.

[106] (1773) 2 Black W 860, 865; 96 ER 507, 510.

[107] *Marshall v Sharland* (1850) 15 QB 1050, 1058; 117 ER 757, 760 (Lord Campbell CJ).

[108] *Pendlebury v Walker* (1841) 4 Y & C Ex. 424, 440; 160 ER 1072, 1079: 'these … bargains are … founded on entire good faith; and … if such good faith be not observed the whole transaction is void' (Alderson B); *Howden v Haigh* (1840) 11 AD & E 1031, 1039; 113 ER 706, 709: 'The principle of the cases is entire good faith, which the creditors have a right to expect from each other and from the debtor. There is to be no collusion between the debtor and the favoured creditor, and each creditor is to stand on the same footing' (Coleridge J); *Knight v Hunt* (1829) 5 Bing 430, 433; 130 ER 1127, 1128: 'these agreements for composition with creditors require the strictest good faith' (Best CJ); *Ex Parte Stokes* (1802) 2 Ves Jun Supp. 50, 50 and 54; 34 ER 992, 992 and 994 (where a commission of bankrupt is tainted by good faith, it will be superseded). In *Ex Parte Brown* (1812) 1 V & B 58, 65; 35 ER 23, 25 Lord Chancellor Eldon considered whether a party who took out a commission of bankruptcy did so without good faith; *Freise v Randall* (1795) TR 145, 147; 101 ER 480, 481 (court report referring to good faith in the context of some creditors receiving proportionately more than others).

[109] *Cadogan v Kennett* (1776) 2 Cowp 432; 98 ER 1171.

[110] *Biddlecombe v Bond* (1835) 4 Ad & E 332; 111 ER 811.

[111] *Belcher v Magnay* (1843) 12 M & W 102; 152 ER 1128 (interpreting bankruptcy legislation).

[112] *In Re A Debtor; Ex Parte Official Receiver v Morrison* [1965] 1 WLR 1498, 1505 (Stamp J).

and good faith require that the contract be rescinded'.[113] In *Howden v Haigh and Another*,[114] Coleridge J stated

> the principle of the cases is entire good faith, which the creditors have a right to expect from each other and from the debtor. There is to be no collusion between the debtor and the favoured creditor and each creditor is to stand on the same footing.[115]

Another interesting context related to bankruptcy proceedings.[116] Creditors of the debtor met to discuss a common concern that some others were attempting to obtain priority by taking property of the debtor and having it sold. The meeting agreed steps would be taken to stop creditors obtaining inappropriate priority through such means. Both the plaintiff and defendant were creditors, and were represented at the meeting. It was agreed that one means of doing so was for one of the creditors at the meeting to commence formal legal proceedings in relation to their debt. The plaintiff declined to immediately act in this manner, but the defendant (whose security ranked second in priority at the time) did so. The effect of doing so apparently was to move that security to first in priority of payment. The plaintiff, whose security had ranked first but which now ranked second, argued that the defendant's conduct was in breach of good faith.

The House of Lords agreed. It found the defendant could not use the plaintiff's delay in commencing proceedings to thereby obtain a benefit for himself, of the very kind that all creditors at the meeting had resolved to be unacceptable and against which joint action was required. The House found the defendant had acted with a lack of good faith. It stated it was the duty of every court exercising equitable jurisdiction to ensure parties acted in good faith.[117]

In another bankruptcy case, creditors agreed to accept 17 shillings in the pound as a compromise of the debts owed to them. Unbeknown to one creditor, other creditors took steps to obtain further security to ensure more of their debt would be repaid than debt owed to other creditors. The court found this was a breach of good faith. Creditors had to be dealt with upon equal terms. No creditor should make out that they were bound by an agreement to accept a certain compromise, only to be secretly making arrangements to obtain a better compromise.[118]

[113] *Inglis v Usherwood* (1801) 1 East 515, 524; 102 ER 198, 202 (Lord Kenyon CJ).

[114] (1840) 11 Ad & E 1033; 113 ER 706; *Mallalieu v Hodgson* (1851) 16 QB 689, 712; 117 ER 1045, 1053: 'the requirement of good faith among the creditors and the preventing of gain by agreement for preference has been uniformly maintained' (Erle J).

[115] (1840) 11 Ad & E 1033, 1039; 113 ER 706, 709.

[116] *Beveridge v Smith* (1839) Maclean & Robinson 806, 818–19; 9 ER 299.

[117] (1839) Maclean and Robinson 806, 818–19; 9 ER 299, 304: 'it is the duty of every court exercising equitable jurisdiction to confine the parties to that situation to which they ought to have confined themselves, if they had acted with good faith towards each other and consistently with the arrangements they had made' (Lord Chancellor).

[118] *Ex Parte Sadler and Jackson* (1808) 15 Ves Jun 52; 33 ER 675; see also *Adams v Sworder* (1863) 4 Giff 287, 293; 66 ER 714, 717: 'if it appears that the composition (with creditors) was not in fact made bona fide, the plaintiff's right to sue does not exist' (Sir John Stuart, VC).

Elsewhere, the court discusses dishonest dealings in bankruptcy context in terms of a lack of good faith.[119]

Good faith was discussed in two contexts in a case where the plaintiff contracted to sell goods on credit to the defendant purchaser. The defendant became insolvent before the goods were delivered. The question was whether the plaintiff was required to complete the contract. The court held that good faith permitted the vendor in such cases to stop delivery. The court further noted that in a case where the insolvent had transferred their rights to purchase to an innocent third party acting in good faith, the seller would in such a case be required to deliver the goods to them.[120]

X. Partnerships

It was also applied in the partnership context in relation to a partner receiving partnership money personally. The court suggested if the partner had agreed not to so receive such money, but then did so, this would be contrary to good faith.[121] The court referred to partners' general obligation to 'keep good faith towards each other'.[122] Lack of good faith within a partnership would be grounds for dissolution.[123] Similarly, it would be contrary to good faith for a third party to insist that members of a partnership were liable on a debt where it was obvious to the third party that the individual partner sought to transact personally.[124]

XI. Agents

It was also applied in the context of a claim by an agent.[125] In *Quebec and Richmond Railroad Company v Edward Quinn*, an advocate noted the 'principal of law of universal application that where an agent acted in good faith and within the

[119] *Mace v Cammel* (1790) Lofft 782; 98 ER 917 (woman passes as man's wife in public but then denies it when he goes bankrupt and her property becomes potentially available to creditors as the bankrupt's wife).

[120] *Hawes and Another v Watson and Another* (1823) Ry & Mood 6, 9; 171 ER 923, 924.

[121] *Foster v Donald* (1820) 1 Jac & W 252; 37 ER 371; another example is *Peacock v Peacock* (1809) 16 Ves Jun 49, 51; 33 ER 902, 903: 'in the case of partnership the court acts upon this principle: that the good faith of the partners is pledged mutually to each other' (Lord Chancellor Eldon). See also *Coventry v Barclay* (1863) 3 De G J & S 320, 329; 46 ER 659, 663: 'I derive this conclusion from the partnership articles, the uniform understanding and practice of the partnership, and the good faith and honour of the dealings between the partners' (Lord Chancellor).

[122] *Rowe v Wood* (1822) 2 Jac.& W 554, 558; 37 ER 740, 742 (Lord Chancellor Eldon).

[123] *Chapman v Beach* (1820) 1 Jac & W 594; 37 ER 494; *Marshall v Volman* (1820) 2 Jac & W 266, 268; 37 ER 629, 630 (Lord Chancellor Eldon).

[124] *Leverson v Lane* (1862) 13 C B (NS) 278, 284; 143 ER 111, 114.

[125] *Bristow v Whitmore* (1861) IX HLC 390; 11 ER 781. There the agent took on further work without authority, thereby incurring greater expenses. The owner took the benefit of the further work but denied liability to reimburse the agent. The Court, in finding for the agent, noted he had acted 'with perfect good faith for the benefit of his principal': (1861) IX HLC 390, 400–01; 11 ER 781, 784 (Lord Campbell).

supposed limits of his authority, the principal is bound'.[126] In another agency case involving the Factors Act, a question arose as to the extent to which an agent's actions bound the principal for whom he purported to act. The Court articulated one of the issues as being whether the third party ought to have been aware as a reasonable person that the agent lacked authority to so engage the principal. The Court explained that the legislation protected agents who had in good faith pledged and exchanged securities. It also protected third parties who had acted in good faith and without notice that an agent lacked authority or was themselves acting in bad faith. The Court explained that where such bad faith existed, it would be contrary to the interests of commerce and 'mere honesty' to enforce the transaction.[127]

In another case involving agents, the court considered whether, when the agent exercised a power of sale in order to reclaim moneys owed to them, they had done so in good faith.[128] And in a case where an agent in fact lacked authority, the court considered whether they were acting in good faith, in determining whether or not an action for misrepresentation would lie against them.[129] Where an agency agreement is ambiguous, an agent that has acted in good faith on one interpretation will not be bound to be acting without authority if the principal later claims the other interpretation was intended.[130]

The Court interpreted the Factors Act, 5 & 6 Vict. c. 39 in relation to the right of a purchaser of property sold to them by an agent representing themselves as the true owner of the property sold. The court found that the third party could derive good title to the property through the agent, provided they purchased in good faith, and were not aware of the fact that the agents were not in fact the owners.[131] The legislation had specifically conditioned the third party purchaser's rights upon them acting in good faith.

XII. Contracts for Services

Good faith was evident in cases involving a contract for services. In *Fechter v Montgomery*,[132] the plaintiff managed a London theatre. He engaged the

[126] (1858) XII Moore, 231, 251; 14 ER 899, 907; another example is *Gobin Chunder Sein v Ryan* (1861) XV Moore, 231, 244; 15 ER 482, 487 (PC).

[127] *Gobind Chunder Sein v Valentine Ryan* (1861) XV Moore, 231, 254–55; 15 ER 482, 490–91 (Knight-Bruce LJ, for the Privy Council).

[128] *De Comas v Prost* (1865) III Moore NS, 157, 170; 16 ER 59, 64 (Milford J, in the Supreme Court of New South Wales). The report of the Privy Council appeal from this case quoted this aspect of the judgment. In a case from Victoria, submissions made to the Privy Council suggested that an agent had acted contrary to good faith by not acknowledging they were acting for a principal: *Wilson v Thrall* (1869) VI Moore NS, 247, 258; 16 ER 719, 723. Another one involved the 'good faith' of accounting entries prepared in relation to an agency relationship: *Murtunjoy Chuckerbutty v Cockrane* (1865) X Moore Ind App 230, 245; 19 ER 959, 965 (Turner LJ, for the Privy Council).

[129] *Collen v Wright* (1857) 8 El & Bl 647, 662; 120 ER 241, 247 (Cockburn CJ).

[130] *Ireland v Livingston* (1872) LR 5 HL 395, 416 (Lord Chelmsford).

[131] *Navulshaw v Brownrigg* (1852) 2 De G M & G 441; 42 ER 943.

[132] (1863) 33 Beav 21; 55 ER 274.

defendant, an actor. During negotiations, the defendant expressed a desire to feature in plays shown in London, to build his profile. Shortly thereafter, the parties completed a written agreement which nominated a weekly payment for services and a length of two years. It did not specify precisely the extent to which the defendant would be utilised. Nor did it expressly state that the defendant would not act in other venues during the period of the agreement. However, a stage manager of the plaintiff gave evidence that it was typical industry practice that, when an actor was engaged to perform at a particular theatre, they implicitly agreed not to perform at rival theatres. As it happened, the plaintiff commenced running another play in which the defendant did not feature. It was very successful, and the plaintiff kept running it. After five months of the defendant's engagement, he had not been called upon to act, though he was paid his weekly agreed fee. He wished to perform elsewhere, and the plaintiff sought an injunction to prevent him from doing so. The Court declined to issue the injunction.

The Court held that, when interpreting an agreement, it was necessary to consider the express terms, but also the position and situation of the parties, and the nature of the contract.[133] The Court held it was part of the parties' agreement (though not expressed) that the defendant would not work elsewhere, and that the plaintiff would engage the defendant within a reasonable time to act. The purpose of the agreement from the defendant's perspective was to increase his profile in London, and it would be contrary to that to permit the plaintiff to not offer him any work (though continuing to pay him). Thus, the court effectively let the defendant out of his contract with impunity. The court mentioned good faith, acknowledging it was required,[134] but holding there was no lack of good faith on the plaintiff's part, because he intended to avail himself of the actor's services and giving him ample opportunity to perform. Thus, the case is useful in reflecting that the court accepted contracting parties owed good faith obligations to the other (though they were not breached in this case), and was willing to rely on materials other than the express terms in determining the parties' contractual rights.

XIII. Company Liability

The court also applied good faith in determining whether or not company directors had acted ultra vires. A company had been established to build a hotel for the purposes of engaging in hotel/tavern operations. Before it was opened, company directors resolved to temporarily let part of the premises for business offices. In

[133] (1863) 33 Beav 21, 26; 55 ER 274, 276.
[134] (1863) 33 Beav 22, 29; 55 ER 274, 277 (Sir John Romilly MR). The Court cited *Lumley v Wagner* (1852) 5 De G & Sm 485 for the good faith requirement.

rejecting an argument that the resolution was ultra vires, the court noted that the directors were acting in good faith in making the decision they did.[135] In relation to a company struggling financially, a shareholder who feared he would face some personal liability transferred his share to a bankrupt person. The court set aside the transfer, on the basis it lacked good faith. The court noted that the extent, if any, of consideration was relevant in determining whether or not a transaction was in good faith.[136]

Similarly in relation to a company, plaintiffs advanced moneys to it on the understanding that the company directors had power to, and did, authorise the transaction on behalf of the company. Later the company argued the contract was not valid and binding upon them. Finding for the plaintiffs, the court noted they had acted in good faith in making the advance. There was nothing to put them upon notice that the directors might lack the power to make this transaction on behalf of the company.[137]

The court applied good faith in relation to determining the rateable value of a railway company's assets. Issues arose concerning the extent to which it could deduct certain expenditure, and whether it or property owners neighbouring the company's activities were entitled to particular deductions. The court noted:

> It is our business, however, only to lay down the general rule, and in applying it, much must be left, not only to the experience and acuteness, but also to the good sense and good faith and candour of the parties concerned, whose interests will be found in the end to be best consulted by this mode of dealing.[138]

The court also noted good faith in relation to a claim against a railway company for loss suffered by the company conducting works. Cockburn CJ noted that before the plaintiff sent in his claim 'he ought to have considered honestly and deliberately, and with good faith, what was the amount of damages he had sustained and what damage was likely in future to accrue … from the … works'.[139]

Good faith was also considered in relation to the exercise of a discretion regarding shares in a company. A deed of settlement of a life insurance company permitted shareholders to transfer their interests to another, provided the Board agreed. The Board refused to grant permission, and this was challenged. The Court said it must be presumed that the Board acted in good faith, and it was for the challenger to demonstrate that it had acted in an arbitrary or capricious fashion in the exercise of its discretion.[140]

[135] *Simpson v Westminster Palace Hotel Co* (1860) 2 De G F & J 141, 149–50; 45 ER 575, 579 (Knight Bruce LJ).

[136] *Re Mexican and South American Company* (1860) 2 De G F & J 302, 308–09; 45 ER 638, 640 (Turner LJ).

[137] *Royal British Bank v Turquand* (1855) 5 El & Bl 248; 119 ER 474.

[138] *The Queen v Great Western Railway Co* (1852) 15 QB 1085, 1089; 117 ER 770, 772 (Lord Campbell).

[139] *Re Hayward and Metropolitan Railway Company* (1864) 4 B & S 787, 796–97; 122 ER 655, 659.

[140] *Re Gresham Life Assurance Society* (1872) LR 8 Ch App 446, 450 (Sir WM James LJ).

XIV. Admiralty

It was utilised in this context.[141] Both the appellant and respondent referred to it in an admiralty case.[142] The court used it an admiralty case involving a limitation of liability clause. It would be effective if the law of England applied, but not effective if the law of France applied. The court found that the parties must be presumed to intend that English law applied, so giving the clause some effect. To do otherwise would be to impute lack of good faith on the part of the party that had proposed the clause.[143] Thus, a presumption (or expectation) of good faith was utilised to help determine a choice of law question based on the intention of the parties. It was also utilised in a case where it was alleged that merchants acted beyond the scope of their licences in entering into particular transactions.[144] It was also utilised in the context of the validity of the actions of a master who sold some of the cargo they were contracted to carry,[145] and a contract for the towing of a vessel.[146]

A court was not satisfied of the good faith of the master of a vessel. It was claimed the ship was sailing to Italy, a neutral country at a time of war, but the court concluded that it had always been intended that the ship would sail to France, against whom Britain was at war at the time. The court would not permit this party to utilise legal principles permitting neutral countries to continue to trade their native produce during times of war, because it concluded it had never been intended that the ship would sail to Italy as relevant documents claimed.[147] The court refused to intervene in a situation where the plaintiff's ship was captured and confiscated by others, only to be sold and re-sold. It subsequently ended up being owned by a British merchant. The court was satisfied he purchased in good faith, and refused an action by the original owner.[148]

[141] *The Ship Carpenter* (1810) II Acton, 11; 12 ER 160 (advocates for both sides referred to good faith in relation to the transaction: II Acton, 11, 15 and 17; 12 ER 160, 161–62). The brief judgment does not; *Harmer v Bell* (1851) VII Moore 267, 285; 13 ER 884, 891 (PC).

[142] *Alexander Duranty v Judah Hart and Company* (1863) II Moore, NS 290, 310 and 316; 15 ER 911, 918 and 920.

[143] *P. and O. Steam Navigation Co v Shand* (1865) III Moore NS, 272, 292; 16 ER 103, 111 (Turner LJ, for the Privy Council).

[144] *The Cosmopolite* (1801) 4 C Rob 7, 13; 165 ER 516, 518 (Sir W Scott); *The Vrow Cornelia* (1811) II Acton, 66, 72–73 and 84; 12 ER 181, 184 and 188 (the references are in the advocates' submissions, not the judgment).

[145] *Australasian Steam Navigation Co v Morse* (1872) VIII Moore NS 482, 491; 17 ER 393, 397 (appears in the judgment of Chief Justice Stephen of the New South Wales Supreme Court, quoted without disavowal in the Privy Council judgment in the case delivered by Sir Montague Smith). Good faith was also considered in relation to a sale of the ship itself: *The 'Glasgow', Otherwise 'Ya Macraw'* (1856) Swab 145, 151; 166 ER 1065, 1068 (Dr Lushington) and *Hayman v Molton* (1803) 5 Esp 65; 170 ER 739.

[146] *'The Kingalock'* (1854) 1 Sp Ecc & Ad 263, 265; 164 ER 153, 154 (Dr Lushington).

[147] *The 'Sarah Christina'* (1799) 1 C Rob 240; 165 ER 162; see elsewhere in the admiralty context at war time *The 'Rosalie and Betty'* (1800) 2 C Rob 343, 344; 165 ER 338, 339.

[148] *The 'Helena'* (1801) 4 C Rob 3; 165 ER 515.

XV. Intellectual Property

It was utilised in the context of an intellectual property claim. A patent holder wished to extend their patent beyond the initial statutory period. The Court noted it had discretion whether or not to extend the patent beyond the mandated time. In exercising its discretion, it could consider various factors. The good faith of the holder was one factor named as being relevant.[149] In *Sturz v De La* Rue Lord Chancellor Lyndhurst stated 'it is a principle of patent law that there must be utmost good faith in the specification. It must describe the invention in such a way that a person of ordinary skill in the trade shall be able to carry on the process'.[150]

The case of *Hogg v Kirby*[151] pertains, albeit loosely, to intellectual property, and good faith was discussed there. The plaintiff was the owner of a monthly publication published by the defendant. The publication adopted a particular appearance, and contained numerous articles (some of which continued on through various editions). A dispute arose between the plaintiff and defendant, and the defendant refused to publish the publication any more pursuant to the parties' agreement. However, he then developed a publication with a new name but of virtually identical appearance to the original, and which continued some of the articles left unfinished from previous editions of the plaintiff's work. The plaintiff sought an injunction to restrain the defendant. On a preliminary motion to issue the injunction, which was granted, the court utilised good faith concepts. It noted that it was open to any person acting in good faith to publish a similar work to that of the plaintiff, provided it was in fact new.[152] The court asked itself what constituted good faith between the plaintiff and defendant. It would breach good faith if the defendant published the work, not as a new work, but as a continuation of the work of another.[153]

XVI. Legal Proceedings

There is also evidence of the use of good faith in the law more generally. This includes a judge commenting that conscription was 'contrary to good faith and common honesty',[154] actions by foreign governments,[155] actions taken by barristers

[149] *In Re Hills' Patent* (1863) I Moore NS, 258, 265; 15 ER 698, 701 (Sir John T Coleridge, for the Privy Council).

[150] (1828) 5 Russ 322, 327; 38 ER 1048, 1050.

[151] (1803) 8 Ves Jun 214; 32 ER 336.

[152] (1803) 8 Ves Jun 214, 222; 32 ER 336, 339 (Lord Chancellor Eldon).

[153] (1803) 8 Ves Jun 215, 223; 32 ER 336, 339 (Lord Chancellor Eldon). See also *Perceval v Phipps* (1813) 2 V & B 19, 25; 35 ER 225, 228 where the Vice Chancellor considered the good faith of a person to whom a letter had been addressed. That person had publicised it. It was argued they had breached the copyright of the author.

[154] *Hillier v Fletcher* (1778) 2 Black W 1207, 1210; 96 ER 711, 712.

[155] *The 'Snipe' and Others* (1812) Edw 381, 386 and 396; 165 ER 1145, 1147 and 1151.

on behalf of their client,[156] court proceedings found to be tainted by a lack of good faith[157] and justices of the peace asserting jurisdiction when they were aware that the conditions under which they had jurisdiction did not exist.[158] In one case a defendant caused delays but then sought to rely on them in making a technical argument against the plaintiff. The court found to do so was against good faith.[159] The court considered whether the appellant was acting in good faith in making an appeal, in determining costs after it was unsuccessful.[160]

In relation to a court process, the court re-affirmed that, subject to a possible exception relating to legal professional privilege, parties were required to observe discovery practices, to disclose documents in their possession to the other side relevant to proceedings, including those contrary to their interests. Failure to do so, including active concealment of such documents, would amount to a lack of good faith.[161] Other proceedings involved a cognovit, where the parties agreed that the plaintiff would not seize the defendant's goods if the defendant honoured a bill of exchange. The defendant honoured it in a timely manner, but the plaintiff still took legal proceedings to seize the goods. The court held the proceedings were tainted by bad faith.[162] Where parties agreed to dispense with jury trial and with the use of a judge, rather than a commissioner, the case was decided. The unsuccessful party then sought to impugn the validity of the proceedings on technical grounds. The court struck this out on the basis it breached good faith.[163] The court asserted its jurisdiction to strike out any plea it regarded as having been made with a lack of good faith.[164]

Where the plaintiff's attorney had written to the defendant demanding payment of money owed to the plaintiff. The defendant then proceeded to pay the debt directly to the plaintiff. This meant the attorney missed out on his fees. He had not at the time of the demand issued a writ, which would have entitled him to payment of his fees. He did that the day after the defendant had paid the plaintiff directly. The court found the defendant's actions, in paying to the plaintiff directly

[156] *Swinfen v Lord Chelmsford* (1860) 5 H & N 888, 921; 157 ER 1436, 1449 (Pollock, CB, for the Court).

[157] *Drury and Another v Johnson* (1824) 13 Price, 478; 147 ER 1058; *Cocker v Tempest* (1841) 7 M & W 501; 151 ER 864; *Wade v Simeon* (1845) 1 CB 610, 620; 135 ER 680, 684; *Biddlecombe v Bond* (1835) 4 Ad & E 332, 338; 111 ER 811, 814; *Gould v Whitehead* (1839) 6 Bing (NC) 144; 133 ER 57; *Wakley v Cooke and Another* (1847) 16 M & W 822, 824; 153 ER 1424, 1425 (Parke B).

[158] *Pease and Others v Chaytor* (1861) 1 B & S 658; 121 ER 859.

[159] *Ouchterlony v Gibson* (1842) 4 Man & G 459, 465; 134 ER 189, 191 (Tindal CJ).

[160] *Simpson v Westminster Palace Hotel Co* (1860) VIII HLC 712, 718; 11 ER 608, 611 (Lord Campbell). Costs were awarded to a plaintiff who acted as a witness in his own case, partly because he 'acted with perfect good faith': *Howes v Barber* (1852) 18 QB 588, 592; 118 ER 222, 224 (Lord Campbell CJ). Travel costs of an attorney were fully reimbursed because he had paid them himself in good faith: *Hale v Bates* (1858) El Bl & El 575, 582; 120 ER 623, 626 (Erle J).

[161] *Flight v Robinson* (1844) 8 Beav 22, 36; 50 ER 9, 14 (Lord Langdale, MR).

[162] *Cash v Wells* (1830) 1 B & D 375; 109 ER 826.

[163] *Andrews v Elliott* (1855) 5 El & Bl 502, 504; 119 ER 567, 568 (Lord Campbell CJ); similarly *The Queen v The Justices of Salop* (1859) 2 El & El 386; 121 ER 146 and *Carpenter and Another v Hall* (1849) 8 CB 84; 137 ER 440.

[164] *Bartlett v Wells* (1862) 1 B & S 836, 840; 121 ER 924, 925 (Crompton J).

and not the attorney, was a breach of good faith.[165] Elsewhere it was seen as requiring that an appellant give full particulars of relevant facts.[166] A party making false allegations against another was found to have acted without good faith and with malice.[167]

And the court applied it to itself. Where a court was involved in a sale under decree, it noted it was itself required to 'keep good faith with purchasers'.[168] It was relevant in determining whether or not costs should be granted against an applicant.[169] An appellate court considered whether proceedings in an inferior court were 'regular or (in) good faith'.[170] A court asked itself if it would be contrary to good faith to make an order permitting a defendant to use personal property to pay advances and debts of a partnership of which he was a member, and then to further call upon him to pay partnership debts, when the personal property may have been utilised to raise such funds.[171] It was applied to the behaviour of a sheriff in relation to a demand for money,[172] a sheriff in failing to prevent goods he had seized from being taken by another,[173] and a government excise officer.[174] In relation to a statute regulating court orders, it was to be carried out 'with good faith'.[175] A court would not permit proceedings in one court to be taken simply in order to obtain an advantage in another court. This was found to be contrary to good faith.[176] The court expressed that good faith was pivotal in relation to bail.[177] The court interpreted early divorce legislation, permitting one of the parties to claim relief where the other had 'deserted' them for at least two years. The court found relief was not available where the party who had left had made a bona fide offer to return and provide for the other partner.[178]

XVII. Statute

Good faith appears elsewhere in statute. Examples include in relation to a railway company that had taken compulsory possession of land previously belonging to

[165] *Morrison v Summers* (1830) 1 B & Ad 559; 109 ER 895.
[166] *The Queen v Inhabitants of Bridgewater* (1841) 10 Ad & E 693, 698; 113 ER 263, 265 (Coleridge J); *The Queen v Justices of Carnarvonshire* (1841) 2 QB 325, 329; 114 ER 127, 129 (Coleridge J).
[167] *Heath v Heape* (1856) 1 H & N.477; 156 ER 1289.
[168] *Osborne v Foreman* (1856) 8 De G M & G 122, 125; 44 ER 336, 337 (Turner LJ).
[169] *In Re Windham* (1862) 4 De G F & J 53, 71; 45 ER 1102, 1110.
[170] *Parbury's Case* (1861) 2 De G F & J 80, 87; 45 ER 808, 811 (Lord Campbell).
[171] *Richardson v Bank of England* (1838) 4 My & Cr 165; 41 ER 65.
[172] *Jefferies v Sheppard* (1820) 3 B & Ald 696; 106 ER 815.
[173] *Thomas v Pearse* (1818) 5 Price, 578; 146 ER 699.
[174] *Sugars v Brinkworth* (1814) 4 Camp 46; 171 ER 15.
[175] *The Queen v Latchford* (1844) 6 QB 567, 578; 115 ER 212, 217 (Coleridge J).
[176] *Williams v Bank of England* (1836) 2 Y & C Ex. 265, 267; 160 ER 396, 397 (Lord Chief Baron); similarly *Wakley v Cooke* (1847) 14 M & W 1424; 153 ER 1424.
[177] *The 'Corner'* (1863) Br & L 161, 165; 167 ER 324, 326 where Dr Lushington referred to the 'scrupulous good faith which must be required of all parties in the observance of the rules relating to bail'.
[178] *Cargill v Cargill* (1858) 1 Sw & Tr 235, 237; 164 ER 708, 709 (The Judge Ordinary).

another. They were generally prohibited from taking possession until they had paid either purchase money or compensation. If they did so, they were liable to financial penalties under the Act. However, the Act created an exception where such possession was in good faith and without collusion.[179]

XVIII. Succession

Good faith was noted in relation to the execution of a will. It was not the basis of the decision, but in passing judgment against an executor who had not realised all of the assets of the estate in a timely manner, instead working some of the assets to produce revenue, the court found the executor had failed in his duty to the residuary beneficiary although he 'acted with perfect honesty and good faith throughout the whole transaction and probably did the best that he could'.[180] Elsewhere in relation to wills, the court noted that a plaintiff had an action in respect of moneys advanced to the estate in good faith.[181]

Further in the will context, the court found that an executor had acted with a lack of good faith. The executor had obtained the signature of a beneficiary on a release document. The beneficiary had recently attained majority. She had not been accurately informed about her rights under the will, and been led to believe (falsely) that there was no money in the estate available to honour a larger claim than that dealt with in the release. The executor was privy to advice to the contrary, but did not share that with the beneficiary. The beneficiary did not have access to independent advice; she relied on advice given by her uncle (the executor) whose personal interests were contrary to that of the beneficiary. The beneficiary's mother had on one view been 'paid off' by the executor granting her an annuity under the will to which she was not strictly entitled. The court concluded the executor had acted with a lack of good faith.[182]

XIX. Good Faith, 'Negligence' and Other Torts

At times, good faith seems to have some relevance to what we would today regard as an action in negligence. Obviously, these references occurred well prior to recognition of a generalised duty of care, and the action for negligence was in relatively

[179] *Hutchinson v The Manchester, Bury and Rossendale Railway Company* (1846) 15 M & W 314; 153 ER 869.

[180] *Wightwick v Lord* (1857) VI HLC 217, 234; 10 ER 1278, 1285 (Lord Wensleydale); cf *Buxton v Buxton* (1835) 1 My & Cr 80; 40 ER 307 where an executor was excused for a substantial delay in selling the testator's assets, leading to a reduction in sale price, because he had acted in good faith.

[181] *Gavin v Hadden* (1871) VIII Moore NS, 95, 119; 17 ER 247, 257 (James LJ, for the Privy Council).

[182] *Harvey v Cooke* (1827) 4 Russ 34, 52–53; 38 ER 717, 725; see in the context of an executor making frivolous claims and against prior promises *Pickup v Wharton* (1834) 2 C & M 401; 149 ER 816.

primitive state applicable to a narrow class of cases. We must also be careful about the sense in which the word 'negligence' is used, not assuming it meant the same previously as it does today.

So in *Shiells and Thorne v Blackburne*,[183] the defendant was a merchant who wished to send some products overseas. He agreed to also deliver goods belonging to another to the same destination. He packed them together, but made a mistake regarding the customs declaration for the goods. As a result they were confiscated. The owner of the goods included with the defendant's brought an action against him for the loss of his product. The court rejected the claim.

In so doing, Heath J noted the defendant 'was not guilty either of gross negligence or fraud; he acted bona fide'.[184] Heath J added the defendant did not profess any special skill in relation to what he did, and acted gratuitously. Wilson J agreed. He said where someone promised to perform a task gratuitously, provided they acted in good faith, it was not consistent with the spirit or policy of the law to make them liable for loss occasioned to another as a result.[185] The defendant was not guilty of gross negligence. Lord Loughborough agreed with this conclusion. And in *Oxley v Young and Another*,[186] the court found that a guarantor might have an action on the case against another if 'wilful neglect could be shown, contrary to all good faith', whereby they had incurred a loss.[187] In the negotiable instrument case of *Gill v Cubitt*, members of the court considered whether the plaintiff had exercised due caution and diligence in making inquiry, in determining whether he had acted in good faith.[188] This was repeated by members of the House of Lords in *London Joint Stock Bank v Simmons*.[189] In *Derry v Peek*, it was suggested 'want of care' may be relevant in determining whether defendants acted in good faith.[190] Obviously, this is the language (at least today) of negligence. I will return to the overlap between good faith and negligence in chapter ten.

There is also evidence of good faith in relation to cases of slander. In one case based on slander of title, the defendant wrote to an intending purchaser of the plaintiff's land. The defendant claimed the plaintiff was insane, and so his title would be in dispute. As a result, the intending purchaser ended the contract. When the plaintiff land owner accused the defendant of slander in title, the court found that the answer would depend on whether the defendant said what he said in good faith, believing it to be true,[191] or with malice. In other cases involving

[183] (1789) 1 H Bl 158; 126 ER 94.

[184] (1789) 1 H Bl 158, 161; 126 ER 94, 96.

[185] (1789) 1 H Bl 158, 161; 126 ER 94, 96.

[186] (1796) 2 H Bl 613, 616; 126 ER 734, 736 (Lord Ch J Eyre, with whom Heath and Rooke JJ agreed).

[187] See similarly *Oliver v Hinton* [1899] 2 Ch 264, 274 (Lindley MR) (with whom Sir FH Jeune and Rigby LJ agreed).

[188] (1824) 3 B & C 466, 476 (Bayley J) and 477 (Holroyd); 107 ER 806, 810 (Bayley and Holroyd JJ).

[189] [1892] AC 201, 221 (Lord Herschell) and 225 (Lord Macnaghten).

[190] (1889) 14 App Cas 337, 359 (Lord Fitzgerald).

[191] *Pitt v Donovan* (1813) 1 M & S 639, 644; 105 ER 238, 240 (Lord Ellenborough CJ); similarly *Pater v Baker* (1847) 3 CB 831; 136 ER 333.

alleged slander of an individual, again the view is expressed that it is a defence to a slander action if the defendant uttered the words in good faith, believing them to be true.[192] The court noted that a defence of privilege may apply to communications, in a case involving alleged libel, where they were made in good faith.[193]

This discussion has sought to demonstrate the very broad range of contexts in which notions of good faith were accepted and applied by English courts. This occurred over many years. It was commonly applied in relation to contracts, and other commercial arrangements including negotiable instruments, financial arrangements, agency and company dealings. It was applied to court proceedings and the behaviour of court personnel. It was utilised in statute. It has also demonstrated the possible overlap between notions of good faith and 'negligence'.

XX. Variable Meaning of Good Faith in these Contexts

The question of the meaning of good faith in these various contexts is an important one. At one level, any breach of contract is a breach of good faith.[194] More specifically, at times, it seems as if it is a synonym for honesty.[195] It is often contrasted with intentional fraud or wrongdoing,[196] or 'wilful default'.[197] A sham transaction would be contrary to good faith.[198] Sometimes it is clear that it means more than a lack of dishonesty.[199] At other times, it seems to mean reasonableness.[200] A 999-year

[192] *Blake v Pilfold* (1832) 1 M & Rob 196, 200; 174 ER 67, 68 (court reporter's explanation of Taunton J's summing up in the case).

[193] *Dickson v Earl of Winton* (1859) 1 F & F 419, 425–26; 175 ER 790, 793 (Lord Campbell CJ); similarly in relation to a journalist's reporting of a court matter, where libel was alleged: *Woodgate v Ridout* (1865) 4 F & F 202; 176 ER 531; allegations of wrongdoing against an employee: *Toogood v Spyring* (1834) 1 C M & R 181; 149 ER 1044; *Somerville v Hawkins* (1851) 10 CB 583, 589; 138 ER 231, 234 (Maule J, for the Court).

[194] *Harries v Thomas* (1836) 2 M & W 32, 39; 150 ER 656, 659 (Lord Abinger C.B.).

[195] *Lawson v Weston* (1801) 4 Esp 56, 57–58; 170 ER 640, 641 (KB) (Lord Kenyon); *Uther v Rich* (1839) 10 AD & E 783, 791; 113 ER 297, 300 (Lord Denman CJ); *Backhouse v Harrison* (1834) 5 B & Ad 1098, 1105; 110 ER 1099, 1102 (Patteson J); *Sheen v Bumstead* (1863) 2 H & C 193, 196; 159 ER 80, 82 (Cockburn CJ); *Hunt v Fripp* [1897] 1 Ch 675, 682 (Byrne J); *Northern Development (Holdings) v UDT Securities* [1976] 1 WLR 1230, 1235 (Megarry J).

[196] *Stewart v Stewart* (1838–1839) VI Clark & Finnelly 911, 932; 7 ER 940, 949; *Perry v Holl* (1860) 2 De G F & J 38, 50; 45 ER 536, 540–41; *Derry v Peek* (1889) 14 App Cas 337, 357–58 (Lord Fitzgerald).

[197] *Coope v Carter* (1852) 2 De G M & G. 292, 298; 42 ER 884, 887 (Knight Bruce LJ); *Jones v Smith* (1841) 1 Hare 42, 56; 66 ER 943, 949 'fraudulent or wilful blindness' (Sir James Wigram, VC).

[198] *Re Mexican and South American Company* (1860) 2 De G F & J 302, 308; 45 ER 638, 640 (asking whether the transaction was 'a mere colourable and unsubstantial transaction') (Turner LJ).

[199] *Baud v Farrell* (1855) 7 De G M & G 628, 632; 44 ER 245, 246 concluding the executrix 'conducted herself with good faith, nor entertained any dishonest or improper intention'.

[200] *The Apothecaries' Company v Harrison* (1840) 12 Ad & E 643, 644; 113 ER 958, 959 (Lord Denman CJ, for the Court) concluding that it was effectively implicit in a compromise agreement between the parties that the plaintiff would only enforce one of the penalties available to it. Later the defendant issued a writ of error in respect of this agreement. The court found such action was a breach of good faith having regard to the only reasonable construction of the agreement, which presumably meant that the parties intended that the compromise agreement would not be the subject of a writ of error.

lease was set aside on the basis that the lessee was not acting in good faith.[201] There is also evidence it was interpreted to include whether the person accused of a lack of good faith had done something to prevent the other party from performing their contractual obligations.[202] It was described as meaning acting 'in the fair and ordinary course of business'.[203] In the context of court proceedings, the court described good faith as including something that, although 'strictly regular', was oppressive or for (at least partly) illegitimate purposes.[204] It has been described as something that would defeat the intention or understanding of the parties to an agreement, were it to be permitted to occur.[205] It includes behaving in a manner that seems contrary to the original purpose/s of the contract,[206] or the conferral upon them of a power.[207] It is assimilated to the question of proper motives (or otherwise).[208]

In *In Re Windham* (1862) 4 De G F & J 53, 67–68; 45 ER 1102, 1108 (Turner LJ) the Court considered whether there were reasonable grounds for the petitioner's belief in determining whether or not they were acting in good faith; *The Queen v Nunneley* (1858) El Bl & El 852, 860; 120 ER 728, 731: 'when the objection is reasonable they are not entitled to say that they choose to disbelieve the bona fides (of the one raising the objection)' (Coleridge J). The court agreed that justices of the peace had no reasonable grounds for believing they had jurisdiction over a matter; this meant they had acted with a lack of good faith: *Pease v Chaytor* (1861) 1 B & S 658, 672; 121 ER 859, 864 (Wightman J, with whom Blackburn J agreed (674, 865); *Kendall v Alken* (1834) 10 Bing 437, 440; 131 ER 974, 975: 'the demand of the plaintiff is most unreasonable … her action now is a breach of good faith' (Tindal CJ); PS Atiyah, *The Rise and Fall of Freedom of Contract* (Oxford, Clarendon Press, 1979) 761–62: 'ideas of good faith did often lead the courts to protect expectations which were not expressly bargained for, but were nevertheless reasonably entertained'. He cites *Ebrahimi v Westbourne Galleries Ltd* [1972] 2 All ER as a factual example; similarly *Esso Petroleum v Mardon* [1976] 2 All ER 5 and *English v Dedham Vale Properties Ltd* [1978] 1 All ER 382.

[201] *Attorney-General v Green* (1801) 6 Ves 452, 452: 'It is impossible that a person taking in good faith would take such a lease as that' (Lord Eldon, cancelling the lease).

[202] *Parry v The Great Ship Company* (1864) 4 B & S 557, 565; 122 ER 568, 571. The case of *Benson v Blunt* (1841) 1 QB 870, 113 ER 1364 is somewhat similar. There the court reasoned that the plaintiff had exercised a contractual discretion arbitrarily and acted capriciously in denying the defendant an opportunity to perform their contractual obligations, to the advantage of the plaintiff in terms of contractual remedies. However, the Court did not expressly refer to good faith in so deciding.

[203] *Uther v Rich* (1839) 10 Ad & E 784, 788 (submission of counsel).

[204] *Siderfield v Thatcher* (1848) 11 Beav 201, 201; 50 ER 793, 794 (submission of counsel).

[205] *Sherborn v Tollemache* (1863) 13 CB (NS) 742, 749; 143 ER 293, 296: ('contrary to the spirit and intention of the instrument … therefore … against good faith' (Erle CJ); to like effect Williams Willes and Keating JJ (749, 296).

[206] *Eastern Counties Railway Co v Hawkes* (1855) V HLC 331, 365; 10 ER 928, 941 (Lord Brougham). The Court considered the good faith of directors in a case where it was alleged the company acted for purposes beyond those for which it was established: *Simpson v Westminster Palace Hotel Co* (1860) VIII HLC 712, 718; 11 ER 608, 611 (Lord Campbell).

[207] *Portland v Topham* (1864) XI HLC 31, 54; 11 ER 1242, 1251 stating that the donee (appointor) was required to act with good faith and sincerity and not for the purposes of achieving ulterior objectives in the sense of acting beyond the purpose and intent of the power originally conferred (Lord Chancellor, with whom Lord Cranworth and Lord Chelmsford agreed). In *Stockton and Darlington Railway Co v Brown* (1860) IX HLC 245; 11 ER 724 the Court considered the situation of a railway company authorised to purchase property needed for the purpose of constructing a particular railway. The Court required that the directors exercise the power bona fide with the object of using them for the purposes authorised by the legislature, not for purposes outside that ambit: (1860) IX HLC 245, 254 (Lord Campbell) and 256 (Lord Cranworth); 11 ER 724, 727 and 728.

[208] *In Re Windham* (1862) 4 De G F & J 53, 67; 45 ER 1102, 1108: 'it is necessary to consider whether (the relevant conduct) was (done) for any improper motive, or whether it was really and bona fide made

At times it seems to be something like the lack of unconscionable behaviour, as we would today describe it.[209] It is also described as something of a mutuality of obligation. Where there is a lack of such mutuality, the court has concluded there is a lack of good faith.[210] In that case, lack of disclosure of material facts relevant to the transaction is also discussed as indicating a lack of good faith,[211] as is taking advantage of the vulnerability of the other.[212] On the other hand, the fact that full disclosure did occur was noted as evidence of good faith.[213] Where a party has discretion under a contract, there seems to be an expectation it will be exercised reasonably, as opposed to capriciously or arbitrarily.[214] This is sometimes connected with good faith.[215] It was distinguished from gross negligence, but acknowledged that gross negligence could be evidence of bad faith.[216] At other times, references to good faith may suggest an equivalence with gross negligence,[217] or negligence.[218] Sometimes it is said that a person who takes an interest without providing valuable consideration acts with a lack of good faith, though there is no evidence of fraud.[219] Sometimes it is said that, in circumstances where the facts would put a reasonable person upon inquiry as to something (for example, the authority of a person purporting to act as agent), the failure of a person to make any inquiry is suggestive that they are acting

with a view to his interest and benefit' ('his' being the subject of a court application) (Turner LJ). In the context of a defamation claim, too, (where traditionally motive was relevant), where the court considered the good faith of an utterer of a statement that might be defamatory if the defence of privilege did not apply), it is likely that good faith in this context meant lack of malicious motive (though concededly this is speculation on my part, because the court did not explain the sense in which it used good faith, and it is not entirely clear from the express words used): *Harrison v Bush* (1855) 5 El & Bl 344; 119 ER 509.

[209] *Beaven v M'Donnell* (1854) 9 Ex 307; 156 ER 131 (contract made by a lunatic, court took into account the other party to the transaction was not aware of this and so did not have to refund a deposit paid); in *Ex Parte Brown* it was described as one of the parties seeking to counteract an endeavour designed to avoid a double expense in the context of bankruptcy proceedings: (1812) 1 V & B 58, 65; 35 ER 23, 25 (Lord Chancellor Eldon).

[210] *Pickett v Loggon* (1807) 1 Ves Jun Supp 551, 551–52; 34 ER 916, 916–17.

[211] *Harvey v Cooke* (1827) 4 Russ 34, 53; 38 ER 717, 725 (Sir John Leach MR); *King v Hamlet* (1834) 2 My & K 456, 476; 39 ER 1018, 1026 (Lord Chancellor Brougham); *The Queen v Inhabitants of Bridgewater* (1841) 10 Ad & E 693, 698; 113 ER 263, 265: 'there ought to be strict good faith, and full information given' (Coleridge J); *Lord Howden v Simpson* (1839) 10 Ad & E 791, 801; 113 ER 300, 303: 'to conceal such an agreement from the legislature was … a fraud upon it, and any contract founded on such concealment contrary to good faith' (Lord Denman CJ, for the Court).

[212] *Harvey v Cooke* (1827) 4 Russ, 53; 38 ER 717, 725.

[213] *King v Hamlet* (1833) Coop T Brough 281, 285; 47 ER 100, 102 (Lord Chancellor); *The Queen v Justices of Carnarvonshire* (1837) 2 QB 325, 329; 114 ER 127, 129 (Coleridge J) (it was also relevant that the party accused of non-disclosure knew less about the particular matters than the one claiming lack of disclosure to them).

[214] *Pope v Lord Duncannon* (1838) 9 Sim 177, 179–80; 59 ER 326, 327 (Sir L Shadwell, VC).

[215] *Barrow v Isaac and Son* [1891] 1 QB 417, 419 (Lord Esher MR).

[216] *Goodman v Harvey* (1836) 4 Ad & E 870, 876; 111 ER 1011, 1014 (Lord Denman CJ).

[217] *Shiells and Thorne v Blackburne* (1789) 1 H Bl 158, 161; 126 ER 94, 96: 'the defendant in this case was not guilty either of gross negligence or fraud; he acted bona fide' (Heath J).

[218] *Gill v Cubitt* (1824) 3 B & C 466, 476–77; 107 ER 806, 810 (Bayley and Holroyd); *London Joint Stock Bank v Simmons* [1892] AC 201, 221 (Lord Herschell) and 225 (Lord Macnaghten).

[219] (1839) 10 Ad & E 784, 791; 113 ER 297, 300 (Lord Denman CJ, for the Court).

without good faith.[220] It can sometimes appear to be similar to estoppel.[221] It is on occasion equated with fairness.[222]

Where a contract is attended by a condition precedent, good faith requires that a contracting party with the ability to influence whether or not the condition is met take reasonable steps to achieve it.[223] To do so would be to act in good faith. Unwillingness to use best endeavours to achieve the condition precedent is evidence of bad faith.[224] As a corollary, a party who contracted on the basis of a condition precedent, where they had no reasonable belief that the condition would be met, would be acting in bad faith.[225]

O'Connor attempts a definition of good faith:

> The principle of good faith in English law is a fundamental principle derived from the rule pacta sunt servanda, and other legal rules, distinctively and directly related to honesty, fairness, and reasonableness, the application of which is determined at a particular time by the standards of honesty, fairness and reasonableness prevailing in the community which are considered appropriate for formulation in new or revised legal rules.[226]

It should again be conceded that the way in which judges express themselves can be somewhat confusing in relation to their understanding of the meaning of the context. As one example of something that appears frequently in the judgments, in *The Queen v Inhabitants of Bridgewater*, Coleridge J opines that 'there ought to be strict good faith, and full information given'.[227] Of course, when a reader is trying to determine the sense in which the judge means 'good faith', at least two

[220] *Gobind Chunder Sein v The Administrator-General of Bengal* (1861) IX Moore Ind App 140, 169; 19 ER 695, 705 (Knight Bruce LJ, for the Privy Council).

[221] *Swan v North British Australasian Co* (1863) 2 H & C 175, 177; 159 ER 73, 74: 'parties shall not be permitted to aver, against equity and good faith, the invalidity of a deed which either by words or conduct they have asserted to be valid, and upon which the others have acted' (Mellor J); *Polglass v Oliver* (1831) 2 C & J 15; 149 ER 7 (plaintiff did not originally object to the bank notes offered by the defendant to make a tender, but later raised an objection – held precluded from doing so because did not raise any objection at the time the notes were accepted).

[222] *The 'Vrow Margaretha'* (1799) 1 C Rob 336, 339; 165 ER 197, 198 considering a question 'whether it was a bona fide transfer or not. It think the time is a strong circumstance, to prove the fairness of the transaction' (Sir W Scott); *The 'Cosmopolite'* (1801) 4 C Rob 8, 13; 165 ER 516, 518; *Salomons v Nissen* (1788) 2 TR 674, 681; 100 ER 363, 366 where Buller J, after stating that good faith was the basis of all mercantile transactions, considered whether the purchaser had acted 'fairly and honestly, or with a design to deceive and defraud'.

[223] *Bain v Fothergill* (1873) LR 7 HL 158, 175 (Baron Pollock) and 200 (Baron Pigott).

[224] *Malhotra v Choudhury* [1980] Ch 52, 72–73 (Stephenson LJ, with whom Cumming-Bruce LJ agreed).

[225] *Bain v Fothergill* (1873) LR 7 HL 158, 212 (Lord Hatherley).

[226] JF O'Connor, *Good Faith in English Law* (Aldergate, Dartmouth, 1990) 102.

[227] (1841) 10 Ad & E 693, 698; 113 ER 263, 265. Another appears in *Ormrud v Huth* (1845) 14 M & W 651, 663–64; 153 ER 636, 642 where Tindal CJ asks whether the seller knew of the fraud that occurred during packing or had acted in good faith or with a fraudulent purpose. This passage seems to suggest good faith is distinct from fraud, but the judgment proceeds then only to consider whether there was fraud (ie whether the defendant knew of the mismatch between the sample provided and the product given).

interpretations of the phrase are possible, bearing in mind the conjunction 'and'. First, Coleridge J may have intended to mean that an aspect of good faith was that full information must be given. Second, Coleridge J may have used the concept of good faith as a separate and distinct one from a requirement of full information. Typically, judgments of this era are succinct, and a reading of the broader judgment does not clarify the intended meaning any further. The best that can be said of such phrasing is that no hard and fast rule can be applied when judges link two concepts with the conjunction 'and', one of which is good faith. The judgment and the passage must be read in individual context, and to some extent there is (educated) guesswork required as to the relation that the judge intends between the multiple concepts to which reference is made.[228]

XXI. The Start of a Shift Away from Good Faith

By the mid-nineteenth century, there is evidence of a shift in the law away from good faith and towards the strict letter of the contract. In *The Company of Proprietors of the Leominster Canal Navigation v The Shrewsbury and Hereford Railway Company*,[229] the court considered a situation where earlier promises upon which reliance had been placed were not kept. The plaintiff sought to bind the defendant to these promises. In refusing, the Court noted that experience had shown that no reliance could be placed upon good faith and common honesty; instead, parties should protect themselves by the written terms of the contract.[230] Further, in *Gibson v Small*, Baron Martin stated 'it is an established rule of law that a written contract (subject to certain known exceptions) shall be taken to contain and express the entire contract between the parties'.[231] Harrison points to a period around the 1870s where she suggests that the law turned against good faith.[232]

[228] More recent definitions appear to include both honesty and reasonableness, as well as fairness, and emphasise the use of community standards at any given time in formulating the content of good faith: O'Connor (n 226) 102: 'the principle of good faith in English law is a fundamental principle derived from the rule pacta sunt servanda, and other legal rules, distinctively and directly related to honesty, fairness and reasonableness, the application of which is determined at a particular time by the standards of honesty, fairness and reasonableness prevailing in the community which are considered appropriate for formulation in new or revised legal rules'.

[229] (1857) 3 K & J 654; 69 ER 1272.

[230] (1857) 3 K & J 654, 673; 69 ER 1272, 1280 (Sir W Page Wood, Vice Chancellor).

[231] *Gibson v Small* (1852–1853) IV HLC 352, 368; 10 ER 499, 505; similarly Lord Chief Baron Pollock: 'our duty is to expound contracts according to the lawful intentions of the parties who make them, expressed by the language they have used; and we are not at liberty to insert or imply a condition of seaworthiness (on account of what we may deem to be its general importance or its beneficial public results) unless we are satisfied that such was the undoubted meaning of the contracting parties' (409, 521); cf Baron Parke 'in the common law of England … a warranty or condition of seaworthiness at the commencement of the risk is implied in all voyage-policies, whether it has been adopted originally from the law merchant or implied from the very nature of the contract itself' (397, 517) (to like effect Williams J (379, 510).

[232] Harrison (n 5) 7.

However, still around this time there are numerous references to courts considering whether parties have acted in good faith.[233] In *Coaks v Boswell* the House of Lords reconfirmed that an ordinary purchaser of property was 'bound to observe good faith in all that he says or does, with a view to the contract'.[234]

It is interesting to speculate as to why this move against good faith occurred. It was not expressly explained.[235] Harrison points to a range of factors.[236] They include the passage of the Judicature Act 1873 (UK), fusing the administration of law and equity. She suggests that some of the common law judges were ambivalent about some equitable doctrines. Good faith had come to be recognised as an equitable doctrine, though it had been applied in various other courts other than Chancery. She suggests that some of the common law judges may have taken an exaggerated view regarding the extent to which Chancery court in fact exercised significant discretion around unfair terms and good faith. She also refers to a greater willingness by parliament to enact statutory reforms to deal with pressing problems. Some judges may have concluded that the increased willingness of parliament to enact needed social reforms, often based around notions of fairness, reduced the felt need for courts to defend and protect such notions. She also points to the Vendor and Purchaser Act 1874 (UK), which provided a remedy for disputes particularly around the title of property. It also limited the court's role in intervening on the basis of good faith, by strictly limiting the basis upon which a contract could be declared invalid. She speculates that the judges might have taken a broader message from legislation on this kind, making them more willing to uphold the literal wording of contracts, and less willing to intervene. There was obviously also an intellectual tradition around this time, about which more will be said in the next chapter, more conducive to freedom of contract, and less conducive to courts' having a supervisory jurisdiction over parties' behaviour regarding contract formation and performance.

XXII. Conclusion

This chapter has discussed a large number of cases where English courts accepted and applied concepts of good faith in the period up to the mid-nineteenth century. It was applied in many contract cases, and in other commercial contexts including negotiable instruments, finance, bankruptcy, agency, company dealings and

[233] *Harper v Hayes* (1860) 2 De G F & J 542, 550; 45 ER 731, 734 (Lord Chancellor); *Hunt v Elmes* (1860) 2 De G F & J 578, 585; 586; 45 ER 745, 748 (Knight Bruce LJ); *Dilkes v Broadmead* (1860) 2 De G F & J 566, 574; 45 ER 740, 743 (Lord Campbell).

[234] (1886) 11 App Cas 232, 235 (Earl of Selborne) (with whom Lords Blackburn Watson Bramwell and Fitzgerald agreed). The context there was the failure of a party to the contract to bring the attention to the court, in the case of a court-ordered sale, of information of which they were aware that was relevant to the fair market price of the thing sold.

[235] Harrison (n 5) 137.

[236] ibid 7–10.

intellectual property. For a time, it did seem that Lord Mansfield's holding in *Carter v Boehm* that good faith was applicable to all contractual dealings, not just those involving insurance, would come to pass. It is conceded that there were a broad range of understandings of what good faith meant and what it required parties to do. This, together with developments in society outside the legal system, may have undermined it. But the discussion tends to contradict some of the more wild assertions that good faith is some kind of alien, and anathema, to our system of common law. The courts and society of the eighteenth and early to mid-nineteenth century did not think so. The next chapter will consider the reaction against good faith in the law during the freedom of contract era, and then the 'reaction against that reaction'.

3

Freedom of Contract: The Courts and the Philosophy

I. Introduction

It will now be demonstrated that, from a legal system which broadly embraced good faith and fairness principles in many different areas, the law shifted away from such concepts, in search of greater certainty.[1] There are many reasons for this. Chief among them would be the Industrial Revolution of the later eighteenth and early to mid-nineteenth century. The exponentially increased level of mercantile activity resulted in a vast increase in the number of contractual engagements. Business demanded some certainty and consistency in the recognition and enforcement of their contracts. Liberalism was an ascendant political philosophy, and legal positivism an ascendant legal one.[2] There was criticism of the arbitrariness of equitable rules, including notions of good faith. It is noteworthy, for example, that the first English treatise on contract, Powell's *Essay Upon the Law of Contracts and Agreements* (1790) claimed:

> It is absolutely necessary for the advantage of the public at large that the rights of the subject should … depend upon certain and fixed principles of law, and not upon rules and constructions of equity, which when applied … must be arbitrary and uncertain, depending in the extent of their application, upon the will and caprice of the judge.[3]

Powell argued that parties were bound to honour contractual promises they had made, despite the fact it would be difficult for the party to do so, would be extremely unfair, and so on.

[1] *Manifest Shipping Co Ltd v Uni-Polaris Ins Co Ltd* (*The Star Sea*) [2003] 1 AC 469, [45]: 'Lord Mansfield's universal proposition (of good faith) did not survive. The commercial and mercantile law of England developed in a different direction preferring the benefits of simplicity and certainty which flow from requiring those engaging in commerce to look after their own interests' (Lord Hobhouse); Sir A Mason, 'Contract, Good Faith and Equitable Standards in Fair Dealing' (2000) 116 *Law Quarterly Review* 66, 66.

[2] W Tetley, 'Good Faith in Contract: Particularly in the Contracts of Arbitration and Chartering' (2004) 35 *Journal of Maritime Law and Commerce* 561, 569.

[3] At x; HK Lucke 'Good Faith and Contractual Performance' in PD Finn (eds), *Essays on Contract* (Sydney, Law Book Co, 1987) 157: 'common lawyers retreated to the familiar territory of strict precedent, concrete categories, precise rules, literalist interpretation and conservative legalism in which good faith cannot flourish'.

In one case, the court expressed the view that a broad definition of good faith to include due diligence and reasonable inquiry would 'paralyse' trade and commerce.[4]

Gordon talks about a three-stage approach to the development of the modern law of contract.[5] He states that stage one involved community custom, local hierarchical relations of social groups (family household-based small business, the village) tempered by 'equitable norms of community'. In the next stage (the focus of this chapter), he says economic actors won their freedom from status hierarchies, local customs and state control to become involved in free exchange. This was the time at which contract law as we today know it was forged. He says that system assumed anything could be commodified and the subject of exchange; virtually any terms agreed to by the parties were possible, and the law would 'blindly' enforce it. He discusses as the third stage the evolution from discrete exchange to more continuous contract relations (more of which in chapter seven and eight), and increased market regulation impacting freedom of contract to try to respond to 'market failure', including power and information imbalances.

Horwitz states it was 'only in the nineteenth century (that) judges and jurists finally reject(ed) the longstanding belief that the justification of contractual obligation is derived from the inherent justice or fairness of an exchange'.[6] He also notes that, with the development of markets in the nineteenth century, there was a move away from acceptance of an objective theory of value, in favour of acceptance of a subjective theory of value. This made courts less willing to intervene in parties' bargains, for instance because of as supposed undervalue or overvalue. This became impossible because there was no inherent value of something – it depended on the worth that subjective individuals placed upon it. Provided they had voluntarily entered into the transaction and were of capacity, the role of the law of contract was to enforce their bargains, as an expression of the parties' will.[7]

Eric Holmes summarises as follows:

> A reaction against the obligation of good faith and fair dealing occurred with the advent, during the late nineteenth century, of the pure theory of contract, characterized

[4] *Lawson v Weston* (1801) 4 Esp 56, 57; 170 ER 640, 641 (Lord Kenyon) (KB).

[5] R Gordon, 'Macaulay, Macneil and the Discovery of Solidarity and Power in Contract Law' [1985] *Wisconsin Law Review* 565, 577.

[6] M Horwitz 'The Historical Foundations of Modern Contract Law' (1974) 87(5) *Harvard Law Review* 917, 917. One example appears in *Barnardiston v Lingood* (1740) 2 Atk 133, 134; 26 ER 484, 485 (Ch). There Lord Hardwicke states that 'in the case of a hard bargain, where it is not absolutely executed, but executory only, the constant rule of the court is, not to carry it into execution'; another *Savile v Savile* (1721) 1 P Wms 745; 24 ER 596 (Ch) (court setting aside a contract involving an inflated price for real property).

[7] 'The role of contract law was not to assure the equity of agreements but simply to enforce only those willed transactions that parties to a contract believed to be to their mutual advantage. The result was a major tendency toward submerging the dominant equitable theory of contract in a conception of contractual obligation based exclusively on express bargains' (947); similarly J Oldham, 'Reinterpretations of 18th-Century English Contract Theory: The View from Lord Mansfield's Trial Notes' (1952) 76 *Georgetown Law Journal* 1949, 1982 notes the 'sharp nineteenth-century reaction against Mansfield's willingness to allow equitable notions to infiltrate contract cases'.

> by notions of freedom of contract, freedom from contract performance, judicial non-intervention, caveat emptor, and bargained-for-exchange. The whole doctrine of contract was said to be formal and external, purged of social facts and duties.[8]

Many historical observations about the law run the risk of oversimplification and generalisation. Horwitz pinpoints the eighteenth century as the time where the equitable conception of contract arose, before being usurped in the nineteenth century. Certainly, there is some evidence for this view. On the other hand, it has not escaped criticism from other legal historians.[9] Others have pointed out the importance of the use of the jury in previous times, and the decline in its use in the nineteenth century.[10] This forced the court to be more transparent in its decisions. The use of merchants as special jurors also disappeared in the nineteenth century.[11]

There is also evidence of notions of good faith and equity prior to the eighteenth century, and during the nineteenth. It would be a mistake to think the only evidence of freedom of contract philosophy appears in the nineteenth century.[12] It would be a serious oversimplification to characterise the eighteenth century as being based on equitable principles, including good faith, and the nineteenth century as a freedom of contract century. Typically in the common law, change is gradual, sometimes not perceptible at times. It is no respecter of centuries, or definitive time frames. Atiyah, for example, asserts that freedom of contract was at an end by the 1870s. On other hand, it is apparent that if this is in fact the case, some of the judges, as will shortly be shown, 'did not get the memo'. And leading advocate of good faith, Justice Leggatt, in 2016 (as he then was) referred to the 'paramount importance' commercial law continues to attach to freedom of contract.[13] Others differ.[14]

II. Freedom of Contract in the Cases

The classic case in which principles of freedom of contract were espoused is *The Printing and Numerical Registering Company (Ltd) v Sampson*.[15] The case involved

[8] E Holmes, 'A Contextual Study of Commercial Good Faith: Good-Faith Disclosure in Contract Formation' (1978) 39 *University of Pittsburgh Law Review* 381, 450.

[9] AWB Simpson, 'The Horwitz Thesis and the History of Contracts' (1979) 46(3) *University of Chicago Law Review* 533.

[10] JH Baker, 'From Sanctity of Contract to Reasonable Expectation' (1979) 32(1) *Current Legal Problems* 17, 20–21.

[11] Oldham (n 7) 1982.

[12] For example, Simpson notes that 'the harsh medieval law of the penal bond was notoriously based on the philosophy that those who made beds should lie in them': (n 9) 540.

[13] *Lecture to the Commercial Bar Association*, 18 October 2016, [10].

[14] For example, in *Andrews v ANZ Banking Group Ltd* (2012) 247 CLR 205, 216 five members of the Australian High Court appeared to reject 'untramelled freedom of contract (as) a universal legal value' (French CJ Gummow Crennan Kiefel and Bell JJ); *Legione v Hateley* (1983) 152 CLR 406, 448–49 (Mason and Deane JJ).

[15] (1875) 19 Eq 462.

the defendant contracting to sell his patent rights regarding patents pertaining to numbering and printing tickets. The contract included an assignment of future patent rights in this field. Subsequent to the contract, the defendant obtained further patents, which the plaintiff claimed under the contract. A dispute arose regarding whether the assignment of future rights was void as against public policy. The defendant argued the class was void, because it would inhibit future intellectual endeavours if the creator knew they would not personally be entitled to the benefits.

In dismissing the defendant's argument, Sir George Jessel MR noted:

> It must not be forgotten that you are not to extend arbitrarily the rules which say that a given contract is void as being against public policy, because if there is one thing which more than another public policy requires, it is that men of full age and competent understanding shall have the utmost liberty of contracting and that their contracts, when entered into freely and voluntarily, shall be held sacred and shall be enforced by courts of justice. Therefore, you have this paramount public policy to consider, that you must not lightly interfere with this freedom of contract.[16]

In another case, Phillimore LJ spoke of a time where

> political philosophy and political economy taught that the interference of the state should be reduced to a minimum, and that liberty was everything, liberty including absolute freedom of contract, that the world was to be regulated by contract, and the duty of the courts was to impress upon everyone the sanctity of contract.[17]

In *Fender v St John-Mildmay* Lord Thankerton referred to freedom of contract as one of the 'constant principles of public policy in the United Kingdom that was the court's duty to maintain'.[18] In *Ertel Bieber and Co v Rio Tinto Company Limited*, in determining the fate of a contract concluded with a war enemy, Lord Sumner considered, in determining the relevant law, that one possible principle would mean that 'freedom of contract is challenged less, the sacrosanctity of commerce is respected more'.[19] In *E Underwood & Son v Barker* Lindley MR (with whom Rigby LJ agreed) stated:

> If there is one thing more than another which is essential to the trade and commerce of this country, it is the inviolability of contracts deliberately entered into; and to allow

[16] ibid 465.

[17] *Herbert Morris Limited v Saxelby* (1915) 2 Ch 57, 81 (dissenting).

[18] [1938] AC 1, 22; see also *Winter Garden Theatre (London) Ltd v Millennium Productions, Limited* [1948] AC 173, 204 (Lord Macdermott). In *Tailby v Official Receiver* (1888) 13 App Cas 523, 545 Lord Macnaghten asked rhetorically 'between men of full age and competent understanding, ought there to be any limit to the freedom of contract but that imposed by positive law or dictated by considerations of morality or public policy?'; *Archer v James and Others* (1859) 2 B & S 65, 88 Baron Bramwell referred to freedom of contract as 'universally regarded as of the greatest benefit'. He cited to Adam Smith's *Wealth of Nations* shortly thereafter (89); see also *Beresford v Royal Insurance Company Limited* [1938] AC 586, 604: 'it is undeniably a principle of public policy that persons who enter into contractual arrangements should be required to fulfil them' (Lord Macmillan).

[19] [1918] AC 260, 287.

> a person of mature age, and not imposed upon, to enter into a contract, to obtain the benefit of it, and then to repudiate it and the obligations which he has undertaken is, prima facie at all events, contrary to the interests of any and every country.[20]

I will now consider freedom of contract philosophy expressed in some specific contractual dispute issues.

III. Liquidated Damages/Penalty Clauses

In the well-known case regarding the enforceability of liquidated damages clauses and whether or not they impose a penalty,[21] a member of the Court considered the matter through the lens of freedom of contract. Lord Parmoor indicated that where the included amount was a genuine pre-estimate of damage from a loss, notwithstanding that it could be applied to a range of types of breach of contract that were likely to lead to significantly different levels of loss to the party seeking to enforce it, it was enforceable. He stated that in such cases the court should not interfere with freedom of contract.[22]

A contract provided for damages to be payable in the event of various breaches of contract, many of which were significant, but some of which could be relatively trivial.[23] The same amount was specified for all breaches. The question was whether this clause was enforceable; it was argued it was a penalty and invalid. The Court determined that in such cases where the relevant clause could apply to a whole range of breaches of contract, it was not likely to be considered a penalty clause. In so deciding, members of the Court reflected on the importance of giving effect to the intention of parties to the contract, on the basis that the Court did not 'know the business' of contracting parties better than the party knew it themselves.[24] Cotton LJ agreed it was not part of the courts' role to remake the parties' contract on the basis of something it considered to be a more reasonable bargain.[25]

In *Astley v Weldon*,[26] Eldon CJ 'lamented' the equitable doctrine that amounts considered 'enormous' and 'excessive' would not be considered to be liquidated damages (and enforceable), but rather a penalty (and so not enforceable). He said it was difficult to apply the word 'excessive' to a contractual provision agreed to by the parties.

[20] [1899] 1 Ch 300, 305; see similarly *Egerton v Brownlow* (1853) 4 HLC 1, 123–24; 10 ER 359, 408–09: 'Prima facie, all persons are free to dispose of their property according to their will and pleasure, and are free to make such contracts as they please, and are morally and legally bound by them, provided in both cases they adopt the formalities required by the common and statute law' (Parke B, with whom Erle and Wightman JJ agreed).

[21] *Dunlop Pneumatic Tyre Co, Ltd v New Garage and Motor Co, Ltd* [1915] AC 79.

[22] ibid 103.

[23] *Wallis v Smith* (1882) 21 Ch D 243 (CA).

[24] ibid 266 (Jessel MR).

[25] ibid 268 (Cotton LJ).

[26] (1801) 2 B & P 346, 351; 126 ER 1318, 1321.

IV. Absolute Nature of Contractual Powers, Not Conditioned by a Requirement of Reasonableness

In *Holme v Brunskill*, the plaintiff agreed to lease a portion of his land to the defendant. The defendant gave the plaintiff a bond to promise that, at the end of the lease, the land and the stock which grazed upon it would be comparable in quality to that which existed at the commencement of the lease. If this did not occur, the defendant would pay the plaintiff compensation. A relative of the defendant acted as surety. The defendant took possession of the parcel of land. More than three years into the lease, the plaintiff gave the defendant a notice to quit the land. The defendant resisted this, and the parties reached a compromise whereby the defendant would relinquish a portion of the land which he had originally leased, in return for the plaintiff abandoning his notice to quit. At the end of the tenancy, the defendant returned the land to the plaintiff. The plaintiff claimed the land and the quality of the livestock had deteriorated. The defendant said that, to the extent it had deteriorated, it was because of the portion of land that had been excised from the original lease. The question was the extent of liability of the surety in relation to the defendant's promise.

The surety argued he should not be bound by his original promise, because there had been a change to the arrangements between the parties of which he was not aware and did not consent. It was argued to the contrary that the change was minimal, not substantial.

A majority of the Court found that the surety was discharged because of the alteration to the terms of the lease, without his approval or knowledge. It was irrelevant that the alteration made may not be material. The surety was the sole judge of whether they would be bound by the new arrangements.[27] In dissent, Brett LJ said the surety was not discharged because the alteration was not material.[28]

Sometimes courts would recognise technical breaches of contract, and give effect to the consequences attaching to them, even though the breach was relatively trivial and inconsequential. So for example in *Barrow v Isaac and Son*, the plaintiff leased premises to the defendant. The lease permitted sub-lease, with the approval of the plaintiff, which could not be reasonably refused. The defendant entered into a sub-lease, without obtaining the required approval. The sub-lease was to a high quality tenant. Although there was no doubt that, if asked, the plaintiff would have approved the sub-lease, the court found it was a technical breach of contract and gave effect to the contractual provision permitting the plaintiff to re-take possession of the premises.[29]

[27] ibid 505–06 (Cotton LJ, with whom Thesiger LJ agreed).
[28] ibid 508–09 (Brett LJ, dissenting).
[29] *Barrow v Isaac and Son* [1891] 1 QB 417 (CA).

The Court gave full effect to clauses in contracts conferring rights on one of the contracting parties in relation to the other. One example involved a case between a property owner and tenant, where the relevant contract included the property owner's right to give the tenant a notice to quit.[30] The property owner did so shortly after the tenant gave evidence in a property dispute between the owner and another tenant. Pearson LJ stated:

> A person who has a right under a contract … is entitled to exercise it and can effectively exercise it for a good reason or a bad reason or no reason at all … if the rule were different … there would be a great unsettlement of property titles and commercial transactions and relationships.[31]

Sometimes, courts stated there was no obligation on a party to a contract to exercise their contractual rights in a reasonable manner.[32]

V. Absolute Focus on Written Terms

Another example occurred in *Bowes v Shand*,[33] where the contract provided for a shipment of rice from India to England. It stipulated that the goods should be shipped during March and/or April of a given year. In fact most of the rice was shipped (in the sense of placed on board) in February of that year. The defendant purchaser refused to accept the shipment, on the basis most of it had been shipped in February. This argument was accepted by the House of Lords. The House stated the simple words of the contract required shipment during specified months. This is not what had occurred. The House speculated that the precise time of shipment might have been of importance to the plaintiff purchaser, without enquiring as to whether it was in fact, or why.

The Court did not concern itself with the motives of the contracting party seeking to exercise their rights: 'any right given by contract may be exercised against the giver by the person to whom it is granted, no matter how wicked, cruel or mean the motive may be which determines the enforcement of the right'.[34]

[30] *Chapman v Honig* [1963] 2 QB 502, 520.

[31] ibid 520–21, with whom Davis LJ relevantly agreed (526) (CA).

[32] *White and Carter (Councils) Ltd v McGregor* [1961] AC 413, 430 (Lord Reid), similarly Lord Hodson (445) (referring to a 'novel' suggestion that parties would only be held to contracts, or contractual provisions, that courts deemed to be reasonable), though others in the case referred to a duty of a contracting party to mitigate losses (Lord Morton (433), Lord Keith (439)), which might find a basis in good faith and/or reasonableness.

[33] (1877) 2 App Cas 455. In *Hutton v Warren* (1836) 1 M & W 465, 475–76; 150 ER 517, 521 Baron Parke seemingly questioned the wisdom of the common law implying terms into a written contract based on custom and usage, but in the end found the practice was too well established to now be overturned.

[34] *Allen v Flood* [1898] AC 1, 46 (Wills J); *Smith v Hughes* (1871) LR 6 QB 597, 607: 'whatever may be the case in a court of morals, there is no legal obligation on (a) vendor to inform the purchaser that he is under a mistake, not induced by fraud by the act of the vendor' (Blackburn J).

VI. Use of Caveat Emptor Principle

Another example of freedom of contract was use of the caveat emptor principle. In *Turner v Harvey*,[35] Lord Chancellor Eldon explained that a person selling property which had a mine under it would not be required to disclose that fact to a would-be purchaser, it being incumbent upon them to make their own enquiries. At one time, a vendor was held to make no implied warranty regarding the title to goods they sold to a purchaser, including a warranty as to their ownership of the goods. It was simply a promise that the vendor would convey such of the title as they possessed. Nor was there any implied warranty regarding the quality of the goods sold, at least generally.[36] A contract to sell a ship for 4000 pounds was valid although, at the time of the contract and unknown to both parties, the ship had foundered and was largely destroyed, now worth 10 pounds. The court held the contract contained no warranty regarding seaworthiness or that the vessel could be used.[37]

In *Parkinson v Lee* the purchaser has held to have no remedy where they purchased a quantity of wheat with no express warranty provided by the seller. The purchaser had relied upon a sample of the product to be purchased; in fact the bulk of what was delivered was of lesser quality. The court found there was no implied warranty regarding the merchantable quality of the bulk to be delivered.[38] In an early case, the court found that there was no remedy, even though the seller, a jeweller, had sold a stone to the plaintiff, stating it was a particular kind of stone. In fact, as the seller knew, it was not that kind of stone. The court found there was no remedy because what the jeweller had said did not amount to a warranty.[39]

A House of Lords decision involved a purchaser of a business who complained about statements made by the vendor concerning the viability of the business.[40] The purchaser unsuccessfully argued the vendor had been fraudulent because some of the statements were not entirely correct. The purchaser also made their own enquiries regarding the relevant issues prior to contract. A majority of the Court dismissed the purchaser's appeal. Lord Brougham spoke generally about honesty and contracting relations, and the very limited circumstances in which a contracting party could escape their responsibilities:

> General fraudulent conduct signifies nothing; … general dishonesty of purpose signifies nothing; … attempts to overreach go for nothing; … an intention and design to deceive may go for nothing, unless all this dishonesty of purpose, all this fraud, all this intention and design, can be connected with the particular transaction (and) … must be made to be the very ground upon which this transaction took place, and must

[35] (1821) Jacob 168, 178; 37 ER 814, 817–18.
[36] *Morley v Attenborough* (1949) 3 Ex 500; 154 ER 943 (Baron Parke).
[37] *Barr v Gibson* (1838) 3 M & W 391; 150 ER 1196.
[38] (1802) 2 East 314; 102 ER 389; *Burnby v Bollett* (1847) 16 M & W 644; 153 ER 1348.
[39] *Chandelor v Lopus* (1603) Cro Jac 4; 79 ER 3.
[40] *Attwood v Small* (1838) 6 Cl & F 232; 7 ER 684.

> have given rise to this contract. If a mere general intention to overreach were enough, I hardly know a contract, even between persons of very strict morality, that could stand; we generally find the case to be that there has been an attempt of the one party to overreach the other, and of the other to overreach the first; but that does not make void the contract … (in order to avoid the contract, the seller) must have given instructions to the agent to deceive, … the agent must … have made a representation deceiving the purchaser, and moreover the purchaser must have trusted to that representation, and not to his own acumen.[41]

O'Connor refers to the 'exaggerated deference to freedom of contract (which in many cases allowed the imposition of unfair and unreasonable terms on the weaker party)'.[42]

VII. Narrow View of Public Policy Exception to Freedom of Contract

As Solicitor-General Lord Mansfield argued a case involving a contract to borrow money, involving a bond as security. The bond was for a substantially larger sum than the amount borrowed. Lord Mansfield railed against arguments that the freedom of an individual to borrow should be constrained by notions of the public good:

> Then what is this public good, this rule they so much insist on, that no man shall spend above his annual income? How can that be prevented? Is it in human nature? He will spend it; men of the best sense have done it; where will be the publick utility? Where the encouragement to industry? Will the court consider every man as a lunatic who exceeds his income? Another end, perhaps to lock up property for another age; is that desirable? Will it procure money on easier terms? It is directly to the contrary.[43]

There was a range of opinion regarding the extent to which courts should or would set aside contracts or other legal documents on the basis of 'public policy'. Obviously, this jurisdiction would impinge on freedom of contract, and the associated will theory of contracting emphasising the mutual consent of contractual arrangements, as a justification for the enforcement of promises contained therein.[44] A good example is provided in the 1853 decision *Egerton v Brownlow*.[45] It involved a question of the enforceability of an unusual provision in a will. Clearly this is not a contract, but there is evidently strong overlap regarding a freedom of contract philosophy and one pertaining to freedom to draft a will as one wishes.

[41] *Attwood v Small* (1838) 6 Cl & F 232, 447–448; 7 ER 684, 765 (Lord Brougham).
[42] JF O'Connor, *Good Faith in English Law* (Aldershot, Dartmouth, 1990) 19.
[43] *Chesterfield v Janssen* [1750] 1 Atk 301, 335; 26 ER 191, 214.
[44] DJ Ibbetson, *A Historical Introduction to the Law of Obligations* (Oxford, Oxford University Press, 1999) 249.
[45] (1853) 4 HLC 1; 10 ER 359.

In this case, a majority of the Court emphasised freedom of contract (and will making), provided formalities were met. The court's jurisdiction to interfere with such freedom was very limited, in the view of the majority. It should not lightly set aside such a document on the basis it was contrary to public policy.[46]

VIII. Refusal of Relief for Hard Bargains

A mortgage contract provided for a minimum 40-year length. The mortgagor sought to set aside the contract on the basis that the length was unreasonably long. The court rejected the argument.[47] In the Court of Appeal, Greene LJ noted that the argument that a clause was void because it was unreasonable

> requires the closest scrutiny for if it is correct, it means that an agreement made between two competent parties acting under competent advice, and presumably knowing their own business best, is one which the law forbids them to make on the ground that it is not 'reasonable' … we are not prepared to say that such an agreement cannot be lawfully made. A decision to that effect would … be contrary to the freedom of business men to enter into contracts best suited to their interests and would impose on them a test of 'reasonableness' laid down by the courts without reference to the business realities of the case.[48]

While traditionally equity would give relief against forfeiture, some courts applied this rule strictly, not permitting it to extend beyond forfeiture for failure to pay rent. So when a lessee had not maintained the premises in good repair, and failed to do so within a stipulated three-month time period the lessor had given them to bring the premises into good repair, the court refused relief from the lessor's exercise of contractual power to take back the property.[49]

Another example of a party being held to a harsh bargain occurred in *L'Estrange v F Graucob Ltd*.[50] There the plaintiff commenced an action, arguing that the

[46] Parke B, with whom Erle and Wightman JJ agreed; cf Pollock CB. Of similar ilk, the court found in *Scott v Avery* (1856) 5 HLC 810; 10 ER 1121 that a contractual clause between parties requiring them to engage in arbitration before bringing disputes to court was valid and enforceable; an argument that the clause was contrary to public policy, curbing the jurisdiction of the courts, was rejected. A freedom of contract philosophy prevailed. See also *Richardson v Mellish* (1824) 2 Bing 229, 252; 130 ER 294, 303 where public policy was derided as 'unruly horse' that, once unbridled, had an unpredictable destination (Burrough J).

[47] *Knightsbridge Estates Trust v Byrne* [1939] Ch 434.

[48] ibid 454 (Greene LJ, for the Court of Appeal). Greene LJ indicated equity would interfere if the bargain were oppressive or unconscionable, but neither was applicable here.

[49] *Hill v Barclay* (1811) 18 Ves Jun 56; 34 ER 238.

[50] [1934] 2 KB 395. Powell suggests the case might prompt support for a good faith requirement, which would include an obligation for a contracting party relying on their standard form contract to explain to others in plain terms the contents of such contract, including the parties' respective rights and responsibilities, in easily understood language: 'Good Faith in Contracts' (1956) 9(1) *Current Legal Problems* 16, 27.

machine she had been supplied by the defendant was not fit for its intended purpose. The defendant successfully relied on small print in the contract excluding any implied warranties in relation to the machine. The Court found for the defendant, enforcing the small print.

IX. Fraud

Freedom of contract was also evident in the narrow way in which the House of Lords conceived of fraud. In the classic case of *Derry v Peek*,[51] directors claimed in a prospectus that the company had a right to do something, which was recognised as having value. In truth, their right to do this particular thing was conditional upon government approval, but the prospectus did not allude to this. The House of Lords rejected a claim of deceit. It limited fraud narrowly to cases where someone intentionally set out to deceive another or was reckless as to whether their words or conduct did so. It was not enough, in itself, that there was no reasonable basis for the defendants to believe as they did. Lord Bramwell said it would be 'disastrous' to have only true statements made, and the fact a statement was unreasonable was not the basis of an action.[52]

X. Employment

Freedom of contract arguments were prevalent in relation to employment. One aspect was the right of employees to form combinations, or unions. This implicated freedom of contract in at least two ways – firstly, to the extent that the members of the proposed combination agreed on joint activity, this curbed their freedom of activity. If some members agreed to strike, for example, or to minimum rates of pay for particular work, they would not look kindly on other members continuing to work, or accepting work at a different rate of pay. It also potentially interfered with the freedom of an employer to engage on agreed terms with employees. The Court eventually found that a trade union was illegal because the content of the agreement among members was essentially a restraint of trade.[53]

Contracts of employment were also interpreted in a strict manner. For example in *Addis v Gramophone Co Ltd*,[54] an employee had been wrongfully dismissed, not being given the required notice. The House of Lords held damages were not available for the manner in which an employee was dismissed, nor for the resulting

[51] (1889) 14 App Cas 337.
[52] ibid 352.
[53] *Hornby v Close* (1867) LR 2 QB 153 (Queen's Bench).
[54] *Addis v Gramophone Co Ltd* [1909] AC 488.

difficulties in obtaining alternative employment. Later cases would explain that the decision had been made during the 'heyday' of market individualism, including in relation to employment, which might have artificially limited the ability of an employee to obtain compensation for loss flowing naturally from breach of their employment contract by the employer.[55]

XI. Anti-Competitive Practices

Relatedly the common law did not provide a remedy in cases where businesses formed alliances or combinations, with detriment to the public interest. Business owners were able to freely make agreements to fix prices, sellers could control the price at which a purchaser subsequently sold the goods, competitors could agree on quotas and make arrangements regarding market share. In one case competitors agreed not to quote on a project, on the basis they would share in the benefits of the contract with the nominated sole tenderer.[56] This was held valid. Other arguably anti-competitive behaviour, including predatory pricing and agreements among competitors about a fixed incentive for customers who exclusively dealt with those party to the agreement, and demands that agents work only for companies within the arrangement, was considered. The House of Lords found that the participants were engaged in a legitimate objective of increasing and protecting their trade interests, and were not utilising unlawful means in so agreeing.[57] Lord Bramwell said it was not appropriate for courts to judge whether contracts provided for fair or unfair competition, or were reasonable or unreasonable.[58] In many other cases too, courts upheld clearly anti-competitive arrangements on the basis of freedom of contract.[59] It was not until the mid-twentieth century that the legal tide would turn against such arrangements.[60]

[55] *Johnson v Unisys Ltd* [2003] 1 AC 518, 531 (Lord Steyn).

[56] *Jones v North* (1875) LR 19 Eq 426.

[57] *Mogul Steamship Co v McGregor, Gow and Co* [1892] AC 25 (HL). The case involved a rival trader not part of the association who alleged an unlawful conspiracy against the participants. It was this claim that was dismissed. The court did not rule directly on the legality and/or enforceability of the agreement. Lord Field found the contracting parties were acting bona fide to further legitimate business interests (57).

[58] ibid 49 (quoting Fry LJ in the Court of Appeal judgment in this case: (1889) 23 QBD 598, 625–26)).

[59] This includes resale price maintenance (*Elliman Sons & Co v Carrington & Son Ltd* [1901] 2 Ch 275); exclusive dealing requirements (*United Shoe Machinery Co of Canada v Brunet* [1909] AC 330)), a collective boycott (*Sorrell v Smith* [1925] AC 700), price maintenance agreements among competitors (*Thorne v Motor Trade Association* [1937] AC 797). The Privy Council struck out Australian legislation designed to inhibit cartel behaviour to artificially restrict output and maintain price levels: *Attorney-General of Australia v Adelaide Steamship Co* [1913] AC 781.

[60] *Esso Petroleum Co Ltd v Harper's Garage* (Stourport) Ltd [1968] AC 269; *A Schroeder Music Publishing Co Ltd* v Macaulay [1974] 1 WLR 1308.

XII. Other Contexts

A defendant contracted with a business, in a situation where the ownership of the business changed. For example, in *Robson & Sharpe v Drummond*,[61] the defendant entered into a five-year lease of a coach from a business owned by the plaintiffs. Three years into the lease, Sharpe retired from the business, and transferred his rights in the business, including in respect of the lease. When Drummond learned of the transfer, he refused to continue with the lease. The Court found for the defendant. Tenderden CJ opined the defendant *might* have entered into the contract only because Sharpe was involved; this was speculation. Evidence of this does not appear in the report. As a result, Drummond was within his legal rights to terminate when the partnership arrangements changed.[62]

The court would sometimes not assist parties with a remedy where the terms of a contract were clear but which led to something of a stalemate. So for example in *Milnes v Gery*,[63] the contract provided for the sale of a particular property. The price was to be agreed by nominees of two parties. In the event that the nominees arrived at different valuations, they would nominate a third person, whose determination as to price was final. The nominees did not agree on price, but they could not agree either as to a suitable third person. The Court concluded in this case there was no contract. It declined to appoint a suitable third party, claiming it had no jurisdiction to do so.

XIII. Approach to Contract Interpretation

Contracts were interpreted in accordance with what was presumed to be the parties' intentions. The parties' intent was considered objectively, in terms of what a reasonable person would take the parties to mean by their agreement, rather than subjectively, or what the parties actually did mean by their agreement, as will be elaborated upon below. An objective approach to intention was inevitable given that, as Swain notes, procedural restrictions in the superior common law courts barred parties with an interest in the suit from directly testifying until 1843, and the actual parties in dispute were not competent witnesses until later.[64] Apathy was expressed in situations where it was clear the written agreement did not match the reality of the parties' contractual intentions. A good example of a highly formalistic response is found in *Peekay Intermark Ltd v Australia and New*

[61] *Robson & Sharpe v Drummond* (1831) 2 B & Ad 303; 109 ER 1156.

[62] See similarly *Boulton v Jones* (1857) 2 H & N 564; 157 ER 232 (buyer ordered goods from a shopkeeper. The goods were supplied by a purchaser of the shopkeeper's business. The buyer then refused to pay for the goods. The Court found he was not required to pay for them, though he had used them, because of the change in the identity of the seller).

[63] *Milnes v Gery* (1807) 14 Ves Jun 400; 33 ER 574.

[64] W Swain, 'Reshaping Contractual Unfairness in England 1670–1900' (2014) 35 *Journal of Legal History* 120, 124.

Zealand Banking Group Ltd.[65] There Moore-Bick LJ stated 'there is no reason in principle why parties to a contract should not agree that a certain state of affairs should form the basis for the transaction, whether it be the case or not'.

The courts were not really interested in arguments that the contents of a contract were substantively unfair.[66] Instead, interest was typically focussed on whether the way in which the contract was formed was fair nor not. There was a general lack of an obligation to disclose relevant information to the other side, though fraud and misrepresentation (narrowly defined) were not permitted. The court is not generally concerned whether there is relatively equal bargaining power between the parties. This reflected the will theory of contract law – that the role of the law of contract was to give effect to the product of the exercise of the voluntary will of the parties.[67] There were limited attempts to try to reconcile principles of freedom of contract, including mistake and frustration, with the parties' intent.[68]

XIV. Freedom of Contract – The Philosophy

There was significant intellectual support for a freedom of contract approach. Even in 1905 Dicey stated:

> Once admit(ted) that A, B or C can each, as a rule, judge more correctly than can anyone else of his own interest, and the conclusion naturally follows that, in the absence of force or fraud, A or B ought to be allowed to bind themselves to one another by any agreement which they choose to make ie which in the view of each of them promotes his own interest, or in other words, is conducive to his own happiness.[69]

Max Weber noted a strong relationship between capitalism and 'formal rationality'.[70] Formal here is taken to mean a legal system that denies ethical ideals based on conceptions of the good or distributive justice, seeing to maximise individual freedom.[71] He argued that for capitalism to do best, the legal system (particularly as it relates to commercial activity) had to provide certainty and predictability. This approach would clearly frown upon courts intervening in commercial

[65] *Peekay Intermark Ltd v Australia and New Zealand Banking Group Ltd* [2006] EWCA Civ 386, [56].

[66] *White and Carter (Council) Ltd v McGregor* [1961] AC 413, 445 where Lord Hodson said that equity would not rewrite an improvident contract, absent disability. It is telling that articles about unfairness in contracts often focus only on procedural unfairness doctrines such as undue influence and unconscionability: W Swain, 'Equitable Doctrine, Fairness and the Law of Contract in Australia' in J Eldridge and T Pilkington (eds), *Australian Contract Law in the 21st Century* (Sydney, Federation Press, 2021).

[67] PS Atiyah, *The Rise and Fall of Freedom of Contract* (Oxford, Clarendon Press, 1979) 406–08.

[68] J Beatson and D Friedmann, 'Introduction: From "Classical" to Modern Contract Law' in Jack Beatson and Daniel Friedmann (ed) *Good Faith and Fault in Contract Law* (Oxford, Clarendon Press, 2002) 10.

[69] Albert Venn Dicey, *Lectures on Law and Public Opinion in England During the Nineteenth Century* 2nd edn (London, Macmilllan and Co, 1914) 150–51.

[70] *Economy and Society: An Outline of Interpretive Sociology* (Berkeley, University of California Press, G Roth and C Wittich ed, reprinted 1978).

[71] AT Kronman, *Max Weber* (California, Stanford University Press, 1983) 95.

arrangements on the grounds of lack of good faith, or unfairness.[72] This would create uncertainty. The will and choice of free individuals was entitled to utmost respect. Weber lauded this approach because it seemed as if the law were value-neutral. It made law rational.[73] This process was inevitable.

However, it has been noted that Weber was at times contradictory. He did not laud this 'inevitable' shift of the law to a value-neutral position. He acknowledged that the 'formal' contract may not accurately reflect parties' intent, and acknowledged that freedom of contract would benefit those with superior bargaining power/skill/knowledge over those without. He saw that 'freedom of contract' could in practice lead to coercion. He lamented that formality was 'contrary to all the elementary forms of human relationship' and an 'abomination to every system of fraternal ethics'.[74] This portends the research much later on relational contract theory, which I will discuss in chapters seven and eight, which recognises that such a formalist approach is also generally contrary to the contracting parties' intention. As Collins notes:

> The drive for doctrinal coherence and the separation of legal reasoning from moral, political, and economic thought pushes the legal system towards the closure of formal legal reasoning. Yet if the law of contract is to achieve the purpose favoured by business of supporting expectations arising from transactions and their surrounding context, the legal system must eschew closed reasoning in favour of doctrines which render the facts of these expectations central to its determinations. This purpose can only be achieved by open-textured rules, the supplementation and qualification of contractual entitlements by custom and expectation, and the interpretation of events and terms in the light of those expectations.[75]

As such, formalism is not consistent with the then-dominant will theory, as it purported to be, because it fails to capture the totality of the parties' *actual* intentions and expectations.[76]

The work of Adam Smith[77] and Ricardo[78] were typically relied upon to support freedom of contract. Individuals were rational utility maximisers who could and

[72] DM Trubek, 'Reconstructing Max Weber's Sociology of Law' (1985) 37 *Stanford Law Review* 919; D Trubek, 'Max Weber's Tragic Modernism and the Study of Law in Society' (1986) 20 *Law and Society Review* 573; D Campbell, 'Truth Claims and Value-Freedom in the Treatment of Legitimacy: The Case of Weber' (1986) 13 *Journal of Law and Society* 207.

[73] It has been observed that there may have been an attempt to apply methods of science to the law. This explains a focus on objectivity and rationality, and a de-emphasis on individuality and fairness: M Eisenberg, 'The Responsive Model of Contract Law' (1984) 36 *Stanford Law Review* 1107.

[74] (n 70) 636–37.

[75] H Collins, *Regulating Contracts* (Oxford, Oxford University Press, 1999) 196.

[76] D Campbell and H Collins, 'Discovering the Implicit Dimensions of Contract' in D Campbell, H Collins and J Wightman (eds), *Implicit Dimensions of Contract: Discrete Relational and Network Contracts* (Oxford, Hart Publishing, 2003) 47: 'if, as the principle of freedom of contract maintains, the job of the law is to enforce the agreement of the parties, this task can only be achieved by looking at the "real deal", which is not necessarily the same as the written contract. Assuming that respect for freedom of contract has the alleged desirable utilitarian consequences or at least ensures respect for individual rights, it does not follow … that legal reasoning should eschew reference to the implicit dimensions of contractual relationships … by incorporating implicit dimensions into legal analysis … the legal system can achieve a greater capacity for upholding freedom of contract and its consequential benefits'.

[77] *The Wealth of Nations* (New York, Bantam Classic, 2003) 413–14. The *Wealth of Nations* was originally published in 1776.

[78] David Ricardo *The Principles of Political Economy and Taxation* (London, John Murray, 1821).

should be left to their own devices to enter into contractual arrangements that moved them to higher levels of utility.[79] This placed great importance on individual interests, and the ability of parties to effectively make decisions that would be in their best interests. Smith believed that, through this model, the public interest would be advanced, without the need for significant government intervention. He viewed such intervention with suspicion, believing it would tend to favour particular lobby groups, at the expense of the general public.[80]

Of course, a belief that contracting parties were rational utility maximisers would support the non-intervention of a court where it was alleged that the consideration for a contractual promise was inadequate.[81] The role of contract law was limited; it set the ground rules upon which parties could engage in 'self-maximising private ordering'.[82] It reflected a period of liberalism in which courts were not interested in questions of reasonable expectations or legitimate interests of contracting parties.[83]

However, even Smith did not believe in the absolute sanctity of freedom of contract:

> To restrain private people, it may be said, from receiving in payment the promissory notes of a banker, for any sum whether great or small when they themselves are willing to receive them, or to restrain a banker from issuing such notes, when all his neighbours are willing to accept of them, is a manifest violation of that natural liberty which it is the proper

[79] 'Every man, as long as he does not violate the laws of justice, is left perfectly free to pursue his own interest, his own way, and to bring both his industry and capital into competition with those of any other man, or order of men. The sovereign is completely discharged from a duty, in the attempting to perform of which he must always be exposed to innumerable delusions, and for the proper performance of which no human wisdom or knowledge could ever be sufficient; the duty of superintending the industry of private people, and of directing it towards the employments most suitable to the interest of society' (Smith (n 77) 873–74); M Cohen, 'The Basis of Contract' (1933) 46 *Harvard Law Review* 553, 558 who observed that the will theory of contract rests 'on the political doctrine that all restraint is evil and that the government is best which governs least. This in turn is connected with the classical economic optimism that there is a sort of preestablished harmony between the good of all and the pursuit by each of his own selfish economic gain. These politico-economic views involve the Benthamite hedonistic psychology, that happiness consists of individual states of pleasures and that each individual can best calculate which will please him most'.

[80] He would limit the role of government to (a) protecting the nation from external threats; (b) protecting members of society from injustice or oppression at the hands of other members of society (ie administering justice); and (c) creating and maintaining public institutions and public infrastructure: 874.

[81] The case *Griffith v Spratley* (1787) 1 Cox Ch C 383; 29 ER 1213 considered an argument by an impoverished seller, who argued that his contracts to sell items ought to be set aside because they were at an undervalue. His argument was rejected, with Baron CJ stating: 'I know of no such principle: the common law knows of no such. The consideration more or less supports the contract. Common sense knows no such principle. The value of a thing is what it will produce, and admits of no precise standard. It must be in its nature fluctuating, and it will depend upon … circumstances. One man …. (may) sell it for less than another would; he may sell it under pressure of circumstances, which may induce him to sell it at a particular time. Now if Courts of Equity are to unravel all these transactions, they would throw everything into confusion and set afloat all the contracts of mankind. Therefore I never can agree that inadequacy of consideration is in itself a principle upon which a party may be relieved from a contract which he wittingly and willingly entered into': (1787) 1 Cox Ch. C 383, 388–89; 29 ER 1213, 1215.

[82] JM Feinman, 'Relational Contract Theory in Context' (2000) 94 *Northwestern University Law Review* 737, 738.

[83] B Dixon, 'Common Law Obligations of Good Faith in Australian Commercial Contracts – A Relational Recipe' (2005) 33 *Australian Business Law Review* 87, 88.

> business of law, not to infringe but to support. Such regulations may, no doubt, be considered as in some respect a violation of natural liberty. But those exertions of the natural liberty of a few individuals, which might endanger the security of the whole society, are, and ought to be restrained by the laws of all governments … the obligation of building party walls, in order to prevent the communication of fire, is a violation of natural liberty, exactly of the same kind with the regulations of the banking trade here proposed.[84]

Later he made observations about the behaviour of nations engaged in trade:

> Nations have been taught that their interest consisted in beggaring all their neighbours. Each nation has been made to look with an invidious eye upon the prosperity of all the nations with which it trades, and to consider their gain as its own loss. Commerce, which ought naturally to be, among nations, as among individuals, a bond of union and friendship, has become the most fertile source of discord and animosity. The capricious ambition of kings and ministers has not, during the present and the preceding century, have been more fatal to the repose of Europe, than the impertinent jealousy of merchants and manufacturers. The violence and injustice of the rulers of mankind is an ancient evil, for which … the nature of human affairs can scarce admit of a remedy. But the mean rapacity, the monopolizing spirit of merchants and manufacturers, who neither are, nor ought to be, the rulers of mankind, though it cannot perhaps be corrected, may very easily be prevented from disturbing the tranquility of any body but themselves.[85]

Smith noted the tendency of merchants and manufacturers towards creating monopolies, and this was contrary to the best interests of the public (and, by implication, ought to be prevented).[86] Campbell notes that Smith favoured regulation of the quality and quantity of goods in some cases, limitation of interest rates, excessive speculation, and control of the amount of currency in circulation.[87] However, it has been emphasised that the approach favoured by these economists should not be interpreted as focussing on individual interests to the exclusion of the interests of others.[88]

[84] Smith (n 77) 413–14. In an earlier work, Smith had lauded justice as a higher value than self-interest: 'Justice … is the main pillar that upholds the whole edifice. If it is removed, the great, the immense fabric of human society, that fabric which to raise and support seems in this world … to have been the peculiar and darling care of Nature, must in a moment crumble into atoms. In order to enforce the observation of justice, therefore, Nature had implanted in the human breast that consciousness of ill-desert, those terrors of merited punishment which attend upon its violation, as the great safeguards of the association of mankind, to protect the weak, to curb the violent, and to chastise the guilty': *The Theory of Moral Sentiments* (Oxford, Raphael and Macfie ed, Oxford University Press, 1976) 86. He emphasised the need for 'fair play', noting that a person 'in the race for wealth and honours and preferments … may run as hard as he can, and strain every nerve and muscle, in order to outstrip his competitors. But if he should jostle or throw down any of them, the indulgence of the spectators is entirely at an end. It is a violation of fair play, which they cannot admit of' (83).

[85] Smith (n 77) 621.

[86] ibid 622.

[87] D Campbell, 'Adam Smith and the Social Foundation of Agreement: *Walford v Miles* as a Relational Contract' (2017) 21(3) *Edinburgh Law Review* 376, 389.

[88] Atiyah (n 67) 260: 'The fact that the classical economists and utilitarians wanted to free people to follow their interests, their wills, did not mean that they were indifferent to what people did with these new-found freedoms. Still less did it mean that they advocated or approved a society in which everybody selfishly pursued their own interests in total disregard to the interests of everyone else'.

Campbell also notes that Smith's consideration of exchange was relatively limited. However, he reasons that Smith's approach was not pursuit of pure self-interest. Rather, it was tempered by a moral, other-regarding requirement of mutual recognition in exchange.[89] An example of this is Smith's view that

> for one man to deprive another unjustly of anything or unjustly to promote his advantage by the loss of another, is more contrary to nature than death, than poverty, than pain, than all the misfortunes which can affect him either in his body or his external circumstances.[90]

It has been observed that classical economics traditionally ignores the role of the social institutions within which market exchange takes place.[91] Campbell says we should recognise that

> welfare-enhancing exchange necessarily rests on a moral framework institutionalized in law. It is not really that the court intervenes to inject morality and law into the economy in order to limit opportunism; it is that without the moral and legal framework there is no economy.[92]

This demonstrates the fallacy of the assumption of classical economic theory, of zero transaction costs.[93] Macneil pointed out that, if it were in fact true that transaction costs were zero, no contracting would take place at all. All contracting takes place through relations, and they involve transaction costs.[94]

Jeremy Bentham's utilitarianism is often typically seen as supportive of freedom of contract.[95] He would naturally support contracts, facilitating the movement of resources from less efficient to more efficient uses. He believed that individuals were best placed to know, and did know, what was in their best interests, and that collectively this would produce the greatest happiness for the greatest number. So,

[89] Campbell (n 87) 388.

[90] A Smith, 'The Theory of Moral Sentiments' (Glasgow, R Chapman, 1809). Campbell states this passage was likely taken from *De Officiis*, iii, 21: Cicero, *On Duties* (EM Atkins ed, Cambridge, Cambridge University Press, 1991) 108.

[91] R Coase, *The Firm The Market and the Law* (Chicago, University of Chicago Press, 1987) 7–8: 'markets are institutions that exist to facilitate exchange; that is, they exist in order to reduce the cost of carrying out exchange transactions. In an economic theory which assumes that transaction costs are non-existent, markets have no function to perform, and it seems perfectly reasonable to develop the theory of exchange by an elaborate analysis of individuals exchanging nuts for apples … this analysis certainly shows why there is a gain from trade, but it fails to deal with the factors which determine how much trade there is or what goods are traded. And when economists do speak of market structure, this has nothing to do with the market as an institution but refers to such things as the number of firms, product differentiation, and the like, *the influence of the social institutions which facilitate exchange being completely ignored*' (emphasis added).

[92] D Campbell, 'The Incompleteness of our Understanding of the Law and Economics of Relational Contract' [2004] *Wisconsin Law Review* 645, 673; similarly K Arrow, 'Economic Development: The Present State of the Art', 6 *Collected Papers of Kenneth Arrow* (Cambridge, Harvard University Press, 1984) 183: 'in many ways the prevailing neoclassical paradigm … is deficient because it ignores the social-structural basis'.

[93] J Kostritsky, 'Taxonomy for Justifying Legal Intervention in an Imperfect World: What to do When Parties Have Not Achieved Bargains or Have Drafted Incomplete Contracts' [2004] *Wisconsin Law Review* 323, 334.

[94] I Macneil, 'Efficient Breach: Circles in the Sky' (1982) 68 *Virginia Law Review* 947, 961.

[95] Baker (n 10) 18.

for example, Bentham criticised laws forbidding usury on the basis they interfered with free choice of individuals to arrangements.[96] Mill took a similar view.[97]

Many lawyers at this time had significant exposure to economic ideas, particularly in the early to mid-nineteenth century.[98] This might help to explain the extent to which the courts embraced freedom of contract philosophy, as demonstrated above.

Associated with freedom of contract was the emergence of the will theory of contract, whereby contracts were seen as an example of a mutual agreement between the parties, entered into voluntarily.[99] This significantly limited the role of the courts in contract disputes. Once it had been determined that the parties had voluntarily entered into a contract, the court's role was limited to determining what in substance the contract provided for, and to give effect to the promises made.[100] In other words, the concern of the law was with procedural justice, not substantive justice. The fact that the contract has been formed in a procedurally fair manner, with no coercion or undue influence, was sufficient. The court would not concern itself with the substantive fairness of the terms of the contract.[101] Case examples of this were cited earlier in the chapter.

Of course, it was eventually realised that the will theory was an inadequate basis for explaining the existing rules of contract. Many rules did not fit the will theory model.[102] Its assumptions were often not accurate in particular cases. Often, parties are not able to foresee future events. This had been known for centuries, as material in chapter one suggests. However, application of the will theory meant that the way in which the court resolves issued surrounding such events would often not in fact be based on the parties' will,[103] despite the law

[96] *Jeremy Bentham's Economic Writings* (London, Stark ed, 1952): 'no man of ripe years and of sound mind, acting freely, and with his eyes open, ought to be hindered, with a view to his advantage, from making such bargain, in the way of obtaining money as he thinks fit; nor (what is a necessary consequence) anybody hindered from supplying him, upon any terms he thinks proper to accede to' (129).

[97] JS Mill, *On Liberty* (London, Longman, 1859).

[98] Atiyah (n 67) 293.

[99] Ibbetson (n 44) 220–21.

[100] Atiyah (n 67) 408.

[101] H Collins, 'Introduction: The Research Agenda of Implied Dimensions of Contracts' in D Campbell, H Collins and J Wightman (eds), *Implicit Dimensions of Contract: Discrete Relational and Network Contracts* (Oxford, Hart Publishing, 2003) 10–11.

[102] For example, the rule against penalties in contracts. Courts are willing to find that a particular clause is penal, and unenforceable, although the parties have apparently agreed that it is, in contrast, a liquidated damages clause and genuine pre-estimate of likely damage in the event of breach. This legal principle is contrary to the will theory of contracts. See for discussion S Williston, 'Freedom of Contract' (1921) 6 *Cornell Law Quarterly* 365, 371–74. Beatson and Friedmann (n 68) refers to the paradox of classic contract law involving incongruity between the will theory and the quest for certainty. The will theory should mean that if consent were not real, there was no contract; on the other hand, the need for certainty led to a limiting of doctrines like mistake misrepresentation and duress. This meant that contracts were upheld on the will theory although the reality was that there was no genuine consent (citing *Bell v Lever Bros Ltd* [1932] AC 161 as an example).

[103] Cohen (n 78) 575–78; Ibbetson (n 44) 221: 'what appeared to be a perfect agreement concealed a more ragged mixture of things on which the parties agreed, things on which they disagreed and things to which one or both of them had given no thought'. An example is *Lloyds TSB Foundation for Scotland v Lloyds Group Plc* [2013] 1 WLR 366 (parties' agreement referred to pre-tax profits. A regulation made after the agreement was executed required parties to disclose unrealised gains. The parties differed as

blindly presuming otherwise. Further, of course parties may make cognitive errors in their judgments.[104]

XV. Conclusion

An exact timeframe of events is notoriously difficult, given the slow and sometimes imperceptible manner in which the common law develops, but there is clear evidence in the nineteenth century of English courts' embrace of notions of freedom of contract and, as a corollary, the marginalisation of formerly important concepts such as good faith. This was argued to be necessary to provide the needed certainty and predictability of legal principle, and to avoid 'arbitrariness' in decision making. The chapter has documented instances where freedom of contract was strongly asserted. This included providing a contracting party with absolute discretion in relation to contractual powers (even if its exercise would be 'arbitrary', seemingly replacing one allegedly arbitrary decision with another), a strict focus on the wording of the contract (at the expense of its spirit), apparently in the belief it was possible to reduce agreements to a complete written form, a refusal to provide relief from harsh bargains, refusal to set aside clauses not reasonably necessary to protect a contracting party's legitimate interests, narrow conception of the fraud and public policy exceptions to freedom of contract, acceptance of anti-competitive contract practices, and employer favourable approaches to employment contract situations.

There was at the time apparently strong philosophical support for this position. It was confidently asserted that individuals were rational utility maximisers, willing and able to make agreements favourable to themselves, which it was the court's role to respect and enforce, and not second guess. A certain and predictable approach to contractual interpretation and enforcement was thought to be conducive to capitalism and the industrial revolution. Contracts that were voluntarily entered into should be enforced against the parties, according to the will theory of contract. However, a closer consideration of some of the supposed intellectual adherents to this approach, including Smith and Weber, suggests they did not advocate unbridled freedom of contract; they seemed acutely aware that a consequence of this would be unfairness and exploitation; they were aware that some of the assumptions made by the freedom of contract did not accord with reality, and expressed this. However, it would take some time for the courts' jurisprudence to reflect this, a matter to which I turn in chapter four.

to whether such a gain should be included in pre-tax profits. The regulatory change was not anticipated or reasonably anticipatable by the parties at the time they made their agreement).

[104] R Scott, 'Conflict and Co-operation in Long-Term Contracts' (1987) 75 *California Law Review* 2005, 2010. There is of course a question as to the extent, if any, to which courts should 'rescue' parties in this situation.

4

The Decline of Freedom of Contract

I. Introduction

A reading of some of the cases in chapter three would suggest the dominance of freedom of contract philosophy in the law. However, the law evolved again. Freedom of contract began to be questioned, including from the bench. Sir John Byles wrote extra-judicially that perfect freedom in contracts was 'specious and seducing … (in) its simplicity'.[1] He explained his position in *Mumford v Gething*:

> It is a popular, but in my judgment a mistaken notion, that parties ought to be at liberty to enter into contracts after their own fashion. The legislature has not thought this expedient; for it has, in numerous instances, interfered in the way of limitation or prohibition … there are many cases in which it is expedient for the law to interpose for the protection of the ignorant or of those who would otherwise by subjected to undue influence or pressure.[2]

With the benefit of hindsight, it might be suggested that the courts seemed to take the numerous examples of statutory relaxation of freedom of contract principles and seek to apply them more broadly, also sidelining or reducing freedom of contract philosophy in areas of the common law not subject to legislation.

II. Statutory Abrogation of Freedom of Contract

As Byles noted, increasingly statute began to impinge upon freedom of contract.[3] By and large, these statutes were enforced by the courts,[4] despite apparent

[1] *Observations on the Usury Laws* (London, 1845) 54.

[2] *Mumford v Gething* (1859) 7 CB (NS) 305, 325–26; 141 ER 834, 842.

[3] For example, the Bills of Sale Act 1882 (UK) restricted the right to repossession and the applicability of bills to goods acquired after the agreement was executed; Factors Act 1889 (UK); Sale of Goods Act 1893 (UK); Moneylenders Act 1900 (UK); Hire Purchase Act 1938 (UK); Consumer Credit Act 1974 (UK); Landlord and Tenant Act 1927 (UK); Supply of Goods (Implied Terms) Act 1973 (UK); Unfair Contract Terms Act 1977 (UK); Unfair Terms in Consumer Contracts Regulations 1994 (UK) (general requirement of 'fairness' in consumer contracts); Consumer Rights Act 2015 (UK).

[4] For example, the court accepted strict statutory regulation of the contents of a promissory note: *Parkfield Trust Limited v Curtis* [1934] 1 KB 685. In the Law Times Report of this judgment, but not the KB version, Slesser LJ noted 'I do not think that the fact that its provisions invade the common law freedom to contract can be relied upon': [1934] 150 LT 437.

grumbling from some quarters.[5] So, for example, the courts enforced a statute which provided for the maximum price a railway company could charge for carriage, though it interfered with freedom of contract.[6] The courts noted that freedom of contract might be applied variably, with more scope given to it in the context of buyer and seller, as compared with employer and employee.[7] It also noted it made more sense in the context of a commercial arrangement with a company as opposed to a contract with an individual, given that the risk of oppression and/or unfairness was reduced.[8] It might apply differently to an employer/employee relationship than one involving business partners.[9] Lord Denning noted that, while the common law did respect freedom of contract, it would not allow it to be abused.[10] The court would assume the parties intended the contract to be reasonable, and interpret it that way.[11]

By the early years of the twentieth century, statutory interference with freedom of contract was well established and generally accepted by the courts.[12] This included in relation to the rent that a landlord could charge,[13] the extent of a landlord's right to evict a tenant,[14] the term of shipping contracts,[15] bills of sale,[16] limits on the ability of a lender to take possession of the goods to which the credit related when the borrower defaulted,[17] ways in which wages should be calculated,[18] workers' compensation statutes[19] and the contents of a promissory note.[20] An important area of statutory reform was working conditions, including working hours, minimum rates of pay and workplace health and safety. Later,

[5] For example, in *Archer v James and Another* (1859) 2 B & S 65, 88; 121 ER 998, 1006 noting an 'important objection' to government legislation limiting deductions from a worker's wages on the basis that it interfered with freedom of contract, which was 'universally recognised as of the greatest benefit'.

[6] *The Midland Railway Company v Myers, Rose and Co* (Limited) (1908) 24 TR 446.

[7] *Mason v Provident Clothing and Supply Company (Limited)* [1913] AC 724, 738 (Lord Shaw).

[8] *Knightsbridge Estates Trust, Limited v Byrne and Others* [1940] AC 613, 623 (Viscount Maugham, with whom Lords Atkin and Wright agreed).

[9] *Nordenfelt v Maxim Nordenfelt* [1894] AC 535, 565 (Lord Macnaghten).

[10] *John Lee and Son (Grantham), Limited v Railway Executive* (1949) 65 TLR 604, 606.

[11] *McCallum v Hicks* [1950] 2 KB 271, 275 (CA).

[12] In *Dewhurst v Salford Guardians* Sargant LJ noted the 'general tendency of certain classes of legislation today … to ignore the extraordinary sanctity of freedom of contract': [1925] 41 TR 478, 480.

[13] *Phillips v Potter* (1925) 41 TR 460; *Winchester Court, Limited v Miller* [1944] KB 734; *Briddon v George* [1946] 1 All ER 609.

[14] *Barton v Fincham* [1921] 2 KB 291 (CA).

[15] *The Torni* (1932) 48 TR 471; *Hughes v Sutherland* (1881) 7 QBD 160, 162 noting relevant provisions of the Merchant Shipping Act 1854 (UK) 'interfere with freedom of contract in order to protect a class of persons peculiarly subject to imposition' (in this specific context, apprentices) (Lord Coleridge CJ).

[16] *Ex Parte Stanford; Re Barber* (1886) 17 QBD 259 (CA); *Hetherington v Groome* (1884) 13 QBD 789 (CA).

[17] *Smart Brothers, Limited v Ross* [1941] AC 84. When this case was decided by the Court of Appeal, McKinnon LJ stated that the legislation (limiting the right of a lender to seize goods purchased on hire purchase in the event of default) represented 'the greatest possible interference with our preconceived ideas of freedom of contract': [1942] Ch 158, 172.

[18] *Netherseal Colliery Company v Bourne* (1889) 14 App Cas 228, 247 (Lord Macnaghten).

[19] *Coe v London and North Eastern Railway Company* [1943] KB 531, 547 (Scott LJ) (CA).

[20] *Parkfield Trust Limited v Curtis* [1934] 1 KB 685 (CA).

anti-discrimination legislation would further regulate this area. Eventually it was realised that freedom of contract was a mirage in this context, with most employment contracts not a result of negotiation between parties of roughly equal bargaining power. Previously, employment contracts were seen as ordinary examples of commercial contracts where party autonomy was paramount. The arrangements were assumed to be a reflection of a voluntary agreement reached between free and equal parties. Eventually it was recognised this did not reflect reality, leading to legislation to curb the ability of an employer to dismiss an employee.[21]

As Atiyah notes, what underpinned these statutory reforms was a realisation of the importance of fair exchange in contractual relationships, coupled with an acknowledgment that market-based negotiations do not inevitably or even typically represent fair exchange,[22] acknowledging that such a concept is subjective and somewhat uncertain.

A dispute concerned whether an employee was entitled to superannuation with respect to a wartime bonus he had received.[23] The employer had made it clear when they made the (gratuitous) payment that it was not intended to have superannuation applied to the bonus, to which the employee did not dissent. A majority of the House of Lords interpreted the legislation such that he was so entitled.[24] A dissenting judge in the House of Lords, Lord Sumner, said that the legislation should not be interpreted to obviate the common law right to contract for waiver of rights,[25] and the trial judge referred to freedom of contract in finding for the employer. However, the employee eventually prevailed in the House of Lords.

Some courts adopted the position that, in the event of ambiguity in a statute, it should be interpreted so as not to interfere with freedom of contract.[26] For example, in a landlord-tenant situation, where a statute placed some fetters on the right of a landlord to refuse renewal of a lease, the court noted that the legislation infringed upon freedom of contract, and should be interpreted, in a situation of ambiguity, in a way that was defensive of common law rights, to the extent possible.[27] In *Admiralty Commissioners v Owners of the M/V Valverda* the trial judge noted:

> It has been said, not once but many times, to be a cardinal principle of public policy that the freedom of contract between persons sui juris should not be held to have been

[21] This is discussed in *Johnson v Unisys Ltd* [2003] 1 AC 518, 547–48 (Lord Millett).

[22] PS Atiyah, *The Rise and Fall of Freedom of Contract* (Oxford, Clarendon Press, 1979) 649.

[23] *Dewhurst v Guardians of the Salford Union* [1926] AC 619.

[24] Viscount Cave LC, Lord Shaw, Lord Parmoor and Lord Blanesburgh.

[25] Lord Sumner (633).

[26] *Barlow and Another v Teal* (1885) 15 QBD 501 (CA); *Board of Trade v Baxter; The Scarsdale* [1907] AC 373, 384–85: 'it is very much to be depreciated that the court should be subtle to find implications of illegality, having the effect of hampering the freedom of contract in business matters, where no express prohibition can be found' (Lord Collins); *Morris and Bastert Limited v Loughborough Corporation* [1908] 1 KB 205, 218 (Lord Alverstone CJ).

[27] *Clift v Taylor* [1948] 2 KB 394, 400 (Scott LJ, for the Court of Appeal); similarly *H. Morell and Sons, Limited v Canter* [1947] 2 All ER 533.

> interfered with unless the statute which is said to interfere with it does so in express and unequivocal terms. That, at all events, is a doctrine of public policy as to which there can be no doubt.[28]

This bears obvious similarity (and relationship) with the principle of legality, under which a statute is interpreted, in cases of ambiguity, so as not to interfere with fundamental common law rights. In other words, it might fairly be said that freedom to contract was traditionally seen as in effect a common law right.

The trial judge in this case held that the parties' attempt to contract out of the provisions of the relevant statute prevailed. This also occurred in *Griffiths v Earl of Dudley*.[29] There the Employers' Liability Act 1880 (UK) had been passed. It was introduced partly to remove the doctrine of common employment.[30] It relevantly provided that, in cases where an employee was killed at work, their estate's rights would be the same as if they were not an employee. Griffiths was killed in a work accident. His employer had maintained a system whereby employees paid money into a common bank account. Proceeds in that account were used by the employer to compensate the families of those killed at work. When the legislation was introduced, Griffiths and other workers signed an agreement to the effect that, in the event they were killed or injured at work, they would not bring a claim under the legislation. Griffiths' widow sought to bring a claim under it. The Court found that the agreement Griffiths had made with his employer was binding upon his widow. The Court effectively permitted parties to contract out of legislation that would otherwise have benefitted them. Field J said there was no fraud, pressure or duress applied in relation to the agreement. He disagreed with the suggestion in a lower court that it ought be struck out as contrary to public policy.[31] Field J said that as a general rule employees were able to make reasonable agreements for themselves. Field J noted that in other cases where statute had impinged upon freedom of contract of parties to contract out of it, the statute had made parliament's intention very clear. However, 'as a general rule freedom of contract has been preserved; it has only been interfered with to obviate great public injustice'.[32] Cave J took a similar view.[33]

It is noteworthy that the view of the trial judge in *Admiralty Commissioners* did not prevail. The House of Lords determined that it was the intention of parliament that the relevant provisions of the Merchant Shipping Act 1894 (UK) not be able to be excluded by agreement of the parties.[34]

[28] [1936] 1 KB 724, 733 (Branson J). This judgment was overturned on appeal: [1937] 1 KB 745 (CA) and [1938] AC 173 (HL). The view of the appellate courts was that it was clear that parliament did not intend that the relevant provisions be subject to contracting out by the parties.

[29] (1882) 9 QBD 357.

[30] *Priestley v Fowler* (1837) 3 M & W 1; 150 ER 1030.

[31] (n 29) 362–63.

[32] ibid 364.

[33] ibid 365. In *Admiralty Commissioners v Owners of the M/V Valverda* [1938] AC 173 Lord Wright doubted the correctness of the decision in Griffiths (185), but distinguished the case on its facts and did not overrule it.

[34] [1938] AC 173.

Unfair contractual terms legislation of today directs the court to a range of factors to help determine whether or not a particular clause is unfair.[35] A theme running through these statutory interventions is that they seek to remedy a perceived shortcoming of the traditional contract law in the area of substantive unfairness of contractual terms, related to inequality of bargaining power between contracting parties.[36] This cannot be papered over by an insistence that a contract reflects mutual agreement by parties.

III. Implied Terms

At times, the court utilised implied terms to go beyond the express wording of a contract in order to give effect to a just outcome. For example, in *The Moorcock*,[37] the defendant wharfowner permitted the plaintiff to moor their boat at their wharf. Due to the depth of the water in that place, it was inevitable that the bottom of the plaintiff's boat would strike the sea bed. When it did so, the plaintiff sustained significant damage to their vessel. The Court implied into their agreement a term to the effect that the plaintiffs would be able to moor their boat at the defendant's wharf without sustaining damage. This was on the basis that 'honest business could not be carried on' between persons such as the plaintiff and defendant without the implied term.[38] Bowen LJ said inferences were based on the parties' presumed intention, based on what was reasonable given the nature of the transaction. He took into account that the matter was peculiarly within the means of knowledge of

[35] For example, the strength of the parties' bargaining positions, alternative ways in which the customer's requirements might have been met, whether the consumer had choice to enter into a contract without the offending term, whether they received an inducement to agree to it, whether the customer knew or ought reasonably to have known of it (based on custom or previous business), whether the term excludes or restricts liability if a condition is not met, whether it was reasonable at the time of contract to expect it would be practical to meet the condition, and whether the goods were produced to the precise order of the consumer: Unfair Contract Terms Act 1977 (UK) (Schedule 2). See similarly the Unfair Terms in Consumer Contracts Regulations 1994 (UK). Section 4 defines an unfair term as one which is contrary to good faith, causing significant imbalance in the parties' relative rights under the contract, to the detriment of the consumer. Schedule 2 (Regulation 4(3)) states that in assessing good faith regard should be had to the above factors. Schedule 3 (Regulation 4(4)) gives examples of terms that might be regarded as unfair. They include situations where a pre-condition to the contract coming into existence is in control of one of the parties, one-sided contracts where one party can keep moneys paid in the event the contract does not proceed, disproportionate sums to be paid in the event of breach, permitting unilateral termination or unilateral alteration of terms, giving one party the sole right to determine whether performance meets expectations or what the contract price will be. This is further expanded in the Consumer Rights Act 2015 (UK) Schedule 2 Part I.

[36] C Mitchell, *Contract Law and Contract Practice: Bridging the Gap Between Legal Reasoning and Commercial Expectation* (Oxford, Hart Publishing Ltd, 2013) 8: 'many of these legislative interventions were required precisely because of the deficiencies of classic contract law in addressing substantive unfairness in contract terms or inequality manifest in the contracting relationship. In championing the virtues of freedom and sanctity of contract, voluntariness and consent, the common law of contract lacked the doctrinal tools to deal in economic power and potential for abuse'.

[37] (1889) 14 PD 64 (CA).

[38] ibid 67 (Lord Esher, MR).

the defendant;[39] the plaintiff could not have made independent inquiries or tested the depth themselves.[40] Terms were also implied via custom where there was nothing in the written contract to exclude them.[41] A view that implications were made solely to reflect the parties' intentions was clearly meant to minimise the objection that to imply such terms was to interfere with party autonomy.[42]

In *Liverpool City Council v Irwin* the House of Lords read into an agreement between landlord and tenant that the landlord would keep the common property in reasonable condition, so that the tenants could enjoy the fruits of the tenancy agreement.[43] This was an implication based on the parties' (presumed) intentions, based on notions of necessity.[44]

IV. Restraint of Trade Clauses

Courts considered clauses in contracts that restrained the ability of one of the parties to engage in trade. Originally the common law refused to recognise the validity of such clauses, on the basis they were a breach of the right of an individual to engage in trade as they saw fit.[45] This was obviously very similar to a freedom to contract. However, the courts began to accept restraints on freedom to contract in this space 'within reasonable limits'.[46] A court would accept such clauses, despite their effect on freedom of contract, provided they were not larger than reasonably required to protect the promisee's legitimate business interests.[47] This was on the grounds of public policy. As Viscount Haldane put it:

> It is no doubt as a general rule wise to leave adult persons to make their own agreements and take the consequences, but in the present class of case considerations of public policy come in and make it necessary for the court to scrutinize agreements like the one before your Lordships jealously.[48]

The onus was placed on the one challenging the restraint of trade clause as being unreasonable. This was stated to be because they were the one seeking to impose

[39] ibid 70.
[40] ibid 69.
[41] *Hutton v Warren* (1836) 1 M & W 466; 150 ER 517.
[42] E Peden, '"Cooperation" in English Contract Law – To Construe or Imply?' (2000) 16 *Journal of Contract Law* 56, 57.
[43] *Liverpool City Council v Unwin* [1977] AC 239.
[44] ibid 254 (Lord Wilberforce) (with whom Lord Fraser agreed), 259 (Lord Cross) and 266 (Lord Edmund-Davies), following *The Moorcock* (1889) 14 PD 64 (CA).
[45] *Attorney-General of the Commonwealth of Australia v Adelaide Steamship Co Limited* [1913] AC 781, 794 (Lord Parker, for the Privy Council); *Nordenfelt v Maxim Nordenfelt* [1894] AC 535, 556 (Lord Ashbourne).
[46] *Attorney-General of the Commonwealth of Australia v Adelaide Steamship Co Limited* [1913] AC 781, 795 (Lord Parker, for the Privy Council).
[47] *McEllistrim v Ballymaceltigott Co-Operative Agricultural and Dairy Society* [1919] AC 548, 597 (Lord Parmoor).
[48] *Mason v Provident Clothing and Supply Company (Limited)* [1913] AC 724, 734 (with whom Lord Dunedin agreed).

a restriction on freedom of contract. It was incumbent upon them to prove that freedom of trade required freedom of contract to be restricted.[49]

V. Enlarged Use of Public Policy to Excuse Contractual Obligation

More generally, courts became increasingly prepared to refuse to enforce contracts voluntarily and freely entered into on the grounds of public policy. They overcame their hesitation to do so, explained in chapter three. So for example in *Beresford v Royal Insurance Company, Limited*[50] the court held that the deceased had contracted to obtain life insurance in the event of his death, including by suicide. The deceased committed suicide, and his estate sought to claim upon the policy. Although that is what the parties had agreed, the court refused to enforce it, on the basis it was contrary to public policy for a person (or their personal representative) to obtain benefit from wrongdoing, and at that time the law regarded suicide as a crime.

VI. Warranties by Sellers of Goods

I noted in chapter three that originally, courts refused to find that a seller of goods had made implied promises to the purchaser in respect of those goods. If no promise were expressed, the court would be unlikely to find one was implicit. This is demonstrated by *Attwood v Small*.[51] However, just a few years after the case, the Court determined that a retail store owner did warrant that they had title to sell goods displayed in their store.[52] And a party who paid a certain amount for a bar of silver after having it inspected by a third party to estimate the amount of silver it obtained received a remedy for money had and received, when a subsequent inspection found the first inspection had significantly over-estimated the amount of silver it contained.[53]

A purchaser also had a remedy when they purchased copper to sheath a ship, a purpose known to the vendor. The vendor assured the purchaser they would supply suitable material. In fact the material supplied only lasted four months, rather than the four years that was expected. All members of the Court found in favour of the plaintiff, on the basis either that the defendant had made an express warranty regarding suitability for purpose, or alternatively that there was an

[49] *Haynes v Doman* (1899) 2 Ch 13, 31 (Romer LJ).
[50] [1938] AC 586.
[51] (1838) 6 Cl & F 232.
[52] *Eichholz v Bannister* (1864) 17 CB (NS) 708; 144 ER 284 (Erle CJ Byles and Keating).
[53] *Cox v Prentice* (1815) 3 M & S 344; 105 ER 641.

implied warranty that goods supplied would be fit for some purpose, and if the purchaser had explained the purpose for which the purchased good was required, that they would be suitable for that purpose.[54]

The court would eventually reach the position that, at least where a contract to purchase goods of a particular nature (rather than a specific item)[55] was concerned, there was an implied warranty that they would be reasonably fit for the purpose for which they were provided.[56] It would accept that, at least where a purchaser had no opportunity to inspect the purchased goods beforehand, there was an implied warranty that the goods to be supplied were fit for purpose and of merchantable quality. In such cases, caveat emptor did not apply.[57]

VII. Fettering Contractual Discretion

The courts' attitude towards contractual discretion began to change. For example, in *Re Gresham Life Assurance Society*[58] the Court had assumed that a body given discretion to consent to a transfer of ownership would exercise it in good faith and not in an arbitrary or capricious fashion. It was for another asserting otherwise to demonstrate. In *Andrews v Belfield*, the court upheld a contractual clause whereby a contractor promised to attend to all of the purchaser's requirements as to the quality of goods supplied. The purchaser had declined the supplied goods because of supposed defects in quality. The court held he was entitled to do so, noting he was not acting with a lack of good faith and/or capriciously.[59] And in *Stadhard v Lee*, where a building contract required the contractor to work as quickly as the client required, the court upheld the clause, though conceding it might appear unfair:

> however unreasonable and oppressive a stipulation or condition may be, the one party intended to insist upon and the other to submit to it, a Court of Justice cannot do otherwise than give full effect to the terms which have been agreed upon between the parties.[60]

VIII. Imposition of Reasonableness Standards

Contract provisions requiring notices were supplemented by the court when a strict interpretation of them would clearly have worked injustice. So for example

[54] *Jones v Bright* (1829) 5 Bing. 533; 130 ER 1167.
[55] As to which see *Chanter v Hopkins* (1838) 4 M & W 399; 150 ER 1484 (Court of Exchequer).
[56] *Bigge v Parkinson* (1862) 7 H & N 955; 158 ER 758; *Ollivant v Bailey* (1843) 5 QB 288; 114 ER 257; *Brown v Edgington* (1841) 2 M & G 279; 133 ER 751.
[57] *Laing v Fidgeon* (1815) 6 Taunt 109; 128 ER 974; *Jones v Just* (1868) LR 3 QB 197 (Cockburn CJ Blackburn and Mellor JJ); *Shepherd v Pybus* (1842) 3 M & G 868; 133 ER 1390.
[58] (1872) LR 8 Ch App 446.
[59] *Andrews v Belfield* (1857) 2 CBNS 779; 140 ER 622.
[60] *Stadhard v Lee* (1863) 4 B & S 364, 372; 122 ER 138, 141 (Cockburn CJ).

in *Toms v Wilson and Another*,[61] the contract provided for a debtor to repay money to the creditor 'immediately upon demand'. The Court interpreted this to require a reasonable time to elapse. The parties did not intend, the Court determined, that the payment would have to be made at the instant demand was made.

Similarly in *Massey v Sladen*,[62] the plaintiff executed a bill of sale in favour of the defendant. The contract permitted the defendant to serve notice on the plaintiff requiring immediate payment of the total amount contained in the bill, failing which the defendant was entitled to seize and sell property. The defendant gave the plaintiff's son the notice. The Court interpreted the notice provision as to require a reasonable time to elapse between when the notice was given and when seizure and sale could occur. The Court noted potentially ridiculous results otherwise – the defendant would be able to seize and sell five minutes after having provided the plaintiff notice. This was not what the parties intended, the Court found. The Court did not use the language of good faith, but its decision is clearly consonant with it.

Similarly, in *Moore v Shelley and Another*, the Privy Council found that where a mortgage permitted the mortgagee to enter into possession following demand and default, a reasonable time must elapse between the demand and entry into possession. In that case, the reasonable time was necessary so that the mortgagor could ascertain whether a person purporting to act as agent for the mortgagee had the necessary authority.[63]

Mortgages were a fertile field for a slightly different approach to contractual interpretation, less reliant on the literal terms. The principle that, despite a contractual term to the contrary, there must be no clogs on the equity of redemption, is one.[64] Another good example of this is the 3–2 decision of the House of Lords in *Bradley v Carritt*.[65] There a mortgage provided that the mortgagor, a holder of shares in a tea company, would 'always thereafter' use his best endeavours to ensure that tea sold by the business would take place through the mortgagee, and would pay the mortgagee the commission they otherwise would have earned if this did not occur. The mortgagee paid off the mortgage, and the issue arose as to the extent to which the obligation to use the mortgagee as broker continued. The contract literally provided that this obligation would apply 'always thereafter', but a majority of the Court interpreted it to be confined to a time when the mortgage remained on foot. Once it was paid off, the obligation ended.[66] Traces of freedom of contract philosophy appear in the judgment of the dissenting justices, on the basis parties of sound mind should be held to the literal terms of their bargain.[67]

[61] *Toms v Wilson and Another* (1863) 4 B & S 442; 122 ER 524 (Court of Exchequer).

[62] *Massey v Sladen* (1868) LR 4 Ex 13 (Court of Exchequer).

[63] *Moore v Shelley and Another* (1883) 8 App Cas 295 (Privy Council, on appeal from New South Wales).

[64] *Noakes and Co Ltd v Rice* [1902] AC 24.

[65] [1903] AC 253.

[66] Lords Macnaghten, Davey and Robertson.

[67] (n 65) 263 (Lord Shand) and 279 (Lord Lindley).

Relief against forfeitures was another area in which the law clearly departed from freedom of contract principles. As Lord Simon noted in *Shiloh Spinners Ltd v Harding*:

> The last hundred years have seen many examples of relaxation of the stance of regarding contractual rights and obligations as sacrosanct and exclusive of other considerations: though these examples do not compel equity to follow – … they do at least invite a more liberal and extensively based attitude on the part of the courts … equity has an unlimited and unfettered jurisdiction to relieve against forfeiture and penalties.[68]

Some freedom of contract sentiment is also evident in *G & C Kreglinger v New Patagonia Meat and Cold Storage Company Limited*,[69] but the court considered whether the contractual term sought to be enforced was 'unfair and unconscionable', apparently prepared to grant relief in such a case.[70]

IX. Estoppel

The court recognised an exception to freedom of contract in cases that we would now recognise as estoppel, though some of these cases themselves do not use the term. In *Hughes v Metropolitan Railway Co*,[71] Lord Cairns noted:

> If parties who have entered into definite and distinct terms involving certain legal results, afterwards by their own act or with their own consent enter upon a course of negotiation which has the effect of leading one of the parties to suppose that the strict rights arising under the contract will not be enforced … the person who otherwise might have enforced these rights will not be allowed to enforce them when it would be inequitable having regard to the dealings which have taken place between the parties.[72]

The case of *Central London Property Trust Ltd v High Trees House Limited*[73] is an interesting one regarding freedom of contract. In 1937, the parties had entered into a 99-year lease at a rent of 2500 pounds per year. In early 1940 due to the war the defendant lessee was not able to sub-let many of the flats in the property. As a result, the parties agreed in writing that the rent would be 1250 pounds per year, backdated to the commencement of the lease. The report does not mention that the parties made any specific agreement regarding the term of this reduction of rent. By 1945, the defendant was able to sub-let virtually the entire building. The lessor sought payment at the original rent; the lessee claimed to be liable only

[68] [1973] AC 691, 726.
[69] *G & C Kreglinger v New Patagonia Meat and Cold Storage Company Limited* [1914] AC 25.
[70] ibid 61 (Lord Parker, with whom the Earl of Halsbury, Lord Atkinson and Lord Mersey agreed).
[71] *Hughes v Metropolitan Railway Company* (1877) 2 App Cas 439.
[72] ibid 448; O'Connor says it is 'difficult to conceive of a better example of the application of good faith in the sense of reasonableness and fairness' than this decision (*Good Faith in English Law* (Aldershot, Dartmouth, 1990) 27) though the judges did not base their decision expressly on the basis of good faith; see also *D & C Builders v Rees* [1966] 2 QB 617, 625 (Lord Denning MR).
[73] *Central London Property Trust Ltd v High Trees House Limited* [1947] KB 130.

for the reduced amount. Lord Denning famously recognised an estoppel principle whereby one party makes a promise to the other intending that it be acted upon. If the other party does so act, the promisor is bound by the promise despite the absence of consideration. The case report is not entirely clear one way or the other, but there is no evidence that the variation was expressly time limited. Thus, on one view of freedom of contract, the lessee would be bound merely to pay the reduced amount for the entirety of the 99 years, particularly given it was back-dated. However, Lord Denning did not give effect to this interpretation, permitting the lessee to have the reduced rent only while the property's occupancy was being affected by the war effort. On one view, this is an example of a court not giving effect to freedom of contract philosophy, and in the direction of good faith.[74]

X. Liquidated Damages/Penalty Clauses

The court also considered freedom of contract in relation to clauses purporting to reflect an agreement between parties in advance as to damages payable in the event of breach of contract. The law has made a distinction between clauses that reflect a genuine pre-estimate of the damage that the innocent party will likely suffer from the breach (even if the estimate turns out to be inaccurate), and penalty clauses, which do not reflect such genuine pre-estimate. The court will enforce the former type of clause, but not the latter. In the leading older case on this, *Dunlop Pneumatic Tyre Coy Ltd v New Garage and Motor Company Ltd*,[75] members of the House of Lords noted that, in determining whether or not a clause did reflect a genuine pre-estimate of damage likely to flow from the loss, the words used by the parties was not conclusive. Lord Parker said the question was whether the clause was a good faith pre-estimate of damage, and indicated a preparedness to look beyond the terms used.[76] Lord Parmoor agreed the clause would not be enforced if it were 'extravagant or unconscionable'.[77] This indicates the preparedness of the courts to depart from freedom of contract principles in some cases.

XI. Making Sense of the Change

Atiyah explains that one of the reasons for the court's change of position was that the nature of contracts had changed. They were becoming less about what had

[74] JF O'Connor *Good Faith in English Law* (Aldershot, Dartmouth, 1990) 20: 'the invention of the doctrine of promissory estoppel to given effect to promises unsupported by consideration is another … example of the judicial imposition of good faith (referring to the *High Trees Case*) … to enforce a gratuitous promise because, in the particular circumstances of the case, good faith in the sense of honesty, fair dealing and reasonableness required that it be kept'.

[75] [1915] AC 79.

[76] ibid 97–98; as did Lord Dunedin (86).

[77] ibid 101. Lord Atkinson considered whether there was anything 'unreasonable, extravagant or unconscionable' about the clause (97).

already occurred and was occurring (executed), and more about promises of what would occur in the future (executory). This was important because it was generally difficult to get the court to do something; the default was always the status quo. At a time when contracts were generally executed, the default was that parties would continue to do what they were doing, and the party seeking the court's intervention would have to provide a strong reason and justification for the court intervening to excuse future non-performance. The courts' reluctance to do so was reflected in freedom of contract principles. As contracts became more executory in nature, it was the party seeking to enforce the contract who might need the court's intervention, through an order for specific performance or damages, for example.[78] Further, it was recognised that many contracts were not, in fact, 'free' in the economic sense,[79] and that promise of freedom of contract of certainty and predictability of result was, in many respects, an illusion.[80]

Atiyah notes, explaining the courts' change in attitude, that

> Change may have been developing in people's expectations as a result of changing commercial customs and practices. As greater regularity and order came into business, as records began to be better kept, as manufactured products began to become more reliable and less risky, as the volatility of the early years of the industrial revolution passed away, contracting parties may well have grown used to having their expectations fulfilled. Prices would naturally have tended to be adjusted upwards as buyers began to expect goods to be more reliable or to expect manufacturers to replace defective goods without further charge. This in turn may have reacted on the law; higher expectations deserved higher protection, partly at least because they were likely to be paid for in higher prices.[81]

Reiter explains it thus:

> The reintroduction of good faith into descriptions of contract represents part of the process of the resocialization of contract law (or law generally) required after the nineteenth century's attempts to disembarrass contract of complicating elements of morality. Where this nineteenth century attempt failed to exert significant influence on contract-in-fact, it did make its mark on descriptions and theories of contract. There, the very aim of contract was seen to be the freeing of individuals from the bonds of societal limitations on their activities, expressed through such restrictive institutions as the guilds, closed towns, custom, convention and natural law, as perceived through reasoned reflection.[82]

Atiyah writes that freedom of contract was effectively finished as a political principle by the 1880s. One of the reasons he ascribes to its death is the evolution

[78] Atiyah (n 22) 478–79.

[79] JH Baker, 'From Sanctity of Contract to Reasonable Expectation' (1979) 32(1) *Current Legal Problems* 17, 21.

[80] A Mason, 'Contract, Good Faith and Equitable Standards in Fair Dealing' (2000) 116 *Law Quarterly Review* 66, 70.

[81] Atiyah (n 22) 479. Atiyah also notes that in the first half of the nineteenth century there was significant anxiety over public safety and law and order. He said it reflected a government that was over-reliant on private contracts rather than government employees to maintain law and order (516).

[82] BJ Reiter, 'Good Faith in Contracts' (1983) 17 *Valparaiso University Law Review* 705, 730.

in democracy and the extension of the franchise to a much broader range of individuals. Freedom of contract presumed satisfaction with the status quo in terms of distribution of wealth and property. Many were not satisfied; this in turn undermined freedom of contract.[83] Other factors were also at work. The late nineteenth century saw the rise of significant monopolies. The free market had not prevented these from developing, and the free market had limited ability to prevent such monopolies taking advantage of their market strength. Laws did not prevent them from occurring. Further, trade associations sought to limit competition among suppliers. The law did not curb these with the same vehemence with which it had sought to curb employee combinations.

It was realised that the market would not always create 'perfect' results. Externalities may not be taken into proper account. The assumption that individuals had access to the kind of information that the classic freedom of contract model required was accepted to be unrealistic. It was difficult to price future wants with accuracy, given that different people would apply a different discounting rate. This could lead to what Arrow called 'adverse selection'.[84] Rationality was, at the very least, bounded.[85] A person's cognitive abilities had limits.[86] If individuals could not be trusted to make rational decisions regarding present and future wants, the rationale for freedom of contract evaporated. Individuals may not adequately research their options prior to making business decisions. Keynes provided significant intellectual ballast for such conclusions.[87]

Eisenberg sums up a range of research in this space. He states a significant body of work has illustrated the limitations of the traditional economic model:

> The action that would maximise a substantive actor's utility may not even be considered, because actors limit their search for and their deliberation on alternatives. Furthermore, actors are unrealistically optimistic as a systematic matter. Moreover, actors systematically utilize heuristics that are irrational or pathological (and) … yield systematic errors … actors make decisions on the basis of data that is readily available to their memory, rather than on the basis of all the relevant data; in particular, actors

[83] Atiyah (n 22) 589–90.

[84] K Arrow, 'The Organization of Economic Activity: Issues Pertinent to the Choice of Market Versus Nonmarket Allocation', 2 *Collected Papers of Kenneth Arrow* (Cambridge, Harvard University Press, 1984) 142–44.

[85] D Campbell, 'The Incompleteness of our Understanding of the Law and Economics of Relational Contract' [2004] *Wisconsin Law Review* 645, 666–67.

[86] H Simon, 'A Behavioural Model of Rational Choice' (1955) 69 *Quarterly Journal of Economics* 99; Christine Jolis, Cass Sunstein and Richard Thaler, 'A Behavioural Approach to Law and Economics' (1998) 50 *Stanford Law Review* 1471, 1477.

[87] JM Keynes, *The End of Laissez-Faire* (London, Hogarth Press, 1926): 'It is *not* true that individuals possess a prescriptive "natural liberty" in their economic activities. There is no compact conferring perpetual rights on those who have or on those who acquire. The world is *not* so governed from above that private and social interest always coincide. It is *not* so managed here below that in practice they always coincide. It is *not* a correct deduction from the Principles of Economics that enlightened self-interest always operates in the public interest. Nor is it true that self-interest generally is enlightened; more often individuals acting separately to promote their own ends are too ignorant or too weak to attain even these. Experience does *not* show that individuals, when they make up a social unit are always less clear-sighted than when they act separately'.

> systematically give undue weight to instantiated evidence as compared to general statements, to vivid experience as compared to pallid evidence, and to concrete evidence as compared to abstract evidence ... actors are systematically insensitive to sample size, and erroneously take small samples as representative samples ... the sample consisting of present events is often wrongly taken to be representative – and therefore predictive – of future events. Actors also have faulty telescopic faculties ... they give too little weight to future benefits and costs as compared to present benefits and costs (and) ... actors underestimate most risks.[88]

Further, the assumption that individuals always preferred options that were in their best interests ignored the 'payoff' that individuals might obtain from being other-regarding. People often care about fairness. They care about being treated fairly, and often treat others fairly, particularly if that person treats them fairly.[89] They may forego short-term gain in favour of maintaining long-term, strong contracting relationships.[90]

Further evidence of this has emerged from studies into human behaviour, including the 'Ultimatum Game'. This involves two parties. One is given a pot of money. That person must agree with the other regarding an allocation of the funds between them. If the offeree accepts the offeror's offer, both parties keep the amounts suggested. If the offeree rejects the offeror's offer, neither gets anything. Obviously, it would be most rational for the offeror to offer the offeree a negligible sum, on the basis they keep the lion's share. Rationally, the offeree will accept the meagre sum offered, because they are aware that, if they do not, they will get nothing. Something is better than nothing. Yet the research tends to suggest that the offeree offered a negligible sum rejects the offer. They must generally be offered something substantial in order to accept. This result has been replicated. It is said to reflect parties' adherence to norms of fairness, even though it may be costly. The offeree in such cases clearly shows an overriding concern for what they consider to be a fair distribution, not rational self-interest.[91] Obviously, ideas of bounded

[88] M Eisenberg, 'Relational Contracts' in Jack Beatson and Daniel Friedmann (eds), *Good Faith and Fault in Contract Law* (Oxford, Clarendon Press, 2002) 301; see also Mitchell (n 36) 44.

[89] Jolis, Sunstein and Thaler (n 86) 1479; M Rabin, 'Incorporating Fairness into Game Theory and Economics' (1993) 83 *American Economic Review* 1281.

[90] See for example *George Mitchell (Chesterhall) Ltd v Finney Lock Seeds Ltd* [1983] 2 AC 803. There the Court heard evidence that it was standard practice in the trade to limit a supplier's liability, in cases where good supplied were defective, to replacement cost. Liability for consequential losses caused by the defective goods was excluded. However, the House of Lords heard evidence that it was usual in the industry that, if the loss claim were genuine, the guilty party would pay more than the contract price by way of compensation. The Court took judicial notice of this fact, and used it to determine the appropriate remedy in the case before them.

[91] E Hoffman and ML Spitzer, 'The Coase Theorem: Some Experimental Tests' (1982) 25 *Journal of Law and Economics* 73; C Camerer and R Thaler, 'Anomalies: Ultimatums, Dictators and Manners' (1995) 9 *Journal of Law and Economics Perspectives* 209; J Morgan, *Contract Law Minimalism: A Formalist Restatement of Commercial Contract Law* (Cambridge, Cambridge University Press, 2013) 58–59. Morgan concludes that 'in contract law, the paradigm of self-interested parties negotiating a one-off transaction at arm's length would seem increasingly untenable' (59). Mitchell agrees: (n 36) 44: 'while there are conditions under which attention to self-interest would be warranted as opposed to any other regarding behaviour, this should not be taken to be the governing and underpinning norm that either fully explains or should explain exchange behaviour'.

rationality and bounded self-interest weaken some of the intellectual foundation of freedom of contract arguments.

XII. Conclusion

What originally appeared to be a complete adoption by the common law of freedom of contract principles turned out to be a mirage. In the early- to mid-twentieth century, in particular, courts became more prepared to intervene in contractual disputes. Courts viewed their role as more than simply enforcing the parties' written agreement. Courts may have been influenced by the extent to which statute law altered the common law rules in particular areas. Unbridled freedom of contract was rejected. Courts were more prepared to intervene, for example by implying terms into contracts to fill gaps, conditioning apparently open-ended contractual powers and discretions on reasonableness, limiting parties' use of restraint of trade clauses, providing relief from unfair contractual clauses, and increasingly subjecting contracts to public policy considerations.

At the heart of this evolution was a realisation that a simple freedom of contract approach does not always lead to outcomes most think are just. That approach makes unrealistic assumptions in relation to contracts. Parties often do not have complete information when negotiating a contract, and are often not in a position of relatively equal bargaining power. Parties do not always choose what economists would regard as optimal choices. And parties are not always the hard-nosed business people that classical economies would presume. There is evidence that parties place value on fairness, and have reasonable expectations regarding the behaviour of those with whom they contract, which are hard to take account of in the classical view of contract.

If classical freedom of contract and will theory were an inadequate basis for the law of contract, naturally other options are considered. Chapters seven and eight will consider a significantly different way of viewing contractual relations in a way that is said to typically reflect much more accurately the realities of contracting and parties' reasonable expectations regarding contracting behaviour. The decline of freedom of contract certainly provided a possible platform for the re-introduction of good faith into contract law. Chapters five and six now consider the extent to which this has occurred in the common law world.

5

Introduction to Good Faith in Modern Times, and Good Faith in the United Kingdom in the Twentieth and Twenty-First Centuries

I. Introduction to Good Faith in Modern Times

It is often argued that, at least in most cases, those engaged in business in fact operate consistently with good faith.[1] This will be explored in more detail in chapter seven. Of course, given the sentiment that commercial law should broadly reflect commercial practice, if it is true that business people typically act in good faith, and legitimately expect that of another, that is an argument for the law of commerce to reflect good faith,[2] in one way or another.

There is a very lively debate as to whether the common law needs a doctrine of good faith. One argument is that there is no need for such a doctrine, because the common law has other doctrines that, to a significant extent at least, can accommodate the kinds of arguments that might today be considered through the lens of good faith.[3] The results will in many cases be similar.[4] David Richards LJ specifically noted rescission for fraudulent representation and unconscionability as examples.[5] I have referred in an earlier chapter to examples such as

[1] R Brownsword, 'Two Concepts of Good Faith' (1994) 7 *Journal of Contract Law* 197, 197.

[2] ibid 202: 'one might argue that English common law would be more effective (more instrumentally rational) in regulating commercial dealing if a good faith requirement were incorporated, because this would bring the law more into line with the expectations and understandings of commercial practice'.

[3] G McMeel, 'Foucault's Pendulum: Text, Context and Good Faith in Contract Law' (2017) 70(1) *Current Legal Problems* 365, 390; Lord Steyn, 'Interpretation, Legal Texts and their Landscape' in BS Markesinis (eds) *The Clifford Chance Millennium Lectures* (Oxford, Hart, 2000) 79; *Esso Australian Resources Pty Ltd v Southern Pacific Petroleum NL and Ors* [2005] VSCA 228, [2] (Warren CJ); G Kuehne, 'Implied Obligations of Good Faith and Reasonableness in the Performance of Contracts: Old Wine in New Bottles' (2006) 33 *University of Western Australia Law Review* 63, 107; *Service Station Association Ltd v Berg Bennett & Associates Pty Ltd* (1993) 117 ALR 393 (Gummow J).

[4] R Powell, 'Good Faith in Contracts' (1956) 9(1) *Current Legal Problems* 16; W Tetley, 'Good Faith in Contract: Particularly in the Contracts of Arbitration and Chartering' (2004) 35 *Journal of Maritime Law and Commerce* 561, 583; M Hiscock, 'The Keeper of the Flame: Good Faith and Fair Dealing in International Trade' (1996) 29 *Loyola Los Angeles Law Review* 1059, 1070.

[5] *Times Travel (UK) Ltd v Pakistan International Airlines* [2019] EWCA Civ 828, [106] (with whom Moylan and Asplin LLJ agreed).

promissory estoppel, and relief against penalties and forfeitures, and implied terms.[6] Unconscionability and the requirement to mitigate losses might be others. The court might utilise its power of interpretation in this regard. In contrast, Brownsword indicates that, if adopted, good faith would lead to some different results, though not radically so.[7]

However, this argument can cut another way. The argument might be that the law is dishonest, in simultaneously denying the general applicability of good faith, but then countenancing outcomes that are very similar, but sometimes through tortured reasoning or unnatural twisting of facts. So, for example, Summers criticises courts on the basis they are sometimes less than frank about the true basis of their decisions:

> Some courts at times refuse to enforce some unconscionable contracts or contract clauses. But, except in a relatively few areas, they seldom do this openly. Rather than invalidate openly in the name of public policy, fairness or good faith, they more often resort to back door techniques – for example they base their decisions on contractual interpretation or construction (or other contractual doctrines) … this is all a notoriously open secret.[8]

It is possible that much of this jurisprudence could be explained through the prism of a generalised contractual principle of good faith, a doctrine that unites these doctrines.[9] As Bingham LJ (as he then was) noted:

> The tendency of the English authorities has … been to look at the nature of the transaction … and the character of the parties to it; to consider what notice the party … was given of the particular condition … and to resolve whether in all the circumstances it is fair to hold him bound by the condition. This may yield a result not very different

[6] Sir Anthony Mason refers to 'various means by which the courts have sought to fill the void caused by the absence of a general good faith doctrine', before referring to fiduciary obligations, unconscionability, estoppel and restitution: 'Contract, Good Faith and Equitable Standards in Fair Dealing' (2000) 116 *Law Quarterly Review* 66, 84; 'the cause of action in unjust enrichment may also be described as a reflection of good faith and fair dealing standards' (94).

[7] One context in which results would differ relates to pre-contractual negotiations. Brownsword (n 1) notes that 'English judges seem to think that commercial people have few scruples about being economical with extrinsic (collateral market-sensitive) information known to be material to the other side' (226) and that the 'rugged English view, generally permitting deception by silence during negotiation, is out of line with good faith as the rule' (227).

[8] R Summers, '"Good Faith" in General Contract Law and the Sales Provisions of the Uniform Commercial Code' (1968) 54(2) *Virginia Law Review* 195, 231. He refers to offer and acceptance, want of 'mutuality', lack of consideration and mutual mistake as examples of other contractual doctrines utilised in this context.

[9] Mason (n 6) 94: 'recognition of good faith and fair dealing concepts would bring a greater coherence and unity to the varied array of principles which are presently available in the area of contract performance'; Tetley (n 4) 584: 'the time may well have come to consider introducing a general good faith duty into English common law of contract, if only to ensure greater unity and consistency in the law, greater international legal harmony, and to better protect the interests of contracting parties by a general principle which, over time, would no doubt be developed by the common law and absorb some of the piecemeal solutions that have hitherto held sway'; JF O'Connor, *Good Faith in English Law* (Aldershot, Dartmouth, 1990) 99–101; PD Finn, 'Equity and Contract' in PD Finn (ed), *Essays on Contract* (Sydney, Law Book Co, 1987).

> from the civil law principle of good faith, at any rate so far as the formation of contract is concerned.[10]

Another example of the way in which existing legal principles might be re-interpreted as a good faith doctrine appears in *Panchaud Freres SA v Etablissements General Grain Co.*[11] There the bill of lading for the goods incorrectly stated the goods had been shipped at the end of July. In fact, other documents suggested the goods had been shipped in mid-August. When the goods arrived, the purchaser argued the goods were not of the required quantity. That claim was upheld. During an appeal process against that finding, the purchaser first raised the argument that they could reject the goods because they had been shipped late. All members of the Court of Appeal found that the purchaser could not raise this argument later, after initially not raising the matter at the time they received the shipping documents relating to the goods.

In so deciding, Winn LJ referred to a nascent legal principle requiring that contracting parties engage in 'fair conduct'. Winn LJ referred to the manifest convenience of consistency in pragmatic affairs, denying that parties could 'blow hot and cold' in commercial affairs.[12] Lord Denning MR referred to situations where it was unjust or unfair to allow a party to a contract to depart from a state of affairs the other party has taken to be settled or correct.[13] These sentiments could be incorporated in a generalised contractual doctrine of good faith.

The fact that the common law often provides outcomes that are similar to what application of a generalised good faith doctrine would leads some scholars to view English law's ambivalence towards good faith as a 'rhetorical flourish'. They claim the reality is that good faith and fair dealing are in substance overarching concepts in the law, as a result of various principles of contractual construction and vitiating factors.[14] Brownsword calls the current approach a 'noble lie' that makes the law

[10] *Interfoto Picture Library Ltd v Stiletto Visual Programmes Ltd* [1989] QB 433, 445; similarly Lord Steyn (n 3) 79.

[11] [1970] 1 Lloyd's Rep 53 (CA).

[12] ibid 59.

[13] ibid 57.

[14] McMeel (n 3) 396, adding he did not believe adoption of an overriding principle of good faith and fair dealing in commercial transactions would harm the English legal system, even if its adoption was unlikely; similarly Mason (n 6) 94: 'good faith and fair dealing concepts are already substantially in place under our general law'; *CTN Cash and Carry Ltd v Gallaher Ltd* [1994] 4 All ER 714, 718: 'the aim of our commercial law ought to be to encourage fair dealing between parties' (Steyn LJ, with whom Farquharson LJ and Sir Donald Nicholls V-C agreed). David Campbell concludes that 'the law of contract contains an extensive set of other-regarding duties constituting a framework for facilitating agreement, and … a clear understanding about this may best be reached through a concept (not a general doctrine) of good faith … contractual agreement is not based on solipsistic self-interest but on self-interest which recognises other regarding duties': 'Adam Smith and the Social Foundation of Agreement: *Walford v Miles* as a Relational Contract' (2017) 21(3) *Edinburgh Law Review* 376, 401; J Carter and A Stewart, 'Interpretation, Good Faith and the "True Meaning" of Contracts: The *Royal Botanic* Decision' (2002) 18 *Journal of Contract Law* 182, 192: 'examination of virtually every rule of contract law would show that is embodies such a requirement, or what has been termed a "good faith function"'.

less rational.[15] There is an air of the law seeking to bend traditional contract law doctrine to try to obtain what the court considers to be correct outcomes. It leads it to irrationality, can lead to the court considering peripheral issues and missing critical ones and, in the language of Brownsword, avoids 'snarl' in the law.[16] An example might be the law of implied terms. It is sometimes argued there is an air of artificiality in deeming that parties consented to terms that the court implies in law or in fact,[17] based on existing tests.[18] Some explain English law of implied terms as being necessary because it lacks a general duty of good faith.[19] That convinces Brownsword that, rather than muddle on with classical contract law doctrine and attempt to fit just results around such doctrines, the better approach would be to adopt a general requirement of good faith. This would be a general rule, not an exception.[20]

[15] Brownsword (n 1) 203: 'the courts have tended to maintain the rhetoric of the classical law of contract while discreetly qualifying its substance – this has been a noble lie but, in the long run, a practice that has impaired the rationality of the law'.

[16] Brownsword (n 1) 203–07.

[17] C Mitchell, 'Contracts and Contract Law: Challenging the Distinction Between the 'Real' and 'Paper' Deal' (2009) 29(4) *Oxford Journal of Legal Studies* 675, 682.

[18] This is most evident in the test to imply terms in fact, based on *The Moorcock* (1889) 14 PD 64 (CA). There the Court noted five requirements in order that a term be implied in fact into a contract: (a) the proposed term must be reasonable and equitable; (b) it must be necessary to give 'business efficacy' to the contract, so a term will not be implied if the contract would be effective without it; (c) it must be so obvious that it goes without saying; (d) it must be capable of clear expression; and (e) it must not contradict any written terms of the agreement; see also *BP Refinery (Westernport) Pty Ltd v Shire of Hastings* (1977) 180 CLR 266, 282–83. This approach is consistent with the then-prevailing will theory of contract, whereby implied terms had to be connected with the parties' actual intention in order to be incorporated into the parties' agreement. As Hugh Collins explains, this was thought to maintain adherence to freedom of contract principles prevalent at the time: 'Implied Terms: The Foundation in Good Faith and Fair Dealing' (2014) 67 *Current Legal Problems* 297, 305. Collins continues 'either in the rule-making of terms implied in law or the adjustment of risks through terms implied in fact, a court is typically venturing beyond the terms expressed by the parties'. He makes cogent criticisms of the requirement of 'business efficacy', noting *Equitable Life Assurance Society v Hyman* [2002] 1 AC 408 (HL) where the Court implied a term based on business efficacy. Collins agrees that the term should be implied, but argues the business efficacy test was not actually met on the facts. The contract would have functioned effectively without the suggested implied term: 316–17. Adherence to this approach is also evident in *Attorney-General of Belize v Belize Telecom Ltd* [2009] 1 WLR 1988 where the Court stated that implied terms were simply an amplification of what the parties would reasonably have understood the express terms to mean: [21](Lord Hoffmann); cf *Marks & Spencer Plc v BNP Paribas Securities Services* [2016] AC 742, 756 where the Court emphasized implication of terms was quite separate from interpreting express words of a contract (Lord Neuberger, with whom Lords Sumption and Hodge agreed).

[19] Justice Steyn, 'The Role of Good Faith and Fair Dealing in English Contract Law: A Hairshirt Philosophy?' [1991] 6 *Denning Law Journal* 131, 133: 'in the absence of a doctrine of good faith English law has to resort to the implication of terms by reason of the nature of the contract (and) in the absence of a doctrine of good faith the specific and general rules of estoppel are needed to deal with demonstrated problems of unfairness'.

[20] Brownsword (n 1) 211–16. See to like effect D Percy, 'The Emergence of Good Faith as a Principle of Contract Performance' in S Degeling, J Edelman and J Goudkamp (eds), *Contract in Commercial Law* (Sydney, Law Book Co, 2016) 254: 'the weakness of the common law is its tendency to deal with good faith only indirectly through devices that do not directly confront the issues at stake' (referring to implied terms and sometimes tortured interpretation of contracts).

Leading contract law scholar Hugh Collins is also of this view. He views the classical view of contract as unduly restrictive:

> The traditional map of the law of contract developed in the nineteenth century, confounded by the mesmerizing quality of the sanctity of contracts, confined its intervention to the use of two steering mechanisms. In a few instances, it could tolerate the invalidity of the contract, as in cases of fraud, incapacity and duress, but this form of intervention could not be permitted to multiply in such directions as mistake and unfairness for fear of endangering the binding quality of contractual commitments. An alternative method was to insert terms into contracts in order to qualify or expand the obligations, but again the technique could only enjoy a marginal existence for extensive use threatened to remove from the parties their choice of obligations. The traditional map of the law of contract therefore offered only an impoverished list of tools for constructing a social market.[21]

Warren CJ of the Victorian Court of Appeal is of this view, as is former Chief Justice of the Federal Court, James Allsop.[22] Warren CJ also countered one of the reasons for the traditional reluctance to embrace good faith, that it was uncertain and thus unhelpful in resolving commercial disputes:

> Underlying most contractual principles is a concern to promote good faith, and despite the underpinning of freedom in contractual relations, there is a chief concern on the part of all concerned that parties to a contract must act in good faith, and that it is in seeking to hold another contracting party to an obligation of good faith that certainty in contractual performance might be sought.[23]

Paul Finn, professor then judge, tied good faith in with notions of relational contracting, as well as the general desirability of moral behaviour in contracting, in this way:

> Commerce has its economic concerns and these are vital ones to our wellbeing. But commerce is founded on relationships with others … not only one interest is

[21] H Collins, 'The Sanctimony of Contract' in Richard Rawlings ed *Law, Society and Economy: Centenary Essays for the London School of Economics and Political Science 1895–1995* (Oxford, Clarendon Press, 1997) 81. See similarly Tetley (n 4) 584: 'the time may well have come to consider introducing a general good faith duty into English common law of contract, if only to ensure greater unity and consistency in the law, greater international legal harmony and to better protect the interests of contracting parties by a general principle which, over time, would no doubt be developed by the common law and absorb some of the piecemeal solutions that have hitherto held sway'; HK Lucke, 'Good Faith and Contractual Performance' in PD Finn (ed), *Essays in Contract* (Sydney, Law Book Company Limited, 1987) 158.

[22] J Allsop, 'Good Faith and Australian Contract Law: A Practical Issue and a Question of Theory and Principle' (2011) 85 *Australian Law Journal* 341, 352: 'our law, including the law of contract, is littered with principles, rules and approaches which have as their elements what can be seen as the elements of good faith. What might be said to be absent is the recognition of an expressed norm reflecting its presence as an informing principle'.

[23] 'Good Faith: Where Are We At?' (2010) 34 *Melbourne University Law Review* 344, 349; see similarly Sir A Mason (n 6) 89: 'why is emphasis on the need for good faith and fair dealing not likely to lead to the resolution of business disputes?'; S Burton, 'Breach of Contract and the Common Law Duty to Perform in Good Faith' (1980) 94 *Harvard Law Review* 369, 380: 'it is the potential for a lack of clarity and completeness that necessitates the implication of the good faith covenant in every contract'.

> involved here. And if this be acknowledged, and if it be accepted as a worthwhile value to afford limited protection to the vulnerable, then an accommodation … must be struck. To harken back to a golden age, to the law of the late nineteenth century, is to give almost complete primacy to one interest and is to accept that casualties to that interest should be tolerated because of its importance. We may be able to afford this in economic terms. But there is a moral cost. And would its acceptance be socially deleterious?[24]

It must be emphasised again that good faith should not be analogised to a fiduciary obligation. It is not an obligation to subordinate one's own interests to those of the other contracting party. It does not require that parties abandon self-interest. However, self-interest is bounded. Parties must be 'other-regarding'.[25] Contracting parties must have due regard to the legitimate expectations of others with whom they contract.[26] A party should not be heard to complain they 'lose' something by having to have regard to the legitimate interests of the other contracting party. Of course, it is a two-sided coin. Just as one contracting party has a duty to be other-regarding, so they have a right to expect the other contracting party to be other-regarding. A good faith obligation ensures that these legitimate expectations are given effect.[27]

There are numerous instances where courts resort to contractual interpretation, reaching controversial (to put it mildly) interpretations of clauses, in order to achieve what they consider to be a good outcome. In so proceeding, frankly the court can avoid looking as if it is rewriting parties' bargains, though on a reasonable view of the matter it is (or might be). A good example appears in *Bank of Credit and Commerce International SA v Ali*.[28] There the employer bank made particular employees redundant. It agreed to pay such employees a severance payment. In return, employees signed a general release. It was stated to be a 'full and final settlement of all or any claims … of whatsoever nature that exist or may exist' against the bank. Later the bank went into administration, and the corrupt

[24] P Finn, 'Commerce, the Common Law and Morality' (1989) 17 *Melbourne University Law Review* 87, 98–99; cf J Morgan, *Contract Law Minimalism: A Formalist Restatement of Commercial Contract Law* (Cambridge, Cambridge University Press, 2013) 87: 'there is an unshakable desire to invest contract law with moral purpose, substantive principles, social values. But in the end this is futile and utterly misguided'.

[25] Brownsword (n 1) 210.

[26] BJ Reiter, 'Good Faith in Contracts' (1983) 17 *Valparaiso University Law Review* 705, 714: 'the role of contract law can usefully be described as the protection of reasonable expectations … a substantial element of what constitutes reasonable expectations is "good faith", defined as what the makers of "right conduct" (the parties, the industry, custom, relevant social expectations) accept as being properly done in this sort of case'; Collins (n 18) 315.

[27] R Pound, *Jurisprudence* (St Paul, West Publishing, 1959) 413 stating that good faith reflects that 'justice demands one should not disappoint well-founded expectations'; A Farnsworth, 'Good Faith Performance and Commercial Reasonableness Under the *Uniform Commercial Code*' (1963) 30 *University of Chicago Law Review* 666, 669 stating that good faith requires 'cooperation on the part of one party to the contract so that another party will not be deprived of his reasonable expectations'; A Duke, 'A Universal Duty of Good Faith: An Economic Perspective' (2007) 33 *Monash University Law Review* 182, 197.

[28] *Bank of Commerce and Credit International SA v Ali* [2002] 1 AC 251.

way in which the bank had been run came to light. An employee who signed a release sought further compensation, arguing that the illegal manner in which the bank had been run had caused him difficulties in obtaining further employment, for which he should be compensated. He claimed to be unaware of this at the time he signed the release. A majority of the House of Lords found in his favour, on the basis the parties did not intend the general release would apply to a claim of this nature.

With respect, on one view the terms of the release were very clear that it was intended to apply to all or any claims that exist or may exist. However, by carving out this particular kind of loss from the release, the majority justices thereby gave the employee a remedy for the loss they had suffered. The result might be 'just', but it is certainly questionable that it reflected the parties' contractual intention. However, it is seemingly dressed up in this manner to avoid any suggestion the courts are altering the parties' actual agreement in order to deliver what it considers to be the fair outcome in a particular case.

II. Not a Fiduciary Obligation

Care must be taken to distinguish good faith from a fiduciary obligation. A fiduciary obligation requires the party who owes the obligation to avoid any potential conflict of interest between the obligor's personal interest and that to whom the obligation is owed. The obligor must subordinate their own personal interests in favour of the person to whom the obligation is owed. It is difficult to apply fiduciary obligations to a commercial context, and the High Court of Australia has eschewed doing so.[29] I do not quibble with this reluctance here. However, it does not present an obstacle to the acceptance of good faith in commercial contracting, because there is no equivalence between good faith and a fiduciary obligation, despite an occasional suggestion to the contrary.[30] Good faith does not require the party who owes the obligation to subordinate their interest to that of the other contracting party.[31] It requires them to meet the reasonable expectations of the parties in terms of how the other will act. It requires fidelity to the parties' bargain.[32] It has been noted that the considerations relevant to interpretation of

[29] *Hospital Products Ltd v United States Surgical Corporation* (1984) 156 CLR 41.

[30] *Hamsard 3147 Ltd v Boots UK Ltd* [2013] EWHC 3251 (Pat) where Norris J explained he did not favour a general obligation of good faith in contracting, equating it to a duty to subordinate one's commercial interests to those of the other contracting party: [86].

[31] Justice Leggatt, 'Lecture to the Commercial Bar Association', 18 October 2016, [41].

[32] Brownsword talks of a party to a contract acting in a particular way for good reason, to protect legitimate interests and/or loyalty to the contract. He view *Arcos Ltd v EA Ronaasen and Son* [1933] AC 470, where a purchaser was able to rely on highly technical grounds to avoid being bound by a contract to purchase timber, when clearly their motivation to do so was to take advantage of a substantial reduction in market prices and where the timber supplied was suitable for their purpose, as one where application of good faith principles would likely lead to a different result: 'Individualism, Co-operativism and an Ethic for European Contract Law' (2001) 64 *Modern Law Review* 628, 638.

an implied duty of good faith will be similar to those applied to interpretation of an express duty of good faith.[33]

III. Good Faith Makes Economic Sense

> One of the characteristics of a successful economic system is that the relations of trust and confidence between principal and agent are sufficiently strong so that the agent will not cheat even though it may be 'rational economic behaviour' to do so.[34]

One of the reasons that some object to good faith is that it seems to cut across the kind of private ordering that the law of economics traditionally assumes is best in order that parties increase their satisfaction levels. It confines parties' presumed interests to their own. However, scholars have challenged this assumption. It may be that individuals also have 'fairness receptors' which guide their behaviour, and their expectations of the behaviour of others. Economics may be traditionally blinkered in its focus on external motivators of behaviour (legal rules), rather than intrinsic motivators (acting in accordance with one's own personal morality and values).[35]

IV. Good Faith and Negligence

Some similarities might be observed between good faith and a duty to take care. In the classic negligence decision of *Donoghue v Stevenson*,[36] Lord Atkin noted that liability in negligence was based on general public sentiment of moral wrongdoing.[37] The duty of care applied to a legal 'neighbour' – one who was so closely and directly affected by the defendant's acts that the defendant ought to have had them in contemplation as being so affected when turning their mind to the relevant acts or omissions.[38] The case broadened the extent of a duty of care, taking it beyond previous limits. Previous cases had traditionally only imposed a duty of care when parties were in a pre-existing relationship.[39] Thus, Donoghue extended liability in negligence beyond contract. But traditionally, liability for what we now regard as negligence was limited to the contractual

[33] *Mid Essex Hospital Services NHS Trust v Compass Group UK and Ireland Ltd* [2013] EWCA Civ 200, [150] (Beatson LJ).

[34] K Arrow, 'The Economics of Moral Hazard: Further Comment' (1968) 58(2) *American Economic Review* 537, 538.

[35] Duke (n 27).

[36] [1932] AC 562.

[37] ibid 580.

[38] ibid 580; with whom Lord Thankerton agreed (604); Lord Macmillan similarly (620).

[39] *Winterbottom v Wright* (1842) 10 M & W 109, 152 ER 402; *Le Lievre v Gould* [1893] 1 QB 491, 497 (Lord Esher).

context. Liability in contract and in negligence can clearly overlap. These matters are further explored in chapter 10.

For present purposes, the point is that if strangers can be considered legal neighbours to whom legal obligations to take care are owed, so much stronger is surely the argument with respect to parties who know one another – parties in a contract. It is well established that parties to a contract can owe each other duties of care, to have the other party in contemplation as being so affected by their actions that it might curb their actions. In other words, to have regard to the interests of others before acting. If that obligation can be imposed with respect to strangers, there is surely a stronger argument for imposing the obligation in respect of parties who are in a contract.[40]

V. Good Faith and the 'Socialisation of Private Law'

Recognition of such a principle might be consistent with the trend observed by Jason Varuhas of the increasing 'socialisation of private law'. He argues private law has moved away from a pure vindication of individual rights, and has increasingly accepted the need to temper such rights in favour of broader societal interests.[41] In the specific context of good faith, it might be argued that recognition of such a concept would be socially beneficial, permitting parties to place more faith in the promises of another, and reducing the need to take preventative action to reduce the risk of opportunistic behaviour by the other side, and reflecting parties' legitimate contractual expectations.

VI. Common Law Hostility to Good Faith

Somewhat paradoxically though, it is argued that there is no need for a generalised good faith concept in the common law because we already have sufficient alternative doctrines that will lead to the same result in most cases, it is also argued that there is no need for a generalised good faith concept because it is anathema to the common law.

So, it has been observed that English law is traditionally 'hostile' to good faith.[42] The English courts emphatically declined to accept an argument that good faith

[40] Finn (n 24) 92. To like effect see PJ Millett, 'Equity's Place in the Law of Commerce' (1998) 114 *Law Quarterly Review* 214, 216: 'there has never been a greater need to impose on those who engage in commerce the high standards of conduct which equity demands. The common law insists on honesty, diligence and the due performance of contractual obligations. But equity insists on nobler and subtler qualities: loyalty, fidelity, integrity, respect for confidentiality and the disinterested discharge of obligations of trust and confidence'.

[41] J Varuhas, 'The Socialisation of Private Law: Balancing Private Right and Public Good' (2021) 137 *Law Quarterly Review* 141.

[42] Johan Steyn, 'Contract Law: Fulfilling the Reasonable Expectations of Honest Men' (1997) 113 *Law Quarterly Review* 433, 438. He noted that, in sharp contrast, neither businesspeople nor 'people

applied to contract negotiations.[43] Walford suggests that good faith is repugnant to the adversarial nature of would-be contracting parties during negotiations (the factual context of the case in which he made the comments). And Lord Ackner did not draw a sharp distinction between behavioural expectations during negotiations and during the performance of the contract, so it might reasonably be inferred that he would carry through his expectation of self-interested behaviour (short of fraud/misrepresentation) during contract performance. Referring to Walford and another case, Morgan states that the 'English judges traditionally ascribe to hypothetical contractors a virtual caricature of atomistic/selfish/Hobbesian behaviour'.[44]

This can be hard to square with suggestions that there is no need for good faith in English law because the results to which it leads will in almost all cases be arrived at by the application of traditional contract law principles. It is conceded again, however, that the context in Walford was the suggestion of good faith in pre-contractual negotiations, not contractual performance, though it is not easy to articulate why norms of behaviour should radically differ at the pre-contractual and contractual performance stages.

A former Lord Chancellor of the United Kingdom explained and defended such 'hostility' in the following terms:

> The English law of contract is the international law of choice over a wide range of areas, particularly in finance, shipping and insurance. It contributes significantly to the earnings of the United Kingdom and thereby promotes the prosperity of the European Union … you could say that the English common law of contract is now a world-wide commodity. It has become so because it is a system that people like. It provides predictability of outcome, legal certainty, and fairness. It is clear and built upon well-founded principles, such as the ability to require exact performance and the absence of any general duty of good faith … this has made the common law without rival as the law of choice in commercial transactions.[45]

Scepticism and/or apparent resistance to notions of good faith is also evident. In *Candey Limited v Bosheh and Salfiti*, Coulson LJ stated that 'the elusive concept

on the Underground' had difficulty with the concept. Similarly, 'judges in the greater part of the industrialised world would usually have no great difficulty identifying a case of bad faith. It is not clear why it should perplex judges brought up in the English tradition' (438–39).

[43] *Walford v Miles* [1992[2 AC 128, 138: 'the concept of a duty to carry on negotiations in good faith is inherently repugnant to the adversarial position of the parties when involved in negotiations. Each party to the negotiations is entitled to pursue his (or her) own interest, so long as (they) avoid making misrepresentations' (Lord Ackner, with whom all other Lordships agreed). Sir A Mason, former Chief Justice of the High Court of Australia, disagrees: 'the notion that a party is entitled selfishly to pursue self-interest as long as misrepresentation is avoided is at odds with equitable principles governing the making of contracts': 'The Impact of Equitable Doctrine on the Law of Contract' (1998) 27 *Anglo-American Law Review* 1, 6. He cites the Privy Council decision in *Queensland Generating Board v New Hope Collieries Pty Ltd* [1989] 1 Lloyd's Rep 205 three years prior to *Walford*, in which there was implied an obligation to use reasonable endeavours to agree on a contract for the supply of coal in the future.

[44] Morgan (n 24) 67.

[45] Lord Falconer, Opening Speech for the European Contract Law Conference, London (2005).

of good faith should not be used to avoid orthodox and clear principles of English contract law'.[46] In *MSC Mediterranean Shipping Co SA v Cottonese Anstalt* Moore-Bick LJ stated: 'there is in my view a real danger that if a general principle of good faith were established it would be invoked as often to undermine as to support the terms in which the parties have reached agreement'.[47] There is also resistance in academic writing. Teubner referred to good faith as 'foreign' to English law, introducing a 'fundamental irritation' and 'outside noise'.[48] Bridge stated:

> Good faith and fair dealing ... is an imperfect translation of an ethical standard into legal ideology and legal rules. However much it might stimulate research or encourage inquiry into theories underlying contract law, its appropriate home is the university where it can perform these functions without wreaking practical mischief. In the form in which it is cast in s205 of the Restatement (Second), good faith is an invitation to judges to abandon the duty of legally reasoned decisions and to introduce an unanalytical incantation of personal values.[49]

Bridge argued that introducing a general principle of good faith would be akin to 'letting a bull loose in a china shop'.[50] One commentator alleged good faith was likely to cause 'practical mischief', was 'vague to the point of meaninglessness' and likely to produce 'idiosyncratic judgments' at odds with the proper role of a court.[51] Another suggests the doctrine lacks legitimate and principled origins,[52] and lacks clarity, certainty and structural integrity.[53]

Some who express negative sentiment against good faith, including Lord Burrows in *Pakistan International Airline Corporation*,[54] Lord Hobhouse in *The*

[46] *Candey Limited v Bosheh and Salfiti* [2022] EWCA Civ 1103, [32] (with whom Arnold and Phillips LLJ agreed).

[47] *MSC Mediterranean Shipping Co SA v Cottonese Anstalt* [2016] EWCA Civ 789, [45].

[48] G Teubner, 'Legal Irritants: Good Faith in British Law or How Unifying Law Ends Up in New Divergences' (1998) 61 *Modern Law Review* 11, 12.

[49] M Bridge, 'Does Anglo-Canadian Contract Law Need a Doctrine of Good Faith?' (1984) 9 *Canadian Business Law Journal* 385, 412–13. He added it could work 'practical mischief' if introduced into Canadian contract law (426) (obviously, it subsequently was); see also C Gillette, 'Limitations on the Obligation of Good Faith' (1981) 4 *Duke Law Journal* 619 (rejecting a broad definition of good faith).

[50] M Bridge, 'Doubting Good Faith' (2005) 11 *New Zealand Business Law Quarterly* 430, 448. He stated 'there is no general duty of good faith and fair dealing in English contract law and there is no reason why there should be' (450).

[51] Bridge (n 49) 412–13: 'good faith and fair dealing ... is an imperfect translation of an ethical standard into legal ideology and legal rules. However much it might stimulate research or encourage inquiry into theories underlying contract law, its appropriate home is the university where it can perform these functions without wreaking practical mischief ... good faith is an invitation to judges to abandon the duty of legally reasoned decisions and to produce an unanalytical incantation of personal values. Far from involving the community ethic in the day-to-day task of law-making and decision-making, with the attendant fruits of such a democratization, good faith is more likely to produce idiosyncratic judgments'; 'good faith becomes vague to the point of meaninglessness, and quite possibly destructive in the hands of a court that does not know how to handle it but does not feel free to ignore it' (396).

[52] T Carlin, 'The Rise (and Fall?) of Implied Duties of good Faith in Contractual Performance in Australia' (2002) 25(1) *University of New South Wales Law Journal* 99, 122.

[53] ibid 122–23.

[54] *Pakistan International Airline Corporation v Times Travel (UK) Ltd* [2021] UKSC 40.

Star Sea[55] and commentators such as Michael Bridge and Tyrone Carlin, do so on the basis of the uncertainty it creates. Certainly, it is suggested that, above all else, what commerce seeks from the law is certainty, or at least as much certainty as possible.[56] Business people should in almost all instances be able to predict what the result would be if their dispute were to go to court. This certainty helps to minimise transaction costs. It fosters the running of businesses,[57] which are typically beneficial for society in terms of providing needed products and services, providing employment, and contributing to taxation revenue.

On the other hand, as Collins notes, an exclusive focus on certainty 'always keeps the gate shut tight against practical considerations in business'.[58] It might encourage sham transactions, where there is little or no resemblance between the contract as written and the contract as intended to be, and actually is, performed. It assumes the court has no role in policing unfairness or unreasonableness in contractual terms. It assumes parties are equally able to look after their own contracting interests, are fully informed of the risks and benefits of the contract. It is trite to observe that, if these assumptions ever were an accurate reflection of business conditions, they no longer are.

Sir Anthony Mason noted that the classic theory of contract, though it promised certainty and predictability, often did not deliver it.[59] Former Justice Steyn, writing extra-judicially, stated that the assertion that current common law principles provided more certainty than application of a general standard of good faith was 'unproven'.[60]

Of course, there are many other concepts in the law which are cast in general terms, including reasonableness and unconscionability. The courts have found a way to interpret these concepts in a manner which provides some acceptable level of certainty, while also permitting justice to be done in particular cases.

In sum, a main argument for a generalised concept of good faith as applied to contracts is that it simply reflects the parties' legitimate expectations of the contracting behaviour of the other party. It is considered to have significant potential as a unifying concept in this area of the law, bringing together disparate legal principles into a coherent body of law. However, the law has not (yet) taken this step. The arguments against such general application seem potentially

[55] *Manifest Shipping Co Ltd v Uni-Polaris Ins Co Ltd* (*The Star Sea*) [2003] 1 AC 469, [45]: 'Lord Mansfield's universal proposition (of good faith) did not survive. The commercial and mercantile law of England developed in a different direction preferring the benefits of simplicity and certainty which flow from requiring that those engaging in commerce to look after their own interests'.

[56] *Herculito Maritime Ltd and Others v Gunvor International BV and Others* [2024] UKSC 2, [74] (Lord Hamblen, for the Court).

[57] M Weber, *Economy and Society* (Berkeley, University of California Press, G Roth and C Wittich ed, 1978) 883.

[58] Collins (n 21) 67.

[59] (n 6) 70: 'the classical theory of contract offered predictability and certainty, though it later emerged, as is the case with many legal concepts rooted in formalism, that the element of certainty was illusory'.

[60] (n 19) 140.

contradictory – it is argued that it is not needed because the common law already provides a remedy for situations where good faith could be useful, but also that it is anathema to the common law. It is difficult to have it both ways. And even worse, it is sometimes suggested there is intellectual dishonesty going on, with courts sometimes achieving the kind of results that would ensue from good faith application by making 'brave' calls about parties' intentions that might struggle to match up with reality, all in order to avoid the impression the court is intervening in parties' agreements in order to enforce good faith norms, when in reality that is what it is doing. Given the documented use of good faith in English legal history over centuries, it can be difficult to accept the argument it is anathema to the essence of English law. Of course, the claim that English law (without good faith) delivers certainty, predictability and fairness may be open to serious challenge.

The volume of commercial litigation suggests that parties regard the outcome of particular disputes as somewhat uncertain. If they did believe the outcomes were certain, as rational utility maximisers (as discussed, the intellectual basis of the anti-good faith, freedom of contract philosophy), the parties would surely not embark on contested litigation. And fairness is surely in the eye of the beholder. Many of the outcomes produced by the freedom of contract laissez-faire type philosophy may be questioned on the basis of fairness, acknowledging the subjectivity of the concept.

I will now sketch the somewhat piecemeal development of good faith in the English law to date.

VII. Good Faith in English Law

> Business men habitually … trust to luck or the good faith of the opposite party.[61]

A starting point for discussion of the modern view of good faith in English law is *Interfoto Picture Library Ltd v Stiletto Visual Programmes Ltd*.[62] There Bingham LJ stated:

> In many civil law systems, and perhaps in most legal systems outside the common law world, the law of obligations recognises and enforces an overriding principle that in making and carrying out contracts parties should act in good faith. This does not simply mean that they should not deceive each other, a principle which any legal system must recognise; its effect is perhaps most aptly conveyed by such metaphorical colloquialisms as 'playing fair', 'coming clean', or 'putting one's cards face upwards on the table'. It is in essence a principle of fair dealing … English law has, characteristically, committed itself to no such overriding principle, but has developed piecemeal solutions in response to demonstrated problems of unfairness.

[61] *Phoenix Insurance Co v De Monchy* 141 LTR (NS) 439, 445 (House of Lords, 1929) (Lord Atkin).
[62] [1989] 1 QB 433, 439.

Bingham LJ said that good faith might require on the facts that one of the contracting parties bring to the attention of the other the existence of a clause providing for a significant payment in the event that items were not returned in a timely manner. Though he said that English law had not committed itself to this doctrine as such, he went on to decide that the party wishing to rely on that clause could not do so because the contents of the clause were extortionate and unreasonable, and sufficient care was not taken to explain the clause to the party against whom it was sought to be enforced.[63] In other words, though the Court clearly did not expressly apply good faith to resolve the situation per se, effectively its substance was applied to provide a contracting party with relief against an oppressive clause, providing a result very similar to the result if good faith had been applied. This is an example of the point made in the first section of the chapter about similar outcomes whether a generalised good faith doctrine or particular currently accepted contract law rules are applied (though the precise legal basis of the decision in this case may be questioned in terms of orthodox contract law doctrine).

In the context of insurance, in *Banque Financiere de la Cite SA v Westgate Insurance Co Ltd*,[64] Slade LJ for the Court of Appeal explained that contracts of the utmost good faith, including contracts of insurance, fiduciary relationships and partnerships, tended to be characterised by the fact that one of the parties was likely to have the command of means of knowledge not open to the other.[65]

Of course, this is not an entirely satisfactory rationale for separating these kinds of cases from others, because in many cases of contracting, one party may have more knowledge than the other, and the other might struggle to have access to that information. For example, one party wishing to procure goods or services ('purchaser') might have approached a particular supplier ('supplier'). That purchaser may be aware that they have no realistic alternative supplier; that possible alternative sources have indicated they are not interested in supply, or will only do so at prohibitive prices. That purchaser might be aware that, because of differences in product, only the product of the supplier meets their needs. All of this kind of information is only known, and likely only knowable, by the purchaser. Yet the fact they likely have this knowledge exclusively has not traditionally been a reason to insist that they disclose it to the supplier. Thus, with respect, the attempted rationale for distinguishing *uberrimae fidei* in the context of insurance contracts, fiduciary obligations and partnerships, on the one hand, and other contracts, which are said not to generally contain an implicit good faith obligation, is considered unsatisfactory. This point will be further elaborated upon below.

In *Abu Dhabi National Tanker Co v Product Star Shipping Ltd*,[66] the court considered a contract which gave discretion to one of the parties to act in a

[63] ibid 445.

[64] [1990] 1 QB 665.

[65] ibid 769 (citing *Bell v Lever Bros Ltd* [1932] AC 161, 227 (Lord Atkin) for the articulation of these three categories of case). This rationale was also mentioned in the House of Lords: [1991] 2 AC 249, 281 (Lord Jauncey).

[66] [1993] 1 Lloyd's Rep 397.

certain way if they believed the alternative was dangerous. That party exercised its discretion. There was a dispute as to whether that party really did believe that the alternative was dangerous, and suggestions that the exercise of the discretion may have been for other reasons. Leggatt LJ (with whom Balcombe and Mann LJJ agreed) indicated that, where a contract provided one of the parties with a discretion:

> The authorities show that not only must the discretion be exercised honestly and in good faith, but having regard to the provisions of the contract by which it must be conferred, it must not be exercised arbitrarily, capriciously or unreasonably. That entails a proper consideration of the matter after making any necessary enquiries.[67]

In *Ludgate Insurance Company Ltd v Citibank NA*,[68] Brooke LJ (with whom Mummery and Russell LJJ agreed) stated that Abu Dhabi and other cases had established that

> Provided that the discretion is exercised honestly and in good faith for the purposes for which it was conferred, and provided also that it was a true exercise of discretion in the sense that it was not capricious or arbitrary or so outrageous in its defiance of reason that it can properly be regarded as perverse, the courts will not intervene.[69]

Lord Bingham (with whom Lord Steyn agreed) observed that contracting parties 'will assume the honesty and good faith of the other; absent such assumption they would not deal'.[70] Elsewhere Lord Bingham equated good faith with 'good standards of commercial morality and practice'.[71] Lord Steyn stated extra-judicially that 'the aim of any mature system of contract law must be to promote the observance of good faith and fair dealing in the conclusion and performance of contracts'.[72] He said it required observance of reasonable commercial standards.

[67] ibid 404 (CA); in *Lymington Marina Limited v Macnamara* [2007] EWCA Civ 151, Pill LJ [70] expressly agreed with that approach (with whom Sir Martin Norse agreed: [63]); see earlier *Selkirk v Romar Investments Ltd* [1963] 1 WLR 1415, 1422 where Viscount Radcliffe for the Privy Council noted that a contracting party exercising a contractual discretion must not do so arbitrarily, capriciously, unreasonably or in bad faith.

[68] [1998] Lloyd's Rep IR 221.

[69] ibid 239–40; similarly *Socimer International Bank Limited (In Liquidation) v Standard Bank London Ltd* [2008] EWCA Civ 116, [66] (Rix J, with whom Lloyd and Laws LLJ agreed); *Paragon Finance Plc (formerly National Home Loans Corp) v Nash* [2001] EWCA Civ 1466, [41] (Dyson LJ, with whom Thorpe LJ and Astill LJ agreed)(CA); *Horkulak v Cantor Fitzgerald International* [2004] EWCA Civ 1287, [30] (Potter LJ, with whom Carnwath and Bodey LLJ agreed) (CA); *JML Direct Ltd v Freestat UK Ltd* [2010] EWCA Civ 34, [14] (Moore-Bick LJ, with whom the Master of the Rolls and Toulson LJ agreed). Focus on purpose is not confined to the exercise of a contractual power. The court considered whether disclosures claimed to be in the public interest in the employment context were made for proper purposes in *Street v Derbyshire Unemployed Workers' Centre* [2004] EWCA Civ 964, [47] (Auld LJ) (with whom Jacob LJ agreed); [63] (Wall LJ).

[70] *HIH Casualty & General Insurance Ltd v Chase Manhattan Bank* [2003] UKHL 6, [15]. Lord Hoffmann agreed that contracting parties expected honesty of the other.

[71] *Director-General of Fair Trading v First National Bank Plc* [2002] 1 AC 481, 494 (he also referred to fair and open dealing).

[72] (n 19) 131. In 'Contract Law: Fulfilling the Reasonable Expectations of Honest Men' (n 42) 439 he noted: 'as long as our courts always respect the reasonable expectations of parties our contract law can be left to develop in accordance with its own pragmatic traditions. And where in specific contexts

He indicated that businesspeople and everyday individuals 'ha(d) no problem' with the concept of good faith or fair dealing.[73]

Similarly, Steyn LJ (as he then was) stated that a theme of the law of contract was that reasonable expectations of honest individuals required protection.[74] In *Socimer International Bank*, Rix J said that an implication of good faith and rationality, and lack of arbitrariness or perversity, 'are standard, for they represent the very essence of business (and other) relationships'.[75] These might be seen as terms implied in law.[76] A term implied by law applies to a particular category of contracting relationship. On one view they apply regardless of party intention, reflecting public policy.[77] A term implied in fact is ad hoc in nature, based on the situation of the particular parties before the court. They are said to reflect party intention.[78]

Good faith can apply to employment contracts. It might require, for example, an employer not to act to destroy or damage a relationship of confidence between employer and employee,[79] connected with the general implied term of mutual trust and confidence in such relationships. Members of the House of Lords in *Johnson v Unisys Ltd* entertained the possibility that this duty and/or a good faith duty might provide a remedy in cases where an employee had been wrongfully dismissed, in a way that led to hurt feelings and difficulties for the employee finding new employment.[80] However, in that specific circumstance, the Court was persuaded that a statutory provision precluded development of the common law in that manner.[81]

duties of good faith are imposed on parties our legal system can readily accommodate such a well-tried notion. After all, there is not a world of difference between the objective requirement of good faith and the reasonable expectations of parties'.

[73] (n 42) 438.

[74] *First Energy (UK) Ltd v Hungarian International Bank Ltd* [1993] 2 Lloyd's Rep 194, 196; see also JH Baker, 'From Sanctity of Contract to Reasonable Expectations' (1979) 32 *Current Legal Problems* 17.

[75] [2008] EWCA Civ 116, [106] (with whom Lloyd and Laws LLJ agreed).

[76] *Mid Essex Hospital Services NHS Trust v Compass Group UK and Ireland Ltd* [2013] EWCA Civ 200, [82] (Jackson LJ).

[77] *Marks & Spencer Plc v BNP Paribas Securities Services* [2016] AC 743, 752 Lord Neuberger (with whom Lords Sumption and Hodge agreed) stated a term otherwise implied by law could be excluded by express terms): 752.

[78] *Scully v Southern Health and Social Services Board* [1992] 1 AC 294, 306–07 (Lord Bridge); *Marks & Spencer Plc v BNP Paribas Securities Services* [2016] AC 743, 752–55 (Lord Neuberger, with whom Lords Sumption and Hodge agreed).

[79] *Imperial Group Pension Trust Ltd v Imperial Tobacco Ltd* [1991] 1 WLR 589, 597 (Sir Nicolas Browne-Wilkinson VC implied obligation of good faith in employment contracts, including mutual trust and confidence, not to act capriciously towards the other). In *Eastwood v Magnox Electric Plc* [2005] 1 AC 503, 523 Lord Nicholls (with whom Lords Hoffmann, Rodger and Brown agreed) found an employer was required to act responsibly and in good faith towards their employees, including in dismissing them; *Mahmud v Bank of Credit and Commerce International SA (In Compulsory Liquidation)* [1998] AC 20 (implied obligation of trust and confidence).

[80] *Johnson v Unisys Ltd* [2003] 1 AC 518, 541 where Lord Hoffmann referred to an implied obligation to exercise a power of dismissal fairly and in good faith (with whom Lord Millett agreed); Lord Steyn noted similar comments in *Imperial Group Pension Trust Ltd* with apparent approval (536).

[81] ibid 526 (Lord Nicholls), 544 (Lord Hoffmann), 550 (Lord Millett). Lord Bingham agreed with Lord Hoffmann.

Although the term of mutual trust and confidence is generally implied into employment contracts, it has limitations as an implied term. Specifically, it cannot override or condition an express term that is (on one view) in conflict with it. For example, in *Reda v Flag Ltd* an employment contract specifically provided that the employer could terminate an employee's employment 'at will', without cause. The employer purported to do so. The employees argued the power was exercised for an ulterior purpose – to prevent the dismissed employees from enjoying the benefits of an employee stock option scheme then under development, and introduced after the dismissal. The Privy Council found in favour of the employer. It applied the literal words of the provision – it permitted the employer to dismiss the employee without cause. As such, arguments about the employer's true purpose were irrelevant.[82]

Where satisfaction of the existence or otherwise of a condition precedent to a contract coming into existence is based on the judgment of one of the contracting parties, that judgment must be exercised reasonably and/or in good faith.[83] On the other hand, it has been held that good faith does not apply where the contract confers an absolute discretion on one of the parties.[84] There is also a suggestion (not supported here) that good faith might apply where a party with a choice has more than two options, but not in cases involving a simple choice between two options.[85]

There are suggestions in previous cases that no legal principle prevents a contracting party from exercising their rights in an unreasonable way.[86] Opportunism loomed large in the factual scenario in *Arcos Ltd v EA Ronaasen and Son*.[87] There the parties made an agreement regarding the sale of timber. Between the time of contract and the time for performance, the market price for timber had dropped substantially. It seems that the buyer was searching for a way out of the contract, to save money. Firstly, they argued that the seller had failed to deliver 'during the summer', as the contract required. This argument failed. Then they argued that the timber supplied did not correspond exactly with the product description. This was technically true, though the slight discrepancy did not affect the suitability of what was supplied for the intended use.

The House of Lords found in favour of the buyer in this case. Lord Atkin acknowledged that, in most cases, if purchasers of goods got substantially what

[82] *Reda v Flag Ltd* [2002] UKPC 38. Hugh Collins notes the courts are typically reluctant to constrain exercise of a power to terminate at will: 'Discretionary Powers in Contracts' in D Campbell, H Collins and J Wightman (eds), *Implicit Dimensions in Contracts: Discrete, Relational and Network Contracts* (Oxford, Hart Publishing, 2003) 249.

[83] *Niarchos (London) Ltd v Shell Tankers* [1961] 2 Lloyd's Rep 496.

[84] *Mid Essex Hospital Services NHS Trust v Compass Group UK and Ireland Ltd* [2013] EWCA Civ 200.

[85] *Myer v Kestrel Acquisitions Ltd* [2015] EWHC 916 (Ch) [61] (Sir William Blackburne); W Courtney, 'Good Faith and Termination: The English and Australian Experience' (2019) 1 *Journal of Commonwealth Law* 185, 193 rejects the suggested distinction as illogical.

[86] *White and Carter (Councils) Ltd v McGregor* [1961] AC 413, 430 (Lord Reid).

[87] [1933] AC 470.

they bargained for, they would not complain. However, in a falling market, the buyer was entitled to rely on the technicality to avoid the contract altogether.[88]

On the other hand, there are apparently references supportive of the application of standards of reasonableness in the contracting environment. For example, in *Hillas and Co Ltd v Arcos Ltd*,[89] Lord Wright referred to reasonableness as running 'throughout the whole of modern English law in relation to business contracts'.[90] Lord Reid stated in *Schuler AG v Wickman Machine Tool Sales Ltd* that the more unreasonable the result of a particular contractual interpretation, the more unlikely it would be that the parties intended it.[91]

In the context of the *Unfair Terms in Consumer Contract Regulations* 1999, Lord Bingham explained that the good faith principle was

> One of fair and open dealing. Openness requires that the terms should be expressed fully, clearly and legibly, containing no concealed pitfalls … appropriate prominence should be given to terms which might operate disadvantageously to the customer. Fair dealing requires that a supplier should not, whether deliberately or unconsciously, take advantage of the consumer's necessity, indigence, lack of experience, unfamiliarity with the subject matter of the contract, weak bargaining position or any other factor listed or analogous to those listed in Schedule 2 to the Regulations. Good faith is not an artificial or technical concept nor, since Lord Mansfield was its champion, is it a concept wholly unfamiliar to British lawyers. It looks to good standards of commercial morality and practice.[92]

In 2003 members of the House of Lords recognised the possibility that an employment contract could be regarded as relational.[93] Lord Millett acknowledged that past assumptions that, at least in this context, contracts were the result of party autonomy, involving free and equal parties, had been found unsatisfactory.[94] In that context, parliament felt compelled to step in. Lord Hoffmann also acknowledged the need to protect employees from the exercise of excessive power by an employer.[95]

[88] ibid 480. Lord Atkin had also noted that non-disclosure during contract negotiations was generally not regarded as a breach of contractual obligation: *Bell v Lever Bros Ltd* [1932] AC 161, 224 (buyers must rely on the written contract for any protection against this kind of behaviour, because of the 'paramount importance that contracts should be observed').

[89] [1932] UKHL 2; 147 LT 503.

[90] ibid 507 (HL); see also *Minister Trust Ltd v Traps Tractors Ltd* [1954] 1 WLR 963, 973 where Lord Devlin stated that conditions in contract relating to satisfaction with the work done pursuant to it were subject to a reasonableness standard; similarly *Stadhard v Lee* (1863) 3 B & S 364, 371–72; 122 ER 138, 141.

[91] [1974] AC 235, 251 (Lord Reid).

[92] *Director-General of Fair Trading v First National Bank* [2002] 1 AC 481, 494 (with whom Lord Hope, Lord Millett and Lord Rodger agreed). Similarly, Lord Steyn noted good faith 'enforce(d) community standards of decency, fairness and reasonableness in commercial transactions' (500); see now Consumer Rights Act 2015 (UK) s 62(4) which establishes a good faith obligation in relation to consumer contracts, and Schedule 2 for examples of unfair terms.

[93] *Johnson v Unisys Ltd* [2003] 1 AC 518, 532 (Lord Steyn).

[94] ibid 547.

[95] ibid 541. He suggested the 'elegance' of a suggestion of an implied term that the power of dismissal (expressly stated in the contract to be without exception) might be conditioned upon a requirement

In 2007, the court considered an agreement between a property developer and property owners.[96] The property developer agreed to make improvements to the owners' land, with a view to increasing its value. They entered into an agreement whereby, if the developer made improvements such as to obtain relevant approvals, and the owner thereby profited by selling, a percentage of the gain would be given to the developer. The developer expended significant effort to increase the value of the land. However, at the relevant time the approvals that would have triggered their entitlement to a share of the proceeds were not in place. The owners decided to sell the land. The developers brought legal action against them, alleging breach of an express good faith clause, and breach of an implied term. The Court found there was breach of the express good faith clause. In doing so, Morgan J defined the requirement of good faith to mean reasonable commercial standards of fair dealing, faithfulness to the parties' agreed purpose, and consistent with the parties' justified expectations.[97] Morgan J took into account that the developer had invested significant time and effort and incurred significant expense pursuant to the parties' agreement, the owner had thereby substantially gained, that the sale at this time did not trigger an entitlement in the property developer to receive any money, and that the purchaser of the property would not be subject to the obligation.[98] The judge found that the sale breached good faith.

The Court in this case also referred to a line of case such as *Mackay v Dick*,[99] where a term was implied that each party to a contract would do all that was necessary to be done for the carrying out of the parties' bargain, even in the absence of express words to that effect.[100] Morgan J found that a term should be implied that the owner would not sell in the circumstances he did, given that the agreement between the parties was long-term and involved the developer incurring substantial expense, and that it was not binding on third parties.[101] Clearly, these arguments were similar to those which convinced the court that the owner was acting in breach of their good faith obligation.

that it be exercised fairly and in good faith. He then found that the specific statutory provisions regarding unfair dismissal made such development of the common law unnecessary.

[96] *Berkeley Community Villages Limited v Pullen* [2007] EWHC 1330 (Ch).

[97] ibid [110] (Morgan J).

[98] ibid [109] (Morgan J).

[99] (1881) 6 App Cas 251.

[100] '(W)here in a written contract it appears that both parties have agreed that something shall be done, which cannot effectually be done unless both concur in doing it, the construction of the contract is that each agrees to do all that is necessary to be done on his part for the carrying out of that thing, though there may be no express words to that effect' (Lord Blackburn) (263); see similarly *Stirling v Maitland* (1864) 5 B & S 840, 852: 'if a party enters into an arrangement which can only take effect by the continuance of a certain existing state of circumstances, there is an implied engagement on his part that he shall do nothing of his own motion to put an end to that state of circumstances under which alone the arrangement can become operative' (Cockburn CJ); *Barque Quilpie Limited v Brown* [1904] 2 KB 264, 271–72 (Vaughan Williams LJ); *Secured Income Real Estate (Australia) Ltd v St Martins Investments Pty Ltd* (1979) 144 CLR 596, 607; *Dynamic Transport Ltd v O K Detailing* (1978) 85 DLR (3d) 19, 27. And similarly, not to impede performance of the objects of the contract: *Shepherd v Felt and Textiles of Australia Ltd* (1931) 45 CLR 359, 372 and 378.

[101] (n 96) [134].

In 2010 in *CPC Group Ltd v Qatari Diar Real Estate Investment Company*, Vos J held that an obligation of good faith (express in that case) required contracting parties to adhere to the spirit of the contract, observe reasonable commercial standards of fair dealing, be faithful to the common purpose of the deal, and act consistently with the justified expectations of the other party.[102] In *Mid Essex Hospital Services NHS Trust v Compass Group UK and Ireland Ltd*, Beatson LJ said that good faith depended on whether the impugned conduct would be regarded as commercially acceptable by reasonable and honest people.[103]

In 2014, the Supreme Court of the United Kingdom confirmed that, in the absence of express words to the contrary, a discretionary power or right under a contract was to be exercised in good faith, and not arbitrarily, capriciously or inconsistently with its purpose.[104] The Supreme Court accepted in *Braganza v BP Shipping Ltd* that a contractual discretion had to be exercised lawfully and in good faith, and consistently with its purpose.[105]

VIII. The Landmark *Yam Seng* Decision

A landmark decision in relation to good faith is *Yam Seng Pte Limited v International Trade Corporation Limited*.[106] It involved a distribution agreement whereby the plaintiff agreed to distribute the defendant's product in particular territories, particularly in duty-free outlets. The distribution agreement of the parties was sparse. It provided for the appointment of the plaintiff to distribute goods that the defendant claimed to have a right to sell. At the time of the agreement, the defendant did not have the relevant right to sell; he only acquired this after the written contract was executed. The contract provided that, in response to orders by the plaintiff, the defendant would ship the required goods to the

[102] [2010] EWHC 1535, [246].

[103] [2013] EWCA Civ 200, [150].

[104] *Telefonica O2 UK Ltd v British Telecommunications Plc* [2014] UKSC 42, [37] (Lord Sumption, for the Court). This has academic support: P Sales, 'Use of Powers for Proper Purposes in Private Law' (2020) 136 *Law Quarterly Review* 384, 395–96: 'it is not a reasonable interpretation of the contract that by incorporation of a discretionary power the counterparty intended to place itself completely at the mercy of the donee of the power as circumstances change. The parties' intention is that the power should be used for proper purposes, the ambit of which is given by what is within the contemplation of the parties … as derived from indications in the text and scheme of the contract and from the business context'.

[105] *Braganza v BP Shipping Limited and Another* [2015] 1 WLR 1661, 1672 (Baroness Hale). Baroness Hale suggested the discretion was limited in a similar way to the exercise of a public power, limited by so-called *Wednesbury* reasonableness: *Associated Provincial Picture Houses Ltd v Wednesbury Corporation* [1948] 1 KB 223, 233–34 (ie whether a decision maker has reached a conclusion that no reasonable decision maker could have reached); similarly Lord Hodge (1677) and Lord Neuberger (1688). Use of a principle of public law to limit discretion contained in a clause in a private contract is not defended here. For criticism of its use in this context see Sales (n 104).

[106] [2013] EWHC 111 (QB); Mr Justice Leggatt, 'Contractual Duties of Good Faith', lecture to the Commercial Bar Association, 18 October 2016.

plaintiff promptly. It also provided for the price at which the plaintiff would sell the goods in duty free stores within the relevant territories. And some of the territories it assigned to the plaintiff were in China.

In fact, at the time of the agreement, the required permissions had not been obtained to sell the product in China, and at the time of the litigation between the parties, it had still not been obtained. There were significant delays in the shipping of product to the plaintiff. The plaintiff was concerned that the defendant had appointed another distributor in the territories, focussed on retail rather than duty-free outlets. The plaintiff claimed that it was expected that retail prices in duty-free stores would be lower than in other outlets, yet the rival retailer was selling at a retail price lower than the price he had agreed with the defendant to charge at retail level. When the plaintiff complained to the defendant, the defendant claimed he had spoken with the relevant rival distributor. He did not pass on information that he had received that it would take time to implement this price increase.

Leggatt LJ considered three reasons for the traditional hostility of the common law to good faith. These were that the common law preferred to develop incrementally rather than by overarching principles, that the common law was based on individualism and the pursuit of self-interest, provided this was not a breach of the contract, and a fear that recognising a general contractual doctrine of good faith would lead to too much uncertainty, because the doctrine is too vague and subjective.[107]

Leggatt LJ noted that the United Kingdom was 'swimming against the tide' in this respect, given that most civil law systems had embraced it. It was (then) part of United Kingdom law as being part of European directives, such as the Unfair Terms in Consumer Contracts Regulations 1999 (UK). It was part of the Restatement (Second) of Contracts and the Uniform Commercial Code.

Leggatt LJ stated that a duty of good faith was implied by law into certain categories of contract, including contracts of employment, partnership contracts and fiduciary relationships. He was in essence labelling these as 'relational contracts', a concept that will be developed further in chapters seven and eight. The law was not (yet) at the stage of implying such an obligation into all commercial contracts. However, it could well be implied by fact into an ordinary commercial contract, based on the presumed intention of the parties. He cited relevant authorities that implication in fact generally require that the provision be so obvious that it goes without saying, and that its implication be necessary to give business efficacy to the contract.

Leggatt LJ noted that, since Belize Telecom, it had been established that the process of implication was a means of interpretation of the contract as a whole.

[107] Others have added an assumption that contracts are a reflection of the allocation of risks between the parties, which legal doctrine ought not disturb: Kuehne (n 3) 98; see also A Wallwork, 'A Requirement of Good Faith in Construction Contracts' (2004) 20 *Building and Construction Law Journal* 257; Carlin (n 52).

This included shared values and norms of behaviour. Leggatt LJ said that contracting parties assumed that such shared values and norms of behaviour would be part of their contract, without expressly stating so. He indicated that such values and norms included expectations of honesty. This might include making statements known to be untrue, deliberately avoiding giving an answer or providing an evasive answer. In some cases, it might include deliberately omitting information relevant to performance of the contract. A contracting party might be precluded from engaging in conduct described as 'improper', 'commercially unacceptable' or 'unconscionable'. It included fidelity to the parties' bargain. This would mean, for example, that where the contract requires something to be done in order that the contract can take effect, parties do not actively seek to thwart the meeting of that condition.

He indicated that good faith might preclude avoiding conduct that is commercially unacceptable by reasonable and honest people. This was consistent with statements of Lord Steyn that the law of contract protected reasonable expectations. He indicated this included cases where a contract provided one of the parties with a power to make decisions. Where this was the case, good faith required that the person exercise the power honestly and in good faith for the purpose for which it was conferred, and it must not be exercised arbitrarily, capriciously or unreasonably (in the sense of irrationally), consistent with case law such as Abu Dhabi. Similarly, where a contractual provision is dependent on the provision by one party of consent. In such cases, it is implied that such consent will not be unreasonably withheld.[108] Another example was where unusual or onerous provisions were found in the contract. In such cases, the party seeking to rely on them would need to bring them to the notice of the other party to the contract.

Leggatt LJ indicated some contracts involved parties making long-term commitments to one another. Such contracts might require minimum levels of communication, cooperation and predictable performance based on mutual trust and confidence. This would be necessary to give business efficacy to such contracts. He gave joint venture agreements, franchise agreements and long-term distribution agreements as examples. That said, he criticised English law for its apparently sharp division between, on the one hand, fiduciary relationships, trustee relationships and partnerships, where higher obligations (for example, in relation to disclosure), and other contractual situations where typically no such duty was owed. Leggatt LJ stated this supposedly sharp division was too simplistic.[109]

Leggatt LJ said that because good faith was based on the presumed intention of the parties, it did not disturb the right of parties to act in their own interests.

[108] See also *Re Audas Group Ltd* [2019] EWHC 2304, [110] (Ch) (HH Halliwell J), stating that where under an agreement the subject of a good faith obligation one party must give their consent to something before it can occur, it was inherent in good faith that consent not be unfairly or capriciously withheld and/or withheld for a purpose beyond the spirit and intent of the parties' agreement.

[109] ibid [142]; this is consistent with the view of Hugh Collins of good faith as a spectrum and criticism of binary views of contractual obligations as failing to respect the reasonable expectations of contracting parties: (n 18) 324.

The essence of contracting was parties making binding promises to each other for mutual benefit. It could encompass a requirement of 'fair dealing'. This did not involve the court imposing its idea of substantive fairness upon the parties; rather, it was based on standards of conduct that the parties must objectively be presumed to have adopted, without the need to express them. He said there was nothing uncertain or subjective about the concept. It created no more uncertainty than already existed in relation to contractual interpretation. He concluded the traditional hostility towards good faith in the performance of contracts subject to United Kingdom law was misplaced.

On the facts, Leggatt LJ found that the defendant had breached the good faith requirement, in particular by being dishonest towards the plaintiff in making statements to them that he would have known were not true.

IX. Subsequent Developments

In *Sheikh Tahnoon Shakhboot Al Nehayan v Kent* Leggatt J elaborated:

> Such relational contracts involve trust and confidence but of a different kind from that involved in fiduciary relationships. The trust is not in the loyal subordination by one party of its own interests to those of another. It is trust that the other party will act with integrity and in a spirit of cooperation. The legitimate expectations which the law should protect in relationships of this kind are embodied in the normative standard of good faith.[110]

In *Astor Management AG v Atalaya Mining Plc* he indicated that good faith required a party to act honestly, and not in a way calculated to frustrate the purpose of the contract, or which would be regarded as commercially unacceptable by reasonable and honest people.[111] On the other hand, others dispute the link between good faith and reasonableness.[112]

In an important extra-judicial speech, Justice Leggatt elaborated on his views:

> There is, I suggest, a case to be made for recognising an obligation of good faith in the performance of contracts as such a default rule. Faithfulness to the agreed common purpose of the contract, adherence to reasonable commercial standards of fair dealing – these are values which protect the integrity of the process of contracting and promote its effectiveness. There are also economic arguments that such a default rule would help to reduce the costs of contracting. Contracting parties are free to choose how much

[110] [2018] EWHC 333 (Comm) [167].

[111] [2017] EWHC 425 (Comm) [98]; similarly *New Balance Athletics Inc v Liverpool Football Club and Athletic Grounds Ltd* [2019] EWHC 2837 (Comm).

[112] J Stapleton, 'Good Faith in Private Law' (1999) 52(1) *Current Legal Problems* 1, 8: 'a requirement to satisfy a standard of reasonable behaviour is more demanding that the requirement of good faith'. Stapleton advocates a narrower view of the scope of good faith, confining it to three situations: (a) dishonesty; (b) where a person fails to comply with a promise they have made; and (c) they exploit a position of dominance over a vulnerable person: 7–8.

> detail to put into their express contract. But negotiating and drafting a long and detailed document which tries to cover every eventuality is time-consuming and expensive. Recognising a default obligation of good faith performance may help to reduce the need for elaborate documents and make short contracts less risky.[113]

Justice Leggatt explained that good faith was rooted in the parties' agreement, not superimposed upon it from an outside source. He indicated it was a fundamental value that, in practice, typically underpinned commerce, and its general acceptance would in his view provide greater coherence to commercial law.[114]

In *D & G Cars Ltd v Essex Police Authority*,[115] Dove LJ found an implied condition of honesty and integrity, related to good faith. The context there was a five-year contract whereby the appellants agreed to dispose of vehicles that had been seized by the respondents. In some cases the seized cars would be destroyed, in other they would be returned to their owners. The contract contained detailed provisions regarding the vetting and selection of staff to work at the appellant's facility, as well as detailed provisions regarding the storage and handling of vehicles and property found within vehicles. It was alleged that the appellants had, without consent, used the body of a seized vehicle to replace one of their vehicles of similar type. This involved a change of number plates and VIN plate to conceal the true identity of the vehicle. When the respondents discovered what the appellants had done, they purported to terminate the contract with them, and disqualify them from a tender panel. It was argued that the appellants had breached an implied obligation of good faith.

Dove LJ characterised the relationship between the parties as one involving a relatively lengthy period of time. It involved a large number of transactions. He characterised it as a relational contract par excellence.[116] This meant that there was an implied term regarding honesty and integrity. Dove LJ described this requirement as containing requirements of fair dealing and transparency. It included, but was not limited to, honesty. It required that parties to the contract not act in a way that would undermine mutual trust and confidence between the parties. In other words, parties could not engage in behaviour that, if asked, they would have identified as obvious acts inconsistent with maintenance of their intended long-term relationship, including fair and open dealing.[117] Dove LJ found that, by substituting one vehicle for another, the appellant had breached this requirement.[118]

In *Bristol Groundschool Ltd v Intelligent Data Capture Ltd & Ors*,[119] the Court found that an agreement between the parties, characterised as a hybrid joint venture/product distribution agreement, contained an implied duty of good faith. Spearman QC (sitting as Deputy Judge of the Chancery Division) found

[113] Lecture to the Commercial Bar Association, 18 October 2016, [30].
[114] ibid [61].
[115] [2015] EWHC 226 (QB).
[116] ibid [176].
[117] ibid [175]–[176].
[118] ibid [197]–[198].
[119] [2014] EWHC 2145 (Ch).

the agreement was relational in nature. He indicated the test of good faith was whether the parties had engaged in commercially acceptable, reasonable and honest behaviour.[120] The Court found that the behaviour of one of the parties, in accessing material to which they were not entitled under the contract, in anticipation of the contracting parties going their separate ways, breached the requirement to act in a commercially acceptable manner.[121]

In the Court of Appeal decision in *Globe Motors Inc v TRW Lucas Varity Electric Steering Limited*,[122] the Court referenced without apparent disapproval the judgment of Leggatt J (as he then was) in *Yam Seng PTE v International Trade Corp Ltd*, including the implication of good faith.[123] Briefly, the facts involved a long-term mutual supply contract between the two parties involving the respondent supplying the appellant with motors. The contract provided that the buyer would advise the supplier of any engineering changes it required. The appellant purchased another company, and then entered into an arrangement for that company to supply them with motors, which they argued were of a substantially different design, and thus not covered by the agreement with the respondents. The respondents sought to enforce the original agreement, arguing it did apply to the new types of motor.

The Court decided the case on other grounds. However, in obiter comments, Beatson LJ made two points of relevant interest: (a) an implication of good faith would only be possible where the language of the contract in context permitted it;[124] and (b) on the facts, involving exclusive supply and a long-term contract, there might be 'considerable force' in an argument that there was an implied obligation on the purchaser (presumably an implied good faith obligation, given the judgment's reference to good faith in the previous two paragraphs of the judgment) to provide the seller with the opportunity to show it could produce the new kind of motor the purchaser sought.[125]

In *Bates v Post Office*,[126] Fraser J set out a list of nine factors to consider in determining whether or not contracting parties were in a 'relational' contract, such that the obligation of good faith might arise.[127] These nine factors were:

(a) Whether there were any specific express terms in the contract preventing a duty of good faith from being implied into the contract;
(b) Whether the contract was a long-term one, with the mutual intention of the parties of a long-term relationship;

[120] ibid [196].
[121] ibid [196]. The Court also implied terms that one party would update materials as reasonably required by the other, and would not do anything to damage the business of the other contracting party ([142]), but did not expressly link these with a good faith obligation.
[122] [2016] EWCA Civ 396.
[123] ibid [67] (Beatson LJ).
[124] [68] (Beatson LJ).
[125] [69] (Beatson LJ) (with whom Underhill and Moore-Bick LLJ agreed).
[126] [2019] EWHC 606.
[127] He connected relational contracts with good faith thus: 'I consider that there is a specie of contracts, which are most usefully termed "relational contracts", in which there is implied an obligation of good faith': ibid [711].

(c) Whether the parties intend that their respective roles be performed with integrity, and fidelity to the parties' bargain;
(d) Whether the parties are committed to collaborating with one another in the performance of the contract;
(e) Whether it is possible to exhaustively express the spirit and objectives of the parties' agreement;
(f) Whether they intend to repose trust and confidence in one another (of a different kind to a relationship regarded by the law as fiduciary);
(g) Whether the contract will involve a high degree of communication, co-operation and predictable performance based on mutual trust and confidence and mutual expectations of loyalty;
(h) Whether one or both parties are making a significant investment, including a financial investment, pursuant to the contract; and
(i) Whether the parties' arrangement is exclusive or non-exclusive in nature.

Fraser J stated the list was not exhaustive. No factor was determinative, but the first was essential.[128] Fraser J stated good faith meant more than honesty.[129]

In *Unwin v Bond*,[130] HHJ Klein indicated that, where good faith applied, it required parties to (a) act honestly; (b) be faithful to the parties' agreed common objective as reflected in their contract; (c) not use contractual powers for a purpose other than that for which they were conferred; (d) deal fairly and openly with the other party; and (e) take into account the other party's interests in deciding upon action.[131] It might include a duty not to mislead the other, as well as a duty to correct errors or false assumptions made by the other party to the contract.[132]

Cases have also required that a party act proportionately in the exercise of their contractual power.[133] The context there was an employment relationship, and the court found one of the contracting parties had acted disproportionately in dismissing an employee, given their alleged misdeeds. They had also breached the express obligation of good faith by failing to accord the employee basic procedural fairness, not sharing the concerns that formed the basis of the dismissal decision, to give the employee a chance to respond to their substance.[134]

[128] ibid [725]–[726].

[129] ibid [710]; in other contexts good faith has been equated with honesty: *Central Estates (Belgravia) Ltd v Woolgar; Liverpool Corporation v Husan* [1972] 1 QB 48, 57 (Megaw LJ) (CA).

[130] [2020] EWHC 1768 (Comm).

[131] ibid [230]. Of course, this is not to equate a duty of good faith with a fiduciary obligation: *Re Compound Photonics Group Ltd; Faulkner v Vollin* [2022] EWCA Civ 1371, [155] (Snowden LJ, with whom Carr and Newey LLJ agreed).

[132] *Costain v Tarmac* [2017] EWHC 619, [124] (Coulson J). D Christie, S Saintier and J Viven-Wilksch 'Industry Led Standards, Relational Contracts and Good Faith: Are the United Kingdom and Australia Setting the Pace in (Construction) Contract Law?' (2022) 43 *Liverpool Law Review* 287, 297 state that in cases such as *Yam Seng*, *Bristol Ground School* and *D & G Cars Ltd*, what was common was that one party acted in their own self-interest, rather than for the success of the project. They failed to be sufficiently 'other-regarding'.

[133] *Re Audas Group* [2019] EWHC 2304 (Ch).

[134] ibid [120] (HH Halliwell J); see similarly *Unwin v Bond* [2020] EWHC 1768 (Comm) regarding lack of proper process prior to termination being considered breach of an express good faith obligation: [246]–[247] (HH Klein J).

In *Essex County Council v UBB Waste (Essex) Ltd (No 2)*, the Court found the relationship between the parties was relational in nature, implying an obligation of good faith. The contract was for the design, construction and management of a waste management facility. Applying the factors identified in Bates, the court noted the length of the contract between the parties (25 years), and that it required a close collaborative working relationship. This in turn required that the parties perform their roles with integrity, fidelity to the bargain and pursuant to their mutually shared objectives. The parties intended to repose trust and confidence in each other. The contract required high levels of communication, and significant investment. It was exclusive in nature.[135] Pepperall LJ applied the same description of good faith as had Leggatt LJ – whether the conduct would be regarded as commercially acceptable by reasonable and honest people.[136]

In *Amey v Birmingham City Council*,[137] Jackson LJ stated that, in the context of a relational contract (obviously, closely aligned with good faith) that the long-term nature of the contract meant there were likely many 'infelicities and oddities'. Jackson LJ admonished the parties to take a reasonable approach in accordance with the purpose of the contract, and warned them not to exploit the infelicities and oddities in order to disrupt the project and maximise their own gain.[138]

In the recent Court of Appeal decision in *Faulkner v Vollin*, members of the Court of Appeal cited to the judgments of Leggatt LJ in which he had explained the imposition of a good faith requirement, and explained its content. No disagreement was expressed with these views. It is acknowledged that *Faulkner* was a case where an express clause imposing a good faith obligation was in issue. That said, Snowden LJ, with whom the other justices agreed, stated that good faith was not limited to a requirement of honesty, and could extend to a requirement to behave in accordance with what was acceptable to reasonable and honest people.[139] Snowden LJ also indicated that the content of any implied obligation of good faith need not be the same as the content of an express obligation of good faith.[140]

Any good faith requirement must be applied sensitively to the context.[141] Snowden LJ was at pains to note:

> Even where thought to be inherent in an obligation of good faith, the concept of fidelity to the bargain or adherence to the spirit of the agreement could only operate to support the common purpose and aims of the parties as objectively ascertained from the express or implied terms of the contract … the shared aims of the parties must be

[135] [2020] EWHC 1581, [112].
[136] ibid [116].
[137] [2018] EWCA 264.
[138] (n 130) [93] (Jackson LJ, with whom Moylan LJ and Sir Stephen Tomlinson agreed).
[139] (n 131) [241] (with whom Carr and Newey LLJ agreed).
[140] ibid [196] (with whom Carr and Newey LLJ agreed); cf *Mid Essex Hospital Services NHS Trust v Compass Group UK and Ireland Ltd* [2013] EWCA Civ 200, [150] stating that Leggatt J's consideration of factors relevant to whether or not an implied obligation of good faith was owed 'are also relevant to interpretation of an express obligation to act in good faith' (Beatson LJ).
[141] [196]; see to like effect *Street v Derbyshire Unemployed Workers' Centre* [2004] EWCA Civ 964, [41] (Auld LJ, with whom Jacob and Wall LJJ agreed); *Manifest Shipping Co Ltd v Uni-Polaris Insurance Co Ltd* [2001] 1 AC 469, 511 (Lord Scott, with whom Lord Steyn and Hoffmann agreed).

> identified by interpretation of the other terms of the agreement, or by implication of terms according to the usual test.[142]

Good faith has also been described as a spectrum of norms.[143] On occasion, it has been limited to a requirement to not act in bad faith.[144] Sometimes it has been explained as 'not playing games' with the other contracting party.[145] Scholars have suggested good faith might deal with behaviour such as 'playing the market', including seeking to take advantage of market movements post-contract in order to get a better deal, 'going through the motions' in tendering, opportunistically re-negotiating contracts, lack of disclosure and unusual and/or unfair terms.[146]

Though a duty of good faith may require a party to exercise a contractual discretion reasonably, there is a difference of opinion regarding how the concept of reasonableness is to be applied here. There is some authority to suggest that the test of reasonableness developed in public law in *Associated Provincial Picture House v Wednesbury Corporation* should be utilised.[147] In other words, whether the discretion was exercised in a manner so unreasonably than no reasonable person could have done so.[148] That test was in the context of review of administrative action. There has been (in my view, well-founded) scepticism that such approach is appropriate in the very different context of the exercise of a contractual discretion in private arrangements between parties, and a refusal to apply such an approach.[149]

[142] (n 130) [212] (with whom Carr and Newey LJJ agreed). Reference to the 'usual test' was to the Supreme Court decision in *Marks v Spencer Plc v BNP Paribas Securities* [2016] AC 742, 754–55 (Lord Neuberger, with whom Lords Sumption, Hodge Carnwath and Clarke agreed). This test considered whether the implied term was reasonable and equitable, necessary to give business efficacy to the contract (in other words, the contract would be commercially or practically incoherent without it), the term must be 'so obvious it goes without saying', must be capable of clear expression and sufficient precision, and must not be inconsistent with the express terms of the contract. The process of implying a term is separate from the process of construction: 757 (Lord Neuberger, with whom Lords Sumption, Hodge, Carnwath and Clarke agreed); cf *Attorney-General of Belize v Belize Telecom Ltd* [2009] 1 WLR 1988.

[143] E Holmes, 'A Contextual Study of Commercial Good Faith: Good Faith Disclosure in Contract Formation' (1978) 39 *University of Pittsburgh Law Review* 381, 402; similarly Collins (n 18) 314–15. Collins says that, at minimum, it includes a requirement of honesty applicable to all contracts. The other end is close to fiduciary duties. He includes unconscionability near the honesty end. He places a requirement to meet the reasonable expectations of honest contracting parties near the middle.

[144] *Manifest Shipping Co Ltd v Uni-Polaris Insurance Co Ltd* [2001] 1 AC 469, [111] (Lord Scott, with whom Lords Steyn and Hoffmann agreed); *Soteria Insurance Limited and CIS General Insurance Limited v IBM United Kingdom Limited* [2022] EWCA Civ 440, [121] (Coulson LJ, with whom Phillips LJ and Zacaroli J agreed).

[145] *Soteria Insurance Limited and CIS General Insurance Limited v IBM United Kingdom Limited* [2022] EWCA Civ 440, [136] (Coulson LJ, with whom Phillips LJ and Zacaroli J agreed).

[146] Brownsword (n 1) 217–31.

[147] *Braganza v BP Shipping* [2015] 1 WLR 1661, 1672 (Lady Hale, with whom Lord Kerr agreed), 1677 (Lord Hodge) and 1688 (Lord Neuberger).

[148] [1948] 1 KB 223, 233–34 (Lord Greene MR).

[149] *Lymington Marina v MacNamara* [2007] EWCA Civ 151, [37] (Lady Justice Arden), [69] (Pill LJ). Sir Martin Norse agreed with both judgments: [63]. In that case, the Court found it was necessary to imply an obligation not to exercise a discretion in bad faith or capriciously, in order to give the contract 'business efficacy': [44]. For more general criticism see Jeffrey Jowell and Anthony Lester, 'Beyond *Wednesbury*: Substantive Principles of Administrative Law' [1987] *Public Law* 368. I make further comment on this in ch 6.

Scholars have sought to explain how constraint of an apparently open-ended discretion is explained by the typical trust inherent in relations between contracting parties.[150]

Recently in *Pakistan International Airline Corporation v Times Travel (UK) Ltd*,[151] five members of the United Kingdom Supreme Court confirmed there was no general, overriding doctrine of good faith in English contract law.[152] Members of the Court agreed with Lord Steyn's previous comments that English law protects the reasonable expectations of honest people entering into contracts.[153] However, it eschewed a general principle of good faith, preferring piecemeal solutions to demonstrated problems of unfairness.[154] Having said that, the joint reasons did consider whether the defendant acted in bad faith in determining whether it had applied lawful act duress.[155] The Court suggested an organisation or individual might act in bad faith either by asserting a pre-existing right which they know does not exist, or in the context of the way in which that organisation or individual asserts their rights, or a combination of the two.[156]

Lord Burrows was hesitant about accepting a generalised principle of good faith. He had just noted that the law regarding lawful act economic duress should develop in a traditional, incremental way, noting the law in this area was still in his infancy. He continued:

> For similar reasons, I do not think that this is an appropriate case in which to rely on a general principle of good faith dealing in so far as that would require a court to try to apply a standard of what is commercially acceptable or unreasonable behaviour. That would be a radical move forward for the English law of contract and the uncertainty caused by it seems unlikely to be a price worth paying. In my view the better strategy at this stage in the law's development is to try to set out a limited but clear and workable boundary for the concept of lawful act economic duress in the context of the facts.[157]

[150] Collins (n 82) 251 noting that the willingness of a party to be subjected to a broad-ranging discretionary power suggests willingness to trust that the party with the potential power will exercise it in a reasonable manner. They are presumably aware of the risks associated with inclusion of such a clause. They have sufficient trust in the other contracting party that the risk of unreasonable use will not materialise, and that the damage to reputation and long-term relationship between the parties will be sufficient to deter opportunistic use of the discretion.

[151] (n 54).

[152] ibid [3] (Lord Hodge, with whom Lords Reed, Lloyd-Jones and Kitchin agreed).

[153] ibid [27] (Lord Hodge, with whom Lords Reed, Lloyd-Jones and Kitchin agreed).

[154] ibid.

[155] ibid [56] (Lord Hodge, with whom Lords Reed, Lloyd-Jones and Kitchin agreed).

[156] ibid [56] (Lord Hodge, with whom Lords Reed, Lloyd-Jones and Kitchin agreed). Agreeing, Burrows J suggested another possibility – that the organisation or person does not genuinely believe it has a defence to the claim being waived by the party being threatened: [102]. Lord Burrows also pointed out that in two previous cases of economic duress by lawful means, a feature of the cases was that the party exerting the duress deliberately created, or exacerbated, a situation where the party threatened was vulnerable: *Borrelli v Ting* [2010] UKPC 21; *Progress Bulk Carriers Ltd v Tube City IMS LLC* [2012] EWHC 273 (Comm).

[157] (n 54) [95]; see similarly *Banque Financiere de la Cite SA v Westgage Insurance Co Ltd* [1990] 1 QB 665, 772: 'in the case of commercial contracts, broad concepts of honesty and fair dealing, however laudable, are a somewhat uncertain guide when determining the existence or otherwise of

Somewhat ironically in the context of an argument about 'certainty', these comments may be interpreted in several ways. One possible interpretation is that Lord Burrows did not need to, and did not, commit to a more generalised notion of good faith; instead he preferred to let the common law to develop in its usual, case by case manner. This leaves open the possibility that, one day, Lord Burrows may be prepared to accept a generalised duty of good faith. Another interpretation is that Lord Burrows disfavours a generalised notion of good faith because of the uncertainty he believes it would create and/or such a step would be 'too radical', in his view. On the other hand, former Chief Justice of the High Court of Australia Murray Gleeson, by no stretch of the imagination a radical, has indicated that today's citizenry place less value on predictability than previous generations might have, and the demands of justice might require something more than a slavish (and likely in vain)[158] attempt at legal certainty.[159]

X. Acceptance in Statute, General Form Contracts

Good faith is referred to in numerous United Kingdom statutes.[160] Section 62(4) of the *Consumer Rights Act 2015* (UK) expresses it as a requirement of *consumer* contracts.[161] It is also applied in commercial contexts not directly involving

an obligation which may arise even in the absence of any dishonest or unfair means' (Slade LJ, for the Court of Appeal). This was a response to comments of the trial judge (Steyn J, as he then was) who asked whether good faith and fair dealing in the particular case (there in the insurance context) require disclosure (702–03). There was no substantive discussion of this point in the House of Lords judgment: [1991] 2 AC 249.

[158] A Gray, *Criminal Due Process and Chapter III of the Australian Constitution* (Sydney, Federation Press, 2016) 21: 'certainty in law is elusive and illusory'; J Dawson, 'Economic Duress and the Fair Exchange in French and German Law' (1937) 11 *Tulane Law Review* 345, 345: 'the system of "free" contract described by nineteenth century theory is now coming to be recognized as a world of fantasy, too orderly, too neatly contrived, and too harmonious to correspond with reality'; R Gordon, 'Macaulay, Macneil and the Discovery of Solidarity and Power in Contract Law' [1985] *Wisconsin Law Review* 565, 566: 'I am always a bit taken aback to hear lawyers argue … that for all its faults the old formal-classical system of rules had the rules of predictability and administrative convenience; its results might be sometimes arbitrary or unjust but at least one knew where one stood. I should have thought that if there was one proof the realist critics had managed to nail down for good it was that of the manipulability and contextual variability of the old-rule system. If the rules are stable and predictable in particular practice meetings … that stability derives from well accepted conventions within the community of regular interpreters of the rule'; A Swan, 'The Obligation to Perform in Good Faith: Comment on *Bhasin v Hrynew*' (2015) 56 *Canadian Business Law Journal* 395, 403: 'certainty in the law of contracts will not be found in narrow rules'.

[159] M Gleeson, 'Individualised Justice – The Holy Grail' (1995) 69 *Australian Law Journal* 421, 430: 'the demands of justice, as seen through modern eyes, are much less likely to be met by formal and inflexible rules which treat hard cases with the dismissiveness sometimes manifested in earlier times. The citizens of the late 20th century have an attitude towards all forms of authority which is questioning, demanding and self-assertive. They seem to place less value upon predictability than former generations'.

[160] For example Companies Act 2006 (UK) s 172 (duties of directors).

[161] Section 62(1) establishes that an unfair contract term in a consumer contract will not be enforced. Section 62(4) states that a term is unfair if, contrary to the requirement of good faith, it causes

contracts. For example, in *Borrelli v Ting*[162] the Court found that Ting, a chairman and chief executive officer of a company, had acted with a lack of good faith in initially opposing a scheme of arrangement in relation to the relevant company. Such an arrangement was necessary in order to realise some value from the company to assist with the company liquidation. Ting (through companies he controlled) agreed to end his opposition to the scheme of arrangement only after the liquidators agreed not to pursue him in relation to alleged breaches of his obligations to the company. The Court found he opposed the scheme of arrangement in order to deny the liquidator of funds, funds which would have been used to investigate his alleged wrongdoing. It found his opposition to the scheme was not made in good faith, but for ulterior and illegitimate purposes.[163]

Good faith is also enshrined in the New Engineering Contracts (NEC) commonly used in industry. For example, Clause 10.2 of NEC 4 contains a good faith obligation, requiring parties to act in a spirit of mutual trust and co-operation.[164] Enterprise contracts, permitting a fluid rather than a static contract situation, are becoming more common.[165]

XI. Reflections on the English Case Law to Date

As earlier chapters of the book have recognised, good faith has a long history in the common law. This occurred over many years, and in a broad range of legal contexts. In this light, the noted 'hostility' of the common law to good faith at present can be hard to fathom. Claims that good faith is anathema to the common law seem ahistorical. Claims that the lack of good faith in English law leads to predictability, certainty and fairness are also open to serious challenge. The volume of commercial law litigation suggests otherwise. Parties as rational utility maximisers, an assumption freedom of contract-like advocates would need to defend, would not embark on expensive, time-consuming commercial litigation in the face of such certainty and predictability. The fact they do so gives the lie to the suggestion that the lack of good faith produces certain and predictable results.

We then have the potentially contradictory argument that there is no need for the doctrine of good faith, because English law already provides an equivalent remedy in cases where otherwise good faith would be useful. It would be difficult to accept both that good faith is anathema to the common law and superfluous

significant imbalance in the rights and obligations of the consumer contract parties, to the detriment of the consumer. A lengthy list of examples of unfair terms appears in Schedule 2 to the Act.

[162] [2010] UKPC 21.

[163] ibid [28] (Lord Saville, for the Council).

[164] See for discussion A McInnis, 'The New Engineering Contract: Relational Contracting, Good Faith and Co-operation – Part I and II' [2003] *International Construction Law Review* 128 and 289.

[165] D Mosey and S Jackson, 'Good Faith and Relational Contracting – Do Enterprise Contracts Offer a Way Through the Woods?', *Society of Construction Law Paper* 2020.

because its essence (if not its name) is soaked through existing legal doctrine. Of the two, I suspect the second one, that good faith (though not by name) underpins some of our existing legal doctrine is closer to the truth. However, there remain gaps which a good faith doctrine would fill. I have demonstrated earlier in the chapter the somewhat tortured attempts to twist facts in order to arrive at just outcomes. The law sometimes resorts to the myth of implying terms in order to do the same. There is a fair and defensible argument that the law is forced into these unacceptable and unsavoury practices in an effort to get around the lack of a generalised good faith principle. In essence, two fundamental questions arise – in what contractual circumstances (if any) will an obligation of good faith arise, and what does it require?

A review of the case law to date in this area suggests a disjunct between the rhetoric and the results. On repeated occasions, judges have commented that the law must reflect the reasonable expectations of commercial business people. It is accepted that generally individuals expect others to act in good faith. There is commercial sense in contracting parties being able to trust the party with whom they are contracting, reducing transaction costs. All of this is suggestive of a generalised good faith doctrine in contract law. Leggatt LJ (as he then was) came closest to advocating this, suggesting there was a good argument for it as a default interpretive principle of the law of contract.

However, the reality has been much more hesitant and piecemeal in terms of development of actual legal principle. English law has not yet recognised a generalised good faith doctrine. Instead, it has reverted to a categories-based approach. It has accepted that in a limited number of commercial contracting contexts, such as joint ventures, partnerships, employment arrangements and long-term commercial relationships, the parties may be seen to be in a 'relational contract' such that good faith might be implied in law into such contracts. This is fairly typical of the common law's piecemeal, case by case method. Courts deal with the precise matter before them, and consider whether in the particular case, the relationship between the parties is 'relational', such that good faith might be implied into their agreement. However, it has not been satisfactorily explained why it is only these types of contracts that parties can have an expectation another will act in good faith. The rhetoric about giving effect to the reasonable expectations of business people is not confined to these narrow categories of commercial relationships. It might be a surprise to an ordinary business person that the law does impose good faith obligations on some of the contracts on which they embark, but not others, and that there can be room for disagreement as to whether the relationship is 'long-term enough' to warrant imposition of the obligation.

In *Bates v Post Office*, Fraser J helpfully set out a list of nine factors to determine whether or not parties were in a relational contract, such that a good faith obligation might arise. It is respectfully suggested that most of these, such as whether the parties intend their respective roles be performed with integrity and fidelity to the bargain, whether parties are committed to collaborating, whether it is possible to reduce the parties' entire agreement in writing, whether they intend to repose trust and confidence in the other, whether the contract will involve a high degree of communication and co-operation might be readily held to exist, at least in default.

Similar uncertainty seems to attend the meaning of good faith. It is tolerably clear that it is not a fiduciary obligation. It requires honesty. What may be regarded as opportunistic behaviour outside the purposes of the contract is frowned upon. Sometimes courts are open that it requires parties to act reasonably; others seem to eschew any obligation towards reasonableness. And the courts seem to have fastened upon the exercise of contractual discretion as being subject to a reasonableness obligation. However, it is not clear why the requirement of reasonableness (perhaps) only extends that far, and not towards other contracting behaviour that many would regard as indefensible but which does not relate to a discretion. Sometimes, the obligation not to deny the other the fruits of the contract, to impede the filling of a pre-condition to contract, and to co-operate in the performance of the contract seems to be regarded as within the good faith obligation; at other times not.

Most recently in *Pakistan International Corporation*, Lord Burrows claimed that introduction of a generalised good faith obligation involving considerations of what is commercially acceptable or unreasonable behaviour would lead to uncertainty. Of course, English law has already adopted good faith (which would typically include considerations of commercial acceptability and reasonableness) in relation to 'relational contracts'. It is not clear why it is acceptable to consider these matters in relation to relational contracts (however defined), but problematically uncertain when applied to other contract types. And of course the law applies concepts of 'reasonableness' in a vast array of contexts without undue difficulty. Even in the context of contracts, as we will see in chapter nine, courts lean away from 'unreasonable' interpretations of contractual clauses. Thus, the expressed concern with reasonableness on the basis it is uncertain is not, with respect, convincing. Similarly, parliament has embraced notions of 'good faith' in relation to statute, and industry standard form contracts embrace it. This is evidence, respectively, of its acceptance by the parliamentary lawmakers and in commercial practice. Frankly, it is an acceptance hard to square with judicial claims of the unworkability of the concept.

6

Good Faith and Reasonableness in Contract Law: Other Jurisdictions

I. Australia

> Commercial law is, or to a significant degree should be, the reflection of society's facilitation, not hindrance, of commercial endeavour. That said, the norms that underpin a just and fair society and its legal system should underpin commerce. It is honest commercial endeavour that is to be facilitated not hindered. And it is the reasonable expectations of honest commercial mean and women that are to be vindicated and protected.[1]

A. Initial Contractual Discretion Cases in Australia

The initial relevant case law in Australia occurred in the context of a consideration of contractual discretion. To be clear, these cases did not expressly use the term good faith to describe the fetter they placed on the exercise of contractual discretion. It was only later in the 1990s when good faith was expressly utilised, as we will demonstrate.

In *Carr v J A Berriman Pty Ltd*,[2] the contract provided that an architect could 'in their absolute discretion' omit work from the originally agreed scope of works. The architect purported to remove work from the original contractor, and give it to a third party. The High Court found that the purpose of the clause was to adjust the scope of the work given to the original contractor as a result of alterations that the architect had made. It was not intended to permit this to be exercised simply to substitute one contractor for another, at the architect's absolute discretion. The court concluded the words used did not go so far (the use of the words 'absolute discretion' were not sufficiently clear). It found that a power to hand over any part of the work at any time to another contractor would be 'most unreasonable', which would require very clear contract wording.[3] Although the court did not refer to

[1] J Allsop, 'Good Faith and Australian Contract Law: A Practical Issue and a Question of Theory and Principle' (2011) 85 *Australian Law Journal* 341, 342.
[2] (1953) 89 CLR 327.
[3] ibid 347 (Fullagar J).

the concept of good faith, this is considered to be an example of it. The court was conditioning a contractual discretion on something like arbitrariness.

The High Court has indicated that where a contract is conditional on the fulfilment of a condition, both contracting parties must do what they reasonably can to ensure that the condition is met. The context there was a contract to sell and lease land which required the consent of a relevant government minister. The Court found there was an implied term in fact that the vendor would do what they reasonably could to ensure the Minister's consent was obtained.[4] This has been connected with good faith.[5]

The High Court has regularly indicated implicit restrictions on the exercise of contractual discretion. For example, in *Godfrey Constructions Pty Limited v Kanangra Park Pty Limited*,[6] the court considered the power of a vendor to rescind the contract if they could not meet an objection or requisition to the title of the property intended to be sold. All members of the Court phrased limitations on the extent to which the vendor could exercise this express power. Barwick CJ (with whom McTiernan J agreed) said that it could not be applied unconscionably.[7] Walsh J indicated it could not be applied arbitrarily or unreasonably.[8] Gibbs J indicated the proposed exercise of the power was unreasonable.[9] Stephen J considered whether the power was being used for improper and extraneous purposes.[10]

Regarding a similar clause in relation to land, legislation provided that generally particular land could not be owned by a corporation, without the Minister's consent.[11] The vendor purported to sell relevant property to a purchaser that was a corporation. The purchaser required them to seek appropriate approvals. The vendor purported to exercise the clause in the contract permitting them to rescind it in the event they were unwilling to comply with a purchaser requisition. The purchaser challenged the validity of the exercise of the contractual right on the facts. In the High Court, Barwick CJ considered the test to be whether the

[4] *Butts v O'Dwyer* (1952) 87 CLR 267, 280 (Dixon CJ Williams Webb and Kitto JJ), 286 (Taylor J). This mirrors the earlier decision of *Butt v M'Donald* (1896) 7 QLJ 68, where Griffith CJ stated it was a general rule applicable to all contracts that parties agree to do all that is necessary to ensure the other party has the benefit of the contract; see also *Secured Income Real Estate (Australia) Ltd v St Martins Investment Pty Ltd* (1979) 144 CLR 596, 607 (Mason J)(with whom Gibbs Stephen and Aickin JJ agreed).

[5] *Alcatel Australia Ltd v Scarcella and Others* (1998) 44 NSWLR 349, 368 (Sheller JA, with whom Powell and Beazley JJA agreed); *Cordon Investments Pty Ltd v Lesdor Properties Pty Ltd* [2012] NSWCA 184, [185] (Bathurst CJ) (with whom Macfarlan and Meagher JJA agreed).

[6] (1972) 128 CLR 529.

[7] ibid 538.

[8] ibid 543.

[9] ibid 547.

[10] ibid 548. Some leading contract law scholars disagree with this, stating that reasonableness should not condition the exercise of discretion, because to do so would 'second-guess' the parties' bargain: J Carter and A Stewart, 'Interpretation, Good Faith and the "True Meaning" of Contracts: The *Royal Botanic* Decision' (2002) 18 *Journal of Contract Law* 182, 193; cf Lord Steyn, 'The Role of Good Faith and Fair Dealing in Contract Law: A Hair-Shirt Philosophy' (1991) 6 *Denning Law Journal* 131, 132: 'throughout the web of English contract law the criterion of the reasonable man's response predominates'.

[11] *Pierce Bell Sales Pty Ltd v Frazer* (1973) 130 CLR 575.

vendor's exercise of contractual discretion was 'unreasonable or unconscionable'.[12] Gibbs J considered whether the vendor's actions were 'arbitrary, capricious or unreasonable'.[13]

In *Meehan v Jones*[14] the High Court considered the validity of clauses in a contract which conditioned the agreement on the purchaser satisfactorily obtaining product supply, and obtaining finance on satisfactory terms. The question arose as to the meaning of these provisions, and in particular whether a term should be implied that the purchaser act honestly and/or reasonably in attempting to meet the conditions and determining whether supply and finance were 'satisfactory' to them. The point was obiter, because the purchaser had in fact obtained finance on satisfactory terms. However, Gibbs CJ stated that the only requirement was for the purchaser to act honestly in determining whether or not supply and finance could be secured on satisfactory terms.[15] Murphy J said the discretion was unlimited, and not even honesty was required.[16] The only other two justices to render judgment were more cautious. Both Mason and Wilson JJ left open the question of whether the question of satisfaction was to be judged honestly and/or reasonably.[17] However, Mason J indicated the discretion was not unbounded. The purchaser was required to do all that was reasonable on their part to obtain suitable finance, and to act honestly and reasonably in determining whether or not offered finance was satisfactory.[18]

B. Express Recognition of a Good Faith Obligation in Australia

In *Commonwealth v Amann Aviation Pty Ltd*[19] the Court considered a clause which permitted the Commonwealth, where the contract administrator considered the contractor had not met contractual obligations, to show cause why the contract should not be cancelled. The Commonwealth would be entitled to compensation from the contractor if this eventuated. Members of both the Federal Court and High Court indicated this discretion was not at large. Davies J said the decision maker was bound to exercise their power without bias and not in a capricious manner, with due regard for the interests of both contracting parties. By inserting a show notice provision, the parties clearly intended that the power of termination would be restricted, that it not merely be exercised having regard to the Commonwealth's interests, and the decision maker should take due account

[12] ibid 589 (with whom McTiernan and Gibbs JJ agreed. Only three justices decided the case).
[13] ibid 591.
[14] (1982) 149 CLR 571.
[15] ibid 581.
[16] ibid 597.
[17] ibid 591 and 598 respectively.
[18] ibid 591 (Mason J) with whom Wilson J agreed (598).
[19] (1990) 22 FCR 527.

of submissions by the contractor prior to exercising their discretion.[20] Sheppard J said the decision maker could not act capriciously, arbitrarily or in bad faith in exercising their discretion.[21] In the High Court, two justices expressly agreed with the interpretation placed upon this clause by the Full Federal Court.[22]

An important development in good faith in Australian contract law occurred in *Renard Constructions (ME) v Minister for Public Works*.[23] The contract contained a clause permitting the principal to a contract, in a case where the contractor defaulted in their performance of it, to suspend payment and issue a show cause notice to the contractor as to why the principal should not terminate the contract, and take back the uncompleted work. The question was whether the power in this clause was limited by an obligation of good faith and/or an obligation to exercise it reasonably. As the court noted, traditionally the law distinguished between two kinds of contractual implications – implications of fact,[24] or ad hoc implications in a particular contractual context, and implications by law, which applied to contracts of a particular class.[25] If the court was considering whether a term should be implied, orthodoxy would require it to analyse whether the requirements for making an implication in fact or in law had been met.

Priestley JA found that all of the requirements existed to imply in fact that the principal's discretion to terminate the contract had to be exercised reasonably.[26] He paid particular attention to the question of business efficacy. He noted that, according to the express words of the contract, the principal might issue a show cause notice for a broad range of alleged breaches, some of which might be serious, but some of which might be trivial in nature. Further, the clause gave the principal apparently unbridled discretion to terminate the contract if the contractor did not respond, or did not respond sufficiently, to the show cause notice, within time. However, there might be a good reason why the contractor did not respond, or respond in time. He indicated that in such cases, for a principal to then be able to terminate the contract would make the contract unworkable. No person or organisation would enter into such a contract. The reasonable contractor, reasonable principal and reasonable third party would all assume that termination would only occur for 'good reason'. Interpreting the termination power to be not

[20] ibid 532.
[21] ibid 542.
[22] (1991) 66 ALJR 123, 135 (Mason CJ and Dawson J).
[23] (1992) 26 NSWLR 234.
[24] The relevant principles were set out in *Codelfa Construction Pty Ltd v State Rail Authority of New South Wales* (1982) 149 CLR 337, 347 (Mason J) (with whom Wilson J agreed); 404 (Brennan J) that (a) the terms must be reasonable and equitable; (b) it must be necessary to give business efficacy to the contract, so no term will be implied if the contract is effective without it; (c) it must be so obvious that it goes without saying; (d) it must be capable of clear expression; and (e) it must not contradict any express contractual terms (applying the Privy Council decision in *BP Refinery (Westernport) Pty Ltd v Hastings Shire Council* (1980) 180 CLR 266.
[25] The implication of terms by law must meet a test of both reasonableness and necessity: *Castlemaine Tooheys Ltd v Carlton and United Breweries Ltd* (1987) 10 NSWLR 468, 486–90 (Hope JA, with whom Samuels JA and Priestley JA agreed).
[26] (n 23) 257.

bounded by reasonableness would be contrary to the promises the contracting parties had made to another. The only way to make the contract workable, in the view of Priestley JA, was to imply reasonableness.[27] Thus, Priestley JA found that an implied term of fact should be made that the discretion be exercised reasonably.

He indicated that similarly, a term could be implied by law. He indicated requirements of necessity and reasonableness were in some respects similar to the requirements of an implication by fact.[28] The test of 'necessity' did not mean the contract could not work without the clause. In cases where it had been implied (Priestley JA referred to contracts of sale, contracts of employment and leases), the court concluded the parties' agreement would work better if a reasonableness standard were applied, in accordance with standards of the time.

Priestley JA explained that the kind of reasonableness he had discussed 'had much in common' with notions of good faith.[29] He also referenced unconscionability, unfairness and lack of good faith as being similarly common. This led him to conclude that:

> People generally, including judges and other lawyers, from all strands of the community have grown used to the courts applying standards of fairness to contract which are wholly consistent with the existence in all contracts of a duty upon the parties of good faith and fair dealing in its performance. In my view this is in these days the expected standard, and anything less is contrary to prevailing community expectations.[30]

Handley JA agreed with the reasoning of Priestley JA, in particular that the power of the principal regarding termination had to be exercised reasonably.[31] He did not base this on the implication of terms. Rather, he suggested that the reference in the clause to 'show cause' suggested that the parties intended that the power would only be exercised reasonably,[32] after noting the potentially very broad ambit of the clause. This is similar to the view of Elisabeth Peden, who rejects good faith as an implied term, preferring to resolve such matters through exercise in construction of the relevant contractual provision.[33] Meagher JA found that the principal's judgment regarding whether the contractor had failed to meet their obligations under the contract was flawed, based on incomplete information and prejudice, such that they could not have been relevantly 'satisfied' of a breach of the contract by the contractor. Thus, the power to terminate was not enlivened.[34]

In *Esso Australia Resources Pty Ltd v Southern Pacific Petroleum NL and Ors*, Warren CJ of the Victorian Court of Appeal also defined good faith in terms of

[27] ibid 258.
[28] ibid 261.
[29] ibid 263.
[30] ibid 268.
[31] ibid 279.
[32] ibid.
[33] Elisabeth Peden, 'Contractual Good Faith: Can Australia Benefit From the American Experience?' (2003) 15(2) *Bond Law Review* 186, 213.
[34] (n 23) 276.

reasonableness.[35] She also agreed with Buchanan J, who defined lack of good faith as involving unreasonableness, capricious behaviour, behaving with an ulterior purpose, and/or preventing performance of the contract by the other party or seeking to deny the other the benefits of the contract.[36]

It has also been suggested that good faith require that parties not utilise contractual power or discretion in a manner other than for the purpose/s for which the power or discretion was conferred.[37] The New South Wales Court of Appeal noted that where a contractual power is expressed in terms wider than necessary to protect the legitimate commercial interests of that party, the court may interpret the clause more narrowly, so as not to extend to the proposed activity. Alternatively, the court might conclude the party is exercising the power in a capricious or arbitrary manner, or for extraneous purposes.[38]

In *Hughes Aircraft Systems International v Airservices Australia*,[39] Finn J was prepared to recognise fair dealing and/or good faith as a organising idea in Australian law. He said it should be recognised as a general standard of conduct to which all contracting parties should be expected to adhere.[40] In *South Sydney District Rugby League Football Club Ltd v News Ltd*, Finn J said that a duty to act in good faith required parties to act reasonably in the protection of their legitimate interests.[41]

In *Burger King Corporation v Hungry Jack's Pty Ltd*[42] a unanimous New South Wales Court of Appeal found that an implied duty of good faith and an implied duty of reasonableness were essentially the same duty.[43] Further, that where such duties are implied, they are implied in law rather than in fact.[44] They apply to a

[35] *Esso Australian Resources Pty Ltd v Southern Pacific Petroleum NL and Ors* [2005] VSCA 228, [3].

[36] ibid [28]; Warren CJ [1] and Osborn AJA [32] agreed.

[37] *Pierce Bell Sales Pty Ltd v Frazer* (1973) 130 CLR 575, 590 (Barwick CJ); *Far Horizons Pty Ltd v McDonalds Australia* [2000] VSC 310, [120]: 'there is to be implied in a franchise agreement a term of good faith and fair dealing which obliges each party to exercise the powers conferred upon it by the agreement in good faith and reasonably and not capriciously or for some extraneous purpose. Such a term is a legal incident of such a contract' (Byrne J); *Garry Rogers Motors (Aust) Pty Ltd v Subaru (Aust) Pty Ltd* (1999) ATPR 41-703, [43008]: 'in appropriate contracts, perhaps even in all commercial contracts, such a term (of good faith) will ordinarily be implied, not as an ad hoc term (based on the presumed intention of the parties) but as a legal incident of the relationship … it will require a contracting party to act in good faith and fairly, not only in relation to the performance of a contractual obligation, but also in the exercise of a power conferred by the contract' (Finkelstein J); see JM Paterson, 'Implied Fetters on the Exercise of Discretionary Contractual Powers' (2009) 35 *Monash University Law Review* 45.

[38] *Alcatel Australia v Scarcella* (1998) 44 NSWLR 349, 368 (Sheller JA, with whom Powell and Beazley JJA agreed); in *Pacific Brands Sport and Leisure Pty Ltd v Underworks Pty Ltd* [2005] FCA 288, Finkelstein J spoke of good faith in terms of proper purpose, whether behaviour was arbitrary and/or capricious, and whether it was unfair and/or oppressive: [65].

[39] (1997) 146 ALR 1.

[40] ibid 37. He elaborated on this in PD Finn, 'Equity and Contract' in PD Finn (ed), *Essays on Contract* (Sydney, Law Book Company Limited, 1987); see for discussion A Phang, 'Tenders, Implied Terms and Fairness in the Law of Contract' (1998) 13 *Journal of Contract Law* 126.

[41] [2000] FCA 1541, [394].

[42] (2001) 69 NSWLR 558.

[43] ibid [169] (Sheller, Beazley and Stein JJA).

[44] ibid [164].

particular class of contract. The court was prepared to make such implications in the current context of a long-term franchise agreement between the parties. The court was concerned that Burger King Corporation, could for relatively slight breaches of the agreement by Hungry Jack's Pty Ltd, terminate the contract.[45] The contract was extremely valuable. Further, the termination clause contained highly subjective criteria for the exercise of the termination power. Other cases have read the class of contracts into which such an obligation is implied broadly, to include 'all commercial contracts'.[46]

Having determined that an implied duty of good faith and reasonableness applied to the facts, the court explained what it required. It did not require that the party that owed the obligation was not entitled to have regard only to its own legitimate interests in exercising the discretion.[47] It was not in the nature of a fiduciary obligation. However, it was necessary that the discretion be exercised reasonably and in good faith, and not for extraneous purposes. There was a suggestion here that Burger King Corporation may have wished to exploit commercial advantages in Australia directly, and not through an agreement with Hungry Jack's under which they would receive a mere royalty.[48]

Elsewhere the Court has clarified that good faith requires fidelity to the parties' bargain, including an obligation to do all things to ensure the other party has the benefit of the contract.[49] Extra-judicially, Sir Anthony Mason explained that good faith comprised three aspects: (a) obligation to co-operate in achieving the objectives of the contract;[50] (b) honest standards of conduct; and (c) standards of conduct that are reasonable having regard to the parties' interests.[51] Other

[45] ibid [183].

[46] *Overlook v Foxtel* [2002] NSWSC 17, [62] (Barrett J); *Pacific Brands Sport & Leisure Pty Ltd v Underworks Pty Ltd* [2005] FCA 288, [64] (Finkelstein J).

[47] (n 42) [185].

[48] ibid [32].

[49] *United Group Rail Services Ltd v Rail Corporation New South Wales* (2009) 74 NSWLR 618, 638 (Allsop P, with whom Ipp and Macfarlan JJA agreed).

[50] In *Peters (WA) Pty Ltd v Petersville Ltd and Another* (2001) 205 CLR 126, 142 four members of the High Court referred to an implied obligation on contracting parties to do all things necessary to permit the other contracting party to have the benefit of the contract, and an obligation not to hinder or prevent fulfilment of the express promises made in the contract (Gleeson CJ Gummow Kirby and Hayne JJ), but did not use the words 'good faith' to describe them.

[51] Anthony Mason, 'Contract, Good Faith and Equitable Standards in Fair Dealing' (2000) 116 *Law Quarterly Review* 66, accepted and applied in *Macquarie International Health Clinic Pty Ltd v Sydney South West Area Health Service* [2010] NSWCA 268. The content of good faith was similarly expressed by Allsop CJ in *Paciocco v Australia and New Zealand Banking Group Limited* [2015] FCAFC 50, [288] to mean an obligation to act honestly, with fidelity to the bargain, not to undermine the agreement or the substantive benefit of the contract, and an obligation to act reasonably and in fairly having regard to the interests of the contracting parties. Suzanne Corcoran discussed at least 12 aspects: 'Good Faith as a Principle of Interpretation: What is the Positive Content of Good Faith?' (2012) 36 *Australian Bar Review* 1, 13–16: honesty, intention, knowledge, freedom from malice, diligence and inquiry, reasonable cooperation, fair dealing and fair consequences, and full disclosure/lack of deceit, adherence to due process, no misuse of power, compliance with statutory and common law obligations and track record of conduct.

cases have emphasised that reasonableness is an important aspect of a good faith requirement.[52] This is inconsistent with some academic commentary suggesting that good faith be limited to honesty.[53]

Peden distinguishes between contractual powers or discretions, and the exercise of contractual rights. She says the former must be exercised in accordance with their purpose, considered in context. In contrast, she argues contractual powers should arguably be completely unfettered.[54]

It has been suggested that co-operation may include disclosure of information to the other side,[55] and to negotiate reasonably in relation to how the contract operates in practice.[56] The former was important on the facts in *Macquarie Bank*, since the court found the defendant had failed to disclose its planning processes on the site, including whether to go ahead with a particular building that they knew was of importance to the other side in its consideration of the project.[57] It will be applied sensitively to the context. In other words, it can mean different things in different contexts.[58]

In *Macquarie Bank*, Allsop P said that the meaning of good faith in Australia was similar to its meaning in the United States. He cited examples from that jurisdiction to indicate that good faith might require that parties not engage in subterfuge or evasion, do not engage in opportunistic behaviour by taking advantage of the other party, for example, because they performed their obligations first, not hindering the other party's performance or impeding the satisfaction of conditions that would trigger one's own obligations, and co-operating to achieve contractual goals.[59] Elsewhere it has been interpreted as the 'spirit' of the contract, supporting the integrity of its character.[60] A party may not cynically resort to the black letter.[61] Capricious behaviour with no rational explanation, and attempts to weaken or destroy the position of the other party to the contract are inconsistent

[52] *Macquarie International Health Clinic Pty Ltd v Sydney South West Area Health Service* [2010] NSWCA 268, [15] (Allsop P), [150] (Hodgson JA) (with whom Macfarlan JA agreed); *Bropho v Human Rights and Equal Opportunity Commission* [2004] FCAFC 16, [103] (French J); *Cordon Investments Pty Ltd v Lesdor Properties Pty Ltd* [2012] NSWCA 184, [145] (Bathurst CJ, with whom Macfarlan and Meagher JJA agreed).

[53] E Peden, 'When Common Law Trumps Equity: The Rise of Good Faith and Reasonableness and the Demise of Unconscionability' (2005) 21 *Journal of Contract Law* 226, 236: 'to equate an obligation of reasonableness and one of good faith is misconceived'.

[54] E Peden, *Good Faith in the Performance of Contracts* (Sydney, LexisNexis Butterworths, 2003) 167.

[55] *Macquarie Bank* (n 52) [16] (Allsop P).

[56] ibid [16] (Allsop P).

[57] ibid [20] (Allsop P), [148] (Hodgson JA) (with whom Macfarlan JA agreed).

[58] ibid [18] (Allsop P).

[59] ibid [19].

[60] *Overlook v Foxtel* [2002] NSWSC 17, [67] (Barrett J).

[61] 'In some circumstances a cynical resort to the black letter or literal meaning of a contractual provision may be taken into account in determining whether there has been a lack of good faith': *Automasters Australia Pty Ltd v Bruness Pty Ltd* [2002] WASC 286, [388]; cf Sir R Jackson 'Does Good Faith Have any Role in Construction Contracts?', Pinsent Mason Lecture, November 2017: '(parties) all need to know what the contract requires and what the contract permits. To that end, they do not speculate about ethics or metaphysics ... they look at the black letter provisions of the contract. That is what the court should do as well': [6.11].

with good faith.[62] So too is the issue of a notice indicating the provider was contemplating taking a course of action, when the evidence suggested they had already decided to do so.[63] The kind of fidelity and loyalty required by good faith is a relational concept.[64]

The Victorian Court of Appeal considered the good faith question in *Esso Australia Resources Pty Ltd v Southern Pacific Petroleum NL and Ors*.[65] There Buchanan JA expressed reluctance to imply a duty of good faith at law. He expressed reservations about declaring that commercial contracts were a class of contract in which such a duty should be implied.[66] He preferred the implied in fact path – that it was possible that an implied term of good faith be inserted, if the tests set out in *BP Refinery* were met.[67] Buchanan JA indicated this was most likely where one of the parties was in a position of vulnerability, where such term could protect them from exploitative conduct not consistent with the purpose of the contract. Osborn AJA agreed. So did Warren CJ, who added that good faith was most likely to be implied where the parties' relationship was unbalanced, involving one party at a substantial disadvantage, and in a vulnerable position.[68]

C. High Court Non-Committal on the Matter

In the High Court, members declined to express a view regarding good faith in *Royal Botanic Gardens and Domain Trust v South Sydney City Council*.[69] In *Commonwealth Bank of Australia v Barker*,[70] the High Court expressly left open the possibility that Australian law might embrace good faith. In that case the Court rejected the suggested implication of a duty of mutual trust and confidence in employment relationships. In so doing, four of the five justices expressly left open the possibility that Australian law might accept an implied duty of good faith, making it clear that the rejection of the implied duty of mutual trust and confidence was not necessarily a rejection of an implied duty of good faith.[71] In *Commonwealth Bank of Australia v Barker* the High Court quickly dismissed

[62] *Overlook* (n 60) [73].

[63] *Bundanoon v Cenric* [2019] NSWCA 87; *Automasters Australia Pty Ltd v Bruness Pty Ltd* [2002] WASC 286.

[64] *Bropho v Human Rights and Equal Opportunity Commission* [2004] FCAFC 16, [91] (French J).

[65] [2005] VSCA 228.

[66] ibid [25].

[67] ibid.

[68] ibid [4].

[69] (2002) 240 CLR 45, 63 (Gleeson CJ Gaudron McHugh Gummow and Hayne JJ) and 94 (Callinan J), although Kirby J indicated 'such an implied term appears to conflict with fundamental notions of caveat emptor that are inherent (statute and equitable intervention apart) in common law conceptions of economic freedom. It also appears to be inconsistent with the law as it has developed in this country in respect of the introduction of implied terms into written contracts which the parties have omitted to include' (75–76). In that case the parties agreed that good faith conditioned and restricted the right of one of the contracting parties to make a rental determination pursuant to the parties' agreement.

[70] (2014) 253 CLR 169.

[71] ibid 195–96 (French CJ Bell and Keane JJ specifically left open whether a general obligation to act in good faith existed and/or whether the exercise of contractual powers and discretions was limited);

an argument about the 'relational' nature of an employment contract, stating the concept was of uncertain application.[72] Some learned commentators believe that the High Court will likely accept a general principle of good faith.[73] Swain supports this, stating that a contract law fit for the early twenty-first century should be more diverse, and should include good faith.[74]

Catterwell has identified four standards of co-operation required under Australian contract law.[75] He says these are implicit, justified by the need to protect the parties' bargain.[76] It is presumed to be what the parties intended.[77] Three members of the High Court described the duty of co-operation as a 'universal implication'.[78] These are:

The 'performance duty', requiring each party to perform acts reasonably necessary to achieve contractual objectives (based on *Mackay v Dick*[79]);

The 'prevention principle', meaning each party must not prevent or delay the other party in performing their obligations under the contract;[80]

The 'benefit duty', requiring each party to all that is reasonably necessary to ensure the other party enjoys the benefit of the contract;[81] and

The 'negative covenant, prohibiting a person from hindering or otherwise preventing the fulfilment of the purpose of their own contractual promises.

D. Acceptance of Good Faith in Statutes

Notions of good faith permeate the statute books in the United Kingdom and Australia. In 2004, one judge counted 154 Commonwealth statutes containing the concept of 'good faith'.[82] The number is not likely to have diminished. The High

Kiefel J also expressly left open the question of good faith, having regard to the 'wider importance' of the topic (214).

[72] (2014) 253 CLR 169, [37] (French CJ Bell and Keane JJ).

[73] W Swain, '"The Steaming Lungs of a Pigeon": Predicting the Direction of Australian Contract Law in the Next 25 Years' in Kit Barker, Karen Fairweather and Ross Grantham (eds), *Private Law in the 21st Century* (Oxford, Hart Publishing, 2017) 96.

[74] ibid 97.

[75] R Catterwell, 'Co-Operation and Prevention in Contract Law' (2023) 47(1) *Melbourne University Law Review* 114.

[76] S Stoljar, 'Prevention and Co-Operation in the Law of Contract' (1953) 31(3) *Canadian Bar Review* 231, 231 referred to 'an obvious corollary' of the parties' agreement was that parties must co-operate to enable the bargain to be realised; E Patterson, 'Constructive Conditions in Contracts' (1942) 42(6) *Columbia Law Review* 903, 929.

[77] E Peden, 'Cooperation in English Contract Law: To Construe or Imply?' (2000) 16(1) *Journal of Contract Law* 56, 56.

[78] *Commonwealth Bank of Australia v Barker* (2014) 253 CLR 169, 189 (French CJ Bell and Keane JJ); Kiefel J recognised a duty to co-operate as an implied term on each party to a contract (201).

[79] (1881) 6 App Cas 251, 262–64 (Lord Blackburn, with whom Lord Selbourne LC agreed (272)).

[80] *Marshall v Colonial Bank of Australasia* (1904) 1 CLR 632, 647 (Griffith CJ, for the Court).

[81] *Butt v McDonald* (1896) 7 QLJ 68, 70–71 (Griffith CJ).

[82] *Bropho v Human Rights and Equal Opportunity Commission* (2004) 135 FCR 105, 129 (French J, as he then was). A key example is s 22 of the Australian Consumer Law. It applies to assessment

Court reflected on various remedial legislation in the context of contract law in Australia in *Andrews v Australia and New Zealand Banking Group Ltd*.[83] It used this fact to suggest caution in dealing with common law 'as if laissez-faire notions of an untrammelled freedom of contract provide a universal legal value'.[84]

This passage suggests an equivalence between statute and common law, that developments in the former might or should lead developments in the latter. That is contentious, but for present purposes the correctness of that point need not be discussed. The point for now is that, if it is true that developments in the statute law should encourage similar developments in the common law, as all members of the Australian High Court accepted in *Andrews*, the fact that good faith is demonstrably so well accepted in statute suggests, at the very least, that the common law of Australia should consider embracing it. Of course, the same point could be made with respect to United Kingdom statute, and the development of common law in the equivalent jurisdictions.

II. United States

Good faith was accepted by the United States Supreme Court in the following terms:

> Corporations as much as individuals are bound to good faith and fair dealing, and the rule is well settled that they cannot, by their acts, representations and silence, involve others in onerous engagements and then turn around and disavow their acts and defeat the just expectations which their own conduct has superinduced.[85]

Similar sentiments were expressed by a New York court:

> In every contract there is an implied covenant that neither party shall do anything which will have the effect of destroying or injuring the right of the other party to receive the fruits of the contract, which means that in every contract there exists an implied covenant of good faith and fair dealing.[86]

whether a party has been guilty of unconscionable conduct, contrary to s 21. Section 22 sets out relevant factors in making this determination, and sub-section (1)(l) and (2)(l) refer to whether the parties acted in good faith. The Franchising Code of Conduct also specifically imposes a duty of good faith on parties to a franchise agreement in its performance, and on would-be parties in relation to its negotiation: Competition and Consumer (Industry Codes – Franchising) Regulation 2014 (Cth) s 6(1). Clause 20 of standard form agreement AS4000 imposes upon a superintendent an obligation to act in good faith. Clause 2.1 of the Proposed General Conditions of Contract AS11000 (2015) would also have imposed an express duty of good faith on contracting parties. Standards Australia did not proceed with AS11000.

[83] (2012) 247 CLR 205.

[84] ibid 215–16 (French CJ Gummow Crennan Kiefel and Bell JJ).

[85] *Railroad Company v Howard* 74 US 392, 413 (1868) (Clifford J, for the Court).

[86] *Kirke La Shelle Co v Paul Armstrong Co* 263 NY 79; 188 NE 163 (1933); *Wood v Lucy, Lady Duff-Gordon* (1917) 118 NE 214, 222 NY 88 (US NY Supp) 91: 'every contract is instinct with an obligation, imperfectly expressed, of good faith' (Cardozo J) (defendant appointed plaintiff as agent to market her products on a profit share arrangement, but then sought to directly market the products herself, keeping all the profits – held to be an agreement subject to good faith); *Carns v Bassick* 187

Of course, freedom of contract retains its adherents.[87]

Section 205 of the Restatement (Second) of Contracts (1981) states that every contract imposes upon each party a duty of good faith and fair dealing in performance and enforcement. Article 1-304 of the Uniform Commercial Code (2011) similarly states that every contract imposes an obligation of good faith in its performance or enforcement. The Code operates in all 50 States. Good faith is also part of the common law of each state.[88] In situations to which the Code applies good faith means honesty in fact and observance of reasonable commercial standards of fair dealing).[89] It was not similarly defined in the Restatement (Second). Notes to the Restatement (Second) indicate a difference in intended meaning of good faith in different contexts. In the context of a pure purchase, it might be limited to honesty,[90] but in the case of performance of contractual obligations, something more than honesty was intended. Here parties must remain faithful to the original purpose of the contract, meet the justified expectations of the other contracting party, and reflecting community standards of decency, fairness and reasonableness.[91]

The notes confirm that the fact the person accused of lack of good faith believed they were justified in what they did does not preclude a finding of bad faith. Further, bad faith can include inaction.[92] The notes further confirm that good faith obligations extend to enforcement. It requires that a contracting party not, for example, artificially contrive a dispute for strategic purposes, falsify information or make claims without believing them to be true, exploiting the other party's 'necessitous circumstances' to extract additional benefits not originally contracted for, rejecting performance for unstated reasons, failing to mitigate losses, and abusing power to determine whether or not the other party has performed, and/or termination.[93] The jurisdiction's long-standing commitment to good faith principles has been lauded as a commitment to fundamental objectives of justice, and justice according to law.[94] It is likely that an attempt to exclude good faith obligations will be held to violate public policy and will thus be void.[95]

App Div 280, 284; NYS 670, 673 (1919): 'the law reads good faith into every contract. Reasonableness is the rule for construing contracts and determining their implications'.

[87] 'Firms that have negotiated contracts are entitled to enforce them to the letter, even to the great discomfort of their trading partners, without being mulcted for lack of "good faith"': *Kham and Nate's Shoes No 2 Inc v First Bank of Whiting* 908 F (2d) 1351, 1357 (7th Cir, 1990) (Easterbrook J).

[88] A Miller and R Perry, 'Good Faith Performance' (2013) 98 *Iowa Law Review* 689, 692–93.

[89] 1-201 states that good faith means honesty in fact and observance of reasonable commercial standards of fair dealing in the trade; see for discussion A Farnsworth, 'Good Faith Performance and Commercial Reasonableness Under the Uniform Commercial Code' (1963) 30 *University of Chicago Law Review* 666.

[90] Farnsworth (n 89) 668.

[91] Section 205 Good Faith, Comment a.

[92] Section 205 Good Faith, Comments b and d.

[93] Section 205 Good Faith, Comment e.

[94] R Summers, 'The General Duty of Good Faith – Its Recognition and Conceptualization' (1982) 67 *Cornell Law Review* 810, 811.

[95] Miller and Perry (n 89) 693. It is also contrary to 1-302(b) of the *Uniform Commercial Code*. Compare *Kham & Nate's Shoes No 2 v First Bank* 908 F 2d 1351, 1357–58 (Seventh Circuit, 1990):

The Uniform Commercial Code also reflects a contextual approach to contractual interpretation.[96] It contemplates that the parties' agreement might be found in the express words of the contract, or by implication, including through past conduct, trade usage or actual performance. The Restatement (Second) reflects a similar sentiment.[97] In other words, it does not strictly apply the parol evidence rule.[98] The approach of the Uniform Commercial Code fits well with the relational view of contracting to be discussed below. As King puts it:

> Under the Uniform Commercial Code, the emphasis is less on there being some entity or thing known as contract. Instead, it is the relationship of the parties that is important. Consequently, the requirement of particular terms being present becomes unnecessary for a contract to be enforced. Once the courts find that there is a spark of consent that creates a general contractual relationship … the bulk of the contract is imposed by law. Hence, the courts may proceed to fill in the necessary missing terms. They may do so by looking to prior dealings, to usage in trade, or course of performance.[99]

It reflects a willingness to impose standards of fairness and reasonableness on contracting parties, particularly where there are gaps in the actual agreement the parties reached.[100]

An example of a context in which good faith has been implied concerns commercial leases. Typically, such leases permit the lessee to transfer their interest to another, provided the property owner gives their consent. United States courts have read in a good faith and fair dealing obligation into this type of clause, requiring that the lessor not withhold their consent arbitrarily and without good reason.[101] Similarly, an appellate court read into a contract apparently providing a lender with limitless discretion regarding the provision of further finance to a borrower that the discretion must be exercised reasonably. The parties had a long-running contractual relationship, and the borrower was in a vulnerable position.[102]

One of the chief scholarly adherents of good faith in contracting in the United States, Robert Summers, says that it is not helpful to attempt to define good faith

'when the contract is silent, principles of good faith … fill the gap. They do not block the use of terms that actually appear in the contract' (Judge Easterbrook) and similarly *Carma Developers v Marathon Developments California* 826 P 2d 710, 729 (Cal, 1992).

[96] S1-201(b)(3).

[97] S202(5). See for example *Nanakuli Paving & Rock Co v Shell Oil Co Inc* 664 F 2d 772 (Ninth Circuit, 1981) where the court referred to trade usage and the course of performance in implying a duty of 'price protection' into the parties' agreement.

[98] D King, 'Reshaping Contract Theory and Law: Death of Contracts Part I: Generalised Consent with Lawmade Obligations' (1994) 7 *Journal of Contract Law* 245, 266–67.

[99] ibid 268–69.

[100] H Dubroff, 'The Implied Covenant of Good Faith in Contract Interpretation and Gap-Filling: Reviling a Revered Relic' (2006) 80 *St John's Law Review* 559, 571–72.

[101] *Kendall v Ernest Pestana, Inc* 40 Cal 3d, 488; 709 P2d 827, 220 Cal Rptr 818 (1985).

[102] *KMC Co v Irving Trust Co* 757 F 2d 752 (Sixth Circuit, 1985). In another discretion case, the New Jersey Supreme Court stated the party with that power must not use it arbitrarily, capriciously and/or unreasonably, with the objective of preventing the other contracting party from enjoying the fruits of the contract. Such behaviour would not meet the parties' reasonable commercial expectations when they entered into the contract: *Wilson v Amerada Hess Corp* 773 A 2d 1121 (2001).

for the purposes of American law.[103] It should instead be seen as a fundamental general principle. It might be better seen as a lack of bad faith. He synthesised from the case law prior to his articles that examples of the kind of conduct that would be considered to demonstrate lack of good faith (bad faith) included evasion of the spirit of the parties' deal, lack of diligence and/or 'slacking off' in relation to performance, deliberately rendering substantial, but not total, performance of contractual obligations, abusing a power to determine whether or not the other party to the contract has met their obligations and/or termination power or attempting to interfere with, or decline to co-operate in, the other party's performance of their obligations.[104] He added over-reaching or 'weasling' contractual interpretations.[105] He added to this list further examples, including concealing defects in something pertaining to the contract, abusing bargaining power to coerce changes to the contract, failure to mitigate damages.[106] He extended it to pre-contractual behaviour, including negotiating without serious intent to contract,[107] abusing a power to break off negotiations, executing contracts without intending to perform them or recklessly disregarding likely inability to perform.[108] He stated his list was not intended to be exhaustive.

Others have argued that what underlies bad faith is the attempt to re-capture opportunities willingly given up when the contract was entered into – for example, the contract might contemplate an exclusive arrangement between parties. If one of them then seeks to do business with another, this would breach a good faith obligation. The party seeking to do this had voluntarily given up this opportunity when they entered into the contract. To now pursue it would be to act in bad faith.[109] On the other hand, it may be difficult to determine which opportunities were foregone in the likely event that the contract does not expressly state what they are.[110]

[103] R Summers, '"Good Faith in General Contract Law and the Sales Provisions of the Uniform Commercial Code' (1968) 54(2) *Virginia Law Review* 195, 215.

[104] Summers (n 94) 813. This list appears in Section 205 Good Faith, comment d.

[105] Summers (n 103) 217.

[106] ibid 203.

[107] He cited *Heyer Product Co v United States* 140 F Supp 409 (Court of Claims, 1956) where a court found that the customer had not invited bids in good faith, having pre-determined their preferred bidder, but sought to conceal this by engaging in an apparently open process.

[108] Summers (n 103) 216.

[109] S Burton, 'Breach of Contract and the Common Law Duty to Perform in Good Faith' (1980) 94 *Harvard Law Review* 369, 387–402; see *Carma Developers (California) Inc v Marathon Developments California Inc* 826 P 2d 710, 727 (Cal 1992) for an example where the Court, applying Burton's approach, stated that a contractual discretion had to be exercised for a purpose reasonably within the contemplation of the parties at the time of contracting; and *Richard Short Oil Co v Texaco Inc* 799 F 2d 415, 417 (Eighth Circuit, 1986) (introduction of a cap on rebates under the contract before parties signed a contract extension held not to be an attempt to recapture foregone opportunities). Miller and Perry (n 89) 710 state it is often difficult to determine whether opportunities have been foregone.

[110] T Diamond and H Foss, 'Proposed Standards for Evaluating When the Covenant of Good Faith and Fair Dealing Have Been Violated: A Framework for Resolving the Mystery' (1996) 47 *Hastings Law Journal* 585, 593–94.

Good faith requires an objective evaluation of the parties' conduct.[111] The Restatement contemplates the use of community standards in order to determine whether there has been a breach of a good faith obligation: 'good faith performance or enforcement of a contract … excludes a variety of types of conduct characterized as involving "bad faith" because they violate community standards of decency, fairness or reasonableness'.[112]

Similarly, Farnsworth states that

> Good faith performance has always required the cooperation of one party where it was necessary in order that the other might secure the expected benefits of the contract. And the standard for determining what cooperation was required has always been an objective standard, based on the decency, fairness or reasonableness of the community and not on the individual's own beliefs as to what might be decent, fair or reasonable. Both common sense and tradition dictate an objective standard for good faith performance.[113]

Industry standards will often be relevant in determining whether or not a party has complied with a good faith obligation.[114]

It should be conceded that United States courts have not been consistent in their understanding of the meaning of good faith, and how it applies to particular cases.[115]

Examples of situations where United States courts have found a lack of good faith have included agreeing with a party that, if they drop their legal claim, the promisor will sell their property and give the other party some of the proceeds. The promisor then delayed the sale for more than eight years. The court found that good faith required the promisor to sell within a reasonable time.[116] Where a contract contained an 'open price' provision,[117] or an 'open quantities' provision, the party exercising the discretion could not act unreasonably.[118] A party who rejects the other's performance without a satisfactory basis was held to be acting in bad faith.[119] Where a contract did not provide for a specific starting date, but delays caused by one of the contracting parties caused the other significant expense, the court found the delaying party had breached good faith.[120] In an insurance context where the insured had mistakenly failed to meet paperwork

[111] Summers (n 103) 204; citing *First National Bank v FC Trebein Co* 59 Ohio St 316, 324–25; 52 NE 834, 837 (1898).

[112] S205 cmt. A.

[113] Farnsworth (n 89) 672.

[114] *Eastern Air Lines Inc v Gulf Oil Corp* 415 F Supp 429, 436 (SD Fla 1975); *Cargill Global Trading v Applied Dev Co* 706 F Supp 2d 563, 581 (DNJ 2010). I am indebted to the article by Miller and Perry (n 89) in bringing many of these cases to my attention.

[115] S O'Byrne and R Cohen, 'The Contractual Principle of Good Faith and the Duty of Honesty in *Bhasin v Hrynew*' (2015) 53 *Alberta Law Review* 1, 25.

[116] *Simon v Etgen* 213 NY 589, 595; 107 NE 1066, 1067–68 (1915).

[117] *Pillois v Billingsley* 179 F 2d 205, 207 (Second Circuit, 1950).

[118] H Havighurst and S Berman, 'Requirement and Output Contracts' (1932) 27 *Illinois Law Review* 1, 13.

[119] *O'Hare v McGee*, 116 Pa Super 318, 323; 176 A 525, 526 (1935).

[120] *Kehm Corp v United States* 93 F Supp 620 (Ct Cl 1950).

requirements in making a claim, good faith required the insurer to assist the insured by explaining what was required, rather than remaining silent.[121] The Court interpreted an apparently open-ended power of one party to cancel a supply contract to require that any cancellation occur within a reasonable time of the contract date, as an aspect of good faith.[122] The Court refused to assist a contractor who, after agreeing to contract terms, walked off the project. He demanded to be paid a bonus in order to come back to the site, and the other party agreed. The Court refused to enforce the promise of a bonus. While clearly the case could have been decided in terms of consideration, the court noted its refusal to enforce the bonus was to avoid placing a premium on bad faith behaviour.[123]

A party was required to mitigate their losses; on a re-sale, after the first contract collapsed, the vendor was required to act with reasonable care, diligence and judgment, as part of a good faith obligation.[124] Courts have required a party exercising a termination at will clause to do so in good faith.[125] One case involved an employment relationship, where an employee was entitled to bonuses if sales were above a certain level. The employer had the power to change that level. The court held the power should not be interpreted to permit the employer to change the level for any reason, including seeking to deny the employee the benefit of a bonus.[126] Where parties formed a joint venture regarding a particular machine, it was a breach of good faith for one of them to subsequently develop an alternative, competing machine. This was an attempt to deny the plaintiff the benefits of the original contract.[127] On the other hand, some courts have declined to provide good faith protection in relation to termination of employment, particularly where the contract provides for terminations at will.[128] They view this as acting inconsistently with the express words of the contract.[129]

III. Canada

In a landmark, unanimous decision of the Supreme Court of Canada in *Bhasin v Hrynew*,[130] good faith was recognised as a general organising principle of the

[121] *Johnson v Scottish Union Insurance Co* 160 Tenn 152, 156; 22 SW 2d 362, 363 (1929).

[122] *Sylvan Crest Sand and Gravel Co v United States* 150 F 2d 642, 644 (Second Circuit, 1945).

[123] *Lingenfelder v Wainwright Brewing Co* 103 Mo 578, 15 SW 844 (1891).

[124] *Obrecht v Crawford* 175 Md 385; 2 A 2d 1 (1938).

[125] *J R Watkins Co v Rich* 254 Mich 82, 84–85, 235 NW 845, 846 (1931); *Busam Motor Sales v Ford Motor Co* 203 F 2d 469, 472 (Sixth Circuit, 1953). I am indebted to Summers (n 103) 195 for the references to these American decisions.

[126] *Tymshare Inc v Covell* 727 F 2d 1145 (DC Cir 1984).

[127] *Universal Sales Corp v California Press Manufacturing Co* 128 P 2d 665, 677 (Cal 1942).

[128] *Guz v Bechtel National Inc* 8 P 3d 1089, 1100 (Cal. 2000) stating that an employer 'may act peremptorily, arbitrarily or inconsistently, without providing specific protections such as prior warning, fair procedures, objective evaluation or preferential reassignment'.

[129] *Brehany v Nordstrom Inc* 812 P 2d 49, 55 (Utah, 1991).

[130] [2014] 3 SCR 494. See for discussion O'Byrne and Cohen (n 115); J McCamus, 'The New General Principles of Good Faith Performance and the New Rule of Honesty in Performance in Canadian

common law of contract. The case concerned a long-term distribution agreement. Bhasin was to sell the products of Can-Am (the defendant) exclusively. Contracts were for a three-year period, and had been rolled over on previous occasions. Bhasin's distributorship had been financially successful. Can-Am entered into discussions with Hrynew, a competitor of Bhasin, regarding a possible merger between those parties. Bhasin was not interested in pursuing this option. The defendant then appointed Hrynew to an auditing position, which entitled him to access private details of Bhasin's business. Bhasin refused to co-operate with Hrynew's requests. Can-Am told Bhasin that Hrynew had an obligation to keep details of Bhasin's business confidential, and that a government regulator had refused his efforts to put someone other than Hrynew in the role. These claims were not true. At the end of the latest three-year agreement, the defendant told Bhasin his distributorship contract would not be renewed, and most of that business was given to Hrynew. Bhasin brought action against the Can-Am, on the basis that it had breached its good faith obligations to him. The Court found in Bhasin's favour.

Cromwell J (for the Court) noted that good faith had 'deep roots' in contract law, and infused many of its current rules.[131] He acknowledged that the common law had generally eschewed adoption of a specific good faith doctrine. He said the consequence of this was unsettled and incoherent, piecemeal legal rules. It sometimes meant that results were not consistent with the reasonable expectations of those engaged in contracting.[132] The law of implied terms was sometimes strained in respect of good faith, given its general requirement of 'business efficacy' in order to imply terms.[133] The traditional distinction between implication in fact or in law was blurred; in some cases it was not clear which of them was being applied.[134]

He indicated that the common law of Canadian contract should now recognise a general organising principle of good faith in contractual performance.[135] Many principles of the common law already had good faith as their underlying

Contract Law' (2015) 32 *Journal of Contract Law* 103; J Robertson, 'Good Faith as an Organising Principle in Contract Law: *Bhasin v Hrynew* – Two Steps Forward and One Look Back' (2015) 93 *Canadian Bar Review* 809.

[131] *Bhasin v Hrynew* (n 130) [32].

[132] ibid [41].

[133] ibid [48]; similarly D Percy, 'The Emergence of Good Faith as a Principle of Contract Performance' in Se Degeling, J Edelman and J Goudkamp (eds), *Contracts in Commercial Law* (Sydney, LawBook Co, 2016) 254: 'the weakness of the common law is its tendency to deal with good faith only indirectly through devices that do not explicitly confront the issues at stake. The adoption of an express principle of good faith forces courts to examine closely the types of conduct that they wish to discourage rather than … through the implication of a term or the manipulative interpretation of the contract which may well not truly reflect the parties' intentions'.

[134] *Bhasin v Hrynew* (n 130) [52].

[135] ibid [33]. On the debate between a 'universalist' approach and a formalist approach, see former Chief Justice of Canada Beverley McLachlin, 'The Evolution of the Law of Private Obligation: The Influence of Justice La Forest' in R Johnson et al, *Gerard V La Forest on the Supreme Court of Canada 1985–1997* (Winnipeg, Canadian Legal History Project, 2000) 22: 'universalism seeks the broad, general principles underlying the imposition of responsibility and the corresponding rights of recovery. It seeks to rationalize both the disparate branches of the law and the doctrine within those branches.

(unstated) rationale.[136] One principle associated with this organising principle was a duty of act honestly in the performance of contractual obligations. This would bring the law closer to meeting the reasonable expectations of contracting parties. Basic honesty was necessary to ensure contracts could function effectively, and dishonesty would be contrary to the parties' reasonable and legitimate expectations.[137] It also required that parties perform their contractual duties reasonably, and not capriciously or arbitrarily.[138] The organising principle of good faith should be applied dynamically and in a context-sensitive manner.[139] It would have more scope, for example, in a long-term contract than a transactional exchange.[140] It was not fiduciary in nature, but it did require that contracting parties not act to undermine the other contracting party's interests.[141] Parties would need to have due regard to the legitimate interests of the other contracting party.[142] Cromwell J was mindful of concerns that the good faith doctrine would lead to uncertainty or subjectivity. He specifically noted it was not a green light to judicial moralism or 'palm tree justice' and should not be used to scrutinize the motives of contracting parties.[143] As such, he viewed any impact of the doctrine on freedom of contract to be minimal.

Because Cromwell J viewed good faith as a general organising principle, he did not need to determine whether it should be implied in fact or in law. That was irrelevant.[144] He said it was a norm which operated irrespective of the parties' intentions.[145] To this end, any attempt by contracting parties to exclude it would be ineffective.[146] He said there was no need for him to exhaustively define the content of the good faith obligation, as it would be developed gradually through the case law, in line with common law tradition. He cited to McCamus' three examples where good faith was held to exist, including where parties must cooperate in order to reach the objectives of the contract, where discretionary contract power

Principle is prime; broad considerations of policy are paramount … (whereas with formalism) … the primary task is to discover the correct rule and apply it'.

[136] *Bhasin v Hrynew* (n 130) [42].

[137] ibid [60].

[138] ibid [63]. This is particularly noteworthy, since Percy (n 133) observes that Canadian commercial leases commonly provide that the property owner's consent is required for any proposed sub-lease of the premises by the tenant, *and that such consent may be arbitrarily withheld* (242). The Canadian Supreme Court's acceptance of a generalised good faith doctrine applicable to all contracts and all exercises of contractual discretion, and an acceptance of a requirement of reasonableness and non-acceptance of arbitrariness, calls that practice into serious question.

[139] *Bhasin v Hrynew* (n 130) [64].

[140] ibid [69].

[141] ibid [65].

[142] ibid [65].

[143] ibid [70].

[144] This was a substantial departure from past cases that had implied good faith into a contract: *Honda Canada Inc v Keays* [2008] 2 SCR 362, 391 (Bastarache J, for McLachlin CJ Binnie Deschamps Abella Charron and Rothstein JJ).

[145] *Bhasin v Hrynew* (n 130) [74].

[146] ibid [75]. In this way, it is similar to a doctrine such as unconscionability: O'Byrne and Cohen (n 115) 11.

existed, and where one contracting party sought to evade contractual obligations, as examples.[147] These were not the only possible applications.

Cromwell J found that Can-Am had breached its honesty obligation in not telling Bhasin the truth about Hrynew's auditing role and its impact on confidentiality. Can-Am was clearly internally moving to a 'merger' of the business of Bhasin and Hrynew or, on one view, a takeover. However, it did not tell Bhasin of its plans. When confronted about it, they were evasive. Their attempts to deflect Bhasin's concerns about the appointment of Hrynew as an auditor were dishonest. The Court awarded Bhasin damages of $87 000, representing an expectation loss – what his business would have been worth if Can-Am had met its honesty obligations.

The Supreme Court applied these principles subsequently in *C M Callow Inc v Zollinger*.[148] There a group of apartment owners enter into a maintenance contract with a contractor. The contract would be terminated without reason with 10 days' notice. The group led the contractor to believe that they were satisfied with the quality of their work, and that a new contract would be entered into when the current one expired. However, when the time came to renew the contract, it was not in fact renewed. Eight of the nine justices found that the group had breached its obligation to act honestly in relation to a contract by leading the contractor to believe they would be retained.[149] The Court reiterated its views in Bhasin about good faith being a general organising principle, encompassing the obligation to act honestly but reaching beyond it. It required parties to have appropriate regard to the interests of the other contracting party, and not to act dishonestly, unreasonably,

[147] ibid [47], citing J McCamus, *The Law of Contracts* 2nd edn (Toronto, Irwin Law, 2012) 840–56. These examples were taken from the Canadian case law. Regarding the first, in *Dynamic Transport Pty Ltd v OK Detailing Ltd* [1978] 2 SCR 1072 the contract required that planning permission be obtained. The vendor was the only party practically able to obtain such permission. The Court implied an obligation on their part to take reasonable steps to obtain it. Regarding the second, in *Mitsui & Co (Canada) Ltd v Royal Bank of Canada* [1995] 2 SCR 187 where the contract provided for the purchase of a leased asset at reasonable market value as determined by the lessor, the Court implied a requirement that this discretion be exercised in an objectively reasonable way. Regarding the third, in *Mason v Freedman* [1958] SCR 483 the contract entitled the vendor to avoid the contract if they were 'unable or unwilling' to remove a particular defect in title. The vendor sought to rely on this clause. The court limited the scope of its application to not include situations where the vendor themselves brought about the failure to satisfy the condition, or where they acted in an arbitrary and/or capricious fashion. In *Honda Canada Inc v Keays* [2008] 2 SCR 362 the Court had implied a duty of good faith into an employment contract, and implied a duty of fair dealing in tendering processes in *Martel Building Ltd v Canada* [2000] 2 SCR 860. Subsequent cases have suggested it might include a duty of disclosure in appropriate cases: *1250264 Ontario Inc v Pet Valu Canada Ltd* [2015] ONSC 29, [58] (Belobaba J). Good faith might explain a case such as *Re Lister Ltd v Dunlop Canada Ltd* [1982] 1 SCR 726 where the court insisted that a creditor, seeking to enforce a contractual clause pursuant to which, in the event of breach, all future monies payable under the contract were immediately owing, must give the debtor adequate notice and opportunity to make good their default before applying this contractual remedy. This reflected a line of cases including *Massey v Sladen* (1868) LR 4 Ex 13; *Toms v Wilson and Another* (1863) 4 B & S 442; 122 ER 524; *Moore v Shelley and Another* (1883) 8 AC 285 (PC).

[148] [2020] SCC 45.

[149] Kasirer J (for Wagner CJ Abella Karakatsanis and Martin JJ, with whom Brown J (for Moldaver and Rowe JJ) agreed; Cote J dissenting.

capriciously and/or arbitrarily.[150] It may include a duty to cooperate.[151] This was an improvement to the piecemeal approach of the previous law. It was not an implied term, and was applied to all contracts and all contractual obligations and rights.[152] It was not possible for parties to contract out of the obligation. Five justices found that the damages payable for breach of the honesty obligation were based on the expectation interest, not the reliance interest.[153] In contrast, three of the justices found such damages should be based on the reliance interest.[154]

A slightly different context arose for the Court's further consideration of the application of the doctrine in *Wastech Services Ltd v Greater Vancouver Sewerage and Drainage District*.[155] There the respondent engaged the appellant to dispose of waste for which it was responsible. The appellant had multiple waste management facilities, and the respondent could direct waste to any of these facilities in quantities it choose. The fees relating to the use of each facility varied. The respondent decided to reallocate waste from one facility to another which was closer. This resulted in a substantial reduction in the fees payable to the appellant under the contract. It meant that the appellant could not meet its profit target for the year. It argued that the respondent had breached its contractual good faith obligation by exercising its discretion in this way. This case gave the court to determine how, if at all, the good faith obligation impacted on an apparently broad, if not absolute, contractual discretion.

Consistently with the previous cases, the Court here determined that a party to a contract who could exercise a discretion or power must do so reasonably.[156] In this context, reasonably meant consistently with the purposes underlying the discretion.[157] The power could not be exercised in an arbitrary and/or capricious fashion.[158] It was not 'reasonable' in the administrative law sense of Wednesbury unreasonableness.[159] It did not require the party with the discretion to subordinate their interests to that of the other contracting party, nor did it require them to confer a benefit on the other contracting party not contemplated at the time of contracting.[160] The Court confirmed the list of existing doctrines reflecting

[150] (n 149) [47] (Kasirer J, for Wagner CJ Abella Karaksatsanis and Martin JJ).
[151] ibid [87] (Kasirer J, for Wagner CJ Abella Karakatsanis and Martin JJ).
[152] ibid [53] (Kasirer J, for Wagner CJ Abella Karaksatsanis and Martin JJ).
[153] ibid [109] (Kasirer J, for Wagner CJ Abella Karaksatsanis and Martin JJ).
[154] ibid [139] (Brown J, for Moldaver and Rowe JJ).
[155] [2021] SCC 7.
[156] ibid [4]–[5] (Kasirer J, for Wagner CJ Abella Moldaver Karakatsanis and Martin JJ).
[157] ibid [4] (Kasirer J, for Wagner CJ Abella Moldaver Karakatsanis and Martin JJ); [129] (Brown and Rowe JJ, for Cote).
[158] In this way, the Canadian approach to the exercise of contractual discretion is similar to the view expressed by the United Kingdom Supreme Court in *British Telecommunications Plc v Telefonica O2 UK Ltd* [2014] UKSC 42, [37] (Lord Sumption, with whom Lords Neuberger Mance Toulson and Hodge agreed).
[159] In other words, exercise of a power or discretion so unreasonable that no reasonable person could have done so: *Associated Provincial Picture Houses Ltd v Wednesbury Corporation* [1948] 1 KB 223, 280 (Lord Greene MR, for the Court of Appeal).
[160] (n 156) [6] (Kasirer J, for Wagner CJ Abella Moldaver Karakatsanis and Martin JJ).

good faith was not closed; it could be developed incrementally if gaps in the law became apparent. However, the Court's role here was limited, having due regard to the importance of private ordering and the need for certainty in commercial affairs.[161] The Court would not overturn the exercise of discretion simply because it believed it to be unfair, unwise or 'morally opportune', as long as it was exercised consistently with the purpose of the discretion.[162] The Court added that, where the discretionary power related to something capable of objective measurement, the scope of 'reasonable' exercise would likely be narrower than where it was not.[163] Again, the duty to exercise discretion reasonably, as an aspect of the duty to act in good faith, was not an implied term. It operated irrespective of the parties' intentions.[164] The Court said the impact on freedom of contract was minimal, because it sought to reflect the parties' bargain and only required discretion to be exercised according to the purposes of the contract as contemplated by the parties in their agreement.[165]

IV. Internationally

Article 1.7 of the UNIDROIT Principles of Contract Law require contracting parties to act in accordance with good faith and fair dealing in the context of international trade. This includes during the negotiation process, and in relation to a request to re-negotiate. Good faith, fair dealing and reasonableness apply to the implication of terms according to these general principles (Articles 4.8 and 5.1.2). Section 7 of the United Nations Convention on Contracts for the International Sale of Goods require its terms be interpreted having regard to good faith in international trade. It is required by section 242 of the German Civil Code.

A. Reflections on Good Faith in Comparable Jurisdictions

The first point to note is the common difficulty among jurisdictions in defining what is meant by good faith, including whether it is limited to a requirement of honesty or whether it extends to reasonableness. The split is evident in *Meehan v Jones* where Gibbs CJ claimed it was limited to honesty, while Mason J stated it included reasonableness. It must be conceded that the court did not expressly use

[161] ibid [51] (Kasirer J, for Wagner CJ Abella Moldaver Karakatsanis and Martin JJ).
[162] ibid [71], [73](Kasirer J, for Wagner CJ Abella Moldaver Karakatsanis and Martin JJ).
[163] ibid [77] (Kasirer J, for Wagner CJ Abella Moldover Karakatsanis and Martin JJ).
[164] ibid [91] (Kasirer J, for Wagner CJ Abella Moldover Karakatsanis and Martin JJ). The judgment of Brown and Rowe JJ (for Cote) took a slightly different position on this. It said the purpose of a discretion was defined by the parties' intentions. By this logic, if it were clear that the parties intended that a contractual discretion be absolute in nature, not conditioned by a requirement of reasonableness, these justices would enforce it in this manner: [133].
[165] ibid [92]–[93] (Kasirer J, for Wagner CJ Abella Moldover Karakatsanis and Martin JJ).

the words 'good faith' there – it was merely considering the exercise of a contractual discretion. It was in the 1990s, and notably in lower courts, where good faith was eventually accepted and applied. Notably, the High Court of Australia has still not indicated whether or not it accepts a doctrine of contractual good faith and, if so, what its contours might be. It has pointedly left the question open. This has had the predictable effect that lower courts continue to divide on whether a good faith obligation exists, and what it might entail. Respectfully, the High Court of Australia must grasp the nettle, and provide definitive guidance. The High Court has in the past criticised lower courts for developing the law. However, the criticism necessarily implies the High Court's willingness to provide the needed leadership and guidance. In this instance, respectfully this has not yet been forthcoming.

The second point is the clear difference of opinion among Australian judges regarding whether, if a doctrine of good faith is to be applied in Australian contract law, it is to be an implied term (and if so, what kind) or whether it is a general organising principle. In *Renard* Priestley JA indicated it would be implied at law or in fact; in *Burger King* the New South Wales Court of Appeal stated it should be implied at law to a particular class of contracts. Doubt attends what that class is or should be. Alternatively, Finn J in *Hughes Aircraft Systems* preferred to view good faith as a general organising idea of Australian contract law, a standard to which all contracting parties would be expected to adhere.

This also seems to have been the approach of the Canadian Supreme Court in Bhasin. Respectfully, there is much to be commended in that decision. The Court there similarly accepted good faith as a general organising principle of the common law of contract, thus obviating application of the narrow rules regarding the implication of terms. That court also rightly observed the long history of good faith in the common law. It was also right in my view to effectively criticise the piecemeal, case by case approach expressly adopted in England, on the basis it led to an incoherent, messy set of rules that did not always meet the parties' reasonable expectations, as it claimed to do. That Court was also right to point out that good faith already implicitly underpinned many principles of Canadian contract law; thus, it was hardly a 'radical' approach (as Lord Burrows claimed in Pakistan International) to expressly adopt it as a general principle.

Another aspect of the Canadian approach that can be supported is its refusal to apply notions of so-called Wednesbury unreasonableness in its consideration of whether good faith obligations had been met. Obviously, notions of Wednesbury unreasonableness were developed in a very different context – to effectively constrain the ability of an individual to obtain a remedy in administrative law for a decision made by a public official. This was in a system of parliamentary supremacy where restrictions on the power of parliament and the executive are notoriously very thin. Though I personally disagree with Wednesbury unreasonableness even in that context, it might have a stronger basis in the context of a system of parliamentary supremacy – a deliberately very narrow basis upon which an individual can effectively challenge the decision of a government official. While one must always consider the possible portability of legal principle from one context to another, it does not make much sense to me to transfer a doctrine conceived in that light and in that context and consistently with parliamentary supremacy to the entirely different context of private law. In its focus on rationality it also bears an uncomfortable similarity to notions of freedom of contract – the assumption being the law should only interfere with the exercise of contractual power where its exercise is irrational. Though views might reasonably differ on this, my own view is that the scope of the court's ability to review contracts must be broader than in the days of freedom of contract – this takes the scope of the court's review jurisdiction beyond bare rationality.

The United States Supreme Court has accepted good faith in relation to contracts since the 1860s and it is reflected in the Restatement (Second) of Contracts and Uniform Commercial Code operative throughout the nation. It embraces notions of reasonableness, fairness and community standards. There are numerous helpful examples of conduct indicating a lack of good faith in the commentary to the Restatement and the case law. While many of these would or may find a remedy under existing doctrines of the common law (other than good faith), not all of them would. Thus, the list is helpful in demonstrating that acceptance of good faith would make some material difference to the law, though not in a radical way. The United States law also appropriately emphasises the parties' relationship, and considers arrangements in their broader context. It is less concerned with terms of the written contract, at least as the exclusive determinant of rights and obligations.

The fact that good faith has been adopted and applied in the UNIDROIT Principles of Contract Law and the UN Convention on Contracts for the International Sale of Goods tends to undercut arguments that adoption of good faith would lead to unacceptable levels of uncertainty in commercial arrangements, as suggested in Pakistan International.

7

Introduction to Relational Contract Theory and the Work of Ian Macneil

I. Empirical Studies

An important empirical study of the behaviour of those commonly engaged in contracting was conducted by Stewart Macaulay.[1] Macaulay interviewed nearly 70 business people and lawyers representing 43 companies and six law firms. He was interested in their views regarding contracting, and resolving contracting disputes. As had been discussed earlier in the book, there is a deep historical experience of commercial law being influenced by commercial practice, typified by the law merchant. Thus, empirical study of the attitudes of business people towards contracting is of particular interest in the current context.

The author himself acknowledged the sample was not purported to be representative, and sample bias was possible. That said, the study contained very interesting findings of high relevance. First, Macaulay concluded that there was much less emphasis on the terms of the written contract than what had been anticipated. Contracts often lack important details.[2] Often parties sought to rely on their own standard terms, which were typically different from that of the other party, without an attempt to reconcile or compromise these different terms.[3] Those engaged in business tend to rely on the parties' established relationship, even when the transaction potentially involves serious risk. They preferred to rely on the 'common honesty and decency' of individuals, not written contractual terms.[4] Though contracts typically outlined the parties' major obligations, they often did not provide detail around consequences if either party did not meet contractual expectations. The parties often expect gaps in the contract to be filled by custom and practice within the industry.[5]

[1] S Macaulay, 'Non-Contractual Relations in Business: A Preliminary Study' (1963) 28(1) *American Sociological Review* 55.

[2] ibid 58–60.

[3] ibid 59.

[4] ibid 58.

[5] ibid 62–63. For doubts about the existence of industry standards see L Bernstein, 'The Questionable Empirical Basis of Article 2's Incorporation Strategy: A Preliminary Study' (1999) 66 *University of Chicago Law Review* 710.

Some business people reported their fear (or, perhaps, lived experience) that if the contract were extremely detailed as to performance expectations, they would experience performance according to the 'letter', rather than the 'spirit' of it. It might also suggest a lack of trust by one of the parties towards the other.[6] Detailed contractual terms might impede the development of a good relationship between the parties. Business people sometimes welcomed a degree of vagueness in contractual arrangements, in order to provide needed flexibility as the contract plays out.

Business people were extremely conscious of their business reputation. They wished to continue in business, and were aware that if they got a reputation for non-delivery, their reputation would be damaged. Promises had to be kept. Similarly, if they got a reputation for being overly-aggressive and/or litigious in relation to contracting disputes, this might negatively impact their business in future.[7] Legal action for breach of contract was extremely rare.[8] One business person pointed out that contractual disputes were better handled by the parties themselves, and that lawyers 'just do not understand the give-and-take needed in business'.[9] Parties would regularly adjust contractual arrangements, perhaps with some informally agreed compensation for losses associated with such adjustment.

Beale and Dugdale reached broadly similar conclusions with their empirical study involving approximately 20 engineering manufacturers.[10] They found that although there was typically express agreement on basic terms, firms typically relied on customs and 'unwritten laws' to fill gaps in their contract.[11] There was a large degree of trust among contracting firms. There was a general belief in mutual fairness. It was important to build and maintain a reputation for acting fairly, as well as being efficient. It was typically expressed that attempts to 'hide behind' express contractual terms would not be well accepted by the other contracting party. Typically, the desire to do business with others in future was paramount in the mind of those surveyed. Survey respondents reported that each side had to give concessions and to do so in a spirit of co-operation, in order to nurture the parties' contractual relationship.[12] For example, parties would sometimes repair damaged goods at no charge, though there was no legal requirement for them to do so.[13]

[6] Macaulay (n 1) 64.

[7] ibid 63.

[8] This finding is replicated elsewhere: F Schultz, 'The Firm Offer Puzzle: A Study of Business Practice in the Construction Industry' (1952) 19 *University of Chicago Law Review* 237, 283.

[9] Macaulay (n 1) 61.

[10] H Beale and T Dugdale, 'Contracts Between Businessmen: Planning and the Use of Contractual Remedies' (1975) 2(1) *British Journal of Law and Society* 45.

[11] ibid 47.

[12] ibid 47–48.

[13] See also T Daintith, 'The Design and Performance of Long-Term Contracts' in T Daintith and G Teubner (eds), *Contract and Organisation: Legal Analysis in the Light of Social and Economic Theory* (Berlin, De Gruyter, 1986) 164, 186: 'in most cases, today, the parties are performing a relationship different from that written in the contract, in which non-contractual norms like fairness in

Like Macaulay, Beale and Dugdale found that those surveyed typically eschewed legal remedies, and lawyers. Again, there was evident sentiment that legal representatives did not understand the needs of business.[14] It was often felt that reliance on customs and 'unwritten laws' was more effective commercially than resort to formal legal rights and duties. Beale and Dugdale concluded that commercial practice should influence the commercial law,[15] obviously reflective of the law merchant and the time of Lord Mansfield.

A study by Arrighetti, Bachmann and Deakin involved 62 firms across mining and kitchen furniture manufacturing in Germany, Britain and Italy.[16] This study reached some similar conclusions as the above two studies, but also found that the written contract played an important part in regulating the parties' relationship. These authors detected the kind of preference for co-operation, give-and-take and flexibility of the other studies, but noted that this attitude was not antithetical to the written contract. It supplemented, but did not replace it, in actual contractual practice.[17] Those surveyed typically reflected the long-term nature of their relationship with numerous contracting parties.

After noting that German and Italian law recognise good faith, but that British law generally has not, the authors observe that there was a significant difference in the stated likelihood of those surveyed to take legal action against a customer or supplier alleged to have committed a breach of contract. According to the survey 60 per cent of British firms surveyed indicated they were 'very likely', 'fairly likely' or 'likely' to take such legal action. For firms in Italy that figure was 21 per cent and for firms in Germany 5 per cent.[18] Admittedly this is from a small sample size. If these figures are broadly reflective of the practice on a larger scale, of course there may be a number of different reasons for this. The researchers point out, for example, that institutional norms of contracting behaviour, including guidelines by trade associations, for example, play a more prominent role in contracting in Germany than in Britain. Thus, it would be simplistic to conclude that the legal attitude of the jurisdictions towards a good faith basis of contracting is somehow related to these apparently significantly different attitudes towards litigation. However, it is an interesting finding in the

quantity reductions, may be more important than contractual ones', and I Ramsay, 'Consumer Redress Mechanisms for Poor-Quality and Defective Products' (1981) 31 *University of Toronto Law Journal* 117, 129.

[14] (n 10) 59.

[15] ibid 60.

[16] A Arrighetti, R Bachmann and S Deakin, 'Contract Law, Social Norms and Inter-Firm Co-Operation' (1997) 21 *Cambridge Journal of Economics* 171.

[17] 'The very stability of the underlying relationships and the expectation that potential contracting partners will respect general norms orientated towards co-operative behaviour creates substantial scope for … flexibility beyond contract in the form of ad hoc understandings, close personal ties and give-and-take in the resolution of disputes … the flexibility here is not achieved in spite of or regardless of the contract, but … built on a foundation of formalised contractual understandings which are underpinned in turn by the stable system of norms external to the contract' (ibid 190).

[18] ibid 187–88.

current context. The authors noted the 'key feature of the concept of good faith … as a bridge between formal contract doctrine and inform norms and standards in the commercial community'.[19]

In the rail freight context, Palay found parties to a contract were often reluctant to take short-term advantages available to them under the strict terms of the contract, if they were likely to have long-term deleterious effects on the parties' contractual relationships.[20] There was evidence parties engaged in behaviour not required by the written contract in order to facilitate the parties' ongoing positive relationships.[21] Parties ranked highly the tendency of contracting parties to be flexible, including in terms of varying contractual arrangements in response to a material change in circumstances.[22]

Lisa Bernstein studied both the cotton[23] and diamond[24] industries in detail. She broadly found that contracting parties placed great value on long-term contracting relationships.[25] Non-legal sanctions, such as loss of reputation, were extremely important motivators towards performance in accordance with the other party's expectations.[26] Parties particularly valued flexibility from the other side, including the willingness to re-negotiate contracts when circumstances had materially changed.[27] Those surveyed indicated their wish to resolve contract breach by requiring the party failing to honour their promise/s to do so, rather than merely being held liable to pay compensatory damages.[28] Transaction costs are lowered in a situation where contracting parties have a high degree of trust in the other.[29] Parties have incentives to engage co-operatively, rather than adversarially, with the other.[30] Written contracts were typically not seen as containing

[19] ibid 180.

[20] T Palay, 'Comparative Institutional Economics: The Governance of Rail Freight Contracting' (1984) 13 *Journal of Legal Studies* 265, 276.

[21] ibid 277.

[22] ibid 282.

[23] Lisa Bernstein, 'Private Commercial Law in the Cotton Industry: Creating Cooperation Through Rules, Norms and Institutions' (2001) 99 *Michigan Law Review* 1724.

[24] Lisa Bernstein, 'Opting out of the Legal System: Extra-Legal Contractual Relations in the Diamond Industry' (1992) 21 *Journal of Legal Studies* 115.

[25] (n 23) 1770: 'Most transactors view contracting relationships as long-term and indeterminate in length. Many trading relationships span entire careers and transactors strongly prefer to deal with people they have done business with in the past'.

[26] ibid 1745.

[27] ibid 1748–49.

[28] ibid 1755.

[29] ibid 1763.

[30] 'Transactors have an incentive not to behave opportunistically. Although a transactor can still obtain a short-term benefit form defection, he will realize that an act of defection will likely trigger a sequence of non-cooperative responses (most likely refusals to deal) both from his transacting partner, and depending on the type of breach, from a certain number of other market participants. Because these noncooperative responses tend to reduce his future trading opportunities, the long-run cost of defection will often be greater than the short-term gain from defection, so a transactor who is not in financial distress is more likely to cooperate than to defect' (ibid 1764).

all of the parties' rights and obligations, needing to be supplemented to take account of changing circumstances.[31]

Russell Weintraub surveyed approximately 80 businesses of various sizes in the United States regarding their contracting practices.[32] Approximately 90 per cent of them responded that they entered into long-term contracts for the purchase or supply of goods or services.[33] Asked what they would do if there were a change in market prices, such that a supplier requested an adjustment to the contract price, 95 per cent said they would not always insist upon the originally agreed price.[34] About 76 per cent said it would depend on whether the request was reasonable according to trade practice, and about 80 per cent said it would depend whether the relationship with the company had been good in the past. More than 80 per cent indicated they had requested modification of the contract terms during the life of the contract.[35] Weintraub emphasised the need for contract rules to mimic and reflect contract practice.

Recently, a survey of more than 250 small and medium enterprises was conducted in Australia in relation to their contracting practice.[36] Unlike many of the surveys above, this survey was not limited to particular industries. It was also significantly larger, thus reducing the risk of sampling error. One of the things it asked respondents about was whether they had ever paid a contractor more than the original contracting price. A significant proportion had. Asked why, typically respondents referred to achieving satisfactory completion of the contract and/or maintaining good relations between the parties. The author concluded that his findings 'corroborate Macaulay's early findings that businesspeople prefer to rely on trust than formalities as the basis of their contractual relationships'.[37] The author also noted great reluctance for contracting parties to resort to legal remedies in the event of an alleged breach of contract. He concluded that such attitudes 'seemingly bespeaks the unwritten conventions of business, which as Macaulay and others have found, favour flexibility, cooperation, and non-legal discourse over resort to the black letter … this foster(s) and maintain good relations'.[38] He reaches a similar conclusion to Beale and Dugdale on the consequences of the findings for commercial law, that 'if decades of research tells us that market players consistently disregard contract law, then it loses its legitimacy and fails in its principal duty of regulating and efficiently facilitating market exchange'.[39]

[31] 'By using written contracts and varying them through extra-legal understandings that may be better tailored to the needs of work-a-day interactions, transactors may be able to capture execution cost savings and reduce the likelihood of relationship breakdown' (ibid 1780).

[32] R Weintraub, 'A Survey of Contract Practice and Policy' [1992] *Wisconsin Law Review* 1.

[33] ibid 16.

[34] ibid 18.

[35] ibid 22.

[36] M Giancaspro, 'Renegotiation in the Real World: A Study of Australian Small to Medium-Sized Enterprises, Contract Variation and the Law' (2022) 41(3) *University of Queensland Law Journal* 299.

[37] ibid 319.

[38] ibid 321–22.

[39] ibid 324.

This empirical work is closely aligned with relational contract theory. This is because relational contract theory reflects how humans typically do behave in contracting situations, seeking to explain why they do so.[40] This is in contrast to traditional contract law rules, based on will theory and that individuals are rational utility maximisers in an abstract, non-empirically based manner. It is to a discussion of relational contract theorists that this chapter now turns.

II. Scholarship of Ian Macneil

Ian Macneil, together with Stewart Macaulay, are the chief architects of the theory of relational contracting.[41] The theory suggests a very different way of considering contractual relations than the traditional model. Macneil would embrace the kind of empirical work referred to above. He would consider it supportive of his idea that traditional rules of contract fail to reflect the reality of many commercial transactions. Before we consider the ways in which Macneil and others argue that they fail to reflect the reality of commercial transactions, let us consider the implications of the premise, if it were true. If it were the fact that commercial law does not reflect common commercial and contracting practice, this would generally lead to suggestions that commercial law should change to better reflect common commercial practice. This is on the assumption that law should be broadly reflective of the society it serves. The argument has a particular cogency in the context of commercial law, given the deep historical links between commercial practice and commercial law, through the law merchant. Judges and scholars have often made the point about the difficulty that would arise if there is a large gap between commercial law and commercial practice, though concededly some dismiss the problem, even after acknowledging it. My own view is that it is not a satisfactory situation, if it were found that there is a mismatch between commercial practice and commercial law. It is to a broader consideration of whether that is so that this chapter now turns, primarily through a consideration of the views of expert scholars in the field. Macneil and Macaulay deserve special recognition for their leadership in this space.

Macneil's very significant and influential academic writings in this space are heavily cited.[42] It has been suggested that 'most legal scholars accept the core

[40] I Macneil, 'Values in Contract: Internal and External' (1983) 78(2) *Northwestern University Law Review* 340, 408.

[41] Earlier authors had developed similar themes in France: G Renaud, *La Theorie de L'Institution* (1930); R Savatier, *Les Metamorphoses Economiques et Sociales Du Droit Civil D'Aujourd'hui* (2nd ed, 1952), cited and discussed in G Gottlieb, 'Relationism: Legal Theory for a Relational Society' (1983) 50 *University of Chicago Law Review* 567, 585–88.

[42] Some of the leading contributions are I Macneil, 'The Many Futures of Contracts' (1974) 47 *Southern California Law Review* 691; 'Contracts: Adjustment of Long-Term Economic Relations Under Classical, Neoclassical and Relational Contract Law' (1978) 72(6) *Northwestern University Law Review* 854; 'Economic Analysis of Contractual Relations: Its Shortfalls and the Need for a "Rich Classificatory

insight of what is called relational contract theory'.[43] I will summarise his views as succinctly as I can.

III. Discrete versus Relational Contracting

Macneil states that traditional contract law assumes the parties are in a one-off, discrete transaction (also known as a 'transactional' view of contracting). This is also the basis of traditional microeconomics.[44] They have no prior relationship, and no planned future relationship. In this environment, an adversarial relationship exists between contracting parties, each seeking to maximise their own benefit under the contract, at the expense of the other contracting party. Parties are rational utility maximisers, and able to negotiate with others on the basis of broadly equal bargaining power, equal levels of information, and so on. This means that the fact that terms of the contract are on one view unfair is irrelevant.[45] In other words, it is of assistance to those who in fact have superior bargaining power, by effectively assuming that it does not exist.[46]

Macneil suggests this assumption is misplaced. He says that, instead, most contracts are not discrete in nature, but relational. It is more nuanced than this – Macneil speaks of a spectrum, with an entirely discrete transaction at one end, and an entirely relational one at the other.[47] Contracts will typically comprise both discrete and relational aspects.[48] They are made between parties who have often had past contractual relations, and are likely to do so in future. He says a 'vast amount' of economic activity is conducted at least partly on the relational model,[49] and it is the 'dominant mode' of economic organisation.[50] He further claims that a fully discrete transaction does not exist,[51] because at the very least a transaction takes place in the existing environment of legal rules pertaining to contract,

Apparatus"' (1981) 75(6) *Northwestern University Law Review* 1018; 'Relational Contract: What We Do and Do Not Know' (1985) *Wisconsin Law Review* 483; 'Restatement (Second) of Contracts and Presentiation' (1974) 60 *Virginia Law Review* 589; 'Relational Contract Theory: Challenges and Queries' (2000) 94(3) *Northwestern University Law Review* 877; *The New Social Contract: An Inquiry Into Modern Contractual Relations* (New Haven, Yale University Press, 1980).

[43] CF Cimino, 'The Relational Economics of Commercial Contract' (2015) 3 *Texas A & M Law Review* 91, 91.

[44] Macneil, *The New Social Contract: An Inquiry Into Modern Contractual Relations* (n 42) 10.

[45] M Boyle, 'The Relational Principle of Trust and Confidence' (2007) 27 *Oxford Journal of Legal Studies* 633, 634.

[46] Macneil, *The New Social Contract: An Inquiry Into Modern Contractual Relations* (n 42) 64.

[47] Macneil, 'Contracts: Adjustment of Long-Term Economic Relations Under Classical, Neoclassical and Relational Contract Law' (n 42) 865.

[48] H Collins, *Regulating Contracts* (Oxford, Oxford University Press, 1999) 141–42 makes a similar point. He suggests that a discussion of discreteness can be misleading because it might obscure the fact that three dimensions – the parties' business relationship, the economic deal and the contract together operate to explain parties' contracting behaviour.

[49] Macneil 'The Many Futures of Contracts' (n 42) 718.

[50] ibid 757; Macneil, 'Relational Contract: What Do We Know and Do Not Know' (n 42) 490.

[51] Macneil, 'Relational Contract Theory: Challenges and Queries' (n 42) 896.

and societal expectations of behaviour. He also denounces discretism as a 'smoke-screen and apologia for the exercise of raw power'.[52] He says the failure of the classical economic model to account for the reality of power imbalances within a contract make it much less useful as an accurate descriptor of what typically occurs in exchange.[53]

Macneil says that because traditional contract law implements a discreteness norm, it treats the identity of the parties as irrelevant to the transaction. Further, it commodifies as much as possible the subject matter of the contract. For example, an employee is just another provider of labour. As Morgan puts it, neoclassical models assume that goods, services and contracts are fungible.[54] Third, it means that the sources utilised to determine the parties' agreement is strictly limited – typically, to the written wording of the contract. And fourth, contract remedies are limited.[55]

The fact that contractual relationships are typically relational, rather than discrete, has important consequences. First, it explains why many contracts (if written at all) do not contain all elements of the parties' bargain.[56] It would justify a court considering a broad range of evidence, of which the parties' written deal is merely one aspect. Second, it might provide more support and justification for a court re-considering the substance of the bargain made by the parties.[57] A court would no longer be limited to intervening in cases of fraud or deceit. Macneil says a move away from traditional discrete contracting explains the development of doctrines such as duress and unconscionability.[58] Obviously, acceptance of a relational model of contract would likely encourage broader interpretation of doctrines such as these. In summary, while traditional principles of contract law assume that contracting is discrete, in fact it contains both relational elements and discreteness. This fact places strain when we attempt to apply such principles to contracts with strong relational elements.[59]

[52] ibid 901.

[53] Macneil, 'Economic Analysis of Contractual Relations: Its Shortfalls and the Need for a "Rich Classificatory Apparatus"' (n 42) 1055.

[54] J Morgan, *Contract Law Minimalism: A Formalist Restatement of Commercial Contract Law* (Cambridge, Cambridge University Press, 2013) 62: 'goods, services and contracts are frequently not fungible, as neoclassical models assume. On the contrary, relationships and the identities of the parties are highly significant'.

[55] Macneil, 'Contracts: Adjustment of Long-Term Economic Relations Under Classical, Neoclassical and Relational Contract Law' (n 42) 863–64. In particular, courts are generally loath to award specific performance of a contract, usually contained to provide a (limited) remedy in money compensation for breach of contract.

[56] Macneil 'The Many Futures of Contracts' (n 42) 718.

[57] P Devlin noted that traditionally 'the common lawyers hardly recognized the principle of fair dealing as one that needed independent support. For them free dealing was fair dealing. So long as fraud and deceit were kept out of the ring, it was up to each party to fight for the best bargain he could get; a fair fight meant that a fair bargain would result': *The Enforcement of Morals* (Oxford, Oxford University Press, 1965) 47.

[58] Macneil *The New Social Contract: An Inquiry Into Modern Contractual Relations* (n 42) 85–86.

[59] P Gudel, 'Relational Contract Theory and the Concept of Exchange' (1998) 46 *Buffalo Law Review* 763, 766.

Macneil also draws upon the history of business in this respect. Clearly, business in early times in England was based on the household. Workers, many of whom were family members, would work in a small business, producing goods that would then be traded with other family businesses. These 'cottage industries' were classically relational, rather than discrete, in nature.[60] On one view, the industrial revolution, including massive increase in the size of business operations, separation of ownership or business and control, and an evolution of businesses away from being home or cottage based has partly obscured the traditionally relational view of contracting. This does not mean that business is not conducted on this relational plane any more; indeed, the above surveys highlighted its continuing relevance, notwithstanding the evolution in business size, structure and typical mode of operation. It has been observed that since the developing economy associated with the Industrial Revolution of the nineteenth century, business has evolved in a way that has become more relational once more. Examples include long-term supply contracts, franchise agreements, agency agreements. And the employment contract has evolved to become more relational in nature.[61]

IV. Presentiation

Related to discreteness is 'presentiation'.[62] Macneil states that traditional contract law also assumes presentiation. This is the ability of parties to exchange promises now about future activity and performance. This became part of the law of contract when contracts became generally executory, rather than executed, in nature. However, again Macneil says this assumption is incorrect. It is in fact not possible, or at least usually not possible, for parties to reduce all of their agreement to writing, because they cannot anticipate events in the future, many of which are outside the parties' control.[63] Further, there is a limit to the number of matters that a person can properly focus upon.[64] As a result, presentiation is just not possible, and the paper deal may only ever capture a portion of the real deal.

He criticises existing contract law for assuming that the parties could plan the entirety of their agreement prior to activity occurring, on the basis it is just not realistic.[65] Relatedly, he criticises it for assuming that the exclusive source of the parties' obligations is the written agreement between the parties.[66]

[60] I Macneil, 'Exchange Revisited: Individual Utility and Social Solidarity' (1986) 96(3) *Northwestern University Law Review* 567, 591.

[61] H Collins, *Relational Contracts* (Oxford, Oxford University Press, 1999) 199.

[62] Macneil (n 42) 864.

[63] The Supreme Court noted this in *Wood v Capital Insurance Services Ltd* [2017] AC 1173, 1180 (Lord Hodge, for the Court), referring to causes such as the parties' having different and competing aims, communication problems, different drafting practices, and time constraints on negotiations.

[64] Macneil, *The New Social Contract: An Inquiry Into Modern Contractual Relations* (n 42) 8.

[65] Macneil, 'The Many Futures of Contracts' (n 42) 774.

[66] ibid 783.

He uses the example of an employment contract. The mere fact that an employee accepts an offer of employment does not mean they necessarily believe that all of the parties' rights and obligations are found in the employment agreement. He says that, even if some kind of 'consent' model of contracting is taken, the employee cannot be taken to consent to a whole range of behaviours upon which an employer might embark in future in relation to the employee. He says that consent in such a case is 'inevitably tentative, and subject to future 'supervening events'. It is 'fuzzy'.[67]

He criticises the will theory that underlay development of the contract law in the nineteenth and first third (approximately) of the twentieth century:

> The response of 19th and early 20th century contract theory and its socioeconomic analogs was to try to transactionalize the past and future as well as all the present, not just the conscious present. Striving for transactional immortality as well as transactional inclusivity, contract scholars sought to bring everything into the transactional present, and keep it there. Their great vehicle was the abstract but brilliant conception of consent: that to which consent is given is included, everything else is excluded: consent, once given, remains immutable. Thus were the ghosts of the past, present and future to be brought into the clear sharp focus of the discretely perceived conscious present.[68]

Both lack of discreteness and lack of presentiation lead Macneil to the following conclusion:

> Contracts have never approximated the pure independent promise that transactionism would suggest … understanding even heavily transactional contracts requires recognition of the factors external to the promise fragment of the transaction. This is not the grudging recognition afforded by such doctrines as implications … rather it is a full recognition that contracts consist of a variety of components, of which truly communicated promise, brought to maximum present effect, is but one co-equal component, and not always even that … (and further, that) … contract is a very useful word to describe the totality of economic exchange relations whether promises are the dominant or even a significant factor in the relation.[69]

He says that the reality of contracting was very different from that assumed under the traditional model. Typically, contracts were of significant duration (citing franchising agreements as an example). They often involved close personal relationships (citing employment contracts as an example). Exchange typically involved aspects that were easy to measure, and aspects that were difficult to measure. The parties typically expected ongoing cooperation (employment). The benefits and burdens of the relation were shared between the parties. Reputation, interdependence, morality and altruistic desire characterised many contract relationships. The parties do not intend that the entire relation between the parties be encompassed

[67] ibid 771.
[68] ibid 756.
[69] ibid 734–35.

in any written agreement they might make; rather relationships are ongoing and it is accepted they will evolve as circumstances change.[70]

In a sense Macneil suggests something of an irony. He is aware of the change in the typical means of manufacture of goods over the centuries, from a household-based enterprise to an era of mass production and specialisation typically associated with the Industrial Revolution. He indicates that the era of the household-based enterprise was much better described as a situation of discrete contracting; in contrast, as production ramped up and individuals took on specialist tasks, contracts became much more relational.[71] The irony is that, according to Macneil, at the very time contracts became in fact more relational, the English common law of contracting, much of which was formed or refined during the Industrial Revolution era, was developing in a manner much more suited to the discrete type of contract.

V. Individuals are Schizophrenic

Macneil did not totally reject the idea underlying the classical view of contract of individuals as rational, utility-maximisers seeking to advance their own interests. It is most accurate to state he believed it was only half the picture. Though he did not deny that individuals put their own interests first, he also stated that individuals were social creatures, and that this tempered their behaviour in particular ways. On some occasions individuals would put their interests first; but on others, they would put other interests first.[72] He says

> It is thus a mistake to think of 'net utilitarian advantage' in its outside-of-society context involving fictional maximizers of individual utility, equally powerful or not. In the real world there are only enhancers of individual utility immersed in relations creating countless countermotives. Exchange is virtually always relational exchange, that is exchange carried on within relations having significant impact on its goals, conduct and effect.[73]

He says that one way we can reconcile, or at least reduce the tension between, these opposites is by recognising the principle of reciprocity. In this way, a party both gets something (meeting their need to improve, if not maximise, utility), and gives something (reflecting their inherently social nature). Relatedly, we recognise solidarity – we can rely on others to meet their promises. This adds a time dimension to reciprocity.[74] Some see reciprocity as a general social norm in our society, which

[70] Macneil, 'Restatement (Second) of Contracts and Presentiation' (n 42) 595.

[71] Macneil, 'Economic Analysis of Contractual Relations: Its Shortfalls and the Need for a "Rich Classificatory Apparatus"' (n 42) 1035.

[72] Macneil, 'Values in Contract: Internal and External' (n 40) 348.

[73] Macneil 'Exchange Revisited: Individual Utility and Social Solidarity' (n 60) 577.

[74] Macneil, 'Values in Contract: Internal and External' (n 40) 349.

might suggest something like a duty to co-operate within a contractual context.[75] Scott states that a substantial body of empirical evidence suggests that

> Many people behave in a reciprocal manner that deviates from purely self-interested behaviour. Reciprocity means that individuals respond cooperatively to generous acts and, conversely, punish non-cooperative behaviour. Individuals will repay generosity and punish selfishness even in interactions with complete strangers, and even if this is costly for them and yields neither present nor future material rewards.[76]

However, it does make problematic the kind of meeting of the minds explanation of contract.[77] It further seriously undermines the traditional assumption of pure rationality underpinning traditional rules of contract and traditional economics,[78] and a purely utilitarian view of contracting.[79] Macneil prefers and will accept 'utility enhancing' as one motivator to contract, but believes that traditional 'utility maximising' is inaccurate.[80] It insufficiently captures the parties' utility from anticipated future exchanges, and does not capture the 'schizophrenia' of a person to use his terms – it completely ignores that part of the individual that is other-regarding. Both Scott and Mitchell adopt the theory of the schizophrenic nature of individuals in the context of contracting.[81]

Further, the fact that an individual is other-regarding is, strangely to some, utility enhancing because, just as we are regarding of others, others are regarding of us when considering their course of action. We gain utility from being able to trust others, and trust that they will have due regard to our interests.[82] Again, classic economics does not capture this utility.

Interestingly, this finding mirrors developments in the law of economics. Traditional economic theory assumed zero transaction costs. This is unrealistic.[83] Newer economic theories that do take into account transaction costs accept that individuals are motivationally complex, not purely driven by self-interest.[84] Further, once transaction costs are factored in, the fact that parties adopt co-operative

[75] R Scott, 'Conflict and Co-operation in Long-Term Contracts' (1987) 75 *California Law Review* 2005, 2040–41.

[76] R Scott, 'The Death of Contract Law' (2004) 54 *University of Toronto Law Journal* 369, 383.

[77] G Gurvitch, *Sociology of Law* (New York, Routledge, 1974) 172–73.

[78] Macneil, 'Values in Contract: Internal and External' (n 40) 411.

[79] Macneil, 'Exchange Revisited: Individual Utility and Social Solidarity' (n 60) 568.

[80] ibid 575.

[81] R Scott, 'A Relational Theory of Default Rules for Commercial Contracts' (1990) 19 *Journal of Legal Studies* 597, 605: 'all commercial parties are egoistic in that they pursue individual self-interest. All parties are also cooperators in that they prefer mutual adjustment'; C Mitchell, *Contract Law and Contract Practice: Bridging the Gap Between Legal Reasoning and Commercial Expectation* (Oxford, Hart Publishing, 2013) 96.

[82] Macneil, 'Exchange Revisited: Individual Utility and Social Solidarity' (n 60) 585; I Bohnet, B Frey and S Huck, 'More Order With Less Law: On Contract Enforcement, Trust and Crowding' (2001) 95(1) *American Political Science Review* 131, 131: 'trust can increase efficiency in the economic and political sphere'.

[83] R Coase, 'The Problem of Social Cost' (1960) 3 *Journal of Law and Economics* 1, 15.

[84] Cimino (n 43) 106.

norms in relation to the contract lowers them.[85] It reduces the need to try to put as many terms of the agreement in the written contract as possible.[86] And recognising transactions costs explains why the reality is that parties typically do not reduce all of their agreement to writing. It might impose unacceptably high transaction costs on parties to expect them to agree ex ante on all aspects of their contractual relationship.[87]

VI. Traditional Approach (Incorrectly) Assumes Only Bilateral Power within a Contract

Macneil suggests that traditional contract law reflects freedom of contract philosophy. It assumes that parties to a contract have bilateral power. This means (equivalent) power to enter into a contract, to negotiate it, to understand all of its implications, and to have it reflect their interests, making them better off than without the contract. However, Macneil suggests this presumption too is misplaced. He says that parties, or potential parties, to a contract have unilateral power. For example, the supplier negotiating to supply their goods or services may have a monopoly. They may for other reasons have superior bargaining power. Parties may have different levels of information in relation to the proposed contract. They may have different levels of advice (if any) available in relation to its signing. They may have different levels of education and understanding. A party may have unilateral power for any of these reasons. Further, as the contract proceeds, power shifts. While at the beginning, both parties have rights to end the contract, once one of the parties performs their end of the bargain, the other party has diminished rights to end the contract, for example, due to non-performance. Macneil says that traditional contract law assumes bilateral, static power that is not reflective of the reality of contracts. Further, unilateral power may come from sources outside of the written contract, for example a person's need to uphold a good business reputation might effectively confer contractual power on the party that contracts with them.

Macneil says that, connected with the reality of unilateral is the need to restrain it. Because traditional common law did not recognise the reality of unilateral power, it struggled to deal with situations where it was exercised. Examples here might be

[85] ibid 114, citing a study by JP Cannon et al, 'Contracts, Norms and Plural Form Governance' (2000) 28 *Journal of Academic Marketing Science* 180, 191.

[86] J Kostritsky, 'Taxonomy for Justifying Legal Intervention in an Imperfect World: What to do When Parties Have not Achieved or Drafted Incomplete Contracts' [2004] *Wisconsin Law Review* 323, 342–43.

[87] Gudel (n 59) 776; R Scott, 'The Case for Formalism in Relational Contract' (2000) 94(3) *Northwestern University Law Review* 847, 862; L Bernstein, 'Merchant Law in a Merchant Court: Rethinking the Code's Search for Immanent Business Norms' (1996) 144 *University of Pennsylvania Law Review* 1765, 1789; D Campbell and H Collins, 'Discovering the Implicit Dimensions of Contracts' in D Campbell, H Collins and J Wightman (eds), *Implicit Dimensions of Contract: Discrete, Relational and Network Contracts* (Oxford, Hart Publishing, 2003) 41.

one party imposing very onerous contract terms on the other, because it effectively can – for example, because of superior bargaining position. It might impose, for example, a clause that purports to provide for liquidated damages in the event of breach, but the stated amount is disproportionate to any conceivable loss they are likely to suffer in the event of breach. Eventually the law turned against such clauses through development of the penalty doctrine. However, Macneil's point is that traditional contract law struggled to provide a remedy in the event of unfair contract terms (a struggle which arguably continues today), because it does not sufficiently appreciate that, quite often, one of the contracting parties, but not the other, has power and discretion under the contract. He associates this (relatively belated) common law recognition of the need to restrain unilateral power with development of doctrines such as unconscionability and good faith.[88]

Thus, Macneil believes that the implication of terms into contracts is not sufficient to reflect the parties' true agreement. Another criticism of current contract law he makes is in the area of remedies. He criticises the fact that the most usual remedy for breach of contract is compensatory damages. This does not seek to restore the relationship between the parties.[89] A relational view of contract that Macneil favours would tend towards a remedy of specific performance and other remedies favouring co-operation, rather than accepting the end of the parties' contractual relationship.[90] Further to this, Macneil reflects on the evidence, discussed in the empirical studies above, that contracting parties are generally loath to enforce their contractual remedies. He says one reason is the 'willingness to sacrifice immediate exchange-gains to increase relational security'.[91]

Macneil argues that existing principles of contract law are inadequate to capture the reality of the relational nature of contracting. He claims that, as a result of this mismatch, existing rules of contract are placed under stress, called upon to deal with situations for which they were never designed. It is a struggle for the existing apparatus to cope, and one way courts do so is by twisting facts and imposing fictions in order to reach acceptable results.[92] This includes inferring

[88] Macneil, 'Economic Analysis of Contractual Relations: Its Shortfalls and the Need for a "Rich Classificatory Apparatus"' (n 42) 1059–62.

[89] Macneil 'The Many Futures of Contracts' (n 42) 737.

[90] G Golding, 'Employment as a Relational Contract and the Impact on Remedies for Breach' (2021) 30(2) *Griffith Law Review* 270, 282–84. An interesting model is presented by M Jennejohn, 'Contract Adjudication in a Collaborative Economy' (2010) 5(2) *Virginia Law and Business Review* 173, who favours a specific dispute resolution model applicable to relational contracts. Rather than awarding an aggrieved party compensation for breach, the model seeks to establish an enforcement mechanism with timeframes for specific contract milestones to be achieved in future. It seeks to preserve the parties' relationship, not accept its demise.

[91] Macneil, 'Economic Analysis of Contractual Relations: Its Shortfalls and the Need for a "Rich Classificatory Apparatus"' (n 42) 1048.

[92] He uses the objective theory of contract as an example, denouncing it as an 'absurdity' when the reality is that parties often do not know or understand the contents of the written agreement: 'Contracts: Adjustment of Long-Term Economic Relations Under Classical, Neoclassical and Relational Contract Law' (n 42) 884.

'consent' and implying terms to, in Macneil's words, preserve the façade of consent and the objective theory of contract.[93]

Macneil's view is that a reset of contract law rules would relieve substantial pressure on existing doctrine.[94] He suggests acceptance of good faith.[95] He says that unconscionability conduct, duress, good faith and 'best efforts' are all relational concepts.[96] He describes 'relational norms' to include role integrity, reciprocity, contractual solidarity, the balancing of power, the propriety of means and harmonizing the parties' relations with the external social matrix within which they take place.[97] They also include implementation of planning, effecting consent, flexibility, and recognising restitutionary, reliance and expectation interests.[98] He concluded that 'every transaction' was embedded in complex relations, and could only be understood and analysed properly in the context of the relations that enveloped the contract.[99]

He suggests that, when interpreting contracts, the court must have regard to the entirety of the parties' relationship, including what has occurred since the contract was entered into, rather than (in all cases) a narrow focus on the written contract.[100] Macneil says the question (at least) must be asked as to the extent to which the written contract actually reflects the parties' bargain.[101] Such must not be assumed, as the will theory of contract and parol evidence rule do. Contractual remedies might reflect more than promise, reliance and breach,[102] including restitution, for example.

How much of a reform, if any, was Macneil calling for? This is an important question. Relational contract theorists are often criticised for declining to follow their theory through to what many would regard as a logical conclusion – to suggest reform to contract law rules to better align contract law with what relational scholars regard as the realities of contractual performance.[103] They are also criticised for failing to appreciate how often parties do not behave as how they ought to behave, and failing to understand the implications of inequality of bargaining power.[104] It should also be accepted that, to a limited extent,

[93] 'Restatement (Second) of Contracts and Presentiation' (n 42) 593.

[94] Macneil, 'The Many Futures of Contracts' (n 42) 815.

[95] 'The burgeoning concept of good faith … is another largely anti-presentiating and very much anti-discrete concept': 'Contracts: Adjustment of Long-Term Economic Relations Under Classical, Neoclassical and Relational Contract Law' (n 42) 885.

[96] 'Relational Contract: What We Do and Do Not Know' (n 42) 498.

[97] ibid 503.

[98] 'Values in Contract: Internal and External' (n 40) 347.

[99] 'Relational Contract Theory: Challenges and Queries' (n 42) 881.

[100] 'Contracts: Adjustment of Long-Term Economic Relations Under Classical, Neoclassical and Relational Contract Law' (n 42) 890.

[101] ibid 894.

[102] ibid 897.

[103] Golding (n 90) 276; D Brodie, 'How Relational is the Employment Contract?' (2011) 40 *Industrial Law Journal* 232, 244–46; Morgan (n 54) 65; Mitchell (n 81) 20, 184; MJ Trebilcock, *The Limits of Freedom of Contract* (Cambridge, Harvard University Press, 1993) 141–42.

[104] Brodie (n 103) 248–53.

exceptions to general rules of contract law can embrace aspects of relational contract theory.[105]

Or for others who subscribe to this theory, how should the law respond? There is a lively debate here. What I would consider the orthodox view is that, at least in broad terms, commercial law should follow commercial practice. This taps into the long history of the influence of the latter on the former, exemplified by the law merchant and the time of Lord Mansfield. Lord Devlin stated that there should be a close match between contract practice and contract law.[106] If it is true that most contracts are relational, it makes sense that general rules of contract law should complement, and not be antagonistic towards, a relational view of contract.[107]

As Mitchell put it:

> The central insights of relational theory – that context is important, that indeterminacy in contract circumstances is rife, that classical law is manifestly unsuitable for some forms of contractual relationship – support the idea that commercial contract law should reflect commercial practice.[108]

On the other hand, not everyone accepts this. Cimino claims that while most legal scholars accept relational contract theory, most of them do not believe it should lead to any reform to the law of contract.[109] Morgan is one such scholar,[110] among Scott[111] and others.[112] He expressly rejects that notion that the law should enforce norms of trust and cooperation.[113]

[105] Mitchell (n 81) 185.

[106] P Devlin, 'The Relation Between Commercial Law and Commercial Practice' (1951) 41(3) *Modern Law Review* 249. There are other adherents. See for example Lord Goff, 'Commercial Contracts and the Commercial Court' [1984] *Lloyd's Maritime and Commercial Law Quarterly* 382; Lord Irvine, 'The Law: An Engine for Trade' (2001) 64 *Modern Law Review* 333; Weintraub (n 32) 2–3: 'there should be a reciprocal relationship between contract rules and business usage. Usage should inform the rule maker; rules should reinforce desirable usage and change as usage and mores change'.

[107] M Eisenberg, 'Relational Contracts' in Jack Beatson and D Freidmann (eds), *Good Faith and Fault in Contract Law* (Oxford, Oxford University Press, 1995) 298: 'the general rules of contract law should fit relational contracts, because contracts that involve a relationship between the contracting parties, beyond the mere relationship of stranger-exchange, comprise the bread and butter of contracting'.

[108] Mitchell (n 81) 199.

[109] Cimino (n 43) 91–92.

[110] Morgan (n 54) 67: 'The traditional reaction of commercial lawyers, faced with the data above (Macneil and Macaulay's work) would be to assume that contract law should be radically reformed to reflect and enforce the cooperation essential to relational contracting. We could term this the 'Mansfield approach' after the father of commercial law, whose overhaul of the late eighteenth-century common law meant incorporation of commercial customs and practices. But, however venerable this assumption, it should be questioned and ultimately rejected'.

[111] Scott (n 87): 'contracts are relational, complex and subjective. But contract law, whether we like it or not, is none of those things. Contract law is formal, simple and … classical'.

[112] D Charny, 'Illusions of Spontaneous Order: "Norms" in Contractual Relationships' (1996) 144 *University of Pennsylvania Law Review* 1841, 1854: 'the rules that parties follow when they play among themselves are not those that the court should attempt to apply'; J Gava, 'Do We Need a Hybrid Law of Contract? Why Hugh Collins is Wrong and Why it Matters' (2004) 63 *Cambridge Law Journal* 605.

[113] Morgan (n 54) 89.

In one paper, Macneil listed four options for contract law, in the face of the realities of relational contract and the disjunct with contract law. He said that the law could (a) ignore these realities; (b) try to force relational contract patterns into existing contract law doctrine; (c) modify contract law doctrine to recognise the impossibility of presentiation; and (d) develop an overall structure of contract law of greater general applicability than that which currently exists, and attempt to merge (at least some of) existing contract law into the new structure.[114] He then goes on to substantially criticise (a), (b) and (c). He declines to elaborate on (d) but it seems clear that this is his preferred option.[115] He claimed that existing contract law (at the time he wrote, the mid-1970s) was similar to English contract law in the eighteenth century, prior to the full acceptance of freedom of contract, will theory, and so on. He says that 'we realise there are common threads, but we have just started thinking about putting them together'.[116] He also says that 'relational contract law should generally track the relational behaviour and norms found in the relations to which it applies … on the whole, the law must generally do this'.[117] However, it must be conceded he appeared unwilling to follow the logical consequences of his ideas in terms of specific reforms to contract law.[118]

Robert Scott is another. After stating that 'we are all relationists now' and accepting that all contracts are 'relational, complex and subjective',[119] he states that contract law has none of those characteristics – it is formal, simple and classical. He does not accept the premise that default rules of contract law need to be reformed to reflect the truly relational nature of contract.[120] Jonathan Morgan reaches similar conclusions.[121]

I will reserve my own comments until the end of chapter eight.

[114] 'Restatement (Second) of Contracts and Presentiation' (n 42) 597.

[115] He suggests some of the reforms made in the Restatement (Second) along the lines suggested in option might prove 'highly subversive of the transactional structure and thereby foster the synthesis of a more comprehensive structure': 'Restatement (Second) of Contracts and Presentiation' (n 42) 610.

[116] 'Restatement (Second) of Contracts and Presentiation' (n 42) 609.

[117] 'Relational Contract Theory: Challenges and Queries' (n 42) 903.

[118] ibid 899: 'I challenge to a duel anyone who … persists in converting my descriptions of relational contract law into prescription of what the law should be, particularly prescriptions of some universal application of relational contract law'.

[119] Scott (n 87) 852.

[120] ibid 847.

[121] Morgan (n 54) 66–69.

8

Other Scholars in the Relational Contract Debate

I. Hugh Collins

Building on the work of Macaulay and Macneil, Collins agreed that the focus needed to be on much more than the express terms of contracts.[1] He developed a model containing three dimensions affecting contractual behaviour. They are the business relation, the economic deal and the contract.[2] The business relation is the relationship between the parties that precedes and will likely succeed this particular contractual engagement. This relation provides the basis of trust between the parties. It includes customary standards of trade and observations as to whether each of the contracting parties typically conform to these. Then there is the economic deal between the parties on this occasion. This interaction is governed by economically rational behaviour. However, this is to be assessed over both the short-term and the long-term.[3] Actions are assessed for self-interest, but care must be applied in this analysis. It might be in the short-term interest of a contracting party to cheat the other on this deal, but it is not in their long-term interest, because such behaviour is likely to end the relationship between the parties. Or there may be an opportunity for short-term profitable opportunism. However, the party able to take the opportunity may decline to do so, because of the long-term consequences for the parties' relationship.

A factual example of what Collins is talking about appears in the case *George Mitchell (Chesterhall) Ltd v Finney Lock Seeds Ltd*.[4] There a contract of supply of seeds included a clause purporting to limit the liability of the provider in the event that the seeds were not of merchantable quality. Their liability was limited to the replacement cost of seeds, and did not extend to any consequential damage the purchaser might suffer from using the defective seeds. As it happened, defective seeds were supplied, and this cost the purchaser more than 60,000 pounds. The purchase price was about 200 pounds. The question was whether the purchaser

[1] H Collins, *Regulating Contracts* (Oxford, Oxford University Press, 1999).
[2] ibid 128–32.
[3] See also D Campbell and D Harris, 'Flexibility in Long-Term Contractual Relationships' (1993) 20 *Journal of Law and Society* 166.
[4] [1983] 2 AC 803.

was limited in terms of remedy, as the express words of the contract suggested, or could claim full consequential damages, as would be their usual common law right. In this case, the court, in reaching its decision that the clause was not fair and reasonable and thus could not be enforced (pursuant to sale of goods legislation), considered standard industry practice in such cases. It found that, where claims were genuine, suppliers would pay compensation well beyond the purchase price for loss to purchasers, even though they were not required to do so under the contract.[5]

Thus, parties are self-interested, but a significant component of this is the expectation of continuing contractual relations between the parties. As a result, Collins states that a myopic focus on what is in the parties' short-term interests will not be a good explainer of behaviour. Collins' third dimension is the written contract itself. This is what the contract law tends to focus on.

Collins says that the behaviour of parties to a contract will likely be influenced to some extent by all three frameworks at the same time. This explains why parties often do not insist on their strict contractual rights when a dispute arises. They are not primarily focussed on the written terms; they are significantly focussed in many cases on the parties' business relationship. Contract law must accommodate this, rather than just be focussed on the written terms, as it typically is.[6] In terms of the priorities, he suggests most emphasis should be placed on the business relationship, then the economic deal, with least emphasis on the written words.[7] He suggests that contract law do this by accepting the concept of 'reasonable expectations' as an additional basis for contractual legal obligations, together with good faith and/or reasonableness.[8] These are beyond the written terms (if any) of the parties' deal. They include expectations derived from past performance, current performance and trade usage. It is an important additional source of information to help describe the standards governing the parties' contractual behaviour.[9]

Collins addresses Weber's influential work. Weber emphasised the need, in order for a system of capitalism to work effectively, for 'calculability' or certainty in business. Collins agrees with this. But Collins says that Weber's error was in assuming that the best way to achieving certainty (or, more likely, the most certainty possible) was to adopt formalism and laser focus on the parties' written agreement. Collins says that the contracting parties typically do not expect that this will occur. Business people would not favour this. Rather they expect that past dealings, current dealings, trade custom, good faith and reasonable behaviour will be relevant in resolving any contractual dispute the parties might have.[10]

[5] ibid 817 (Lord Bridge, with whom all other Law Lords agreed).

[6] Collins (n 1) 144.

[7] ibid 175.

[8] ibid 181. As noted earlier, justices have accepted the idea that 'reasonable expectations' can be a legitimate source of contractual obligations: *First Energy (UK) Ltd v Hungarian International Bank Ltd* [1993] 2 Lloyd's Rep 194, 196 (CA) (Steyn LJ).

[9] Collins (n 1) 146–48.

[10] ibid 180–81.

Finally, Collins responds to concerns about the possible uncertainty caused if good faith and/or reasonableness were to be applied to contracts. As noted above, this concern was recently expressed by Lord Burrows in *Pakistan International Airline Corporation*[11] as a reason for not recognising a generalised concept of good faith. Collins says that such concerns are overstated. Once it is recognised that contracts involve the three considerations (in descending order of importance) of the business relationship, economic deal and the written contract, arguments that good faith and reasonableness undermine legal enforcement run hollow. In other words, such concepts underpin the more important contractual norms associated with the business relationship. This trumps any adverse effect (which is not necessarily admitted) on the certainty of the written terms.[12]

II. More from Stewart Macaulay

Macaulay published numerous further works in this area. He would re-emphasise the large gap between the 'real and the paper deal'.[13] The written contract did not contain the parties' full agreement. If the law really wanted to give effect to the legitimate expectations of contracting parties, it had to take into account matters beyond the written contract.[14] Macaulay rejects the fundamental premise that we can assume that the contractual language as used accurately and completely reflects the parties' intentions. He says that strict application of this rule gives too much power to the party that drafted the contract. The will theory, assuming that contracts were a product of choice and consent, did not reflect the practical reality of many contracts.[15]

He said that, in any event, a formalist approach to contract was destined to fail, because it inevitably produces outcomes that the legal system cannot stomach. And further, it would place the very legitimacy of the legal system in jeopardy.[16] Such a system would reward conduct verging on fraud.[17]

[11] [2021] UKSC 40, [95].

[12] Collins (n 1) 270.

[13] S Macaulay, 'The Real and the Paper Deal: Empirical Pictures of Relationships, Complexity and the Urge for Transparent Simple Rules' (2003) 66 *Modern Law Review* 44.

[14] S Macaulay, 'Relational Contracts: Floating on a Sea of Custom? Thoughts About the Ideas of Ian Macneil and Lisa Bernstein' (2000) 94(3) *Northwestern University Law Review* 775, 801.

[15] Macaulay (n 13) 51; Macaulay (n 14) 779. He dismisses notions of 'bargain' and 'free choice' as 'symbolism' masking some who would use it to mask the achievement of illegitimate ends. He says the formal contract system 'claims to be neutral and autonomous and to rest on simple rationality. A descriptively accurate model of the process challenges these assumptions': S Macaulay, 'An Empirical View of Contract' [1985] *Wisconsin Law Review* 465, 478.

[16] Macaulay (n 13) 79: 'we might decide there is a high cost in legitimacy if the legal system comes to symbolize that contract rests on manipulation of forms and courts reject the substance of the real deal of the parties'.

[17] Macaulay (n 14) 802: 'formal rationality can produce certain but bad law. It can be divorced from the actual and reasonable expectations of transactors in the market place … sometimes it will reward

He rejects arguments that an approach favouring cooperation and good faith creates too much uncertainty. He states that uncertainty already exists in contract doctrine, including waiver, estoppel, substantial performance, distinctions between contractual conditions and warranties, mistake, impossibility and frustration.[18]

Macaulay notes that courts typically engage in awkward practices in order to resolve contractual disputes. In cases where a technical application of the contractual language would lead to unacceptable outcomes, courts are forced to resort to unorthodox interpretations of contractual language, or unrealistic or incomplete views of the facts.[19] They might resort to existing legal doctrine such as waiver, estoppel or implied terms to try to achieve justice in particular cases.

He says that many assumptions made by a classical view of contract are wrong. These include that the parties carefully plan their relationships before entering into them, that this planning is reflected in the written contract, that contracts must be detailed because parties will only perform to the letter of the contract (if to that extent), not the spirit, and the prime importance of contract litigation in resolving contract disputes and deterring non-performance. Macaulay says all of these assumptions are either plain wrong or so overstated as to be misleading.[20]

Macaulay favoured a relational view of contracts. He said discrete transactions did not exist in the real world. He rejected the argument that, if a court were required to apply relational contract principles, this would lead to uncertain results and would be beyond a court's competence.[21] He acknowledged criticism of relational contract theory that it might assume more of a 'common enterprise' than some contracts entailed.[22] On the other hand, a purely individual view of contracting was not accurate either, contrary to much business practice.

If these legal realism-based arguments against traditional contract law have validity, naturally the mind turns to how the situation might be reformed. On that question, just like Macneil, Macaulay was somewhat sceptical that a rival theory could develop that would not be an oversimplification.[23] He acknowledged Macneil's work gave scholars something to think about, if not precise measurable

sophistry. Perhaps submitting to it will give us (cheaper goods) … but people who feel tricked and cheated when the paper deal is substituted for the real deal are part of the cost of this approach'.

[18] Macaulay (n 13) 52.

[19] ibid 47 and 53.

[20] Macaulay (n 15) 467.

[21] MJ Trebilcock, *The Limits of Freedom of Contract* (Cambridge, Harvard University Press, 1994) 141–42.

[22] R Brownsword, 'Individualism, Cooperativism and an Ethic for European Contract Law' (2001) 64 *Modern Law Review* 628, 630: 'there are two plausible ethics for contract law, individualism and cooperativism … it is not easy for contract doctrine (whether through doctrines of good faith, unconscionability, reasonableness, loyalty, legitimate expectation or whatever) to hold strictly to either of these ethics in their most robust form. Doctrinal adherence to individualism will often seem out of touch with business practice (where compromise, adjustment and partnering and the like govern dealing), but equally doctrinal adherence to cooperativism can put too great a strain on the idea of a common enterprise (at any rate, in the sense of an identity of interest)'.

[23] Macaulay (n 13) 45.

reforms.[24] However, it would at least embrace good faith, reflecting the parties' intentions. He concluded:

> If we want our courts to carry out the expectations of the parties to contracts, both those that they express in writing and those that are left unrecorded or even unspoken … we must accept a contract law that rests on standards rather than on clear, quantitative rules. Contract law then will talk of 'good faith', 'duties of co-operation' or 'within limits set by commercial reasonableness'.[25]

III. Other Scholars

A. Jay Feinman

Feinman emphasised the importance of norms in relational contract theory.[26] Macneil suggested norms such as role integrity, reciprocity and implementation of planning. Feinman says the relative importance of each of these norms will vary according to the nature of the contract.[27] Norms external to the contract are also important. These include customs, standard kinds of contracting in particular contexts, third parties and social norms. Feinman states:

> The substantive core of relational contract theory proceeds from two propositions: that contract is fundamentally about cooperative social behaviour, and that contracts containing significant relational elements are the predominant form of contracting. This suggests that there is a baseline of obligation in contracting … that arises out of the contract norms. This position is distinguished from the classical position that there is a baseline of no obligation, or the neoclassical position that there is a core of self-interest affected at the periphery by custom and regulation. The precise content of the obligation is determined by the application of relational method.[28]

Feinman gives the examples of insurance law, landlord-tenant law and products liability law. These have been become largely independent areas of law, but they are spin-offs from, respectively, the law of contract, law of property and law of tort. These areas of law were traditionally areas of classic law. Feinman notes that the spin-off areas have largely created their own rules and principles.[29] A significant

[24] Macaulay (n 14) 803.

[25] S Macaulay, 'The Real and the Paper Deal: Empirical Pictures of Relationships, Complexity and the Urge for Transparent Simple Rules' in David Campbell, Hugh Collins and John Wightman (eds), *Implicit Dimensions of Contract: Discrete, Relational and Network Contracts* (Oxford, Hart Publishing, 2003) 52.

[26] J Feinman, 'Relational Contract Theory in Context' (2000) 94(3) *Northwestern University Law Review* 737.

[27] ibid 742.

[28] ibid 743; J Feinman, 'The Last Promissory Estoppel Article' (1992) 61 *Fordham Law Review* 303.

[29] See similarly on the 'spin-off' theory P Gudel, 'Relational Contract Theory and the Concept of Exchange' (1998) 46 *Buffalo Law Review* 763, 778; R Mangabeira Unger, 'The Critical Legal Studies Movement' (1983) 96 *Harvard Law Review* 561, 617.

part of the content of these rules and principles reflects relational theory. He says they are examples where the law does (even unwittingly) embrace relational concepts, including propriety of means, restraint of power and good faith.[30] One could add to Feinman's list employment law and consumer law, both of which grew out of the law of contract, and both of which also contain significant relational elements (it must be said, typically, though not exclusively, through legislation rather than case law development).

B. Robert Scott

Scott identifies as a relationist. He explains why the traditional assumption underlying classical contract law about individuals being rational utility maximisers does not present a complete picture. Rather, he says parties who contract engage to maximise the expected value of the contract for both parties.[31] Deviation from joint maximisation is inefficient and makes contracts unstable. The joint maximisation objective is jeopardised if parties engage in individualistic behaviour, whether it be wagering, altruism or engaging in opportunistic or strategic behaviour. This is why such behaviour should not be permitted.

C. Catherine Mitchell

Something of a centrist position on these matters is taken by Catherine Mitchell. Mitchell argues that the distinction between the paper deal and the real deal is a simplistic binary.[32] Most contractual relations are complex, involving both the parties' written agreement and all of the surrounding circumstances, including the relationship between them. She argues that many adherents of the theory of Macneil and Macaulay exaggerate the extent to which it damages orthodox contract law. She maintains contract law doctrine continues to play an important role in private ordering of affairs. Contract law needs to embrace both the formal and relational aspects of the agreement. She argues courts can overemphasise the importance that contracting parties place on certainty in commercial dealings.[33] However, in the end she supports use of relational contract theory to make (modest) changes to the law of contract:

> It is nevertheless relational theory … that is best able to comprehend the multifaceted and complex realities of the commercial relationship, and thus provide a suitable framework within which a contract law more aligned with commercial expectations could be

[30] Feinman (n 26) 744–46.

[31] R Scott, 'A Relational Theory of Default Rules for Commercial Contracts' (1990) 19 *Journal of Legal Studies* 597, 602.

[32] C Mithell, 'Contracts and Contract Law: Challenging the Distinction Between the "Real" and "Paper" Deal' (2009) 29(4) *Oxford Journal of Legal Studies* 675.

[33] ibid 699.

developed … there will be costs involved in developing a relational contract law, but the institutional costs in not developing it, particularly in terms of our confidence in contract law's capacity to facilitate commercial dealing and commercial expectations in all their forms, are likely to be greater.[34]

IV. Definition of Relational Contracts

One of the areas of controversy is the precise scope of the meaning of 'relational contracts'. At times, Macneil distinguishes discrete from relational contracts, on the basis that both can exist, but he also indicates that a truly discrete form of contracting is impossible. Others have attempted their own definitions. So Goetz and Scott define a relational contract to mean one where the parties are not capable of reducing important terms of the contract to well-defined obligations,[35] perhaps because the contract is long-term, or there are significant unknowables at the relevant time.

In sharp contrast, Eisenberg says it is very difficult to define a relational contract in a meaningful way, given that Macneil and others viewed contracts as on a spectrum between discrete and relational, with various factors relevant to determining where on the spectrum a particular contract lay. He rejects the mere longevity of a contract as being necessarily indicative of a contract being relational. He also rejects Goetz and Scott's definition, on the basis it is never possible to reduce all important terms to writing. Instead, he settles upon a definition of relational contract as being one 'involving not merely an exchange, but a relationship, between the contracting parties'. However, he goes on to acknowledge that, if this definition were applied, the category of discrete contracts would be largely non-existent, because all contracts involve at least some relationship between the parties.

Komel suggests that

> The crux of the matter is that the relationship in question is such that it has the propensity to generate norms, define or inform parties' expectations, provide sources of reassurance, facilitate cooperation, create interdependence … over and above, indeed potentially instead of, what can be gleaned from the express terms of the contract or contracts to which they are parties, and over and above what is provided by the bare legal norms and legal mechanisms that underlie or support these contracts.[36]

As discussed in chapter five, some judges have attempted to provide guidelines as to when a contract might be considered relational in nature.[37] Some scholars in

[34] C Mitchell, *Contract Law and Contract Practice: Bridging the Gap Between Legal Reasoning and Commercial Expectation* (Oxford, Hart Publishing, 2013) 198, 266.

[35] C Goetz and R Scott, 'Principles of Relational Contracts' (1981) 67(6) *Virginia Law Review* 1089, 1091.

[36] D Kimel, 'The Choice of Paradigm for Theory of Contract: Reflections on the Relational Model' (2007) 27 *Oxford Journal of Legal Studies* 233, 236.

[37] *Yam Seng Pte Ltd v International Trade Corp Ltd* [2013] EWHC 111 (QB) [142] (Leggatt J, as he then was); *Bates v Post Office Ltd* (No 3) [2019] EWHC 606, [725] (Fraser J).

the field have as well.[38] The implication of these suggestions might be that different rules might be applied to contracts identified as having 'relational' nature.[39] Otherwise, with respect, on one view there does not seem to be any point in so identifying them. This is unless the approach of Eisenberg, to be discussed below, is taken, that is to say, that relational contract theory should essentially be applied to all contracts.

It has been observed that the failure (on one view) to adequately define relational contracts, subject to the view in the previous paragraph, represents a weakness of the theory.[40]

V. Implications of a Contract Being Relational or Contracts Typically Being Relational

Another question is the consequence, if any, if we accept that contracts, or certain contracts, are relational. Scholars and judges have identified that some contracting types, including employment agreements, franchising arrangements, distribution arrangements, long-term leases, joint ventures, partners and so on are clearly relational. This does certainly not purport to be an exhaustive list. The question is, what are the consequences of accepting this fact? Does it mean that we need special rules of contracting to deal with such contracts? At times, in the work of Macneil, it does seem as if this is what he is proposing, though it is not clear. The (on one view) failure by Macneil to spell out specifically the implications of his theory for substantive rules of contract law has been noted and criticised.[41]

Another view is based on the premise that all or virtually all contracts are relational.[42] This might mean that the general rules of contract need to be calibrated to reflect this fact. In other words, one question is whether only contracts

[38] H Collins, 'Employment as a Relational Contract' (2021) 137 *Law Quarterly Review* 426, 429 (expectation of a longer-term business relationship, investment of substantial resources by contracting parties, implicit expectations of cooperation, loyalty, mutual trust and confidence) (guides only). Collins said that a hallmark of such contracts was that the parties did not expect that their written contract reflect the entirety of their bargain: 'Is a Relational Contract a Legal Concept?' in S Degeling, J Edelman and J Goudkamp (eds), *Contract in Commercial Law* (Sydney, LawBook Co, 2016) 55; CJ Goetz and RE Scott, 'Principles of Relational Contracts' (1981) 67 *Virginia Law Review* 1089, 1091 say a contract is relational to the extent that the contracting parties are incapable of reducing important parts of their agreement to written form, due to significant future uncertainty or lack of ability to contract precisely on future matters.

[39] For example, in *GEC Marconi Systems Pty Ltd v BHP Information Technology Pty Ltd* [2003] FCA 50, [230] Finn J stated that fairness and commercial reasonableness would be factored in to the interpretation of contracts held to be relational in nature.

[40] Collins, 'Is a Relational Concept a Legal Concept?' (n 38) 37, 38.

[41] ibid 37, 38; R Gordon, 'Macaulay, Macneil and the Discovery of Solidarity and Power in Contract Law' [1985] *Wisconsin Law Review* 545, 551.

[42] D Campbell, '*Arcos v Ronaasen* as a Relational Contract' in D Campbell, L Mulcahy and S Wheeler (eds), *Changing Conceptions of Contract: Essays in Honour of Ian Macneil* (London, Palgrave Macmillan, 2013) 163: 'the main point of the relational theory of contract is not that there is a class of relational

of a particular, relational kind should have 'relational legal principles' applied, or whether relational legal principles should apply to all contracts, because all or most of them are relational in nature. Campbell and Harris state that classical contract principles should be completely rejected as an explanation of long-term contracting.[43]

Prominent here is the work of Melvin Eisenberg. He clearly accepts that traditional classical contract law is based on incorrect premises of the kind identified earlier in this chapter.[44] He embraces relational contract theory, but says proponents of it have made a mistake in suggesting that relational contracts are a sub-category of contracts, with the implication that special rules ought be applied to them, and that non-relational contracts are the norm. He says that, given almost all contracts have relational aspects, there should not be a special sub-category of law dealing with relational contracts. Instead, a relational contract approach should be applied to all contractual scenarios, subject to sensitivity towards individual cases.[45]

This approach has implications for what the contract law should be. Eisenberg states that the general contract law must be flexible enough to govern relational contracts. The traditional classical law of contract did not do this. He gives numerous examples of how the law of contract might be reformed to accommodate this. Apart from requiring parties to perform contracts in good faith, he suggests the following:

- Greater acceptance of agreements to negotiate in good faith;
- Expansion of rules regarding changed circumstances (impossibility, impracticability, frustration) that justify non-performance; clarity regarding clauses such as best endeavours and termination at will;
- Construe contracts so as to reflect a mutual enterprise, not an adversarial relationship;
- Rules favouring keeping the parties together;
- Rules requiring equitable adjustments to the contract when changed circumstances occur; and
- Rules permitting courts to make adjustments to the contract based on changed circumstances to fairly spread any loss/profit that occurs as a result of the change.[46]

contracts which should be recognised in addition to the class of discrete contracts, but that all contracts are relational'.

[43] Campbell and Harris (n 3) 173.

[44] M Eisenberg, 'Why There is No Law of Relational Contracts' (2000) 94 *Northwestern University Law Review* 805, 808.

[45] ibid 821; M Eisenberg, 'Relational Contracts' in J Beatson and D Friedmann (eds), *Good Faith and Fault in Contract Law* (Oxford, Clarendon Press, 2002).

[46] Eisenberg 'Relational Contracts' (n 45) 298–99.

Gounari says a relational interpretation of contracts will more likely give effect to the parties' reasonable expectations than the current contract law,[47] which resorts to context in the event of contractual ambiguity, as will be elaborated upon below. Gounari's approach would favour a contextual interpretation in cases other than identified ambiguity. Gounari specifically cites the *Arcos v Ronaasen*[48] decision as an (unsatisfactory) consequence of a focus purely on the written terms of the contract, in the traditional vein of contract law. She suggests that a relational view of contracting would likely view what the purchaser did in this case as opportunism, contrary to the parties' reasonable expectations.[49] She indicates this would not result in radical change to contract law, because the core tenets of relational contract theory already exist within current rules. For example, the existence of any contract implies that both parties have agreed to abandon ruthless pursuit of self-interest at the expense of all else (and all others), in relation to the subject matter of the contract. The parties have agreed to cooperate to achieve the objectives of the contract. She proposes a 'default legal structure informed by what the parties would have intended if they purported to act rationally'.[50] She concludes:

> The relational interpretation of contracts should not be confined to those contracts which the law treats as quintessentially relational in the sense of an ongoing relationship of mutual reliance, such as the joint ventures which Lord Leggatt addressed in both *Yam Seng* and *Al Nehayan*. Instead, the relational interpretation of contract should be introduced into the current legal framework by simply having classical contract law be re-interpreted contextually, in light of relational norms that made the contract possible in the first place, so as to avoid the kind of arguably anomalous outcomes achieved in cases like *Arcos v Ronaasen*.[51]

Hugh Collins spelled out some implications of a contract being considered relational. They included (a) interpretation of contracts in a deeply contextual way; (b) willingness to adjust contractual obligations, for instance as circumstances change; (c) recognition of binding, intermittent contracts in the context of long-term business relations between parties; and (d) a mandatory contractual obligation to act in good faith.[52] He indicates that the concept of implied terms is the likely way in which the consequences of relational contract theory will be practically translated into legal principle.[53] Implied terms of good faith, co-operation, fair dealing and mutual trust and confidence will be part of relational contracts. These are necessary to avoid parties acting in opportunistic ways

[47] Z Gounari, 'Developing a Relational Law of Contracts: Striking a Balance Between Abstraction and Contextualism' (2021) 41 *Legal Studies* 177, 179.
[48] [1933] AC 470.
[49] Gounari (n 47) 180–82.
[50] ibid 193.
[51] ibid 183.
[52] Collins, 'Employment as a Relational Contract' (n 38) 428.
[53] Collins, 'Is a Relational Contract a Legal Concept?' (n 38) 55.

and/or ways that otherwise do not meet the parties' reasonable expectations and general standards of commercial propriety.[54]

Obviously factors such as past practice, course of performance, 'tacit agreement' including acquiescence will be relevant, if a relational view were applied to contract interpretation.[55]

Zhong Xing Tan identifies three different ways in which relational contract theory might impact contract law.[56] These are (a) re-interpretive relationalism; (b) re-orientative relationalism; and (c) reconstructive relationalism. Re-interpretive relationalism involves largely reinterpreting existing doctrine as being reflective of relational contract theory. For example, the doctrine of consideration could be viewed as an example of reciprocity, the doctrine regarding minors' contracts could be viewed as going to role integrity, in terms of two of Macneil's social norms. This would result in minimal if any change to the law. Reorientative relationism would involve greater change to the law, including an expansion of exceptions (for example, to the parol evidence rule), dilution of certain rules tending towards rigidity, expansion of the concept of implied terms, estoppel, unconscionability, and so on. Reconstructive relationalism is more radical. Tan cites the Canadian Supreme Court good faith decision in *Bhasin v Hrynew* as an instance. Here the Court did not imply a good faith term; rather it accepted good faith as a general organising principle of the common law of contracting. It was an example of a broad-level change to the law.

This approach has the advantage of not having to meet the requirements for implication of terms. As was discussed above, to imply a term in fact, among other things, it must be necessary, in order to give business efficacy to the contract. Necessity is interpreted strictly.[57] A term will not be implied when the contract would be effective without it.[58] In other words, it must be such an obvious term that it goes without saying.[59] Nor can it contradict an express term of the contract. Such implications are ad hoc in nature. In these cases, a term is implied because it is presumed to reflect the parties' intention. If a term is implied in law, it applies only to a class of contracts, and again requires that a test of 'necessity' be satisfied. This kind of implied term may not be connected with parties' intention.

It can be difficult to argue that implication of a term of good faith is required to give business efficacy to a contract. In many cases, frankly the contract would be effective without it. It may not meet a test of necessity. Some courts have concluded

[54] ibid 56–57.

[55] G Gottlieb, 'Relationism: Legal Theory for a Relational Society' (1983) 50 *University of Chicago Law Review* 567, 604.

[56] Zhong Xing Tan, 'Disrupting Doctrine: Revisiting the Doctrine Impact of Relational Contract Theory' (2019) 39 *Legal Studies* 98, 105–13.

[57] *Marks and Spencer Plc v BNP Paribas Securities Services* [2016] AC 742, 755 (Lord Neuberger, with whom Lords Sumption and Hodge agreed).

[58] ibid. Lord Neuberger stated that without the suggested the implied term, the contract would have to lack commercial or practical coherence (with whom Lords Sumption and Hodge agreed).

[59] *The Moorcock* (1889) 14 PD 64 (CA).

that implication of such a term would be necessary to give a contract business efficacy. However, with respect, on occasion there is apparent strain in reaching such a conclusion.[60]

Further, if good faith is implied, it is of course subject to being overridden by the parties' agreement. This might be express, though concededly it would be a rare case where a contract expressly contemplated that parties to it might act in bad faith. It is more likely that it might do so subtly. For example, assume a contract that apparently confers absolute discretion upon one of the contracting parties, for example to terminate the contract. It is certainly plausible to argue that a contractual provision cast in such terms reflects the parties' intention that the discretion be unqualified. This might make it difficult to argue that an implied (in fact) term of good faith (which would have the effect of circumscribing the exercise of that discretion) exists.

VI. Robert Scott

Not everyone accepts that the fact that contracts are relational in character should impact on the law of contract. These are the formalists such as Robert Scott. He is evidently concerned with giving courts too significant a role in setting default rules of contract (or, at least, different default rules of contract than those that currently exist), or in adjusting parties' express agreement in favour of ill-defined and subjective standards of fairness. He is concerned this will interfere with the predictability around contract interpretation. For these reasons, although he acknowledges the difference between the reality of contracts and the rules of contract law, he insists that courts should stick to a formalist approach, giving effect to unambiguous express contract terms. The kinds of norms that Macneil and others identified are better enforced, Scott says, through non-legal, social sanctions.[61] He disagrees with the imposition of 'reasonableness' glosses on the exercise of contractual discretion on the basis that some courts have (ab)used their power in this context, not reflecting the reality of commercial norms, but engaging in speculation or using illegitimate criteria.[62]

[60] H Dubroff, 'The Implied Covenant of Good Faith in Contract Interpretation and Gap-Filling: Reviling a Revered Ethic' (2006) 80 *St John's Law Review* 559, 577: 'the traditional approach to gap filling relied on either strained interpretations of contract language or implication of contract terms based on the presumed intention of the parties. In this manner, courts would enforce gap-ridden express contracts without acknowledging that they were … making contracts for the parties. The technique for gap-filling usually involved no more than stating conclusively what the parties' presumed intent was. Frequently, such presumed intent was by no means self-evident.' Dubroff cites *Taylor v Caldwell* (1863) 122 ER 309 (QB), where a contract provided for a licence to use a music hall. The hall was destroyed by fire. The court read in a term that such an event ended the agreement, based on the presumed intention of the parties.

[61] R Scott, 'The Case for Formalism in Relational Contract' (2000) 94(3) *Northwestern University Law Review* 847.

[62] ibid 868.

VII. Donald King

Professor King did attempt to spell out in more detail the implications of relational contracting theory for the law of contract.[63] He argued that it called for significant reform of that law. Specifically, he fundamentally disagreed with the parol evidence rule, and the view that the parties' contractual agreement was typically bounded by that contained in the written agreement. Rather, he indicated that a 'spark of consent' was needed to establish a contractual relationship between parties. However, in largely rejecting the will theory of contract (apart from the 'spark'), he argued there was no need for parties to attempt to set out precisely the details of that engagement. The expectation would be that the law would fill in the many blanks of the detail of that relationship. This would be, for example, though principles such as fairness, reasonableness, trade usage and course of performance. In other words, there were two parts to every contract – the 'party made' part and the 'law made' part. Application of concepts of fairness and reasonableness would be context specific. Contracts would be valid although no specific provision was made regarding important terms such as price, timeframes, quality, warranties, remedies and so on. This approach would take greater account of evolution in the parties' relationship over time and after the contract was executed.

Obviously the traditional approach to contract already provides some 'law made' aspects. Often contracts do not specify the consequences if particular terms are breached. Contracts may not identify which terms are conditions and which are warranties, for example, or specify that in the event of breach of contract, the innocent party is entitled to consequential damages. There is already a 'law made' part of most contracts. King's suggestion is really to expand the scope of the law-made part of contracts, and shrink the party-made part (or, at least, expectations regarding the scope of the party-made part).

King also points to relational aspects in how the Uniform Commercial Code deals with breach of contract. Traditionally, the response of the common law to breach of contract is the payment of damages and/or a right to termination (if the contract is not already at an end), with specific performance very much the exception. This is of course in marked contrast to civil law systems, where good faith is long-established, where specific performance is the most usual remedy. King points to provisions of the Uniform Commercial Code permitting a party in breach of contract a right 'to cure performance'.[64] He notes this clause supports the parties' continuing relationship. It discourages reliance on minor or technical breaches to end the contract, particularly where the innocent party has found a more appealing contracting partner and wishes to take advantage of such technical

[63] D King, 'Reshaping Contract Theory and Law: Death of Contracts Part I: Generalised Consent With Lawmade Obligations' (1994) 7 *Journal of Contract Law* 245 and 'Reshaping Contract Theory and Law: Death of Contracts Part II: Ending Consideration and Beginning New Performance and Remedies' (1994) 8 *Journal of Contract Law* 16.

[64] S2-508 Uniform Commercial Code (2011).

breach. It gives parties in breach a reasonable chance to fix their error/s. This is consistent with relational contract theory, as opposed to an adversarial approach to contracting where compliance with the letter of the contract is always expected, and parties who depart from this run the risk of being held liable in damages and having the contract prematurely ended.

He also points to the fact that section 2-302 of the Uniform Commercial Code reflects a preparedness to consider unconscionability in a substantive way. This is a contrast with the traditional common law approach to unconscionability which is usually limited to procedural unconscionability. The difference is material – procedural unconscionability is focussed on the time leading up to the parties' agreement – for example, whether one party took advantage of the other's vulnerability to secure an advantage for themselves.[65] It generally declines to consider whether clauses in the actual contract are unfair. This is because to do so would, on one view, unacceptably impinge on the parties' freedom of contract. In contrast, substantive unconscionability does include reference to the actual terms of the contract, and consideration of whether they result in unfairness. This could be, for example, because they are one-sided in nature, conferring one party with rights but not the other, terms that are not reasonably necessary to protect parties' legitimate interests, how common such clauses are in that particular industry etc, whether the contract is a product of genuine negotiation and so on.[66]

VIII. Conclusion

My own view is an orthodox one – that commercial law should be reflective of actual commercial practice, as far as is possible, and recognising that a broad range of commercial practice occurs, making any generalisations potentially difficult. If there is evidence that there is a substantial disparity between commercial law and commercial practice, and the reasonable expectations of those engaged in commerce (or if there typically is such a disparity), I view this as a serious concern that warrants reflection and, perhaps, reform.

Of course, any general rules, principles or assumptions of contract law will run the risk of not being applicable or appropriate to a particular situation. This is unavoidable. That said, given the empirical evidence as to actual contractual practice, it is sensible and defensible to assume, or have a default position, that a particular contract situation is 'relational'. While there is a continuum between discrete and fully relational contracts, it seems reasonable to assume that most contracts will have (or are intended to have) a relational aspect. Thus, this should be the default assumption, and the legal principles should flow from that assumption.

[65] *Commercial Bank of Australia Ltd v Amadio* (1983) 151 CLR 447.

[66] D King 'Reshaping Contract Theory and Law: Death of Contracts II: Ending Consideration and Beginning New Performance and Remedies' (n 63) 28–29.

What would an assumption that contracting parties are typically in a 'relational' arrangement mean practically? It is thought best to be frank about this. First, it would reduce reliance on the written word as reflecting the entirety of the parties' bargain. It is an important piece of evidence, but it should not be permitted to eviscerate other evidence of the parties' relationship. The law must no longer presume or pretend that the written agreement reflects the entirety of the parties' bargain. It never did, and does not. This would open the door to the court considering matters extraneous to the written contract. Prime examples are the parties' conduct after the contract is executed, and what was said during pre-contractual negotiations. It would also support a contextual interpretation of contracts, which is already occurring to some extent. These matters are discussed further in chapter nine.

A relational view of contracting is consistent with the law recognising that parties typically have expectations regarding the behaviour of others with whom they contract. They expect the other party to act reasonably, to support rather than undermine the parties' agreement, and not act capriciously or arbitrarily. They expect honesty. These expectations will not necessarily appear in writing, yet they are vital. The law should respect and enforce them. It is difficult, arguably impossible, to do this without a good faith doctrine.

The law should not assume that individuals are Hobbesian-like, seeking to extract maximum advantage from a particular exchange, without care as to the parties' relationship or ethical values. Individuals are simply not always motivated by immediate material self-interest. The law should not craft rules on the assumption that they are. By doing so, it effectively encourages and rewards opportunistic behaviour.

There are many implications for the law of contract if we were to adopt a relational view of contracts. It is not within the scope of this book to identify them all. For present purposes, it provides significant intellectual support for the application of a generalised obligation of good faith to be applied to contractual relationships. This is submitted to better align, in most cases, with the parties' expectations.

9

Application of Relational Contract Theory: Contract Interpretation

I. General Principles of Contractual Interpretation

A traditional legal starting point in determining the ambit of the agreement between parties is the parol evidence rule. The rule applies as a presumption.[1] It is that

> Where parties agreed to embody, and do actually embody, their contract in a formal written deed, then in determining what the contract really was and really meant, a court must look to the formal deed and to that deed alone.[2]

Traditionally, and consistently with neoclassical contract law, courts took an objective approach to interpretation of the parties' agreement. A court would give effect to the written terms, and give the words their natural meaning, on the assumption that the written terms as used accurately reflected the parties' intention. The question was what a reasonable person would have understood the express terms used in the contract to mean. On this approach, extrinsic evidence could not typically be led to shed further light on the parties' intentions. This prohibition would extend to evidence as to how the contract was actually being performed.

This view is consistent with a view of contracts that assumes that parties are rational utility maximisers, and that they were able to negotiate the terms of a contract that would lead to such maximisation. It assumed parties had full information upon which to make contractual choices, and were in a roughly equal bargaining power, such that they could in reality negotiate an agreement to their liking. As discussed above, it assumed it was possible to reduce the entirety of the parties' agreement to writing, even though contracts had typically become executory in nature, contemplating future performance, sometimes many years after the contract was finalised. Either it tolerated the fact that the form of the contract

[1] *Gillespie Bros & Co v Cheney Eggar and Co* [1896] 2 QB 62 (Lord Russell).

[2] *Inglis v John Buttery & Co* (1873) 3 App Cas 552, 577 (Lord Blackburn, in turn quoting Lord Gifford in an unnamed case); see for discussion R Stevens, 'Objectivity, Mistake and the Parol Evidence Rule' in A Burrows and E Peel (eds), *Contract Terms* (Oxford, Oxford University Press, 2007) 109.

would often differ from the reality in terms of actual contractual performance by ignoring it, or it denied it. The façade of certainty and objectivity was all-important.

However, this model proved to be unsatisfactory. There are now so many exceptions of the parol evidence rule that the rule itself has become marginal. A focus on a contextual interpretation of contracts has become dominant, as will be elaborated upon below. Courts will now regularly consider 'surrounding circumstances' when interpreting contracts. Courts will intervene when a literal interpretation of the contract would lead to commercial nonsense. Courts will regularly interpret contracts having due regard to 'business common sense'. Courts connect this with the reasonable expectations of the parties, and believe it to be their duty to give effect to such expectations. Sometimes courts will imply terms into contracts, though this is logically separate from and not part of the interpretation/construction of the original contract.

II. Relevance of Actual Performance: English Authorities

Traditionally, English courts refused to consider extrinsic material in contract interpretation.[3] In *Whitworth Street Estates (Manchester) Ltd v James Miller and Partners Ltd*,[4] Lord Reid said anything said or done after the contract was entered into was irrelevant to its interpretation.[5] Similarly, the court excluded statements made prior to the introduction of the contract as being of any relevance.

In *Narich Pty Ltd v Commissioner of Pay-Roll Tax*,[6] the Privy Council (on appeal from Australia) considered whether, in determining the scope of the parties' agreement, it was limited to consideration of the express written terms. It noted:

> Subject to one exception, where there is a written contract between the parties whose relationship is in issue, a court is confined, in determining the nature of that relationship, to a consideration of the terms, express or implied, of that contract in the light

[3] In the case of Scotland, see *Bairds Trs v Baird and Co* (1877) 4 R 1005, 1016–17: 'the best exposition of doubtful expressions in a mercantile contract is the manner in which the person who used them carried them into effect' (Lord Justice-Clerk Moncreiff); *Hunter v Barron's Trs* (1886) R 883; *Jopp's Trs v Edmond* (1888) 15 R 271; *Welwood's Trs v Mungall* [1921] SC 911.

[4] [1970] AC 583.

[5] ibid 603, similarly Lord Hodson (606), Viscount Dilhorne (611) and Lord Wilberforce (614). Viscount Dilhorne (611) and Lord Wilberforce (615) agreed that evidence of subsequent conduct might give rise to an estoppel; *Schuler (AG) v Wickman Machine Tools Sales Ltd* [1974] AC 235, 252 (Lord Reid), 260 (Lord Morris), 261 (Lord Wilberforce), 268 (Lord Simon) and 272 (Lord Kilbrandon). Lord Wilberforce stated there that 'the general rule is that extrinsic evidence is not admissible for the construction of a written contract; the parties' intentions must be ascertained on legal principles of construction, from the words they have used. It is one and the same principle which excludes evidence of statements, or actions, during negotiations at the time of the contract, or subsequent to the contract, any of which to the lay mind might at first sight seem to be proper to receive'. This apparently contradicted an earlier Privy Council decision in *Watcham v Attorney-General of East Africa Protectorate* [1919] AC 533 where such evidence was utilised.

[6] [1984] ICR 286.

> of the circumstances surrounding the making of it; and it is not entitled to consider also the manner in which the parties subsequently acted in pursuance of such contract. The one exception to that rule is that, where the subsequent conduct of the parties can be shown to have amounted to an agreed addition to, or modification of the original written contract, such contract may be considered … by the court.[7]

Lord Nicholls was strongly critical of this position:

> It is surely time the law recognised what we all recognise in our everyday lives, that the parties' subsequent conduct, that is, their conduct after they had reached agreement, may be a useful guide to the meaning they intended to convey by the words of their contract. Such conduct … is one of the matters the court should be able to take into account when deciding what … is the meaning the words would reasonably convey to a reader. Judges are well able to identify, and disregard, self-serving subsequent conduct.[8]

The Privy Council also emphasised a substantive view of contracts. It eschewed a focus on labels used in a contract to describe the parties' agreement. The court should focus on the substance of the bargain.[9]

However the Courts' approach began to involve. In *Carmichael v National Power Plc*, the court had to consider whether an employment relationship existed between the parties. The court viewed an exchange of correspondence between them to determine that question. The Court determined that, on the evidence, in fact no agreement existed between the parties. In so deciding, Lord Irvine noted that a lower level decisionmaker might have concluded that the record of written correspondence between the parties did not reflect the entirety of the parties' bargain. Further, that this intention could be discerned by considering other sources. These somewhat innocuous comments, at odds with the traditional laser focus on the written word, seemed to open the door to the possibility of a much broader view of the parties' agreement. Specifically, the fact the contract had been performed might be of relevance in interpreting it, and discovering the true nature of the parties' relationship. The court here demonstrated recognition that the 'paper deal' could well differ from the 'real deal'. Further, it demonstrated a preference to give effect to the 'real deal', to the extent that could be demonstrated through evidence, as opposed to the paper deal. The court was no longer prepared

[7] ibid 291 (Lord Brandon, for the Council); see similarly *Whitworth Street Estates (Manchester) Ltd v James Miller and Partners Ltd* [1970] AC 583. Lord Reid stated in that case that 'it is now well settled that it is not legitimate to use as an aid in the construction of the contract anything which the parties said or did after its was made' (Lord Reid, 603); similarly Lord Hodson (606), Viscount Dilhorne (611) and Lord Wilberforce (614). Similar sentiments were expressed by Lord Wilberforce in *Schuler v Wickman Machine Tools Sales Ltd* [1974] AC 235, 261: 'the general rule is that extrinsic evidence is not admissible for the construction of a written contract; the parties' intentions must be ascertained on legal principles of construction from the words they have used. It is one and the same principle which excludes evidence of statements or actions during negotiations at the time of the contract, or subsequent to the contract'; to like effect Lord Reid (252), Lord Morris (260), Lord Simon (268) and Lord Kilbrandon (272).

[8] 'My Kingdom for a Horse: The Meaning of Words' (2005) 121 *Law Quarterly Review* 577, 589.

[9] (n 6) 291 (Lord Brandon, for the Council).

to assume that they were one and the same, or to ignore the obvious fact that they were not.

In this context, care must be taken to distinguish matters of present relevance with 'sham' contracts. Courts will typically not enforce sham contracts. However, it is critical to note how courts have defined a 'sham' contract. It is typically one where both parties to a contract contrive to make an agreement at a time when they know or intend that the actual performance of the contract will be materially different, such that the written contract does not accurately reflect the parties' agreement. The important thing is that both parties understand the written agreement to be a fantasy; the mere fact that only one of the parties does so is insufficient.

In *Carmichael* recognition that much of the real agreement between the parties may not appear in the written contract was obiter dicta, because there was found to be no written agreement there. However, those sentiments were subsequently adopted in other cases where a written agreement did exist. So, for example, although the parties had called a particular accommodation arrangement a 'licence', the court was prepared to look beyond the written word to the substance, and conclude it was in fact a lease. The facts in the case would not have amounted to a sham, since there was no evidence both parties intended something different than what the written agreement evidenced.

Pauline Bomball calls the situation in that case, and in others, a 'pretence'. There is where one of the parties does not intend that the contract as written will be the same as the contract as performed. Others have defined a 'pretence' situation to mean where the dominant party (in the above case, the property owner) does not intend that the contract, or parts of it, will actually be enforced as written in the contract.

An important decision in the current context is *Autoclenz Ltd v Belcher and Others*.[10] The case involved the engagement of car detailers. The party that engaged the detailers asked them to sign a contract. That contract purported to provide that the relationship between the parties was one of client-independent contractor, rather than an employment contract. It expressly contemplated that contractors could sub-contract work out, provided this occurred according to certain conditions. It required contractors to perform the work at a certain standard. It sought to impose upon them an obligation to obtain appropriate insurance and to pay the relevant taxation. The contract expressly provided there was no obligation upon a contractor to perform any particular service. The contract contained no guarantee that the contractors would receive a minimum amount of work from the client.

The Court was prepared to take a substantive view of the nature of the parties' relationship. It found that, in substance, it was an employment contract, regardless of the fact it had been drafted ostensibly to avoid that outcome, specifically

[10] [2011] ICR 1157.

providing for an independent contractor-client relationship. This was not new – previous cases had similarly been prepared to look beyond labels. What was new was the court's willingness to look outside of the parameters of the contract. The facts did not fit the Narich exception – it was not a case of a contractual variation. The court suggested that the reality of an unequal bargaining power between the parties in cases like this suggested a different approach to contractual interpretation. Such a contract was likely to be one-sided, could be unfair, and may not reflect the reality of the way in which the contract was performed, or even the parties' intention accurately. Specifically, the court indicated it was more prepared to look beyond the four corners of the contract in this context. The Court concluded:

> So the relative bargaining power of the parties must be taken into account in deciding whether the terms of any written agreement in truth represent what was agreed and the true agreement will often have to be gleaned from all the circumstances of the case, of which the written agreement in only part.[11]

On the facts, the Court found that the agreement as written did not accurately reflect the agreement as performed. The detailers were in reality effectively obliged to do work offered to them. And Autoclenz was in reality effectively obliged to offer them work (both of which directly contradicted the written terms of the agreement). Further, contrary to the written terms, detailers were in fact precluded from sub-contracting work out. The Court said that, in such a case, the court should apply the law to the actual factual scenario, not what the written terms might have apparently contemplated.

Following *Autoclenz*, courts became more prepared to look behind the 'paper deal' to find the 'real deal', and to apply the law to it.[12] This has occurred in contexts other than employment relationships.[13]

The United Kingdom Supreme Court reflected on the importance of the *Autoclenz* decision as follows:

> The Autoclenz case shows that, in determining whether an individual is an employee or other worker for the purpose of the legislation, the approach endorsed in the Carmichael case is appropriate even when there is a formal written agreement (and even if the agreement contains a clause stating that the document is intended to record the entire agreement of the parties). This does not mean that the terms of any written

[11] ibid 1168 (Lord Clarke) (with whom Lords Hope, Walker, Wilson and Collins agreed).

[12] *Independent Workers' Union of Great Britain and Central Arbitration Committee and Roofoods t/a Deliveroo* [2021] EWCA Civ 952, [26] that the court was 'alive to the possibility that the terms of the … contract might not reflect the true agreement between he parties' (Underhill LJ, with whom Coulson and Phillips LLJ agreed); *Addison Lee Ltd v Lange & Ors* [2021] EWCA Civ 594, [12]: 'where the provisions of the contract are at variance with the reality of the facts they should be disregarded' (Bean LJ).

[13] *Agnew v Commissioner of Inland Revenue* [2001] 2 AC 710, 730: 'it is not enough to provide in the debenture that the account is a blocked account if it is not operated as one in fact' (Lord Millett, for the Privy Council); *Commissioners for Her Majesty's Revenue and Customs v Atholl House Productions Limited* [2022] EWCA Civ 501, [113] (Sir David Richards, with whom Arnold and Peter Jackson LLJ agreed).

> agreement should be ignored. The conduct of the parties and other evidence may show that the written terms were in fact understood and agreed to be a record, possibly an exclusive record, of the parties' rights and obligations towards each other. But there is no legal presumption that a contractual document contains the whole of the parties' agreement and no absolute rule that terms set out in a contractual document represent the parties' true agreement just because an individual has signed it. Furthermore … any terms which purport to classify the parties' relationships, or to exclude or limit statutory protections by preventing the contract from being interpreted as a contract of employment or other worker's contract are of no effect and must be disregarded.[14]

Extra-judicially, Lord Steyn also supported this broader focus:

> Business people and, for that matter, ordinary people, simply do not understand a rule which excludes from consideration how the parties have in the course of their performance interpreted their contract. The law must not be allowed to drift too far from the intuitive reactions of justice or men and women of good sense: the rule (excluding evidence of) subsequent conduct may have to be re-examined.[15]

Thus, in broad terms, the English position seems to have evolved from a strict adherence to the written terms to a more flexible approach, whereby evidence of subsequent conduct will be readily admitted to assist to explain the parties' agreement. At the risk of simplicity, it will now be shown that the Australian position has apparently moved in the opposite direction, from a flexibility regarding interpretation of the parties' contractual relationship to one focussed more closely on the written term. Many of these issues have arisen in the context of an employment or employment-type agreement.

So for example in *The Queen v Foster; Ex Parte The Commonwealth Life (Amalgamated) Insurances Ltd*,[16] three members of the Court indicated a willingness to consider the true nature of the parties' arrangements, and that clauses in a written contract would not be permitted to obscure that reality. Dixon CJ Fullagar and Kitto JJ stated:

> If in practice the company assumes the detailed direction and control of the agents in the daily performance of their work and the agents tacitly accept a position of subordination to authority and to orders and instructions as to the manner in which they carry out their duties, a clause designed to prevent the relation receiving the legal complexion which it truly wears would be ineffectual.

[14] *Uber BV & Ors v Alsam & Ors* [2021] UKSC 5, [85] (Lord Leggatt, with whom Lord Reed, Lord Hodge, Lady Arden, Lord Sales and Lord Hamblen agreed).

[15] 'The Intractable Problem of the Interpretation of Legal Texts' (2003) 25 *Sydney Law Review* 5, 10.

[16] (1952) 85 CLR 138, 151; see also *Curtis v Perth and Fremantle Bottle Exchange Co Ltd* (1914) 18 CLR 17, 25 where the Court noted that contracting parties 'cannot by a mere consensual label alter the inherent character of the relationship they have actually called into existence. Many cases have arisen where courts have disregarded such labels, because in law they were wrong, and looked beneath them to the real substance' (Isaacs J). This is sometimes noted in the context of estoppel: *Thompson v Palmer* (1933) 49 CLR 507, 547 (Dixon J); *Grundt v Great Boulder Pty Ltd Gold Mines Ltd* (1937) 59 CLR 641, 656–57 (Latham CJ) and 676–77 (Dixon J).

The matter was again considered in *Stevens v Brodribb Sawmilling Co Pty Ltd*,[17] where the Court considered whether a particular worker was a contractor or employee. A close reading of the judgments suggests that, in determining this matter, the Court did not confine itself to the wording of the contract of engagement. Members of the Court considered how the arrangement worked in practice. Judges considered the extent to which an employee actually exercised their own skill and judgment,[18] and the extent of a supervisor's actual authority or the worker's actual right of independent judgment.[19] One said that that 'totality' of the parties' relationship had to be considered in determining the issue;[20] another said the 'substantive content … (not) the technical characterization of (the) relationship', was what was important.[21]

Again in *Hollis v Vabu Pty Ltd*,[22] the question arose as to the nature of an engagement between two parties relating to work to be performed. The case again demonstrates the courts' willingness to go beyond the parties' written terms in order to determine the parties' contractual rights and obligations. It should be conceded that, to some extent at least, this approach was forced on the court by the fact that the written terms of the agreement between the parties were very sparse.

That acknowledged, Gleeson CJ Gaudron Gummow Kirby and Hayne JJ stated that the parties' relationship was not to be deduced merely from the written contractual terms. The system that was actually operated by the engaging firm and the way in which work actually occurred were relevant.[23] Applying this approach, the joint reasons considered whether the workers had much actual control over the way in which their work was performed, to whom work was allocated, whether they actually could delegate tasks to others, whether they actually could work for others, what uniforms they actually wore and whether they referred to the engaging firm, the payment arrangements, who actually provided equipment necessary to do the work, and so on.[24]

In a different contractual context, the Court's emphasis on the literal terms of the contract, rather than evidence of actual performance, was re-asserted. The case *Agricultural and Rural Finance Pty Ltd v Gardiner and Another*[25] involved participants in an agricultural project being offered finance. It was agreed that if they ended their part in the project, they would have an indemnity from liability provided they had met their payment obligations 'punctually' until that time. Some of these participants ended their part in the project, and the issue arose as to the enforceability of the indemnity. It was common ground that some of these

[17] (1986) 160 CLR 16.
[18] ibid 25 (Mason J) (with whom Brennan J agreed).
[19] ibid 26 (Mason J), 37 (Wilson and Dawson JJ).
[20] ibid 29 (Mason J).
[21] ibid 50 (Deane J).
[22] (2001) 207 CLR 21.
[23] ibid 33.
[24] ibid 42–45. McHugh J also considered how the engagement actually operated in practice (48).
[25] (2008) 238 CLR 570.

parties had made payments after the due date (which also potentially triggered an acceleration clause). However, no objection had been taken to the late payments by the lender, and the acceleration clause was never exercised. The issue arose as to whether these payments had been made 'promptly'. The intermediate court had differed on the matter, with two holding that the payments had been made late and therefore not 'promptly', and one finding that because they had been accepted by the lender at the time, they had effectively been made 'promptly'.

It was in that context that members of the High Court re-asserted the primary importance of the written text of the contract, generally eschewing consideration of subsequent conduct of the parties in interpreting it.[26] Specifically, the fact that the lender had accepted late payments in the past without objection and without engaging the acceleration clause did not affect the meaning of the word 'punctually' in the written contract. If payments were made late, they could not be said to have been made 'punctually'.

In its most recent decisions, this time in the employment law context, the High Court took a similar approach in narrowly focussing on the written terms of the contract.[27]

The first case, *CFMMEU*, involved a labour company Construct, which organised workers in the construction industry. It signed a services agreement with an individual McCourt ('M'). The agreement described M as a self-employed contractor. It did not guarantee M work. M could decline offered work, and could accept work with other companies. The contract specifically stated that Construct was not liable to pay M various leave entitlements typically associated with employment, including annual leave, sick leave and long service leave. M acknowledged he was not an employee of Construct. He provided the tools he used at work. Construct liaised on his behalf with construction businesses in terms of possible work. It would negotiate on his behalf as to appropriate remuneration. M was free to negotiate a higher rate with them.

It was arranged that M would work on a site controlled by the firm Hanssen. He was given that company's induction forms and told he would be supervised by an employee of that firm. While Construct attended the work site occasionally, it did not direct M as to the work he should do, how it should be done etc. M would be paid by Construct after submitting an invoice to them. The High Court considered two main questions: (a) how to determine whether or not a worker is an employee or not; and (b) the relevance of the actual working of the contract to its interpretation. It is the second of these questions that is of most importance to us here.

[26] Gummow Hayne and Kiefel JJ referred to the general principle that 'it is not legitimate to use as an aid in the construction of a contract anything which the parties said or did after it was made' (citing *James Miller & Partners Ltd v Whitworth Street Estates (Manchester) Ltd* [1970] AC 583, 603 (Lord Reid)). The court also rejected arguments based on waiver, estoppel or forbearance.

[27] *Construction, Forestry, Mining, Manufacturing, and Energy Union v Personnel Contracting Pty Ltd* (2022) 275 CLR 165 ('*CFMMEU*'); *ZG Operations Australia Pty Ltd v Jamsek* (2022) 275 CLR 254 ('*ZG Operations*').

A split was evident among the justices as to the relevance of the actual working of the contract to its interpretation. For the sake of convenience, I refer to the 'first joint reasons', comprising the views of Kiefel CJ Keane and Edelman JJ, and the 'second joint reasons', comprising the views of Gageler and Gleeson JJ. The first joint reasons took a narrow view of relevant factors in interpretation, eschewing considerations of actual performance:

> Where the parties have comprehensively committed the terms of their relationship to a written contract the validity of which is not in dispute, the characterisation of their relationship as one of employment or otherwise proceeds by reference to the rights and obligations of the parties under that contract. Where no party seeks to (argue that the contract is a sham or should otherwise be held invalid) there is no occasion to seek to determine the character of the parties' relationship by a wide-ranging review of the entire history of the parties' dealings. Such a review is neither necessary nor appropriate because the task of the court is to enforce the parties' rights and obligations, not to form a view as to what a fair adjustment of the parties' rights might require.[28]

The first joint reasons pointed out that, in the United Kingdom, an approach different from the orthodox approach had been taken with respect to employment contracts, citing *Autoclenz*. The first joint reasons declined to follow *Autoclenz* in this respect. These reasons stated that *Autoclenz* was irreconcilable with *Narich*.[29] The first joint reasons did at least concede that their approach did not mean parties could simply put a label on something that was contrary to its substance, and expect the court to recognise and enforce it. To that extent at least, the court favoured a substance approach.

In contrast on these issues, the second joint reasons stated that, while often there would be no real divergence between the contract as written and the contract as performed, in other cases there would be:

> There will be cases where, without any variation to the terms of a written contract, the true character of a relationship in fact established and maintained under the contract will be revealed through the manner of the performance of the contract. That will be so where the terms of the written contract are sufficiently opaque or obscure to admit of different manners of performance. And it will be especially so where such a contract is a standard form written contract couched in language that might arguably have been chosen by the putative employer to dress up the relationship to be established and maintained as something somewhat different from what it might turn out to be.[30]

Gordon J took something of a middle position. She cited the general rule that conduct subsequent to formation was not relevant to interpretation of the contract. She apparently agreed with this. However, she acknowledged that there were occasions where subsequent conduct might be considered for reasons other than interpretation. She gave examples including matters relating to formation of the

[28] (2022) 275 CLR 165, 193.
[29] ibid 193.
[30] ibid 215–16 (Gageler and Gleeson JJ).

contract, to establish what the terms of the contract were, as evidence of discharge or variation of the original contract, to show that the written contract was a sham, or as evidence relating to another possible contract remedy, including estoppel or rectification. She also acknowledged that 'dynamic relationships' existed and in such cases it might be necessary to look at the totality of what occurred, including performance subsequent to formation.[31]

In the case of *ZG Operations*, similar issues were raised regarding the engagement of truck drivers. The appellants had previously employed these truck drivers as employees. A restructure occurred, and the drivers were purportedly re-engaged as independent contractors. The drivers would provide their own vehicles and other equipment to complete assigned tasks. The High Court unanimously found the drivers should be considered to be independent contractors.

The first joint reasons in this decision (again Kiefel CJ Keane and Edelman JJ) reiterated the point made in *CFMMEU* that rejected an approach to contractual interpretation said to reflect the 'substance and reality' of the parties' relationship. The first joint reasons said this was contrary to orthodox contractual interpretation and should not be adopted.[32] Specifically, the fact that a contract may involve a disparity of bargaining power between the parties was not a reason for adopting the 'substance and reality' approach, according to the first joint reasons. These reasons discounted the importance of the fact that the drivers wore uniforms featuring the appellants' logo, and the trucks reflected the appellants' livery. This did not alter the nature of the parties' agreement. Similarly, the reality that, because of the number of hours of work the appellants provided the drivers, they were extremely unlikely to work for anyone else, did not alter the nature of the parties' agreement.[33] For their part, Gageler and Gleeson JJ also took a similar approach to that adopted in *CFMMEU*. They considered how the contractual arrangements worked in practice in characterising the true nature of the relationship between the parties. Specifically, they considered whether a particular driver was required to, and did, perform the required services personally, or whether they could be (and were) given to another, and whether the driver was required to, and did, provide the truck required to provide the service.[34] Gordon and Steward JJ adopted the approach taken by Gordon J in *CFMMEU*, explained above.[35]

Thus, in essence, we see a division among High Court justices as to the extent to which actual performance of the contract and/or the history between the parties is relevant to contractual interpretation. Kiefel CJ Keane and Edelman JJ will generally decline to consider those matters, giving full effect to the written terms of the contract. Gageler and Gleeson JJ will take into account the full picture of

[31] ibid 230–32 (Gordon J). Steward J dissented and did not consider this issue.
[32] ibid 273.
[33] ibid 273–74.
[34] ibid 283–85.
[35] ibid 285–86.

the parties' relationship, including actual performance, in determining the parties' contractual rights and responsibilities. Gordon J (with whom Steward J agrees) occupies something of a middle position, reiterating the orthodox position that focusses on the actual terms of the contract and ignoring realities and/or performance. However, this is a general rule, and subject to exceptions with respect to matters other than interpretation of the contract, or potentially in special cases of 'dynamic' contracts.

III. Academic Support for Consideration of Actual Performance in Giving Effect to the Contract

Most of the academic commentary on these matters supports the position of the English courts in being prepared to consider actual performance in the interpretation of contracts, at least in some contexts. One argument in favour of such an approach is that it reduces the risks associated with situations where there is inequality of bargaining power. In such cases, the stronger party may have room to draft the contract in ways considered favourable to them. This might include presenting a picture of the parties' intended contractual arrangements that is not intended to reflect, and does not reflect, the parties' actual contractual arrangements.

The common law has developed the doctrine of sham, pursuant to which contractual arrangements that are designedly false and misleading may be ignored. However, the courts have interpreted this doctrine narrowly, to apply only to situations where there is a clear dual intention to deceive third parties, and sufficient evidence that both parties never intended their contractual arrangements to proceed as their contract might suggest.[36] This is typically difficult to determine, and again will not apply where it is one party (the one who drafts the contract), but not the other, who has this intention.

So leading Australian labour law scholar Andrew Stewart effectively supports the position taken by the English courts, and effectively disagrees with the first joint reasons in CFMMEU and ZG Operations:

> As Gray J so memorably put it … 'the parties cannot create something which has every feature of a rooster, but call it a duck and insist that everybody else recognise it as a duck. The fact is though that it is possible under Australian law to do just that. If the contract that governs the parties' relationship has enough duck-like features, most courts … will be persuaded that they are looking at a duck – even if the underlying reality of the relationship suggests a rooster. The key to this, and to the success of the drafting strategy just described, is the preoccupation that most judges have with the formal terms of the arrangement they are scrutinising.[37]

[36] *Snook v London and West Riding Investments Ltd* [1967] 2 QB 786, 802 (Lord Diplock).

[37] A Stewart, 'Redefining Employment? Meeting the Challenge of Contract and Agency Labour' (2002) 15 *Australian Journal of Labour Law* 1, 13; similarly A Stewart and S McCrystal, 'Labour Regulation and the Great Divide: Does the Gig Economy Require a New Category of Worker?' (2019) 32

Nothing in the first joint reasons in *CFMMEU* and *ZG Operations* changes Australian law from the position described by Stewart. Gageler and Gleeson JJ are apparently sympathetic to Stewart's position. Gordon J (with whom Steward J agrees) may in an appropriate case be persuaded to consider the practicalities of parties' arrangements.

Pauline Bomball is also alert to the possibility that a party in a strong bargaining position may draft clauses preferential to them. In the context of employment, this might include, for example, clauses that apparently permit the person engaged to do work to delegate the work to another, or those that apparently permit the person engaged to decline work offered to them. Bomball suggests that these clauses may not reflect the reality of the parties' (intended) agreement. A simple focus on the written agreement, ignoring the bigger picture including actual performance, might privilege form over substance. Thus, she suggests that the actual performance of the contract should in appropriate cases be taken into account.[38] This would be in relation to determining the parties' actual agreement, as opposed to an issue of construction.

David McLaughlan would support consideration of actual contractual performance, but only to the extent it sheds light on the parties' intentions at the time the contract was entered into.[39] On his view, the subsequent conduct need not be mutual in order to be beneficial.[40] This approach has judicial support.[41] An obvious advantage of this approach is that it avoids any suggestion that the

Australian Journal of Labour Law 4, 7: 'if weight is given to how the parties have chosen to structure their relationship, this will inevitably make it easier for organisations to evade the cost of employment entitlements by drafting contracts that minimise any appearance of control and emphasise what may be illusory 'freedoms' for the worker; B Langille and G Davidov, 'Beyond Employees and Independent Contractors: A View from Canada' (1999) 21 *Comparative Labor Law and Policy Journal* 7, 15 express a similar view.

[38] 'Statutory Norms and Common Law Concepts in the Characterisation of Contracts for the Performance of Work' (2019) 42 *Melbourne University Law Review* 370, 382; 'Subsequent Conduct, Construction and Characterisation in Employment Contract Law' (2015) 32 *Journal of Contract Law* 149, 158–59.

[39] 'Contract Formation, Contract Interpretation and Subsequent Conduct' (2006) 25 *University of Queensland Law Journal* 77, 88; 'The Continuing Confusion and Uncertainty Over the Relevance of Actual Mutual Intention in Contract Interpretation' (2021) 37 *Journal of Contract Law* 25, 42–44; 'Contract Interpretation: What is it About?' (2009) 31 *Sydney Law Review* 5, 42–44.

[40] This point divided the New Zealand Supreme Court in *Gibbon Holdings Ltd v Wholesale Distributors Ltd* [2008] 1 NZLR 277. There Tipping and Anderson JJ limited the use of such evidence to cases involving mutual post-contract conduct; Elias CJ and Thomas J disagreed. Blanchard J did not decide the issue. See for discussion McLaughlan, 'Contract Interpretation: What is it About?' (n 39) 44–46.

[41] Thomas J in *Attorney-General v Dreux Holdings Ltd* (1996) 7 TCLR 617, 631 commenting that post-contract execution conduct was 'admitted for the purpose of persuading the court that it provides a reliable guide to the meaning which the parties attributed to the contract when it was signed. The proper construction is assisted and not changed by the subsequent conduct. In this manner, the court's ability to give effect to the mutual intention of the parties is undoubtedly furthered'; *Shewchuk v Blackmont Capital Inc* [2016] ONCA 912, [48](Stathy CJO, with whom Weiler and Watt JJA agreed); *Bathurst Resources Limited v L & M Coal Holdings Limited* [2021] NZSC 85, [84]–[89] (Winkelmann CJ and Ellen France JJ, with whom Glazebrook O'Regan and Williams JJ relevantly agreed: [232]).

court is making the contract for the parties, or re-aligning the contract so that it accords with individual justices' views as to what might be a fair arrangement. Many would regard this type of judicial decision-making as having crossed a red line into unacceptable judicial activism. Courts are typically (and understandably) very wary about doing this, or being seen to do this.

An approach to contractual interpretation that takes into account subsequent conduct is also taken in international law. Article 8(3) of the United Nations Convention on Contracts for the International Sale of Goods (UNCISG) states that, in determining the parties' intentions or the reasonable understanding of the contract, all relevant matters must be considered, including the parties' conduct after the contract was entered into and the negotiations. Similarly, Article 4 of the UNIDROIT Principles of International Commercial Contracts (2016) states that the parties' common intentions determine the interpretation to be given to a contract. However, where the parties' intentions cannot be adequately gleaned, a court should apply the interpretation that a reasonable person would make of the contract provisions. In applying Article 4, the conduct of the parties after the contract was entered into is relevant, as are the negotiations.[42]

United States commercial law recognises a doctrine of the 'course of performance'. Section 1-303a of the Uniform Commercial Code (1952) defines a course of performance to mean how a contract is in fact performed by either or both parties, in particular where the other party is aware of how that party is performing their contractual obligations, and has an opportunity to object, but does not do so. In this way, it has similarities to the common law doctrine of waiver, or (arguably) estoppel. The course of performance can be utilised to interpret the parties' agreement. It can assist in interpreting written terms, including to supplement or qualify the express word. Where possible, the written word and the course of performance will be interpreted to have a consistent meaning. Where this is not possible, the written word will prevail over the inconsistent course of performance. Charles has written of the workability of this rule, which readily accommodates consideration of actual performance in interpreting the provisions of a written contract.[43]

IV. More General Principles of Contractual Interpretation

The courts generally prefer an objective approach to contractual interpretation. This means that the courts construe the words used, give them their natural meaning

[42] Section 4(3)(c). Not surprisingly, this reflects the practice in civil law countries: O Razzolini, 'The Need to Go Beyond the Contract: Economic and Bureaucratic Independence in Personal Work Relations' (2010) 31 *Comparative Labour Law and Policy Journal* 267, 274–75.

[43] S Charles, 'Interpretation of Ambiguous Contracts by Reference to Subsequent Conduct' (1991) 4 *Journal of Contract Law* 16, 36.

and determine what the document would convey to a reasonable person.[44] It does not generally consider subjective statements about intent. It generally ignores previous negotiations between the parties.[45]

Notwithstanding this, the Courts have for many years been prepared to look beyond the literal wording of the contract. So, for example, in *River Wear Commissioners v Adamson*, Lord Blackburn said that in seeking to understand the meaning of any written instrument it was necessary to consider the surrounding circumstances to aid in that understanding.[46] In Reardon Smith Line v Hansen-Tangen,[47] Lord Wilberforce said that the surrounding circumstances were relevant in assisting with the interpretation of a contract. This included the commercial purpose of the contract, its background and antecedents, the context, and the market in which the parties were operating. On the other hand, others had interpreted the authority of River Wear narrowly, taking the case as meaning that evidence of the surrounding circumstances was only relevant to the interpretation of a written instrument in cases where there was demonstrated ambiguity in the written terms.[48]

In *Investors Compensation Scheme Ltd v West Bromwich Building Society*,[49] Lord Hoffmann reiterated this position.[50] His judgment drew support from several other judges.[51] He added that 'absolutely anything' which could affect how a reasonable person would interpret the terms of the agreement could be considered.[52] Words should be given their natural and ordinary meaning.

[44] *Reardon Smith Line v Hansen-Tangen* [1976] 1 WLR 989, 996 (Lord Wilberforce, with whom Viscount Dilhorne and Lords Simon and Kilbrandon agreed).

[45] *Prenn v Simonds* [1971] 1 WLR 1381, 1384 (Lord Wilberforce, with whom Lords Reid, Donovan, Pearce and Diplock agreed). Interestingly, Janet O'Sullivan observes that the classic implied terms case of *The Moorcock* (1889) 14 PD 64 involved consideration of 'pre-contractual' material; the parties did not conclude a written contract. The court derived the parties' agreement from this material: 'Implied Terms in Fact and Evidence of Prior Negotiations: An Exploration' (2022) 138 *Law Quarterly Review* 558, 581.

[46] [1877] 2 App Cas 743, 763 (HL), similarly *Bairds' Trs v Baird and Co* (1877) 4 R 1005, 1017: 'the courts are entitled, in reading this contract, to be placed in the position of the parties to it, by ascertaining the surrounding circumstances' (Lord Justice-Clerk Moncrieff). River Wear was referred to with evident approval in *Prenn v Simonds* [1971] 1 WLR 1381, 1383–84 (Lord Wilberforce, with whom Lords Reid, Donovan, Pearce and Diplock agreed). In *Macdonald v Longbottom* (1859) 1 E & E 977, 983; 120 ER 1177, 1179 the contract referred to the thing being sold as 'your wool'. Lord Campbell CJ said everything within the knowledge of both parties before and at the time of contract was relevant to its interpretation. He also took into account of the content of a conversation between the parties prior to the entry into the contract to determine its meaning: 1 E & E 977, 984; 120 ER 1177, 1179; Erle J also expressly took into account the conversations prior to the entry into the contract: 1 E & E 977, 986; 120 ER 1177, 1180.

[47] [1976] 1 WLR 989, 995 (with whom Viscount Dilhorne and Lords Simon and Kilbrandon agreed).

[48] *Great Western Railway and Midland Railway v Bristol Corporation* (1918) 87 L J Ch 414, 418 (Lord Atkinson) and 424–25 (Lord Shaw).

[49] [1998] 1 WLR 896.

[50] ibid 912–13.

[51] Lord Goff (898), Lord Hope (918) and Lord Clyde (918).

[52] Obviously, the words 'absolutely anything' suggest a very large possible scope of relevant material. This sentiment raised questions, for example, about comments in *James Mill & Partners Ltd v Whitworth Street Estates (Manchester) Ltd* [1970] AC 583 that a court should not take into account

Lord Hoffmann added that sometimes 'things go wrong' and the words used do not accurately capture the parties' intention. He said in such cases courts would not ascribe to words a meaning that the parties could clearly not have intended. In other words, it will not reach an interpretation of a contract that 'flouts common sense'.[53]

There has been a significant debate regarding whether Lord Hoffmann's stated views changed the pre-existing law, or substantively confirmed it. It is difficult to reconcile Lord Hoffmann's views that 'absolutely anything' relevant to a reasonable person seeking to determine the parties' intentions, on the one hand, with the law's traditional reluctance to take into account the parties' subsequent conduct in interpreting the contract. Similarly, it is difficult to square the comments with the law's near-equal determination to discount evidence of pre-contractual negotiations, where they can shed light on the parties' actual agreement.

These issues arose again in *Chartbrook Ltd and Another v Persimmon Homes Ltd and Another*.[54] The contract was between a property owner and a property developer. The dispute arose as to payments due under the contract. The contract provided for payment of an 'additional residential payment' involving a number of variables. However, there were different views as to how this amount was to be calculated, and a large variation in amounts that the two parties calculated to be owed/owing under the relevant provision.

The Court reiterated the judgment of Lord Hoffmann in *Investors Compensation Scheme Ltd* regarding general principles of contract interpretation.[55] The court would adopt a common sense position. While it would focus closely on the express terms in the contract, it would avoid an interpretation of these words that would make no commercial sense.[56] This was not a licence for a court to revisit contractual terms because they were unduly favourable to one party. In this case, a literal interpretation of the words used would lead to irrational and arbitrary results.[57] The Court clarified it would not readily assume the parties had made an error; however if it were clear they had done so, the court would correct it if a clear correction (consistent with the parties' intentions) could be made.[58]

The Court reiterated that it must consider what a reasonable person would have understood the parties to have meant by way of agreement. This included the written words, as well as the background and context in which the contract

anything said or done after the contract was entered into in interpreting it: Lord Reid (603), Lord Hodson (606), Viscount Dilhorne (611) and Lord Wilberforce (615). Of course, it can be argued that a reasonable person *would* take into account such sentiments or actions, potentially creating a conflict in the views expressed in these cases.

[53] (n 49) 913.

[54] [2009] AC 1101.

[55] ibid 1112 (Lord Hoffmann), with whom Lord Hope (1109), Lord Rodger (1128), Lord Walker (1136) and Baroness Hale (1136) agreed.

[56] ibid 1112.

[57] ibid 1113.

[58] ibid 1114.

was made.[59] The court's resort to the background and context was not limited to occasions in which there was an ambiguity in the contract. Nor was its solution limited to what some might consider to be an 'available' meaning of the words used.[60] Where more than one interpretation of a particular clause is available, the court should adopt the one that is more consistent with business common sense. This is because it is likely it will reflect the parties' legitimate expectations.[61]

The Court considered an argument that the background and context might include pre-contractual negotiations. It considered past cases that had rejected use of such material in interpreting contracts.[62] One example was *Frederick E Rose (London) Ltd v Williams H Pim Jr & Co Ltd*.[63] There the plaintiff was tasked with securing 'Moroccan horsebeans described here as feveroles'. This was made known to the defendant. The defendant told the plaintiff they were just horsebeans. The written contract reflected a purchase of horsebeans. When the product was supplied, the purchaser discovered the beans were not feveroles. They sought rectification of the contract by addition of the word 'feveroles' after the word horsebeans in the contract. The single judge found in their favour, but this was overturned in the Court of Appeal.

Denning LJ agreed the parties were under a common mistake as to a fundamental aspect of the contract. They both believed that the product to be supplied would be 'feveroles', but they were not. The contract did not specifically provide for this, but it was reflected in the parties' pre-contractual negotiations. The Court of Appeal refused to grant rectification. The defendants contracted to supply 'horsebeans' and this is what they had supplied. There was no error in the contract for which the remedy of rectification could be applied.[64]

In the end the Court in *Chartbrook* did not disturb the orthodoxy here. That said, it did suggest that estoppel by convention might be utilised in appropriate cases where something said in pre-contractual negotiations was relied upon. Further, the court considered the remedy of rectification. It cited with apparent approval an earlier case which had outlined that rectification was available where (a) the parties had a continuing common intention in respect of a contractual matter; (b) there is external evidence of such agreement; (c) this intention existed at the time the parties executed their agreement; (d) by mistake, the written contract did not reflect that continuing common intention.[65] In cases like that, the

[59] Similar views appear in *Rainy Sky SA v Kookmin Bank* [2011] 1 WLR 2900, 2907 (Lords Clarke Phillips Mance Kerr and Wilson) and *Arnold v Britton* [2015] AC 1619, 1627 (Lord Neuberger, with whom Lords Sumption and Hughes agreed).

[60] [2009] AC 1101, 1119.

[61] *Rainy Sky SA v Kookmin Bank* [2011] 1 WLR 2900, 2908 (Lords Clarke Phillips Mance Kerr and Wilson).

[62] [2009] AC 1101, 1115–17.

[63] [1953] 2 QB 450.

[64] ibid 462.

[65] (n 54) 1123, citing the judgment of Peter Gibson LJ in *Swainland Builders Ltd v Freehold Properties Ltd* [2002] 2 EGLR 71, 74, para 33.

court may give effect to the continuing common intention of the parties. Thus, at least to the extent of grounding a possible action of estoppel by convention and/or rectification, evidence of pre-contractual negotiations might be relevant.[66]

In *Arnold v Britton*,[67] members of the Supreme Court explained that the meaning of words in a contract must be interpreted in light of: (a) the natural and ordinary meaning of the words used; (b) other relevant provisions of the contract; (c) the overall purpose of the clause and the contract more broadly; (d) facts or circumstances known or assumed by the parties at the time the contract was executed; and (e) commercial common sense.[68] However, it was emphasised that commercial common sense should not be used to undermine the express terms.[69] Further, the concept must be used sparingly. The mere fact that a bargain has turned out to be an improvident one for one or both of the parties does not mean that the parties' agreement as written necessarily lacked commercial common sense.[70] The objective was to ascertain the parties' intentions, and the orthodox way in which this occurred was by consideration of the words used.[71]

That said, the Court added that the more the words in dispute are ambiguous, the greater the likelihood that it will depart from their natural meaning. This does not mean that courts search for ambiguities in order to drive a departure from the natural meaning of the words used.[72]

The Court also added that, in interpreting a contractual provision, a court could only take into account circumstances that existed at the time the contract was made, and known or reasonably available to both parties.[73] In cases where an event occurs subsequent to the contract having been entered into which was not contemplated by the parties, the court will determine whether the contract is clear as to what the parties' intention would have been in relation to such an event. If so, that intention will be given effect.[74] On one reading, this sentiment can seem to be at odds with the decision in *Autoclenz*, where matters that occurred after the contract was made (actual performance) was taken into account in the course of contractual interpretation.

The Court has noted that the broader context is important in interpreting the terms of a contract.[75] However, a textual and contextual approach to contractual interpretation were not in conflict.[76] Both were useful. Their relative importance

[66] Baroness Hale agreed with Lord Hoffmann, adding that if the language of the contract does not reflect a consensus that parties had earlier reached, the contract should be rectified to reflect it (1137); see also *ING Bank NV v Ros Roca* [2011] EWCA Civ 353; [2012] 1 WLR 472.

[67] [2015] AC 1619.

[68] ibid 1627 (Lord Neuberger, with whom Lords Sumption Hughes and Hodge agreed).

[69] ibid 1628.

[70] ibid 1628–29.

[71] ibid 1628.

[72] ibid 1628.

[73] ibid 1629.

[74] ibid.

[75] *Wood v Capita Insurance Services Ltd* [2017] AC 1173, 1179 (Lord Hodge, for the Supreme Court).

[76] ibid 1180.

may vary. So, for example, a textual approach may have a greater role where contracts were written comprehensively and with the input of legal personnel; a contextual approach may assume greater importance where the written terms are brief, the contractual arrangements are characterised by informality, and/or the parties did not have access to legal advice. However, even when contracts were drafted with the assistance of lawyers, the drafting may be incomplete for various reasons. In such cases, a greater focus on the 'factual matrix' and a consideration of the purpose of equivalent clauses utilised elsewhere would be appropriate.[77]

One of the fears expressed in relation to the English courts' apparent greater willingness to consider the context was that the 'floodgates' would open in relation to the material presented to the court argued to be of assistance in providing context.[78] However, judges have noted that claims about a 'floodgate' of material being submitted to the court as a result have not generally materialised.[79]

In the Australian context, the leading judgment is often considered to be that of Mason J (with whom Stephen and Wilson JJ agreed) in *Codelfa Construction Pty Ltd v State Rail Authority of NSW*.[80] Mason J concluded that

> The true rule is that evidence of surrounding circumstances is admissible to assist in the interpretation of the contract if the language is ambiguous or susceptible of more than one meaning. But it is not admissible to contradict the language of the contract when it has a plain meaning. Generally speaking facts existing when the contract was made will not be receivable as part of the surrounding circumstances as an aid to construction, unless they were known to both parties.[81]

Subsequent authorities have, with respect, not been entirely clear as to the extent to which courts may have regard to extrinsic material in interpreting the contract.

[77] ibid.

[78] J Spigelman, 'From Text to Context: Contemporary Contractual Interpretation' (2007) 81 *Australian Law Journal* 322, 334: 'taking into account the whole of the "factual matrix" … unquestionable expanded to a substantial degree the cost of litigation starting … with the enormous costs of the discovery process, and thereafter the cost of the compilation of the agreed bundle of documents, the proliferation of disputes about what is admissible … and the enormous burden imposed on all involved in litigation … in getting on top of an enormous body of material'.

[79] *Static Control Components (Europe) Ltd v Egan* [2004] EWCA Civ 392, [29] (Arden LJ); Lord Bingham, 'A New Thing Under the Sun? The Interpretation of Contract and the ICS Decision' (2008) 12 *Edinburgh Law Review* 374, 387–88.

[80] (1982) 149 CLR 337.

[81] ibid 352. Earlier Mason J had explained that the parol evidence rule had traditionally sought to exclude the use of extrinsic evidence to vary the language of a written agreement. This was because it was considered that the words used should be given their plain and ordinary meaning. As a result it was unnecessary to consider extrinsic evidence. He acknowledged that it had also been accepted that there was more to the construction of a contract that merely assigning to the words used in it their ordinary meaning (347–48). He apparently sought to reconcile the views with the position that resort could be had to such extrinsic evidence in cases where the contractual language contained an ambiguity. On the other hand, Mason J seemed to take a broader view of the circumstances in which context was relevant to contractual interpretation, not limited to circumstances of ambiguity, in *K & S Lake City Freighters* (1985) 157 CLR 309, 315: 'the modern approach to interpretation insists that the context be considered in the first instance, especially in the case of general words, and not merely at some later stage when ambiguity might be thought to arise' (Mason J).

Specifically, three justices in *Mount Bruce Mining Pty Ltd v Wright Prospecting Pty Ltd and Another*[82] stated that resort to extrinsic material was justified where 'constructional choice' was possible in contractual interpretation.[83] It has legitimately been pointed out that such choice is always possible.[84] The High Court has apparently suggested that resort to extrinsic circumstances is legitimate even where there is no contractual ambiguity.[85] There has also been the suggestion that the matter remains open.[86] This is not satisfactory. The High Court has also acknowledged possible inconsistency with the contextual position taken by the English Court in *Investors Compensation Scheme* and the Australian position in *Codelfa*, where resort to context appears to be more confined. It acknowledged it, but pointedly refused to resolve it.[87] This is also not satisfactory.

It has also been accepted that, where there are 'rival meanings' regarding particular clauses in the contract, the court should be guided by commercial common sense in deciding which of them to apply.[88] Some have interpreted Mason J's views to meant that evidence of 'surrounding circumstances' can include evidence of prior negotiations, if they demonstrate objective background facts known to both parties.[89]

[82] (2015) 256 CLR 104.

[83] ibid 116 (French CJ Nettle and Gordon JJ).

[84] J Carter, 'Commercial Construction and Contract Doctrine' (2009) 25 *Journal of Contract Law* 83.

[85] *CIC Insurance Ltd v Bankstown Football Club* (1997) 187 CLR 384, 408 (Brennan CJ Dawson Toohey Gummow JJ); *Pacific Carriers Ltd v BNP Paribas* (2004) 218 CLR 451, 462 (Gleeson CJ Gummow Hayne Callinan and Heydon JJ) stated that contractual interpretation was based on what a reasonable person would think the contract meant. This reasonable person interpretation was in turn influenced by the text of the contract, surrounding circumstances, and the object and purpose of the transaction. This expression of the test did not condition resort to matters other than the written text on a finding of ambiguity. The High Court confirmed *Pacific Carriers Ltd* in *Toll (FGCR) Pty Ltd v Alphapharm Pty Ltd* (2004) 219 CLR 451, 461–62: 'the meaning of the terms of a contractual document is to be determined by what a reasonable person would have understood them to mean. That normally requires consideration not only of the text, but also of the surrounding circumstances known to the parties, and the purpose and object of the transaction' (Gleeson CJ Gummow Hayne Callinan and Heydon JJ). See similarly *Electricity Generation Corporation v Woodside Energy Ltd* (2014) 251 CLR 640, 656–57 where French CJ Hayne Crennan and Kiefel JJ similarly permitted consideration of surrounding circumstances even without ambiguity; T Cole, 'The Parol Evidence Rule: A Comparative Analysis and Proposal' (2003) 26 *University of New South Wales Law Journal* 680 and J Getzler, 'Interpretation, Evidence and the Discovery of Contractual Intention' in S Degeling, J Edelman and J Goudkamp (eds), *Contract in Commercial Law* (Sydney, Lawbook Co, 2016) 132–33.

[86] *Mount Bruce Mining Pty Ltd v Wright Prospecting Pty Ltd and Another* (2015) 256 CLR 104, 132 (Kiefel and Keane JJ); Spigelman (n 78) 328.

[87] *Royal Botanic Gardens and Domain Trust v South Sydney City Council* (2009) 240 CLR 45, 63: 'it is unnecessary to determine whether their Lordships (in *Investors Compensation Scheme*) took a broader view of the admissible "background" that was taken in *Codelfa* or, if so, whether those views should be preferred to those of this Court. Until that determination is made by this Court, other Australian courts, if they discern any inconsistency with *Codelfa*, should continue to follow *Codelfa*' (Gleeson CJ Gaudron McHugh Gummow and Hayne JJ).

[88] *Royal Botanic Gardens and Domain Trust v South Sydney City Council* (2009) 240 CLR 45, 70 (Kirby J); *Farmer v Honan and Dunne* (1919) 26 CLR 183, 197 (Isaacs and Rich JJ).

[89] *BP Australia Pty Ltd v Nyran Pty Ltd* (2003) 198 ALR 442, [34]; accepted in *Braystock Pty Ltd v Garland* [2004] NSWSC 874, [17] (Hamilton J).

V. Application of Relational Contract Theory to Issues of Contractual Interpretation

There would be consequences for the interpretation of a contract if a relational contract theory were applied. An obvious one would be that the courts would be less focussed upon the written terms of the contract. As has been demonstrated above, the English courts have broadly moved in this direction. The Australian courts have been more ambivalent, and there is a recent strong re-assertion of the dominance, even exclusivity, of the written word in terms of the parties' agreement in *CFMMEU*. This would include serious consideration to conduct subsequent to the entry into the contract, including actual contractual performance.

It is interesting that the leading English case in which the courts accepted the legitimacy of taking subsequent performance into account was an employment contract decision.[90] It has been demonstrated above that, with some exceptions,[91] the English courts have been relatively reluctant to accept relational contract theory. However, they have indicated it might be appropriate in the employment context.[92] Members of the Australian High Court, in rejecting the *Autoclenz* decision, seem to believe that the method of contractual interpretation it favours is confined to the employment context.[93]

It is submitted that the *Autoclenz* approach to interpretation is correct and, further, that there is no logical reason to confine the approach to contractual interpretation favoured in that case to the employment context. The *Autoclenz* decision is of course consistent with relational contract theory. As Macneil stated in relation to contractual interpretation:

> Adjustments of existing contractual relations occur in numerous ways. Performance itself is a kind of adjustment from original planning. Even meticulous performance of the most explicit planning transforms figments of the imagination, however precise, into a new, and therefore different, reality. A set of blueprints and specifications, however detailed, and a newly built house simply are not the same. Less explicit planning is changed even more by performance … the vaguely articulated duties of a secretary are made concrete by (their) actual performance of a day's work. Perhaps this is merely a way of saying that planning is inherently filled with gaps, and that performance fills the gaps, thereby altering the relations as originally planned.[94]

[90] *Autoclenz Ltd v Belcher and Others* [2011] ICR 1157.

[91] A notable exception is, of course, the judgment of Leggatt LJ (as he then was) in *Yam Seng Pte Limited v International Trade Corporation Limited* [2013] EWHC 111, [142].

[92] *Imperial Group Pension Trust Ltd v Imperial Tobacco Ltd* [1991] 1 WLR 589, 597; *Johnson v Unisys Ltd* [2003] 1 AC 518, 541v (Lord Hoffmann, with whom Lord Millett agreed); 536 (Lord Steyn).

[93] *CFMMEU v Personnel Contracting Pty Ltd* (2022) 275 CLR 165, 193.

[94] I Macneil, 'Contracts: Adjustments of Long-Term Economic Relations Under Classical, Neoclassical and Relational Contract Law' (1978) 72 *Northwestern University Law Review* 854, 873; Razzolini (n 42) 298: 'according to relational contracts theory, it goes without saying that the contractual agreement cannot regulate ex ante all the events and changes that occur in the future'; S Macaulay, 'The Real and the Paper Deal: Empirical Pictures of Relationships, Complexity and the Urge for Transparent Simple

Certainly the language used by the court in *Autoclenz* is readily applicable to contexts other than employment. It is true that the context there was an employment situation. The court indicated that in a contract situation such as that, matters such as inequality of bargaining power may feature. This could in turn lead to the contract being one-sided and/or unfair. It may not reflect the reality of the parties' agreement. It may not reflect accurately parties' intent.

Of course, these features may exist in a broad range of other contracts. It is suggested that many, if not most, contractual situations involve an inequality of bargaining power. For example, a large supermarket contracting with its suppliers or deliverers is likely to have significant market power. So is a banking company dealing with customers/clients, an insurance company dealing with customers/clients, a body providing public transport to the public, owners of a football stadium selling tickets to the public or to onsellers, and so on. One could suggest that the reality of unequal bargaining power between contracting parties is likely the norm. This is significant. As has been documented earlier in this book, contract law assumed the opposite – that contracts were typically conceived between organisations and/or individuals of relatively equal bargaining power. The reality should be accepted that contracts are typically between parties of unequal bargaining power, and the law must be ready to accommodate the realities of typical contractual arrangements, not an ideal.

What follows from the fact that contracts are typically characterised by an inequality of bargaining power? Naturally, the party in the stronger position will in many cases be in a position to insist that the contract proceed upon their preferred terms. The supermarket chain will be in a position to insist upon their terms, as will the bank, the insurance company, the public transport provider and the stadium owner. Some may choose to exploit this power. It is likely, given the research above, that many will not – because they value the relationship between the parties, it is a long-term, or hoped to be a long-term, relationship, and so on.

In such cases, at the very least the court should be prepared to consider the reality of the parties' arrangement, by taking into account how the contract is actually being performed. This is a way of preserving the parties' relationship. It avoids the stronger party imposing their will illegitimately and taking unfair advantage by insisting upon the text of a contract when it does not reflect the reality. The parties have a right to expect that, when there is a difference between the reality of how the contract is performed and the written word, that the reality be given effect to. This avoids the kind of textualism that relational contract theory teaches us is better to avoid, because we must not assume that the only source of information concerning the parties' contractual relationship exists in the contract itself.

Rules' in D Campbell, H Collins and J Wightman (eds), *Implicit Dimensions of Contract* (Oxford, Hart Publishing, 2003) 102: 'we might decide there is a high cost in legitimacy if the legal system comes to symbolise that contract rests on manipulation of forms and courts reject the substance of the real deal of the parties'; J Silverstein, 'The Contract Interpretation Policy Debate: A Primer' (2021) 26 *Stanford Journal of Law, Business and Finance* 222, 277.

The court in *Autoclenz* indicated that another reason for its willingness to consider actual performance, rather than simply the written text, was that the written text may not reflect the parties' intention. If this were the case, note that the main theory said to support freedom of contract and the argument for textualism would not apply. Traditionally, the theory utilised to justify freedom of contract and application of textualism was the will theory – the assumption that the written contract was a product of voluntary agreement and that it actually captures the parties' true agreement. Thus the role of the law was simply to give effect to the parties' intentions and wishes, as reflected in the written terms.

However, this theory becomes difficult where there is evidence that the parties' written agreement does not in fact represent the parties' intentions. The will theory justification for enforcing the contract as written disappears. It is not clear what can take its place. In some cases, it is true that where the parties' written agreement does not accurately reflect the parties' intentions, the court might view it as a sham and refuse to enforce it. However, as explained above, the requirements to establish a 'sham' are difficult to meet, and there could be examples where the parties' written agreement is not intended to reflect the reality of performance, yet it does not meet the threshold of a sham.

Of course, there are many other potential reasons why the written contract does not accurately reflect the parties' actual performance. The contract may not have been drafted well. The parties may have poorly communicated the situation to the drafters. It may not have been the product of legal advice. The parties might prefer a more informal manner of doing business. As Macneil and others said, it is often simply impossible, despite the best drafting, to anticipate what might occur over the life of the contract. The broad range of situations that makes it unrealistic to expect the written contract to accurately capture the totality of the parties' agreement makes it sensible, in my view, to broaden the range of considerations in determining the parties' agreement. A court that, as did the first joint reasons in *CFMMEU*, hones in on the written wording of the contract and ignores actual performance is surely reifying form over substance. It is very difficult to satisfactorily justify why the form of something should outweigh the substance. Doing so unduly weighs in favour of the party that happened to draft the form, typically a stronger party. But my argument to give prominence to the substance of a contractual arrangement, not its form, is not sourced in the need to 'level up' between some presumed or possible inequality of bargaining power. It is that, as a principle, the law should reify substance over form, and that the law should not presume that the written contract contains the entirety or even the substantial majority of the parties' real agreement. Such an assumption is demonstrably false and the law should not base itself upon incorrect and wildly unrealistic assumptions.

Respectfully, the first joint reasons in *CFMMEU* was wrong to seemingly conflate a preparedness to consider the actual performance of a contract to interpret it with making 'a fair adjustment of the parties' rights'.[95] This is NOT what a consideration of the actual performance of the contract is intended to achieve. It is intended to determine the reality of the parties' bargain, and to give effect to that substance, not to preside over a triumph of form over substance or to reward the party with the better negotiation tactics/power to draft the contract.

In this vein, the English courts' willingness to accord 'commercial common sense' to transactions is applauded. This is most likely to reflect the parties' (perhaps uncommunicated and expressly not provided for) legitimate expectations of the other. This does not mean the court is re-making the parties' agreement to make it fairer.

The court's jurisdiction to look beyond the written word to the broader context should not be limited, as some courts have suggested, to cases where it is shown that contractual terms contain ambiguity. It is submitted the concept of 'ambiguity' is given undue prominence if it is the gateway that must be navigated in order to apply a contextual interpretation. This gives the concept too much work to do. The rationale for limiting consideration of context to cases of 'ambiguity' is difficult to discern. As contract law expert Carter stated, there can always or almost always be argued to be some ambiguity in contractual terms. It is extremely difficult (or impossible) to draft a contract with no ambiguity. Thus, the concept of ambiguity shades into irrelevance. However, it continues to enjoy support in the English and Australian cases. It should be abandoned in this context.

The question of the use of subsequent conduct to assist in the interpretation of contracts and the question of the use of pre-contractual negotiations to assist in the interpretation of contracts are connected. If the courts have begun to take into account subsequent conduct in the interpretation of contracts, it might logically follow that they should also take into account pre-contractual negotiations.[96] That said, it should also be acknowledged that some judges, perhaps presciently, observed that while the rule forbidding consideration of subsequent conduct in contract interpretation was vulnerable, but the rule forbidding consideration of

[95] (2022) 275 CLR 165, 193: 'where the parties have comprehensively committed the terms of their relationship to a written contract the validity of which is not in dispute, the characterisation of their relationship as one of employment or otherwise proceeds by reference to the rights and obligations of the parties under that contract. Where no party seeks to (argue that the contract is a sham or should otherwise be held invalid) there is no occasion to seek to determine the character of the parties' relationship by a wide-ranging review of the entire history of the parties' dealings. Such a review is neither necessary nor appropriate because the task of the court is to enforce the parties' rights and obligations, not to form a view as to what a fair adjustment of the parties' rights might require' (Kiefel CJ Keane and Edelman JJ).

[96] *L Schuler AG v Wickman Machine Tool Sales Ltd* [1974] AC 235. There Lord Simon pointed out subsequent conduct was not of greater probative value in the interpretation of contracts than pre-contractual negotiations, and it may positively mislead to have regard to the former but not the latter (268). Lord Wilberforce confirmed it was 'one and the same principle' that applied to both (261).

pre-contractual negotiations in contract interpretation less so.[97] This is as it has turned out, to date at least.

In this context, it somewhat puzzling that the English courts continue to refuse to consider, at least generally, pre-contractual negotiations.[98] An objection to these being utilised is of course understandable and justified if it were to contradict the written agreement. This would create intolerable uncertainty as to what the parties' bargain was. However, in cases where there are gaps in the contract, and evidence that the parties considered and perhaps agreed on such matters earlier (with no evidence of a change of heart by both parties in the written terms or as reflected in the actual performance), there is an argument that such conversations should be relevant in interpreting the written agreement. Something somewhat similar was arrived at in *Chartbrook*. However, the court framed this as a remedy of 'rectification', and pointedly refused to overturn its previous case law to the effect that pre-contractual negotiations could not be the basis for contractual obligation. It cited an earlier case for four elements that a party seeking to rely on such statements would need to prove. The fourth of these was that the parties had made a 'mistake' in not including what was agreed into the written contract.

With respect, it is only a mistake if the courts will only consider the written agreement. 'Rectification' implies something has gone wrong. If the courts are willing to consider the broader context, including pre-contractual discussions that don't contradict the written word, in order to determine the parties' agreement, it may not be a mistake that parties do not include it in the written terms. There may be no wrong that needs 'rectification'. It may be that they prefer an informal arrangement and do not wish to reduce every possible term into the written form.[99] This is what relational contract scholars have told us is the reality surrounding most contracts. Or it may be that it is impossible to do so, even if parties wished to. Contract law should listen and respond to these realities, not remain blissfully and determinedly ignorant of them and pretend that things are typically different from what plenty of empirical studies have told us, as well as common sense, is the actuality.

Courts state that they interpret contracts by considering the written words in their context, and having regard to how a reasonable person would interpret the words and the context. If a reasonable person were seeking to interpret a contract

[97] Lord Steyn, *Democracy Through Law: Select Speeches and Judgments* (Ashgate, Routledge, 2004) 46; Bingham (n 79) 390.

[98] It may be added 'at least on the face of it'. Lord Nicholls sagely observed that in his experience, notwithstanding the law as it is, legal representatives typically do seek to include at least parts of the pre-contractual negotiations as evidence, and judges often do in fact take it into account in interpreting the contract: (n 8) 585: 'I suspect that, in practice, despite the exclusionary rule, in one form or another evidence of the actual intentions of the parties often does come to the attention of the judge on disputes about interpretation. I suspect also that in practice the judges are influenced by this evidence when it assists in determining the objective meaning of the words'.

[99] Lord Nicholls similarly states that the remedy of rectification, due to its narrowness, is not a satisfactory solution to the issue: (n 8) 586.

which contained ambiguities, and was aware that the parties had discussed the matter in detail in an earlier conversation or written correspondence, a reasonable person would surely want that detail in order to complete their task. The law does not actually implement the test it itself devised for determining contractual interpretation disputes. It claims to be based on how a reasonable person would interpret the words and the surrounding context, but then refuses to actually take into account important evidence that reasonable person would take into account. As a result, this gives the decision maker (at least notionally, if we assume for a moment the judges apply the law as they have stated or accepted it to be) an incomplete picture.[100]

It is submitted that the result in the *Frederick E Rose (London) Ltd v William H Pim Jnr & Co Ltd* decision is a harsh one. Recall there that the plaintiffs asked their agents to purchase 'Moroccan horsebeans described here as feveroles'. The agents asked the defendant's representatives, who made inquiries, and told the plaintiff's agents that they were just horsebeans, that they could readily supply. The parties executed a contract providing for the delivery of 'horsebeans'. When the product was supplied, the plaintiff realised they were not feveroles. They sought rectification of the contract, by inserting reference to feveroles in the written terms. Although the trial judge found in their favour, the Court of Appeal rejected their argument.

The Court of Appeal conceded that the parties had made a common mistake regarding a matter fundamental to the contract. However, it found that since, for all outwards appearances, the parties had made a complete agreement, the court would not disturb it. It refused rectification:

> In order to get rectification it is necessary to show that the parties were in complete agreement on the terms of their contract, but by an error wrote them down wrongly, and in this regard, in order to ascertain the terms of their contract, you do not look into the inner minds of the parties – into their intentions – any more than you do in the formation of any other contract. You look at their outward acts, that is, what they said or wrote to one another in coming to their agreement, and then compare it with the document which they have signed. If you can predicate with certainty what their contract was, and that it is, by a common mistake, wrongly expressed in the document, then you rectify the document, but nothing less will suffice … a continuing common intention is not sufficient unless it has found expression in outward agreement … (a party) is allowed to prove … that they agreed something different … but not that they intended something different … (on the facts) the parties no doubt intended that the goods should (be feveroles) … they assumed that they would do so, but they made no contract to that effect. Their agreement … was for horsebeans. That is all that the defendants ever committed themselves to supply, and all they should be bound to.[101]

In this case, the parties clearly did make an error. It seems fairly clear that the purchaser intended to purchase feveroles, and the defendant agreed to supply

[100] ibid 583.
[101] (n 63) Denning LJ (461–62), Singleton and Morris LLJ reaching the same conclusion.

them. This is what the parties intended to occur.[102] It seems that feveroles are a type of horsebean, but not of the regular variety. The written contract did not accurately reflect the parties' intentions. To seek to give effect to the parties' intentions is not to adopt a subjective approach – it is not sufficient that the plaintiff testifies that is what they intended.[103] A reasonable person reading the evidence of the communications between the parties would reasonably conclude that was what the parties' intended.[104] In my view, the courts should be concerned with giving effect to the parties' intentions. They should be alert to the reality that, sometimes, the contract as written does not give effect, or full effect, to the parties' intentions, and be prepared to make adjustments, so that it does reflect their parties' intentions.[105]

McLauchlan takes a similar view:

> Of course it is true that in some situations courts do enforce contracts that neither party intended … the courts can only seek to resolve the dispute by reference to the parties' presumed intention … It is entirely another matter, however, to find a contract or adopt an interpretation that reliable evidence shows is contrary to the actual intention of the parties. That would, in effect, be to allow one party to perpetuate a fraud on the other.[106]

A factual scenario such as this surely demonstrates the folly of a myopic focus on the written word, at the expense of the 'bigger picture' or broader context of the parties' relations. The court had clear evidence that what the parties intended differed from the written word. A substantive view would have taken that evidence into account, to seek to give effect to what the parties intended. Instead, the court focussed on the form, and relied on the clear myth that it reflected the entirety of the parties' bargain. The presumption that the written contract reflected the parties' true agreement was clearly wrong in this case, yet the court ignored it.

Extra-judicially, Lord Nicholls pointed out the folly of the current situation. He noted that contractual interpretation involved an objective ascertainment of the meaning of the words the parties used, in the context of the information that a reasonable person would have available to them in interpreting it. This clearly

[102] This factual scenario is clearly different from that in *Smith v Hughes* (1871) LR 6 QB 597. In that case, there was disagreement as to whether the purchaser had specified they wished to purchase a specific vintage of oats, and the court proceeded on the assumption that the purchaser had not so specified, and thus the parties had not reached any agreement to this effect. It did not appear in the written terms, and the vendor denied being aware of the purchaser's requirements in this regard.

[103] See similarly A Burrows, 'Construction and Rectification' in A Burrows and E Peel (eds) *Contract Terms* (Oxford, Oxford University Press, 2007) 82–83: 'to allow in previous negotiations or declarations of intention … is consistent with an objective approach in that one is still ascertaining a party's intentions through objective evidence. In particular, an objective approach would not permit evidence of undeclared intention or of what a party thought the previous negotiations meant'.

[104] An objective approach to rectification is supported here. See for discussion M Smith, 'Rectification of Contracts for Common Mistake, *Joscelyne v Nissen*, and Subjective States of Mind' (2007) 123 *Law Quarterly Review* 116.

[105] Support for this proposition is derived from the statement of Leggatt J in *Blue v Ashley* [2017] EWHC 1928 (Comm), [64] to the effect that 'there is, at least arguably, a limitation on the objective nature of the test where one party's subjective intention is actually known to the other'.

[106] D McLauchlan, 'The Contract That Neither Party Intends' (2012) 29 *Journal of Contract Law* 26, 30.

includes the context and the objectives of the contract. The logic of this principle would surely include evidence as to pre-contractual negotiations. It is something a reasonable person would take into account in seeking to discern the parties' agreement. However, the courts continue to refuse to do this. Lord Nicholls stated that

> although a reasonable person in the position of the parties would have known what had passed between them before the contract was signed, the parties are not permitted to put the court into the same position. It is difficult to see how this exclusion as a rule of universal application can be justified, how it can be sensible rationalised.[107]

Lord Nicholls stated it would not be every, or even most, cases where pre-contractual discussions should be taken into account. They may not shed any light on the matter/s now in dispute, the parties' views about the matter may have differed, or the standard terms of one of the parties might have been utilised. However, on other occasions the content of pre-contractual negotiations could shed valuable light on what the parties intended by the use of the language incorporated into the contract. As he (correctly) points out, this would not be a departure from the objective theory of contract. It would simply enable the reasonable person trying to discern the parties' intention to have regard to more sources of information in order to determine what that intention was. It may in some cases be the very best available evidence of what the parties intended. As such, he viewed it as perverse that the law should continue to refuse to take it into account.

Lord Nicholls gives two examples of cases where evidence of the parties' pre-contractual negotiations was helpful in interpreting the contract. The first is *The Karen Oltmann*.[108] There the contract provided for the charter of a vessel. The contract was for two years. It gave the chartered the option to hand back the vessel 'after 12 months' trading'. The charterer sought to return the vessel about 19 months after the charter was executed. The question was whether their option to terminate the charter could only be exercised at the 12-month mark, or whether it could be exercised at any time on or after the 12-month mark. The court relied on the parties' pre-contractual discussions to determine the parties' intention in this regard. It concluded that the parties mutually intended this clause to mean 'at the expiry of' rather than 'at any time after'.[109] It is said that this decision could not have been justified on the basis of rectification, because there was no mistake to be corrected.[110]

[107] (n 8) 581.

[108] *Partenreederei MS Karen Oltmann v Scarsdale Shipping Co (The Karen Oltmann)* [1976] 2 Lloyd's Rep 708.

[109] David McLaughlan agrees with the decision, stating that any other result would have been 'perverse': DW McLaughlan 'Common Assumptions and Contract Interpretation' (1997) 113 *Law Quarterly Review* 237. Lord Bingham also expressly agreed with it: (n 79) 389.

[110] McLaughlan, 'Contract Interpretation: What is it About?' (n 39) 21–22. He cites for support the statement to like effect of Lawrence Collins LJ (dissenting in the result) in *Chartbrook Ltd v Persimmon Homes Ltd* [2008] EWCA Civ 183, [123].

In *The Pacific Colocotronis*,[111] the court was required to interpret a contractual provision requiring a hirer to 'render assistance' by removing oil from a leaking vessel. The court took into account pre-contractual discussions in establishing the extent of assistance required. Lord Nicholls opined that these precedents ought to have been given greater prominence.

He gave four reasons for his view that pre-contractual negotiations should be taken into account in interpreting a contract:

It would improve coherence in the law;

It would make the law more transparent – he suggests that in practice courts do take this evidence into account in seeking to determine the objective meaning of contractual clauses, even if the law on its face apparently forbids it;

It would make English law consistent with the UN Convention on Contracts for the International Sale of Goods, Unidroit Principles of International Commercial Contracts and the Principles of European Contract Law, as well as the Restatement (Second) of Contracts, all of which require that relevant circumstances be taken into account in interpreting contracts, including pre-contractual negotiations; and

The current rule works injustice be apparently inhibiting courts' ability to consider evidence relevant to determining the parties' intention, which is its task in interpreting contracts.[112]

David McLaughlan expresses similar views. He states that a blanket principle that pre-contractual statements cannot be used to assist in the interpretation of a written contract is 'unprincipled and unworkable'.[113] It is hard to reconcile with the view of Lord Hoffmann that 'absolutely anything' relevant to a reasonable person's interpretation of contractual provisions should be taken into account. This is because a reasonable person would typically take into account the contents of the negotiations.[114]

In arguing that such evidence should be admitted to assist in interpretation, he is at pains to emphasise this does not involve a discarding of the objective approach to contractual interpretation.[115] He defined subjective intentions, which are and should be irrelevant, to mean uncommunicated intentions. On the other hand, he says evidence of actual intentions is highly relevant and should be taken

[111] *Shell Tankers (UK) Ltd v Astro Comino Armadora SA* (*The Pacific Colocotronis*) [1981] 2 Lloyd's Rep 40.

[112] (n 8) 585.

[113] McLaughlan, 'Contract Interpretation: What is it About?' (n 39) 9.

[114] ibid 31.

[115] Andrew Burrows makes a similar point: 'it has sometimes been suggested that the exclusion of previous negotiations and declarations of intention is logically dictated by the objective approach. But that is not so and tends to confuse the approach being applied with the separate question of what evidence is to be permitted in applying that approach. To allow in previous negotiations or declarations of intention … is consistent with an objective approach in that one is still ascertaining a party's intentions through objective evidence … an objective approach would not permit evidence of undeclared intention or of what a party through the previous negotiations meant': Burrows (n 103) 82–83.

into account.[116] So, for example, where there is a dispute about the meaning of a word in a contract, the fact the parties had discussed that point and reached an agreement about it during pre-contractual negotiations is highly cogent and should be considered, as part of the courts' interpretation of the actual agreement. Similarly, where one party to the contract believed a clause meant a particular thing, and had reason to believe the other party accepted that meaning, it should be given effect.[117]

McLaughlan concludes

> There cannot be an absolute rule that evidence of prior negotiations is inadmissible as an aid to interpretation. Such evidence ought to be admissible not only for the orthodox purpose of assisting the court in determining the factual background to the contract but also establishing that the parties reached an agreement or held a common understanding as to the meaning of the words in dispute.[118]

If the courts eventually do reach a position that they will in appropriate cases consider either or both subsequent conduct and pre-contractual negotiations, in order to give effect to the parties' intended agreement, perhaps the approach to general contractual interpretation needs some modification. McLaughlan makes the point:

> The task of a court when resolving an interpretation dispute between the original parties to a contract must be … to give effect to what the parties actually intended the words to mean. This is contrary to received wisdom which states that, while the general object of contract interpretation is to implement the parties' intention, the primary task is to determine the meaning of the words the parties have used. 'It is not an inquiry into intention, but into meaning, as a guide to intention'. Such statements … wrongly assume that words may have a settled meaning without regard to their users. Rather it is some person/s who give meaning to them and, in the case of a contract, it is the meaning that the parties gave to the words in question (or) … the meaning that one party gave where they reasonably expected the other party shared that meaning.[119]

It is submitted that this view warrants serious consideration. Critics may be quick to suggest that McLaughlan is suggesting that a subjective view of interpretation is being suggested, contrary to the established view of intention as objective. As noted above, McLaughlan himself denies that he is suggesting a subjective approach to interpretation. He distinguishes a subjective approach as relating to unexpressed intention regarding the contract, while an objective approach relates

[116] An example might be *Brambles Holdings Ltd v Bathurst City Council* (2001) 53 NSWLR 153. There the Court gave effect to what it regarded objectively as the meaning of 'general commercial waste' to include liquid waste. Evidence that neither party actually intended liquid waste to be included was regarded as irrelevant. Andrew Robertson cites the case as evidence that the law sometimes eschews the clear will of the parties in its obsession with objectivity: *The Law of Obligations: Connections and Boundaries* (London, UCL Press, 2004) 97.

[117] McLaughlan, 'Contract Interpretation: What is it About?'(n 39) 12–13.

[118] ibid 23.

[119] ibid 49.

to matters the parties did discuss (and agree to), or agreed to through means other than communication (ie by conduct), though this may not always be reflected in the parties' written agreement.

In my view, he makes a reasonable criticism that the classical approach, in presuming that the written word of the contract reflects the parties' intentions, can be artificial, particularly where it refuses to consider substantive evidence (whether in the pre-contractual negotiations or in subsequent conduct, or both) that the parties' written agreement does not in fact reflect the parties' intentions. In other words, the law apparently clings to something it knows to be a fallacy, and in effect subverts the parties' intentions, something which it at the same time claims to be enforcing.

VI. Conclusion

The law of contract has already moved, perhaps unwittingly, towards an approach to contractual interpretation that is consistent with good faith and relational contract theory. It has done so by eschewing exclusive reliance on the written word, and applying a contextual approach to contractual interpretation. This is more in evidence in English than Australian law. Recent Australian decisions reflect a lamentable application of freedom of contract principles amidst a refusal to acknowledge that the written wording of the contract does not reflect the reality of how the contract is actually being performed by the parties.

However, the law needs to go further in relation to contract interpretation. First, it must embrace evidence of pre-contractual negotiations, where these shed light on the parties' actual intentions. This avoids the myth that the court is giving effect to the parties' intentions, in the face of evidence it is not doing so.

10

The Boundary between Contract and Tort, and Good Faith and Insurance

I. Introduction

This chapter will argue that some of the developments in tort law in recent times should inform the court's preparedness to accept good faith as a principle applicable to contracts. It asserts there are evident analogies between a duty of care owed to an individual in tort, and the existence of a good faith obligation owed to an individual in contract. In simple terms, if I owe a duty of care to another who is my 'neighbour' as being directly affected by my actions, then by analogy I should owe a duty of good faith to those with whom I contract. This is partly on the basis that I am even more likely to be aware they will be directly affected by my actions. I know them, in a way that is sometimes not applicable in the tort context, increasing the 'neighbour' connection. If my awareness that another will likely be affected by my actions operates (perhaps, with other factors) to curtail my behaviour towards a stranger in tort, surely it should also curtail my behaviour towards a known contracting partner, in contract. There may also be tort consequences. The point was made by Sir Robin Cooke:

> In both contract and tort it may be possible to think of a duty of care as being to do what is reasonable to avoid causing damage to one's neighbour, whether contractual or in sufficient proximity for some other reason … the time has come to recognise that duties of reasonable care are a distinct chapter of the law … it may be more fruitful to think in terms of the liability that should rightly be borne by the person who is in breach of such a duty rather than to begin with whether the particular duty happens to originate in contract, tort or otherwise.[1]

It may also be observed that, traditionally, liability in negligence was highly 'relational' in nature, in that the plaintiff had to demonstrate that their relationship to the defendant was a category of case in which a duty of care obligation had been recognised.[2] Obviously, the argument for recognition of a good faith obligation

[1] 'Tort and Contract' in PD Finn (ed), *Essays on Contract* (Sydney, Law Book Company Ltd, 1987) 231–32.

[2] *Candler v Crane, Christmas & Co* [1951] 2 KB 164, 188 (Asquith LJ) (CA); WL Prosser, *Selected Topics on the Law of Torts* (Ann Arbor, University of Michigan, 1953) 403.

in contracts is based on the 'relational' nature of most contracting situations. It has been argued that contract and tort 'were for much of their history animated by universal moral precepts'.[3]

Writing of the implication of terms by courts, Andrew Robertson notes

> The most strikingly tort-like of implied terms are those requiring parties to act in conformity with community standards such as good faith and reasonableness. These include the implied duty to co-operate in doing all that is necessary for performance of the contract and to ensure that the other party receives the benefits for which he or she has contracted. They also include implied obligations to exercise powers and discretions conferred by a contract in good faith, reasonably and not dishonestly, for an improper purpose, capriciously or arbitrarily.[4]

Further, in *Banque Financiere de la Cite SA v Westgate Insurance Co Ltd*, English courts considered arguments in both good faith and tort. There it was alleged that an insurer had failed its obligations to an insured in failing to tell them that their broker had been engaged in fraud in relation to a previous insurance policy. The allegation was that the insurer had failed their good faith obligation, and breached a duty of care they owed to the insured. At first instance, Steyn J (as he then was) noted the interplay between the claims: 'The existence of a duty of care is consistent with the requirement of good faith and fair dealing which ought to govern the relations between insured and insurer'.[5]

Arguably, Lord Jauncey in the House of Lords also saw the overlap between the good faith obligation and the duty of care obligation. Though clearly in obiter, and reserving the question whether a duty of care could exist in such circumstances, he noted:

> If the obligation of disclosure incumbent upon parties to a contract of insurance could ever per se create the necessary proximity to give rise to a duty of care, a matter upon which I reserve my opinion, it is clear that the scope of any such duty would not extend to the disclosure of facts which are not material to the insured.[6]

[3] J Varuhas, 'The Socialisation of Private Law: Balancing Private Right and Public Good (2021) 137 *Law Quarterly Review* 141, 144.

[4] *The Law of Obligations: Connections and Boundaries* (London, UCL Press, 2004) 99. Finn expresses a similar idea in the same volume: 'one can … take different views of the extent to which a person should be permitted knowingly to exploit another's failure or inability to conserve his own interests in a *contractual* dealing depending upon whether one wishes (a) to curb merely the more gross manifestations of self-interested or exploitative conduct, or (b) to emphasise the social (or relational) nature of contractual activity by imposing some level of '*neighbourhood*' responsibility on the more favoured party for the welfare of the other' (109–10) (emphasis added). Obviously the concept of neighbourhood is pivotal to the owing of a duty of care in tort: *Donoghue v Stevenson* [1932] AC 562, 580 (Lord Atkin). See similarly Varuhas (n 3) 155: 'the method of deciding whether to recognise a standard term (implied by law) increasingly resembles that for determining novel duties of care in negligence'.

[5] [1990] 1 QB 665, 715.

[6] [1991] 2 AC 249, 282 (with whom Lord Brandon (269) and Lord Ackner (281) agreed). Lord Templeman seemed to accept the possible application of tort principles to a factual scenario implicating also the question of the good faith duty of disclosure, but denied there had been a negligent misstatement or reliance (275); C Larkin, 'Uberrima Fides – Quo Vadis? Where to From Here? (1995) 7(2) *Bond Law Review* Article 2, 28: 'The comments of both Lords Templeman and Jauncey indicate

In order to make this argument, it will be necessary to briefly trace the history of the law of contract, and its long association with the law of tort. It will be seen the two areas of law have long-term connections.[7] The boundaries between the two are a matter of continuing conjecture. Some esteemed scholars have argued for greater recognition of their entwined nature,[8] as will be further discussed below. Robertson says it is 'necessary to mis-state the basis of contractual obligations in order to draw a sharp distinction between contract and tort'.[9] Ibbetson says the ambiguity surrounding the distinction between contract and tort was 'never quite resolved' over 700 years of common law legal history.[10] On the other hand, the classical understanding of the law of obligations typically favoured a strict division between contract and tort.[11] It should be acknowledged that

that it is possible for a tortious duty of care to arise in a contract of insurance but as to how and when that duty may arise their Lordships remain silent. It is arguable that the House of Lords did not preclude a tort duty subject to the facts being appropriate. The trial judge's comments that a tortious duty may arise in a pre-contractual setting was not expressly overruled, and therefore remains a live issue'.

[7] GHL Fridman, 'The Interaction of Tort and Contract' (1977) 93 *Law Quarterly Review* 422, 423: 'in terms of legal theory and legal history, tort and contract are far from being independent legal concepts. Whatever may be the position in the modern common-law world, in other legal systems, and at other periods in the course of the development of the common law, there is to be seen a close connection between the idea of relationships or liabilities founded upon what we would now call tortious behaviour and those which arise out of what we would now regard as contractual arrangements'; AC Guest, 'Tort or Contract' (1961) 3 *University of Malaya Law Review* 191, 191–92; P Winfield, *Province of the Law of Tort* (Cambridge, Cambridge University Press, 1931) 47: 'there is not a trace of any reasoned distinction of the one from the other' (referring to tort and contract).

[8] Fridman (n 7); A Robertson, 'On the Distinction Between Contract and Tort' in A Robertson, *The Law of Obligations: Connections and Boundaries* (London, UCL Press, 2004); M Bridge, 'The Overlap of Tort and Contract' (1982) 27 *McGill Law Journal* 872; J Swanton, 'The Convergence of Tort and Contract' (1989) 12 *Sydney Law Review* 40, 74 refers to a 'coalescing' of contract and tort which is beneficial, arguing the distinction between them is artificial and mechanical; Grant Gilmore, *The Death of Contract* (Columbus, Ohio State University Press, 1974) 87–88 stating that contract and tort 'are gradually merging and becoming one … contract is being absorbed into the mainstream of tort'. He said the law was getting to the point that loss incurred as a result of reliance on a defendant's assurances was compensable, and thus that there was no really viable distinction between contract and tort. Leading torts scholar John Fleming noted 'weakening of the borders between contract and tort that were once so clearly delineated by the classical theories of both disciplines': 'Tort in a Contractual Matrix' (1995) 33 *Osgoode Hall Law Journal* 661, 677; cf J Morgan, 'Liability for Independent Contractors in Contract and Tort: Duties to Ensure That Care is Taken' (2015) 74(1) *Cambridge Law Journal* 109 and J Gardner and J Murphy, 'Concurrent Liability in Contract and Tort: A Separation Thesis' (2021) 137 *Law Quarterly Review* 77.

[9] A Robertson, *The Law of Obligations: Connections and Boundaries* (London, UCL Press, 2004) 88; Prosser calls the border between contract and tort 'poorly defined: Prosser (n 2) 452.

[10] D Ibbetson, *A Historical Introduction to the Law of Obligations* (Oxford, Oxford University Press, 1999) 23: 'this ambiguity (surrounding the historical action for covenant) was never quite resolved. One pervasive theme of the next seven centuries of legal history was the friction on the boundaries of the action for breach of contract – on the one hand, between it and the action to give effect to a contractual entitlement and, on the other, between it and a straightforward action in tort. The scars are plainly visible in the common law at the end of the twentieth century'.

[11] Robertson (n 9); J Feinman, 'Critical Approaches to Contract Law' (1983) 30 *UCLA Law Review* 829, 832. This continues to be reflected in Regulation (EU) No 1215/2012 and the Rome I and Rome II Regulations regarding jurisdiction and choice of law rules in contract and tort, which differ: H Stratton, 'The Uncertain Boundary Between Contract and Tort' (2021) 137 *Law Quarterly Review* 222.

differences in contract and tort remain in relation to matters such as limitation periods, the availability of contributory negligence as a defence, contribution rights, choice of law rules, the availability of punitive damages and damages for mental distress and (more controversially) how damages are assessed in the event of breach.[12]

II. Covenant and Debt

Early English law struggled to provide appropriate remedies for what we would today regard as a breach of contract. No general action on contract existed until the eventual recognition of assumpsit in the early seventeenth century. Prior to this, the most likely actions for an action on covenant, and an action on debt.

An action on covenant was based on breach of promise. However, the courts limited the action on covenant to cases where there was sufficient evidence of the agreement between the parties. Specifically, it had to have been made under seal.[13] Because most agreements were not made under seal, in practice the action on covenant was little used.[14] The action on covenant may be based on a tort, and it reflected what we would regard today as tort-like concepts of fault and blame.[15]

An action on debt did not require proof of an agreement made under seal, though some were. However, these actions were as the name suggests limited to cases where a debt existed between the parties – most commonly a loan, or a conditional bond, where one party agreed with another that if they did not do a particular thing by an agreed date, the other party would be entitled to an agreed amount by way of compensation.[16] They were confined to claims for liquidated damages amounts, and were vulnerable to claims that they amounted to penal bonds and should therefore not be enforced. The other limitation was that the plaintiff would be put to wager of law in attempting to prove their claims.[17] The outcome of this in any given case was highly uncertain. Obviously, the use of oath-keepers and/or juries mean there is little on the record to help ascertain the precise legal principles being utilised to resolve these cases.

[12] K Mason, 'Contract and Tort: Looking Across the Boundary form the Side of Contract' (1987) 61 *Australian Law Journal* 228, 229; *Henderson v Merrett Syndicates Ltd* [1995] 2 AC 145, 185 (Lord Goff); *Astley v Austrust Ltd* (1999) 197 CLR 1 (apportionment legislation held to be not applicable to a claim in contract).

[13] F Pollock and F Maitland, *The History of English Law II* (Cambridge, Cambridge University Press, 1895) 217.

[14] It should be conceded that contracts not under seal could be enforced in the local courts, subject to monetary limits on their jurisdiction: J McLaren, 'The Convergence of Tort and Contract: A Return to More Venerable Wisdom?' (1989) 68 *Canadian Bar Review* 30, 32.

[15] Ibbetson (n 10) 23.

[16] (n 13) 202.

[17] (n 13) 212–13. This required the use of oath-helpers who were 'available for hire' in the royal courts: C Donahue Jr, 'The Modern Laws of Both Tort and Contract: Fourteenth Century Beginnings' (2017) 40 *Manitoba Law Journal* 9, 20.

These limited ways in which agreements could effectively be enforced inevitably led to other options being considered, in particular the use of trespass.

III. Trespass

As originally conceived, the writ of trespass included the words 'vi et armis', or with violence. This reflects its history as an offshoot of the criminal law. This would clearly not be appropriate to what we would today regard as a simple contract dispute. Of course, the overwhelming majority of these involve no violence. Cases were sometimes rejected in trespass because they did not utilise these words.[18] However, the trespass writ evolved so as not to require the words 'vi et armis' to be used.[19] It also evolved to embrace actions that would today we would regard as contractual in nature.[20] Arguments concerning warranties in relation to goods were dealt with in trespass.[21] Cases of mis-performance of a contract appeared in writs of trespass.[22]

A well-known example of this is the *Humber Ferryman's Case* (1348).[23] There the defendant agreed to take the plaintiff's horse across the river. It was argued that, due to overloading of the boat, the plaintiff's horse fell into the river, and was lost. There was no agreement under seal between the plaintiff and defendant in relation to the carriage, thus no action on covenant was possible. There was no debt agreement between the parties, so no action in debt could arise. The defendant argued the case should be dismissed on this basis.

The Court found that the plaintiff was entitled to a remedy for their loss. This was for the tort of trespass. The defendant's actions in overloading the boat caused the plaintiff's loss. Thus, at this time, deficiencies in what we today recognise as the law of contract were counteracted by the law of tort. The case is also a good example of how one set of facts may give rise to liability in both contract and tort. The principles often overlap. The origins of the law of contract are found in the law of tort.[24]

[18] *The Surgeon's Case* (*Stratton v Swalond*) YB Hil 48 Edw III, fol 6, pl 11 (KB 1374).

[19] *Farrier's Case* (1372) YB Trin 46 Edw III, fol 19 Pl 19 (CB 1373).

[20] An early example is *Ferriers v Dodford* K.B. 42/189 (Trin 1307). There the plaintiff purchased a horse from the defendant. The defendant apparently guaranteed the horse was healthy and 'unmaimed'. Once the plaintiff purchased the horse and began to ride it, he found the horse was 'maimed' and 'imperfect'. The court found the plaintiff had an action in trespass against the defendant.

[21] *Aylesbury v Wattes* (1382) YB 6 Ric II (AF) 119.

[22] *De Rook v de Hauleye* (1352) ELABD 365, case A14a; *The Oculist's Case* (1329) B & M 340; *De Athelingflet v de Maydeston* (ELABD 329, case A3i) (cases discussed in Ibbetson (n 10)) 45–48).

[23] *Bukton v Tounsende* (1348) B&M 358. I acknowledge assistance with these cases from CHS Fifoot, *History and Sources of the Common Law: Torts and Contract* (London, Stevens & Sons, 1949); JH Baker and SFC Milsom, *Sources of English Legal History: Private Law to 1750* (Oxford, Oxford University Press, 2009) and G O Sayles (ed), *Select Cases in the Court of Kings Bench Under Edward III* Vol 3 (London, Selden Society, 1939).

[24] *Nocton v Ashburton* [1914] AC 932, 956 where Viscount Haldane (with whom Lords Dunedin and Shaw agreed) discussed the question of solicitor liability to clients. He indicated that 'in the early

Court processes were evolving. Courts began to allow plaintiffs to use a particular form of trespass writ permitting the plaintiff to set out in more detail than a typical trespass claim allowed what their case was.[25] This is obviously what we know today as actions 'on the case'. So in *Waldon v Marshall*,[26] the plaintiff took his horse to the defendant veterinarian for treatment. The defendant undertook to treat the animal. As a result of their negligence, the horse died. The defendant's argument that the action was for covenant, which should fail because of the lack of an agreement under seal, again failed. The court found that an action 'on the case' for negligence lay against the defendant. It was not what we would regard today as trespass, because the defendant did not directly kill the animal; rather it was indirect, because the 'cure' administered did not work.

IV. Overlap between Contract and Tort

Traditionally an action in trespass did not lie for cases of non-feasance.[27] However, the court recognised exceptions to this general rule.[28] The court began to express contradictory views as to whether such a claim was possible.[29] Eventually the rule it was not actionable was abolished in respect of claims in contract.[30]

The court accepted a claim in trespass on the case for deceit in relation to a contract.[31] The plaintiff entered into a contract to purchase property from the defendant. Settlement was to be effected within 14 days. Shortly after the contract was entered into, the defendant contracted to sell the property to another at a

history of the action of assumpsit this liability was indeed treated as one of tort'; B Grosman and S Marcus, 'New Developments in Wrongful Dismissal Litigation' (1982) 60 *Canadian Bar Review* 656, 657: 'in its origins the law of contract was very closely aligned with the law of torts'; Bridge (n 8) 874; *Jarvis v Moy, Davies, Smith, Vandervell and Co* [1936] 1 KB 399, 406 (Slesser LJ) (CA); SFC Milsom, *Historical Foundations of the Common Law* 2nd edn (London, Butterworths, 1981) 322; I Jackman, 'Why the History of Restitution Matters' in Justin T Gleeson, J A Watson and E Peden (eds) *Historical Foundations of Australian Law – Volume II Commercial Common Law* (Sydney, Federation Press, 2013) 239: 'it is one of the great oddities of English legal history that the obvious gaps in the medieval law pertaining to consensual or voluntary transactions were filled by what we would now regard as the law of tort'; Prosser (n 2) 381.

[25] AWB Simpson, *A History of the Common Law of Contract* (Oxford, Clarendon Press, 1975) 203.

[26] (1370) YB Mich 43 Ed III, f 33, pl 38.

[27] AWB Simpson, *A History of the Common Law of Contract: The Rise of the Action of Assumpsit* (Oxford, Clarendon Press, 1987) 226; Donahue Jr (n 17) 21–22.

[28] *The Innkeeper's Case (Navenby v Lassels)* YB Easter 42 Edw III, fol 11, pl 13 (KB 1368) (failure to keep guest's property safe from thieves).

[29] In *Watkins' Case* (1425) YB Hil 3 Hen VI fo 36, pl 33 the matter concerned a defendant who had allegedly failed to build a mill by the due date, causing the plaintiff financial loss. Martin J took the orthodox view that an action was not available in assumpsit for non-feasance, while Babington CJ suggested such an action should be available, as did Cokayne J. Assumpsit for non-feasance was rejected by Babington CJ in *Somerton v Colles* (1433) YB Pas 11 Hen VI, fo 25 pl 1.

[30] *Orwell v Mortoft* (1505) YB Mich 20 Hen VII, fol 8, pl 18 (Common Pleas).

[31] *Doige's Case* (1442) YB Trin. 20 Hen VI, f 34, pl 4; similarly *Somerton's Case* (1433) YB Hil, 11 Hen VI, f 18, pl 10.

higher price. The plaintiff brought legal action against the defendant. The defendant argued the claim ought to have been made for breach of covenant. This would not have been successful (again, because of the lack of agreement under seal). However, the court found against the defendant on the basis of deceit. The court circumvented the principle that nonfeasance was not actionable by holding the defendant was liable for misfeasance – namely, transferring the property to another.[32] Ibbetson said it was the acceptance of actions for nonfeasance in trespass that led to breach of the boundary between contract and tort.[33]

Deceit was also useful in cases involving a sales contract where issues arose regarding the quality of what was supplied.[34] The law developed the concept of a warranty, which might be breached if the goods were substandard. This was originally the basis of a tort action, and it was independent of any action for breach of covenant.[35]

It is said that the case of *Skryne v Butolf*[36] is the first case where an action for assumpsit was brought to the court. The somewhat bizarre case seemed to be against a leech. It was alleged the leech undertook (*assumpsiset*) to cure the plaintiff of ringworm, in return for payment. After mentioning this case McLaren states that:

> Assumpsit in its original incarnation was then a mixed action which depended upon the existence of damage or injury flowing from a positive act on the part of the defendant (tort) in the context of an undertaking to take care of the plaintiff or his chattels (contract). The cases normally involved a defendant who exercised a skill or craft, held himself out as such, or who provided commercial services.[37]

Further early inklings of something like an action for breach of promise occurred in 1486[38] and 1558.[39] Assumpsit actions originally betrayed their trespass origins, focussing on the defendant's allegedly wrongful behaviour. It reflected the fact a defendant had 'taken something on'.[40] It was not initially promissory in nature. Eventually the action focussed on the promise they had made.[41] The beginning of

[32] Eventually, the non-availability of trespass for cases of non-feasance would be questioned: Ibbetson (n 10) 129.

[33] ibid 129. He says that actions for breach of contract might conceivably have been viewed as a tort in its own right, as had nuisance, conversion and defamation; alternatively it might break away from tort, though remaining with tort under the umbrella of actions on the case. In fact the law took the latter route (130).

[34] *Langridge v Levy* (1837) 2 M & W 519; 150 ER 863.

[35] McLaren (n 14) 37; Milsom (n 24) 322.

[36] (1387) YB 77 Ric II (AS) 223.

[37] McLaren (n 14) 35. The common calling liability shifted over time from a 'holding out of skill' basis to an 'undertaking of responsibility' basis: Prosser (n 2) 389.

[38] *The Shepherd's Case*, YB 2 Hen VII, HI, f 11 Pl 9 (defendant found liable for injuries to sheep entrusted to their care because he had 'undertaken and executed his bargain'.

[39] *Norwood v Read* (1558) 1 Plow 180 (KB): 'every contract executory is an assumpsit in itself'. I am indebted to McLaren (n 14) 39 for the material about this case and to *The Shepherd's Case*.

[40] J Lidbetter, '"Third Time's a Charm": The Historical Development of Contract Law Through the English Forms of Action' (2022) 51 *Australian Bar Review* 357, 367.

[41] Ibbetson (n 10) 130–31. An example is *Pickering v Thoroughgood* (1533) where the plaintiff alleged the defendant had 'bargained and sold to the plaintiff forty quarters of malt … and assumed and

the recognition of an action for breach of contract in the manner we would now recognise it occurred in *Slade's Case* in 1602.[42] The basis of an assumpsit claim was that a defendant had undertaken to do a particular thing and should be held to that undertaking.[43] This kind of wording is of course similar to the way the House of Lords described one kind of liability for pure economic loss in tort – cases where the defendant has assumed a responsibility to the plaintiff.[44] Indeed, it is noted that Lord Devlin in the case saw analogies between the language used there in a tort liability context to the earlier language describing liability in contract.[45]

The court accepted that where a contract existed between a client/customer and the provider of a service, there would be an obligation on the provider to exercise due care and skill in its provision. This was an obligation in contract, but could also give rise to liability in tort.[46] It was assumed that those pursuing a 'common calling', including common carriers, innkeepers, surgeons, chemists, attorneys, veterinarians, smiths and barbers, could be liable in tort to their customers, according to the custom of the realm.[47] They would obviously be in a contractual relationship with their customers,[48] but liability was generally considered to not depend on that.[49] It would often be related to deceit – that the defendant had deceived the plaintiff in falsely representing they had the required skill and would apply it to the relevant task.[50] However the existence of the

promised to deliver it accordingly' (emphasis added). Sometimes breach of promise is described as a tort: Simpson (n 27) 290 (referring to an unnamed case).

[42] 'Every contract executory imports in itself an assumpsit, for when one agrees to pay money, or to deliver any thing, thereby he assumes or promises to pay, or deliver it, and therefore when one sells any goods to another, and agrees to deliver them at a day to come, and the other in consideration thereof agrees to pay so much money as (sic) such a day, in that case both parties have an action of debt, or an action on the case on assumpsit, for the mutual executory agreement of both parties imports in itself reciprocal actions upon the case, as well as actions of debt': (1602) 4 Co Rep 91a; 76 ER 1072, 1077 (KB).

[43] Bridge (n 8) 880.

[44] *Hedley, Byrne & Co v Heller and Partners* [1964] AC 465, 486–87 (Lord Reid), 494 (Lord Morris), 514 (Lord Hodson) and 528–29 (Lord Devlin).

[45] ibid 529; he cited Lord Shaw in *Nocton v Lord Ashburton* [1914] AC 932, 972 using the phrase 'equivalent to contract' to refer to case where there had been an assumption of responsibility by one party that would, apart from a lack of consideration, amount to a contract'.

[46] *Donoghue v Stevenson* [1932] AC 562, 610 (Lord Macmillan).

[47] *BG Choco International Ltd v British Columbia Hydro and Power Authority* [1993] 1 SCR 12, 59–62 (Iacobucci and Sopinka JJ); JH Baker, *An Introduction to English Legal History* (Oxford, Oxford University Press, 2002) 406; J Blom, 'The Evolving Relationship Between Contract and Tort' (1985) 10(3) *Canadian Business Law Journal* 257, 265.

[48] *Tattan v The Great Western Railway Co* (1860) 2 E & E 844; 121 ER 315 (QB). In *Kelly v Metropolitan Railway Co* [1895] 1 QB 944, 946 (CA) Lord Esher MR stated that in the case of a common carrier, the plaintiff might 'allege' a contract between the carrier and the customer including a provision requiring the carrier to exercise due care and skill in providing the service.

[49] *Bretherton v Wood* (1821) 3 Brod & B 54, 62; 129 ER 1203, 1206 (CP) (Dallas CJ); *Foulkes v The Metropolitan Railway Co* (1880) LR 5 CPD 157 (CA); McLaren (n 14) 35: 'in the earliest period of the application of the action on the case (the mid to late fourteenth century) the pre-existing transaction was mentioned but not emphasised'). This was to avoid an argument the claim ought to have been brought in covenant rather than an action on the case.

[50] Prosser (n 2) 382.

contract (at least at one time) limited the scope of liability in tort to the immediate parties to the contract,[51] subject to exceptions. This did not apply, for example, to businesses such as common carriers, who were recognised as being liable in tort to customers with whom they did not have a contract (for example, the ticket was purchased by a third party for the plaintiff).[52] The liability of common carriers for the carriage of goods seemed to oscillate from tort to contract,[53] and back again.[54] Similarly with bailment, the action was traditionally in tort, but in some cases it could also lie in contract.[55]

Kreitner notes that during this period of the early to mid-nineteenth century, contract was 'inhabited by people in relational pairs'. The nature of the relationship gave rise to a standardised duty in terms of reasonable skill, reasonable diligence and reasonable care. He notes it was failure to meet these standards that triggered contractual liability.[56] This links the relational nature of contracting parties with what we would today regard as liability in tort.

Until this era, liability in assumpsit had more of a basis in detrimental reliance. McLaren states that has this remained the basis of an assumpsit (contract) action, there would have been no need to separate contract and tort.[57] However, the rise of the will theory of contract in the late eighteenth and early nineteenth century caused a significant change. and its focus on the individual agreement between the parties at the expense of societal norms, began to obscure the link between contract and tort, tort often reflecting societal expectations of behaviour.[58] This pushed contract into the private realm, and away from the public realm.[59] The focus was on the parties' presumed intentions, each being a rational utility maximiser, willing and able to maximise their own welfare through private ordering. The role of the law of contract was reduced to the enforcement of the parties' private bargain. It would merely ensure that fair process was followed in the making of the agreement; the court lost interest in the substantive fairness of the contract itself. Development of the consideration doctrine took the

[51] *Winterbottom v Wright* (1842) 10 M & W 109, 114–15; 152 ER 402, 405 (Lord Abinger, CB) (Alderson B agreed, Gurney B concurred). Rolfe B expressed a similar view.

[52] *Marshall v York, Newcastle and Berwick Railway Co* (1851) 11 CB 655; 138 ER 527.

[53] Compare *Tattan v Great Western Railway* (1860) 2 E & E 844 (tort) with *Fleming v Manchester, Sheffield and Lincolnshire Railway* (1878) 4 QBD 81; *Gibbon v Paynton* (1769) 4 Burr 2298, 2302; 98 ER 199, 201 (contract).

[54] *Forward v Pittard* (1785) 1 TR 27; 99 ER 953.

[55] *Turner v Stallibrass* [1898] 1 QB 56; *Legge v Tucker* (1856) 1 H & N 500. Ibbetson notes this created difficulties, because liability in tort typically required fault of some kind, while liability in contract did not: D Ibbetson, '*Coggs v Barnard*' in Charles Mitchell and Paul Mitchell (eds), *Landmark Cases in the Law of Contract* (Oxford, Hart, 2008) 7.

[56] R Kreitner, 'Fault at the Contract-Tort Interface' (2009) 107 *Michigan Law Review* 1533, 1536.

[57] McLaren (n 14) 42.

[58] G Yihan and M Yip, 'Concurrent Liability in Tort and Contract: An Analysis of Interplay, Intersection and Independence (2017) 24 *Torts Law Journal* 148, 150.

[59] Kreitner (n 56) 1541: 'teasing contract and tort apart was one aspect of erecting a firm divide between the public and the private'.

law of contract further away from notions of reliance.[60] Development of the privity doctrine encouraged the courts to see contracts as even more separate from tort.[61]

The rapid advancement of the law of contract in the nineteenth century meant that the earlier connection with the law of tort was virtually lost, and primacy was accorded to contractual obligation. This is reflected in decisions like *Winterbottom v Wright*.[62] There the defendant had contracted with the postal service to provide coaches for the delivery of mail. The contract required the defendant to maintain the coaches in reasonable condition. The plaintiff was engaged by a company retained by the postal service to deliver mail. The plaintiff was injured because the coach the defendant supplied was defective. In rejecting the claim, the court concluded the defendant did not owe the plaintiff a duty of care because the defendant was party to a contract with another regarding the provision of the coach. The plaintiff was not privy to this contract. The court limited the defendant's liability to the party with whom they had contracted. This decision seriously curtailed, if only temporarily, any move towards a generalised duty of care for negligence.[63]

It was in cases such as *Donoghue v Stevenson* that it was accepted that the existence of a contract between two parties did not preclude one of those contracting parties owing a duty of care to a third party,[64] outside the exceptional cases such as common carriers. And obviously, liability in negligence could exist in the absence of a contract between them, though until Donoghue this was limited to particular categories of recognised relationships (usually featuring a contractual relationship).[65]

[60] *Thomas v Thomas* (1842) 2 QB 851; 114 ER 30; this departed from Lord Mansfield's claims of a moral obligation being sufficient to ground a contract.

[61] *Winterbottom v Wright* (1842) 10 M & W 109; 152 ER 402 (Ex).

[62] ibid.

[63] This explains the House of Lord's refusal to provide a remedy for non-fraudulent misrepresentation in *Derry v Peek* (1889) 14 App Cas 337 (HL). In *Le Lievre v Gould* [1893] 1 QB 491 (CA), a defendant surveyor negligently prepared a statement of progress in respect of construction works. He was aware that the statement would be relied upon by a bank in determining whether to advance finance for the project. It was so relied upon. The bank lost money as a result. The court denied him a remedy, because of the lack of contractual relationship between the plaintiff and defendant. It admitted the defendant had been negligent, but denied a remedy to the plaintiff on the basis the defendant owed them no duty. Interestingly Lord Esher had been a member of the Court of Appeal in *Heaven v Pender* (1883) 11 QBD 503 which apparently favoured a generalised duty of care in cases where no contract existed. He apparently took a more limited view in *Le Lievre*, perhaps mindful of the House of Lords decision in Derry in the interval between *Heaven* and *Le Lievre*. Both in the judgment of Brett MR in *Heaven v Pender* (507) and the judgment of Lord Atkin in *Donoghue v Stevenson* [1932] AC 562, 589 there appears disagreement with that part of *Winterbottom* which suggests that a contractual obligation and a duty of care in tort are mutually exclusive.

[64] [1932] AC 562 (Lord Atkin, Lord Thankerton and Lord Macmillan, Lord Buckmaster and Lord Tomlin dissenting). Lord Macmillan said there was 'no reason why the same set of facts should not give one person a right of action in contract and another person a right of action in tort' (610).

[65] *Donoghue v Stevenson* [1932] AC 560, 579–80 (Lord Atkin).

Often there is a recognition that a plaintiff may have overlapping remedies in contract or tort on the one set of facts.[66] Different views were expressed as to non-feasance claims. Traditionally no action was available in tort for non-feasance; it was applicable to misfeasance only.[67] One view was that any claim at this time for non-feasance would need to be brought in contract, not tort.[68] Another at the same time seemed to suggest negligence was an available action for non-feasance.[69]

There are suggestions that any breach of contract is tortious and capable of grounding an action in tort. So in *Brown v Boorman* Lord Campbell states that:

> Whenever there is a contract, and something to be done in the course of the employment which is the subject of that contract, if there is a breach of a duty in the course of that employment, the plaintiff may either recover in tort or in contract.[70]

In the Exchequer Chamber, Tindal CJ had referred to cases against professionals for lack of proper skill as reflecting that 'the contract creates a duty, and the neglect to perform that duty, or the nonfeasance, is a ground of action upon a tort'.[71]

While many of the above cases, and others,[72] accepted the possibility that liability could arise in both contract and tort, legislation effectively forced parties to choose between them, by imposing a costs regime that applied differentially to claims in contract and tort, or otherwise distinguishing claims in contract and tort.[73] Judges complained about this, noting that there was 'debateable ground' between them, and an action could often be brought in either.[74] In the years following, there were suggestions of a sharper division between contract and tort than had previously been determined. So in *Legge v Tucker*,[75] the plaintiff delivered their horse to the defendant so that they would look after it, including separating it from other horses. It was argued that the defendant failed to do this. As a result, the horse was injured by other horses. As a result of the costs legislation, the court had to determine whether the claim was in assumpsit or tort. It found

[66] *Tattan v The Great Western Railway Co* (1860) 2 E & E 844, 852–53; 121 ER 315, 319 (Cockburn CJ); *Taylor v Manchester, Sheffield and Lincolnshire Railway Co* [1895] 1 QB 134, 139–40 (A L Smith LJ); *Kelly v The Metropolitan Railway Co* [1895] 1 QB 944, 946 (Lord Esher MR) (CA).

[67] Prosser (n 2) 388.

[68] *Taylor v Manchester, Sheffield and Lincolnshire Railway Co* [1895] 1 QB 134, 140 (A L Smith LJ); *Kelly v The Metropolitan Railway Co* [1895] 1 QB 944, 947 (A L Smith LJ).

[69] *Kelly v The Metropolitan Railway Co* [1895] 1 QB 944, 946 (Lord Esher MR)(CA).

[70] (1844) 11 Cl & F 3, 44–45; 8 ER 1003, 1018–19.

[71] *Boorman v Brown* (1842) 3 QB 511, 525–26.

[72] *Grant v Australian Knitting Mills Ltd* [1936] AC 85 (PC) is a well-known example.

[73] Small Debts Act 1846 (UK) provided that, if damages awarded were below a certain level, parties would either lose or have restricted ability to claim costs. The threshold was lower for a tort claim than a contract claim, effectively encouraging parties to claim in tort; see also County Courts Act 1867 (UK). Further, the limitations periods differed, as did the contribution rules (liability was several in tort, joint in contract) – both favoured an action in tort over contract: Bridge (n 8) 891; J Plunkett, 'The Historical Foundations of the Duty of Care' (2015) 41 *Monash University Law Review* 716, 720–21.

[74] *Taylor v The Manchester, Sheffield and Lincolnshire Railway Co* [1895] 1 QB 134, 138 (Lindley LJ).

[75] (1856) 1 H & N 500; 156 ER 1298.

that the claim was in substance one in assumpsit. Pollock CB stated that it was only where there was a duty 'ultra the contract' that the plaintiff may proceed in case.[76] It has been suggested that this approach applied to cases not involving the establishing common calling categories – that in such cases, it was necessary to show the existence of a duty of care independently of contractual obligation.[77] However, it has been accepted that, as a result of *Esso Petroleum v Mardon*,[78] one approach should be taken to cases of liability in contract and tort, not dependent on whether the parties are in a relationship traditionally described as one involving a common calling.

Cases had determined that, where an election had to be made as to whether the action was contractual or tortious (for example, because of the relevant legislation), the court should take a substantive view of the matter.[79] However, the effect of the legislation may have been to lead the courts to see cases as being contractual or tortious,[80] against previous acceptance of the fact that one set of facts may give rise to liability in either or both. This attitude has persisted. The case *Bagot v Stevens, Scanlan & Co*[81] involved a question of liability of architects who were arguably in breach of their legal obligations in failing to supervise properly drain work. In obiter dicta, Diplock LJ opined that the claim was contractual in nature, not tortious. He claimed

> I accept that there may be cases where a similar duty is owed both under a contract and independently of contract. I think that upon examination all those will turn out to be cases where the law in the old days recognised either something in the nature of a status like a public calling (such as common carrier, common innkeeper or a bailor and bailee) or the status of master and servant … I do not think that that principle applies to professional relationships of the kind with which I am concerned here, where someone undertakes to exercise by contract his professional skill.[82]

However, subsequent cases would accept that a defendant might be liable both in contract and tort. They are not confined to the limited class of cases to which Diplock LJ refers above. So for example in *Esso Petroleum Co v Mardon*[83] the court found the appellants were liable both in contract and tort. During contractual

[76] (1856) 1 H & N 500, 502; 156 ER 1298, 1299.

[77] *BG Choco International Ltd v British Columbia Hydro and Power Authority* [1993] 1 SCR 12, 63 (Iacobucci and Sopinka JJ).

[78] [1976] 2 All ER 5; noted in *BG Choco International Ltd v British Columbia Hydro and Power Authority* [1993] 1 SCR 12, [65] (Iacobucci and Sopinka JJ).

[79] *Bryant v Herbert* (1878) 3 CPD 389, 390 (Bramwell LJ), 392 (Brett LJ) (Baggallay LJ agreed with both).

[80] Bridge (n 8) 894–95.

[81] [1966] 1 QB 197.

[82] ibid 204–05. In commentary Bridge (n 8) 901 states that 'this represents a clear attempt to fix the twentieth century division between contract and tort by reference to the nineteenth century boundaries of tortious liability and is a perfect example of the fallacious use of the historical method. Besides lumping together a number of relationships which do not have a great deal in common, this dictum ignores altogether the rise in modern times of the tort of negligence'.

[83] [1976] QB 801 (CA).

negotiations, they had communicated an estimate of the likely level of fuel that the respondent would sell during the relevant period. The respondent relied upon this. In fact, while the estimate might have been accurate based on an assumption regarding the placement of the pumps near a busy road, by the time Esso communicated to the respondent, it was aware that Council would not permit them to place the pumps near that road. This would likely materially affect the level of custom. Esso failed to convey this to the respondent. The Court held Esso liable both for a breach of warranty and negligent misrepresentation regarding likely turnover.[84]

A plaintiff claimed damages against his stockbroker, alleging that because he breached his contract in purchasing shares on the plaintiff's behalf at the time he did, the plaintiff suffered loss. One could see a possible case in negligence against the stockbroker, at least in terms of the law today. However, all members of the Court of Appeal found the claim was properly brought in contract (only).[85] The case suggests a rigid distinction between claims in contract and claims in tort.[86] In another professional liability case, the court found that in a case of solicitor-client, the client's remedy for solicitor negligence lay in contract, not tort.[87] Scott LJ was adamant that in cases involving professionals, including solicitors, and their clients, there was a contractual relationship between the parties which would govern claims between the parties. There was generally no duty (in tort), unlike in cases involving common carriers or bailees.[88] This had implications for the damages for which the solicitor was liable; specifically, the court found that

[84] Lord Denning MR Ormrod and Shaw LJJ. The Court found that the damages would be the same, regardless whether the claim was brought in contract or tort: 820 (Lord Denning MR, with whom Shaw LJ agreed). This is contrary to the orthodoxy that the rules regarding remoteness of damage differ between contract and tort, where the former recognises expectation damages in relation to the loss, while the latter focusses on reasonably foreseeable loss resulting from the wrongful behaviour: LL Fuller and WR Purdue, 'The Reliance Interest in Contract Damages' (1937) 46 *Yale Law Journal* 52, 373; *Koufos v Czarnikow Ltd* [1969] AC 350 (HL); *Hadley v Baxendale* (1854) 9 Ex 341; *Overseas Tankship (UK) Ltd v Morts Dock & Engineering Co Ltd* [1961] AC 388; *Overseas Tankship (UK) Ltd v The Miller Steamship Co Pty Ltd* [1967] AC 617; *Wellesley Partners LLP v Withers LLP* [2016] 2 WLR 1351, 1371–72 (Floyd LJ, with whom the other justices agreed) (CA). The Court also accepted the right of a party to elect between remedies in contract and tort in *Batty v Metropolitan Property Realisations Ltd* [1978] QB 554 (CA). In cases where both are potentially applicable, the rules of remoteness in relation to contract law are applied: *Wellesley Partners LLP v Withers LLP* [2016] 2 WLR 1351, 1374 (Floyd LJ), 1394 (Roth LJ) and 1404 (Longmore LJ) (CA).

[85] *Jarvis v Moy, Davies, Smith, Vandervell and Co* [1936] 1 KB 399 (CA) (Greer and Slesser LJJ, with whom Scott LJ agreed).

[86] 'Where the breach of duty allegedly arises out of a liability independently of the personal obligation undertaken by contract, it is tort, and it may be tort even though there may happen to be a contract between the parties, if the duty in fact arises independently of that contract. Breach of contract occurs where that which is complained of is a breach of duty arising out of the obligations undertaken by the contract': 405 (Greer LJ) (with whom Slesser and Scott LJJ agreed). Fridman criticises this rigidity: 'nothing precludes a policy that permits a party to sue in either tort or contract if the facts substantiate such a claim. Nor indeed is there anything in the way of permitting some, if not all, breaches of contract to be treated as torts eg when there is an element of negligence, or fraud, in the way the contract was broken': (n 7) 436.

[87] *Groom v Crocker* [1939] 1 KB 194, 205 (Greene MR), 222 (Scott LJ) (CA).

[88] ibid 222.

damages for injury to reputation and/or feelings were not available in cases involving breach of contract.[89] Yet in other cases the court accepted that solicitors could be held liable both in contract and tort.[90]

In *Lister v Romford Ice & Cold Storage Ltd* the court accepted as axiomatic that those engaged to provide a service could be subject to concurrent obligations in contract and tort.[91] Viscount Simonds said that the duty of care imposed upon the service provider was 'rightly regarded as a contractual obligation'.[92] Lord Radcliffe said it was a mistake to regard liability in contract and tort as necessarily exclusive of one another.[93] On the facts, he said there was 'no real distinction between the two possible sources of obligation' in contract and tort.

Obviously a landmark decision in the area of negligent misstatement in a situation where there was no contract between the parties was *Hedley Byrne and Co Ltd v Heller and Partners Ltd*.[94] The appellant advertising agency made enquiries of the financial position of one of its customers. Its bank contacted the customer's bank, and that bank (the respondent) provided information (with a disclaimer) about the customer's financial position. The appellant relied on that information, and lost money when the relevant customer went into liquidation. There was no contract between the appellant agency and the respondent bank.

Although the respondent was able to successfully rely on its disclaimer, the real importance of the decision is its recognition of the potential actionability of a claim for negligent misstatement resulting in pure economic loss, in circumstances where no contractual relationship existed between the plaintiff and defendant.[95] There had been strong historical resistance to this, based on notions that economic matters were a matter for commercial parties to agree to exclusively by way of express contractual provision. This had been regarded as a matter for private ordering.[96]

Here, in accepting the potentiality of such a claim, the language of the Court becomes important. So for example Lord Reid stated that the defendant who provided such negligent advice could be liable, in a situation where they had undertaken a responsibility to provide the information, where the plaintiff had relied upon it in circumstances where it was reasonable to do so, where the defendant knew or ought to have known it would be so relied upon.[97] Lord Morris also used

[89] ibid 205–06 (Greene MR), 224 (Scott LJ); see also *Addis v Gramophone Co Ltd* [1909] AC 488.

[90] *Nocton v Ashburton* [1914] AC 932, 956 (Viscount Haldane, with whom Lords Dunedin and Shaw agreed); 977 (Lord Parmoor).

[91] [1957] AC 555, 573 (Viscount Simonds).

[92] ibid 576.

[93] ibid 587.

[94] [1964] AC 465.

[95] This overturned an earlier view that damages were not available for mere negligent misrepresentation, that it would be necessary to show that a misrepresentation was fraudulent (in the sense that the person who made it either knew it was untrue or was reckless as to that fact: *Derry v Peek* (1889) 14 App Cas 337.

[96] This explains decisions such as *Candler v Crane, Christmas & Co* [1951] 2 KB 164 (CA) (Lord Denning dissenting).

[97] (n 94) 483.

the word undertaking to describe behaviour of the defendant that would attract liability for negligent misstatement.[98] The significance of the word 'undertaking' should not be missed. It will be recalled that the word assumpsit, the basis upon which the law of contract is historically based, means undertaking.

Lord Devlin was most explicit about this connection. He said that a duty of care would arise in cases that were 'equivalent to contract';[99] in other words, where the defendant had assumed a responsibility to parties such as the plaintiff in relation to that advice. Thus Hedley Byrne is an important case in demonstrating the conceptual closeness between contract and tort.

The Privy Council in *Tai Hing Cotton Mill Ltd v Liu Chong Hing Bank Ltd* suggested that, where contracting parties were in dispute, particularly commercial in nature, the dispute should be resolved by principles of contract law rather than tort law. It claimed this would avoid difficulties inherent in pursuing a concurrent claim, including different limitation periods for different claims.[100]

The House of Lords in *Henderson v Merrett Syndicates Ltd*[101] accepted the possibility of concurrent claims in contract and tort. This was important, since the House reiterated that in contracts for the provision of services, there was an implied promise that services would be rendered with reasonable care and skill.[102] This demonstrates the closeness of contract and tort, where a tortious obligation is being implied into a contract.[103] Frankly, if concurrent liability were not accepted, this would largely sideline the law of negligence in relation to the provision of services. The case did, however, demarcate the boundaries of liability between contract and tort: 'the tortious duty is imposed by the general law, and the contractual duty is attributable to the will of the parties'.[104] Australian courts

[98] ibid 502–03.

[99] ibid 528–30. This is not an isolated occurrence. In establishing that a duty of care was owed in *Junior Books Ltd v Veitchi Ltd* [1983] 1 AC 520, Lord Fraser noted that in respect of the parties 'the proximity between (them) is extremely close, falling only just short of a direct contractual relationship' (with whom Lord Russell agreed). Lord Roskill referred (641) with evident approval to an extract from the judgment of Lord Devlin in *Hedley Byrne* containing the observation that the relationship between the parties was 'equivalent to contract' in determining that a duty of care was owed. In *Smith v Bush* [1990] 1 AC 831, 846 Lord Templeman also quoted Lord Devlin's 'equivalent to contract' speech in *Hedley Byrne* and applied it to determine that a duty of care existed on the facts. Lord Keith and Lord Brandon agreed (840). The court held that a valuer owed a duty of care to a mortgagor. The valuer was engaged by the mortgagee to provide a valuation. The court held the valuer owed a duty of care to the mortgagor, because they knew the mortgagor would likely rely on the result of the valuation.

[100] [1986] AC 80, 107 (Lord Scarman, for the Council) stating that there was nothing 'to the advantage of the law's development in searching for a liability in tort where the parties are in a contractual relationship (particularly) … in a commercial relationship'.

[101] [1995] 2 AC 145, 192 (Lord Goff) (with whom Lords Keith Browne-Wilkinson Mustill and Nolan agreed), 206 (Lord Browne-Wilkinson).

[102] ibid 193 (Lord Goff); see also *Lister v Romford Ice and Cold Storage Ltd* [1957] AC 555, 573 (Viscount Simonds) and 586 (Lord Radcliffe) and 592 (Lord Tucker) and 598 (Lord Somervell); *Manchester Building Society v Grant Thornton UK LLP* [2022] AC 783, 822 (Lord Leggatt).

[103] Another example is *Wong Mee Wan v Kwan Kin Travel Services* [1996] 1 WLR 38, 46 (implied obligation services would be provided with reasonable skill and care) (Lord Slynn, for the Privy Council).

[104] 194 (Lord Goff). This was applied by the High Court of Australia in *Astley v Austrust Ltd* (1999) 197 CLR 1, 36 (Gleeson CJ McHugh Gummow and Hayne JJ); A Burrows, *Understanding the Law of*

have accepted the possibility of concurrent liability in contract and tort, though noting their substantive differences.[105] In contrast, members of the Supreme Court of Canada have noted the desirability of 'reducing the significance of the existence of the two different forms of action' in contract and tort.[106] However, that court has also recognised the possibility of concurrent claims in contract and tort.[107]

Bridge states in conclusion that

> Tort and contract rules are in the process of merging … tort and contract are increasingly to be seen as protecting the same range of interests … it seems to the practical mind of a common lawyer that any attempt to locate precisely the boundary separating contract and tort, or to chart the exact area of overlap of the two, is rather beside the point; it is doomed to be overtaken by events.[108]

Fridman was an advocate of some kind of fusion between tort and contract, calling it the 'ultimate development',[109] and claiming 'the dichotomy has outlived its utility … assuming … it ever had any utility'.[110] He indicated that courts should not enforce a clear-cut distinction between tort and contract.[111]

Fridman points out many substantive areas of law in which tort and contract overlap. He points out that, at one time, non-fraudulent misrepresentation was not actionable. Obviously, the law distinguished between promises that were terms of a contract, and mere representations (without contractual force). He blames this on rigid adherence to the boundaries of contract. Eventually, the law realised that some forms of non-fraudulent misrepresentation, specifically negligent misrepresentation, should be actionable. He uses this evolution as evidence that

Obligations (Oxford, Hart, 1998) 9–10. Andrew Robertson sharply disagrees: 'it is a misconception to suggest that a sharp distinction can be drawn between contractual obligations and obligations in tort on the basis that the former are voluntarily assumed while the latter are imposed. The source of obligation in each case is far more complex'. Murphy points to principles such as the action for inducing breach of contract, and references to assumption of responsibility in the tort context, as reflecting overlap between contract and tort: 'Hybrid Torts and Explanatory Tort Theory' (2018) 64 *McGill Law Journal* 1, 15 and 26. In *Wellesley Partners LLP v Withers LLP* [2016] 2 WLR 1351, 1374 Floyd LJ noted that the 'assumption of responsibility' by the defendants in the case gave rise to liability in both contract and tort. It is noteworthy that the principle of estoppel by convention is enlivened by an 'assumption of responsibility' by a defendant: *Tinkler v Revenue and Customs Commissioners* [2022] AC 886, 909 (Lord Burrows, with whom Lord Hodge, Lady Arden and Lady Rose agreed) (approving *Revenue and Customs Commissioners v Benchdollar Ltd* [2009] EWHC 1310 (Ch), [52]) (Briggs J). These were non-contractual contexts, but the court stated there was no reason not to apply the same principles in the contractual context: *Tinkler* (916–17).

[105] *Astley v Austrust Ltd* (1999) 197 CLR 1, 36 (Gleeson CJ McHugh Gummow and Hayne JJ). In *Perre v Apand Pty Ltd* (1999) 198 CLR 180, 227 McHugh J held that 'developments in negligence should occur in sympathy with the law of contract'.

[106] *BG Choco International Ltd v British Columbia Hydro and Power Authority* [1993] 1 SCR 12, 21 (La Forest and McLachlin JJ, for L'Heureux-Dube and Gonthier JJ).

[107] ibid 30 (La Forest and McLachlin JJ).

[108] Bridge (n 8) 913.

[109] Fridman (n 7) 449.

[110] ibid 436.

[111] ibid 448. Similarly, McLaren concludes there is nothing 'pre-ordained about or deep-rooted in' the division between contract and tort, noting the potential of notions of reliance to unite them: (n 14) 58–59.

> The law has come to accept the greater importance of protecting those suffering loss, as against the niceties and technicalities of older legal principle. Whether you regard the developments that have taken place as a broadening of the concept and scope of negligence, or as an alleviation of the stricter rules of contract, the effect is the same: to render less sharp, and bring closer together, the boundaries of tort and contract.[112]

Fridman uses the example of cases where a third party seeks to take advantage of exemption clauses that appear in contracts to which they are not a party. Typically, such claims are difficult, running up against privity arguments.[113] Fridman refers with approval to the judgment of Lord Denning (dissenting) in *Scruttons*, which purported to use concepts such as *volenti* to consider whether or not the exemption clause should be extended to apply to the third party. In other words, whether the contracting parties intended that one of them would take on a particular risk associated with performance. If so, if that risk materialised through the negligence of a third party, the argument is that the contracting party should be made to bear that loss. This argument would thus justify the third party being able to avail themselves of the advantage of the exemption clause, though it appears in a contract to which they are not a party. Fridman notes, however, that

> What stands in the way of such an analysis … is the hidebound attitude that contract is contract and tort is tort, and the principles of one cannot and should not apply outside its own context and within that of the other. That since the duties and rights in issue arise from a contract, therefore the way to look at any issue that arises from the situation is in terms of contract generally. This … is neither reasonable nor dictated by legal or logical necessity. On the contrary, adherence to such strict, rigid, classification of problems is to frustrate the function of the law, and make the fulfilment of its purposes subservient to the maintenance of archaic distinctions and divisions.[114]

Fridman also uses the examples of collateral contracts and warranties to make his point about (unacknowledged) overlap.[115] He says that essentially the principle of collateral contracts is an attempt to circumvent the ordinary rules of contract in order to give effect to a promise made outside the main contract but which the court believes should be binding on the promisor. Fridman says that this is dressed up as a collateral contract, but this is artificial. The parties do not necessarily intend that the promise be 'contractual' in nature. It is a mere pretence to avoid difficulties in obtaining a remedy for innocent misrepresentation. He says

[112] Fridman (n 7) 440.

[113] *Scruttons Ltd v Midland Silicones Ltd* [1962] AC 446.

[114] Fridman (n 7) 442.

[115] 'The language and ideas which surround both warranty and collateral warranties (contracts) are redolent with the flavour and taste of tort … (after reporting that breach of warranty 'turned into' a contractual wrong) … there was no logical necessity about that … conceptually … it might still be argued that the expression 'warranty still imports connotations of a tortious kind. The warrantor is not exactly promising anything: what he is doing is making a statement which could mislead if it is not true now, or will not be true in the future … courts … should not be allowed to get away with the claim that tort and contract are distinct … (they) themselves … have destroyed or made inconsequential any such distinction': 444.

that the pretence of collateral contract was created because, at the time, no remedy was available for non-fraudulent misrepresentation. Eventual acceptance of the principle of negligent misrepresentation means, he says, that there is no longer a need to maintain the pretence. He says that the real nature of what we call 'collateral contracts' is really tortious behaviour, likely negligent misrepresentation.

He regards 'warranties' similarly.[116] He seems to be talking about things like manufacturers' warranties in relation to goods sold to a consumer by a retailer. Obviously, privity rules would generally deny that these 'warranties' are contractual, though they are related to the contract between dealer and consumer. Again, Fridman views this as abstract, as the law attempting to put a contractual gloss on a promise because, at the time of development, no action was available for non-fraudulent misrepresentation. Eventual acceptance of liability for negligent misrepresentation should have logically led, according to Fridman, to giving substantive meaning to this claim – a claim in negligent misrepresentation against the manufacturer.

Robertson is of a similar view:

> In both contract and tort, rights and obligations are to some extent shaped by the deliberate actions of the parties. Both contract and tort, however, also involve the application of community standards that are 'collective in origin'. Both contract and tort are concerned with what people do, as well as what they intend. Both draw heavily on the notion of reasonableness … in many respects the law of contract also 'eliminates the personal equation' and requires everyone to act as the courts imagine a reasonable person would act.[117]

Robertson quibbles with the will theory of contract. Contracts are based on the appearance of offer and acceptance, and intention to create legal relations. The objective theory of contract emphasises the appearance of consent, not the actuality. Contractual obligations can be imposed in the absence of actual consent and actual will. When a dispute arises regarding contractual interpretation, it will be resolved based on how a reasonable person would interpret the parties' intention, not their actual intention.[118] He says that 'ultimately, contractual obligations, like those in tort, are imposed on the basis of norms of reasonable behaviour'.[119] He indicates that, in both contract and tort, to some extent the parties' obligations to one another are shaped by the agreement between them, to some extent by the actions of one party, and to some extent imposed on the parties by law.[120]

[116] '"Warranty" of course, is a tort concept in origin': 444; to like effect *BG Choco International Ltd v British Columbia Hydro and Power Authority* [1993] 1 SCR 12, [75] (Iacobucci and Sopinka JJ); *Beningsage v Ralphson* (1682) 2 Show KB 250; 89 ER 921.

[117] Robertson (n 9) 91.

[118] *Arnold v Britton* [2015] AC 1619, 1627 (Lord Neuberger, with whom Lords Sumption and Hughes agreed).

[119] (n 9) 95.

[120] 106; see similarly R Kreitner (n 56) 1541: 'objectivism in contract blurs the boundary between liability based on actual consent and liability based on law-imposed standards of behaviour, or, in other

Swanton argues the boundaries between tort and contract have become increasingly blurred.[121] She attacks the traditional distinctions made between them – it is said that tort duties are owed to the world at large, while contractual obligations are confined to the other party to the contract. She says that tort duties are typically confined to an individual or small class of individuals. Another suggests that tort duties are imposed, while contractual duties are voluntarily assumed. Swanton says the distinction is specious – when parties choose to enter into a relationship or do a particular thing in which a duty of care is owed, they may be said to voluntarily assume the duty. And in many cases contractual duties are imposed on the parties and not voluntarily assumed – for example, the law of implied terms, assumptions made about parties' intentions, even when they fly in the face of evidence of parties' actual intentions, and so on. A third suggested distinction is that they protect different interests, as evidenced by the different way in which damages are calculated – the law of contract is said to protect expectation interests, while the law of tort compensates for reasonably foreseeable loss.[122] But Swanton argues in some cases at least tort compensates for the defendant's failure to confer a benefit on the plaintiff,[123] and that sometimes the law of contract does not compensate expectation losses, but rather losses flowing from reliance. She concludes

> The traditional suggested distinctions between contract and tort never were wholly convincing, and are even less so today. The expansion of the tort of negligence has reached the point where observers are asserting that the law is moving towards a principle that every breach of contract which could be avoided by reasonable care is a tort towards a person foreseeably affected thereby.[124]

The cases *White v Jones*[125] and *Hill v Van Erp*[126] have been observed to run counter to the view that tort compensation is not based on expectation losses.[127]

It has been seen that, on one view, the *Hedley Byrne* decision undercuts the rules regarding privity of contract. In some cases, at least, a person who reasonably relies on negligent statements of another has a claim against them, independently

words, blurs the boundary between contract and tort. The protection of reliance where no contract has been concluded again brings contract and tort perilously close to one another' (he is presumably referring to actions such as estoppel). He adds that the rise of claims in restitution gives further credence to the notion that private law is 'infused … with public decision making and a limited role for actual consent'. He concludes that 'contract, like tort, is a mode of social regulation whose rules ought to serve social goals. The idea that the parties own interests, narrowly construed and bargained over, could exhaust the relevant social goals was a pipedream of the late nineteenth-century legal science … socially imposed duties … function as building blocks of contract' (1549).

[121] Swanton (n 8).

[122] The distinction was criticised in *Parsons (Livestock) Ltd v Uttley Ingram & Co Ltd* [1978] 1 All ER 525, 534 (Lord Denning MR).

[123] She cites *Ross v Caunters* [1980] Ch 297 and *Junior Books Ltd v Veitchi Co* [1983] 1 AC 520 as examples.

[124] Swanton (n 8) 42.

[125] [1995] 2 AC 207.

[126] (1997) 188 CLR 159.

[127] *Woolcock Street Investments Pty Ltd v CDG Pty Ltd* (2004) 216 CLR 515.

of contract. Further, doctrines such as promissory estoppel undercut traditional contract rules relating to consideration. Where a person has reasonably relied on promises made by a defendant that create an expectation in the mind of the plaintiff, where the defendant knew or intended the plaintiff would rely on them, at least in cases where the parties had an established legal relationship and the plaintiff suffers detriment as a result of their reliance, they may have a claim.[128] That case involved a situation where the plaintiff was led to believe that a binding contract would be entered into between the parties, acting on that belief by commencing construction work on the relevant land, only for the defendant to refuse to proceed with the transaction. The court held that the plaintiff was entitled to damages from the defendant on the basis of estoppel. Obviously, this decision blurs the lines between terms and representations, and between contractual and non-contractual remedies. It may also be seen as a negligence case.[129]

V. Development of the Tort of Negligence

It will now be necessary to discuss briefly the modern development of the law of negligence. This is with a view to considering analogies between recognition of a duty of care in negligence, and acceptance of good faith in contract. Prior to *Heaven v Pender* and *Donoghue v Stevenson*, a person wishing to bring an action based on a duty of care in negligence had to demonstrate that the case was one that could be fitted within existing categories of case where a duty had been recognised, such as 'common calling' cases.[130]

The first attempt to rationalise a generalised duty of care appears in the judgment of Brett MR in *Heaven v Pender*.[131] Here the plaintiff was a painter. He was employed by Gray. He was injured in the course of painting a ship docked at the defendant's dock. The defendant had placed some staging around the vessel to permit the painting to be done. However, it was alleged the staging was not fit for purpose, and reasonable care had not been taken by the defendant in that regard. The plaintiff sued the defendant for injuries sustained when the staging collapsed. Clearly, there was no contract between the plaintiff and defendant. Thus the action could only proceed in tort. All members of the Court of Appeal found in favour of the plaintiff, but it is in the judgment of Brett MR (with whom the others did not agree) that we find an important attempt to rationalise a generalised duty of care.

Brett MR stated that a generalised duty of care would be owed by person who would, if being of 'ordinary sense', realise that if they did not take reasonable care and skill, the safety of others would thus be placed in jeopardy. The duty would

[128] *Walton Stores (Interstate) Ltd v Maher* (1988) 164 CLR 387.
[129] Swanton (n 8) 53.
[130] *Candler v Crane, Christmas & Co* [1951] 2 KB 164, 188 (Asquith LJ).
[131] (1883) 11 QBD 503.

be owed to those whom he would know would be placed in jeopardy (as a class of individuals, it was not necessary that the defendant know of the identity of particular victims). If a person who owes such a duty fails to exercise ordinary care and skill, they will be liable for the person/s so injured as a result.[132]

In *Donoghue v Stevenson*,[133] Lord Atkin was to rationalise a generalised duty of care based on the neighbour principle. Individuals were required to take reasonable care to avoid acts or omissions which they could reasonably foresee would be likely to injure their neighbour. A neighbour was someone so closely and directly affected by the person's actions that the person should have had them in contemplation as being so affected when they considered the acts or omissions in question.[134]

The law would recognise the viability of a claim for pure economic loss arising from negligent misstatement,[135] in circumstances where the defendant had assumed a responsibility to exercise due care and skill in rendering advice or information,[136] that they were aware or ought to have been aware the plaintiff would rely on it, that it was reasonable for them to do so, they did so and suffered loss as a result.[137] It would attempt to re-frame Lord Atkin's position into a two-stage test.[138] However, in *Caparo Plc v Dickman*[139] the House of Lords apparently settled upon a three-stage test. The stages would consider: (a) whether there was foreseeability of damage to the plaintiff; (b) there existed between the party owing the duty and the party to whom it was owed a relationship of proximity and/or neighbourhood; and (c) the court considers it fair, just and reasonable that a duty of care should be recognised.[140]

Subsequently the United Kingdom Supreme Court denied that the *Caparo* decision meant that a three-stage test ought to be applied to all cases of negligence. It denied that a '*Caparo* test' existed. There was no single test to be applied to determine whether or not a duty of care existed in a particular case.[141] The approach of the common law was to develop the law incrementally and by

[132] ibid 508–09.

[133] [1932] AC 560.

[134] ibid 580–81, with whom Lord Thankerton agreed (604); Lord Macmillan similar (620).

[135] *Hedley Byrne and Co Ltd v Heller and Partners Ltd* [1964] AC 465.

[136] 'The distinction drawn by Lord Hoffmann in SAAMCO between "advice" cases and "information" cases has not proved to be satisfactory': *Manchester Building Society v Grant Thornton UK LLP* [2022] AC 783, 796.

[137] *NRAM Ltd v Steel and Another* [2018] 1 WLR 1190, 1202–03 (Lord Wilson, for the Supreme Court).

[138] *Anns v Merton London Borough Council* [1978] AC 728, 751–52, being (a) whether there was a sufficient degree of proximity or neighbourhood such that, in the reasonable contemplation of the defendant, negligence on their part may likely injure the plaintiff; and (b) whether there are any policy considerations which ought to negative or reduce the scope of the duty or the class of persons to whom it is owed (Lord Wilberforce).

[139] [1993] AC 605.

[140] ibid 617–18 (Lord Bridge) (with whom Lords Roskill and Ackner agreed).

[141] *Robinson v West Yorkshire Chief Constable* [2018] AC 736, 744 (Lord Reed, with whom Baroness Hale and Lord Hodge agreed); *Darnley v Croydon Health Services NHS Trust* [2019] AC 831, 838 (Lord Lloyd-Jones (with whom Baroness Hale, Lord Reed, Lord Kerr and Lord Hodge agreed).

analogy. It distinguished between categories of case in which a duty of care had in the past been found to arise, and novel situations in which a duty of care had not yet been found to arise. The *Caparo* approach might be useful with respect to the latter situations; in particular, whether recognition of a duty of care in such circumstances would be 'fair, just and reasonable'.[142]

Recently the Supreme Court has emphasised the importance of the purpose of the advice rendered by the defendant to the plaintiff.[143] It asks what the purpose/s were for which the advice was given.[144] This helps to frame the scope of the duty of care owed (if any). In that case, the defendant accountants had been asked whether the plaintiff could adopt hedge accounting. This was important to the plaintiff because, if it could use such accounting, it could proceed with a particular enterprise. If it could not, it could not so proceed. The accountant advised them they could use hedge accounting, but this was negligent and wrong. In finding in favour of the plaintiff, the court noted that the purpose of the defendant giving the plaintiff advice was to assist their capital position. The loss they suffered fell within the scope of the duty of care owed to them.

Concurring in the joint reasons, Lord Burrows referred to an earlier decision which had also focussed on the purpose for which the defendant had rendered their advice as critical in framing the scope of the duty of care. He said that the principle in that case 'is best understood as a principle which focusses on the scope of the defendant's duty of care (whether in contract or tort)'.[145] He said the case was based on a policy of seeking to ensure a professional's liability for negligence reflected a fair and reasonable allocation of risk of the loss that has occurred between the parties.[146]

VI. Links between Good Faith and Negligence

Historical links between good faith and 'negligence' are deep, as was explained in chapter two. There are some case examples where legislation provides a defence to what would otherwise be an actionable wrong in circumstances where the defendant acted in 'good faith'. Field notes that a line of cases has required that defendants in such circumstances make a 'real' or 'genuine' attempt to fulfil their functions. A failure to do so can lead to a finding they have acted in the absence of good faith. Obviously, failure to make a genuine attempt to fulfil a function can be analogised to negligence.

[142] *Robinson* (n 141) 746–47 (Lord Reed, with whom Baroness Hale and Lord Hodge agreed); 764 (Lord Mance); 770 (Lord Hughes); *Darnley v Croydon Health Services NHS Trust* [2019] AC 831, 839 (Lord Lloyd-Jones, with whom Baroness Hale, Lord Reed, Lord Kerr and Lord Hodge agreed).

[143] *Manchester Building Society v Grant Thornton LLC* [2022] AC 783.

[144] ibid 798 (Lord Hodge and Lord Sales, with whom Lord Reed, Lord Kitchin and Lady Black agreed); 843 (Lord Burrows).

[145] ibid 840–41.

[146] ibid 841.

So for example in *Mid Density Developments Pty Ltd v Rockdale Municipal Council* a developer complained that the defendant Council had issued the developer with certificates without due regard to recent flood studies pertaining to the property the subject of the certificates. These studies highlighted the dangers of the property being inundated, but the Council's certificates made no reference to this risk. Relevant legislation gave Council a defence for advice furnished in good faith. The Full Federal Court found that this required more than honesty. The Council had not met this obligation here because it had failed to make a 'real attempt' to respond to the developer's queries.[147]

Similarly in *Barrett and Others v South Australia and Another*[148] legislation protected directors from acts done or omissions made in good faith. Bollen J found that the good faith defence did not apply in cases of 'gross negligence' or where the director had made no genuine attempt to fulfil their functions properly.[149] In *South Australia v Clark*, Perry J said liability might arise because of a lack of a genuine attempt to exercise a power, making a good faith defence unavailing.[150]

Developments in the United Kingdom were influential around the common law world. Canada and New Zealand accepted, and continue to accept, the two-stage *Anns* test.[151] The High Court of Australia rejected *Anns*.[152] It did accept the actionability of pure economic loss from negligent misstatement in light of the House of Lords decision in *Hedley Byrne*. It also held that pure economic loss would also be claimable for negligent acts, in circumstances where the defendant was aware that the particular plaintiff (not as a member of a class of individuals, but personally) would or would likely suffer loss if they (the defendant) acted negligently.[153]

The Australian High Court initially accepted notions of proximity as going to establish the existence of a duty of care,[154] although a majority of the Court did not accept the three-stage *Caparo* 'approach' (of which proximity is the second

[147] (1993) 44 FCR 290 (Gummow Hill and Drummond JJ).

[148] (1994) 63 SASR 208.

[149] ibid 209. See for discussion I Field, 'Good Faith Defences in Tort Law' (2016) 38 *Sydney Law Review* 147; I Field, 'Good Faith Protections and Public Sector Liability' (2016) 23 *Torts Law Journal* 210.

[150] (1996) 66 SASR 199, 234. For an argument that some breaches of contract should be seen as lacking in good faith and result in tort liability see T Diamond, 'The Tort of Bad Faith Breach of Contract: When, If At All, Should it be Extended Beyond Insurance Transactions?' (1981) 64 *Marquette Law Review* 425.

[151] *Canadian National Railway Co v Norsk Pacific Steamship Co* [1992] 1 SCR 1021; *South Pacific Manufacturing Co Ltd v NZ Security Consultants & Investigations Ltd* [1992] 2 NZLR 282.

[152] *Sutherland Shire Council v Heyman* (1985) 157 CLR 424.

[153] *Caltex Oil (Australia) Pty Ltd v The Dredge 'Willemstad'* (1976) 136 CLR 529 (dredge operators were aware that the plaintiffs obtained oil through a pipeline operating in their area of operations. The pipeline was not owned by the plaintiffs, thus they suffered no physical damage, but purely economic loss, because the ruptured pipeline was offline for some tie. The High Court held the defendant owed the plaintiffs a duty of care in relation to this economic loss, because they had specific knowledge that *Caltex Oil* would be so affected by negligent dredge operations in the area).

[154] *Bryan v Maloney* (1995) 182 CLR 609, 617–18 (Mason CJ Deane and Gaudron JJ), 656 (Toohey J).

element),[155] with objections particularly expressed over the third aspect of 'fair, just and reasonable'.[156] However, the High Court would eventually turn away from proximity as a general touchstone of a duty of care.[157] It has generally abandoned the attempt to develop a unifying rationale to explain and justify the imposition of a duty of care, reflecting developments in the United Kingdom in cases such as *Robinson*.

In its place, the High Court has adopted a 'salient features' approach, as part of an incremental approach to the recognition of a duty of care in a particular case. These salient features will differ from case to case. However, one feature that has found real prominence is the concept of 'vulnerability'.[158] A plaintiff who can demonstrate that they were in a vulnerable position with respect to the factual scenario is more likely to be able to establish that a defendant in the particular case owes them a duty of care.

So for example in *Perre v Apand Pty Ltd*,[159] the plaintiffs owned land in South Australia on which they grew potatoes. The defendants manufactured seeding for potatoes. It negligently supplied contaminated seed to an owner of farm situated near that of the plaintiffs. The plaintiff sold many of its potatoes in Western Australia. Western Australia law prohibited the sale in that state of potatoes grown on or near a farm affected by contaminated seed. As a result of the defendant's supply of contaminated seed to a neighbour, the plaintiffs were unable to sell their property into Western Australia. They sued the defendant for the pure economic loss they suffered. They were not in a contractual relationship with the defendant, and nor had they suffered physical damage to their crop.

A majority of the Court found that the defendant owed a duty of care to the plaintiff. This was partly because of the presence of 'vulnerability'. Gleeson CJ said that vulnerability could arise in a number of ways. One way was assumption of responsibility, and reliance.[160] Another way was where the defendant knew that the plaintiff individually, or as a member of an identifiable class of individuals, would or would likely be affected by their acts. Here, the defendant knew that the owners of farms within 20 kilometres of a farm with contaminated seed would likely suffer economic loss as a result of the contamination.[161] The plaintiffs were vulnerable because they could do nothing to their own land to prevent

[155] *Sullivan v Moody* (2001) 207 CLR 562, 579 (Gleeson CJ Gaudron McHugh Hayne and Callinan JJ).

[156] *Perre v Apand Pty Ltd* (1999) 198 CLR 180, 211–12 (McHugh J) and 301–03 (Hayne J); *Sullivan v Moody* (2001) 207 CLR 562, 579 (Gleeson CJ Gaudron McHugh Hayne and Callinan JJ). This is with the exception of Kirby J who applied the three-stage process in that case: 285–91.

[157] *Hill v Van Erp* (1997) 188 CLR 159, 177–78 (Dawson J), 189 (Toohey J) and 192 (Gaudron J); *Pyrenees Shire Council v Day* (1998) 192 CLR 330, 414 (Kirby J); *Sullivan v Moody* (2001) 207 CLR 562, 578 (Gleeson CJ Gaudron McHugh Hayne and Callinan JJ).

[158] *Burnie Port Authority v General Jones Pty Ltd* (1994) 179 CLR 520, 551 (Mason CJ Deane Dawson Toohey and Gaudron JJ); *Crimmins v Stevedoring Industry Finance Committee* (1999) 200 CLR 1, 24–25 (Gaudron J) and 40–41 (McHugh J).

[159] (1999) 198 CLR 180.

[160] ibid 194; see McHugh J to similar effect (228).

[161] ibid 194–95.

this loss.[162] Gaudron J emphasised the extent to which the defendant 'controlled' the enjoyment or exercise of a legal right by the plaintiff, acknowledging this was a corollary to the extent to which the defendant depended on the plaintiff.[163] This is obviously highly analogous to questions of vulnerability.

McHugh J stated

> What is likely to be decisive, and always of relevance, in determining whether a duty of care is owed is … how vulnerable was the plaintiff to incurring loss by reason of the defendant's conduct … so also is the actual knowledge of the defendant concerning that risk and its magnitude. If no question of indeterminate liability is present[164] and the defendant, having no legitimate interest to pursue, (knows that their) conduct will cause economic loss to persons who are not easily able to protect themselves against that loss, it seems to accord with current community standards in most … cases to require the defendant to have the interests of those persons in mind before he or she embarks on that conduct.[165]

As McHugh J alludes to above, the Court has also noted that some care must be taken in applying torts in the commercial environment. This is because 'a duty to take reasonable care to avoid causing mere economic loss to another … may be inconsistent with community standards in relation to what is ordinarily legitimate in the pursuit of personal advantage'.[166]

In *Woolcock Street Investments Pty Ltd v CDG Pty Ltd*[167] members of the Court acknowledged the importance of vulnerability as one of the salient features to be considered in determining whether or not a duty of care is owed.[168] Justices elaborated upon its meaning. It did not mean simply that the plaintiff was likely to

[162] Gaudron J noted this specifically (202), as did Gummow J (259) and Callinan J (328).

[163] ibid 201; see also *Graham Barclay Oysters Pty Ltd v Ryan* (2002) 211 CLR 540, 597–99 (Gummow and Hayne JJ) regarding the importance of control.

[164] This is to avoid the spectre of liability in an 'indeterminate amount for an indeterminate time to an indeterminate class': *Ultramares Corporation v Touche* (1931) 225 NY 170, 179; 174 NE 441, 444 (Cardozo CJ).

[165] (n 159) 220.

[166] *Bryan v Maloney* (1995) 182 CLR 609, 618 (Mason CJ Deane and Gaudron JJ); *Van Erp v Hill* (1997) 188 CLR 159, 179 (Dawson J), 192–93 (Gaudron J), 215–16 (McHugh J) and 235–36 (Gummow J); *Perré v Apand Pty Ltd* (1999) 198 CLR 180, 220 (McHugh J) and 258 (Gummow J). McHugh J elaborates at 224–25. He contrasts this with contract, where there may be less vulnerability because contract law assumes that parties are able to protect their legitimate interests through the negotiation process (228). We know that the reality is that parties are often not able to negotiate contract terms, given inequalities of bargaining power. On the facts Gummow J held that imposition of a duty of care on *Apand* in this case would not be inconsistent with its legitimate pursuit of commercial advantage – it was not legitimate commercial advantage to sell defective products, injuring others (258); Hayne J reached a similar conclusion (305–06), as did Callinan J (328); see similarly *Hofstrand Farms Ltd v British Columbia* [1986] 1 SCR 228, 243: 'the realities of modern life must be reflected by the enunciation of a defined limit on liability capable of practical application, so that social and commercial life can go on unimpeded by a burden outweighing the benefit to the community of our neighbourhood historic principle'.

[167] (2004) 216 CLR 515.

[168] ibid 530 (Gleeson CJ Gummow Hayne and Heydon JJ), 549 (McHugh J), 576 (Kirby J) and 588 (Callinan J).

suffer loss if reasonable care were not taken.[169] It considered the extent to which the plaintiff was able to protect itself from the consequences of the defendant's lack of reasonable care.[170] The more the plaintiff was able to do so, the less vulnerable they were, and the less likely it would be that they would be held to be owed a duty of care. McHugh J also suggested that vulnerability could consider social, political or economic constraints operating on the plaintiff in determining their ability or otherwise to protect their own interests.[171] Members of the Court also noted that in cases where the defendant had assumed a responsibility to others in the knowledge they would rely on the defendant, it was more likely that vulnerability would be said to exist.[172]

Apparent differences of view emerged in *Brookfield Multiplex Ltd v Owners – Strata Plan No 61288*[173] regarding the relationship between contract and tort. Hayne and Kiefel JJ acknowledged the possibility that tort might 'outflank' or 'undermine' fundamental doctrines of the law of contract.[174] Gageler J agreed liability in contract and tort could co-exist.[175] On the other hand, Crennan Bell and Keane JJ doubted whether the allocation of economic risks by the parties to a contract could or should be disturbed by tortious liability.[176] All agreed that vulnerability, as evidenced by the inability of a party to take measures to defend themselves from the consequences of a lack of care by another, was relevant in determining whether or not a duty of care should be owed.[177]

VII. Reliance Theory: Atiyah and Others

Atiyah claimed that the distinction between contract and tort was now out of date, reflective of the long-discredited will theory of contracting. He says

[169] ibid 530 (Gleeson CJ Gummow Hayne and Heydon JJ).
[170] ibid 530 (Gleeson CJ Gummow Hayne and Heydon JJ); 552 (McHugh J), 576 (Kirby J) and 588 (Callinan J).
[171] ibid 549.
[172] ibid 531 (Gleeson CJ Gummow Hayne and Heydon JJ).
[173] (2014) 254 CLR 185.
[174] ibid 211.
[175] ibid 241.
[176] ibid 229: 'the common law has not developed with a view to altering the allocation of economic risks between parties to a contract by supplementing or supplanting the terms of the agreement by duties imposed by the law of tort'.
[177] ibid 201 (French CJ), 210–11 (Hayne and Kiefel JJ), 214 (Crennan Bell and Keane JJ), 244 (Gageler J). It has been suggested that the question of the ability of the plaintiff to take steps to protect themselves from the harm caused to them by the defendant's alleged lack of care must take account of the reasonableness of taking such steps, as opposed to the theoretical possibility of it: J Stapleton, 'Comparative Economic Loss: Lessons from Case-Law Focussed "Middle Theory"' (2002) 50(2) *University of California Los Angeles Law Review* 531, 558; *Woolcock Street Investments Pty Ltd v CDG Pty Ltd* (2004) 216 CLR 515, 558–59 (McHugh J) and 576–77 (Kirby J). The willingness of the High Court to assume the ability of a commercial party to adequately protect themselves from such risk, as opposed to a consumer, without regard to the bargaining power of the commercial party has been trenchantly criticised: A Jackman, 'Vulnerability, Autonomy and Protection: The Role of Actual and Hypothetical Contracts in the Duty of Care to Protect Against Pure Economic Loss' (2020) 49 *Australian Bar Review* 82, 93.

that, although will theory is generally now not the accepted basis of contract, its remnants continue to influence contract law doctrine. So, for example, we continue to search for the parties' presumed intentions, on the basis that contracts are about what parties intend, rather than what they do. This is another basis upon which some distinguish contract and tort – that tort, unlike contract, is concerned with what parties do.

Atiyah says that contract law is in fact closely tied in with both benefit and reliance. Contract law reflects reliance in terms of principles such as breach of warranty and estoppel. It also reflects benefit in terms of principles such as consideration. He says that when contract law makes a party liable for something, contrary to the person's intent and/or understanding, it is typically because it has been relied upon by another, to their detriment. This is similar to many cases of tort. He says the breach of contract action is essentially a form of compensation for wrongful harm. Because he views contract law liability in this way, he says the distinction between contract and tort is too sharply drawn. At least a large component of contract law liability is in fact reliance-based. He says the existing view of contract law is based on anachronistic thinking:

> It is the protection of expectations deriving from promises which I regard as associated with a laissez-faire ideology, together with the related idea that a person who has not obtained a promise to protect himself cannot complain of the other party's behaviour. That is indeed a highly individualistic position, and is surely very closely linked with nineteenth century ideology.[178]

Sir Andrew Tipping, formerly of the Supreme Court of New Zealand, has expressed a similar view:

> There is one concept that is helpful in identifying whether obligations should exist in contract, tort and equity. It is the concept of reasonable reliance. With reasonable reliance will usually come a moral obligation to recognise and fulfil that reliance … when parties are in a contractual relationship it is perfectly reasonable for each party to rely on the other to perform their contractual obligations. That is the whole point of having a contract … the whole foundation for both the primary duty (to perform as promised) and the secondary duty (provide compensation in the event of default) is that of reasonable reliance. Commerce could hardly be carried on if contracting parties could not rely on each other to perform their contractual obligations. The law reinforces that reliance. The position with reliance in the tort of negligence is conceptually similar. Whether there is sufficient proximity between the parties depends very much on whether it is reasonable for one party to rely on the other to take care.[179]

[178] PS Atiyah, 'Contracts, Promises and the Law of Obligations' (1978) 94 *Law Quarterly Review* 193, 223.

[179] 'Obligations in Contract, Tort and Equity: Reliance, Responsibility, and the Moral Dimension: Essay in Honour of Sir John McGrath' (2021) 52 *Victoria University of Wellington Law Review* 643, 650.

VIII. Applicability of these Principles to Good Faith Context

It will be recalled that in one of the leading cases in which good faith was held to be applicable to all contracts, Lord Mansfield justified this on the basis that the means of knowledge of a particular thing lay most commonly with one party, the other party trusting that the other has not withheld information.[180] As has been conceded, this did not in fact become a principle applicable to all contracts. But one can see a link between the concept of vulnerability as establishing a duty of care (where the High Court emphasised the ability or otherwise of a party to take steps to defend themselves) and the ability of a party to know of particular facts. On one view, just as the (general) lack of ability of a party to know of particular facts justified the imposition of good faith principles, the general lack of ability of a party to adequately deal with a particular risk justifies imposition of a duty of care.

Others have made the connection between negligence principles and good faith. McGivern has noted (in the context of good faith in the insurance context):

> The duty of utmost good faith as a positive normative obligation arising as an incident of the relationship between the parties can be seen to share key juridical features with the duty of care in negligence. Each duty is imposed as a matter of law, it is designed to hold incumbents to a standard of conduct objectively assessed (informed by notions of fairness, reasonableness and 'community standards'), and is responsive to context; neither arises in the abstract. For these reasons, it is suggested that the juridical approach to identifying and ordering the features of a legal relationship for the purposes of discerning the content of a duty of care is a useful means to import greater certainty into determination of what the duty of utmost good faith requires.[181]

It has been pointed out that the concept of vulnerability is important in terms of determining whether a duty of care is owed. McGivern states that vulnerability is also inherent in insurance contracts, with one party typically with superior knowledge of the risks associated with the insurance.[182] She notes that it was at the heart of Lord Mansfield's initial rationale for the duty of disclosure in *Carter v Boehm*, which he argued was applicable to all contracting situations – the vulnerability of the party with access to less material detail than the other. She says that once the insurance contract has been entered into, the parties are potentially 'vulnerable' in different ways – the insured relies on the insurer to process claims expeditiously and in accordance with standard practices; the insurer relies on the insured to make non-fraudulent claims, and continue to provide relevant disclosures.[183]

[180] *Carter v Boehm* (1766) 3 Burr 1905, 1909; 97 ER 1162, 1164.

[181] B McGivern, 'A Tale of Two Duties: Utmost Good Faith and Reasonable Care' (2016) *27 Insurance Law Journal* 261, 267–68; 'Coming to the Party: The Evolution of Post-Contractual Duties of Utmost Good Faith under the ICA' (2013) 24 *Insurance Law Journal* 159, 173.

[182] McGivern, 'A Tale of Two Duties' (n 181) 270.

[183] ibid 271–72.

Former Chief Justice of Victoria, Marilyn Warren, also referred to the justification for the application of good faith principles being strongest where one party was vulnerable:

> Where commercial leviathans are contractually engaged, it is difficult to see that a duty of good faith will arise … if one party to a contract is more shrewd, more cunning and out-manoeuvres the other contracting party who did not suffer a disadvantage and who was not vulnerable, it is difficult to see why the latter should have greater protection than that provided by the law of contract.[184]

In *Joel v Law Union and Crown Insurance Company* Fletcher Moulton LJ in explaining the duty of utmost good faith utilised classic principles of the law of negligence:

> There is … something more than an obligation to treat the insurer fairly and honestly. There is the further duty that he should do it to the extent that a reasonable man would have done it; and if he has fallen short of that by reason of his bona fide considering the matter not material, whereas the jury, as representing what a reasonable person would think, hold that it was material, he has failed in his duty … this further duty is analogous to a duty to do an act which you undertake with reasonable care and skill, a failure to do which amount to negligence, and which is not atoned for by any amount of honesty or goof intention. The disclosure must be of all you ought to have realized to be material, not of that only which you did in fact realize to be so.[185]

As has been demonstrated in chapters five and six, many who accept the doctrine of good faith equate it to concepts of reasonableness. It requires parties to be other-regarding, which is also required in the field of tort. The argument is thus that the boundaries between contract and tort are not as fixed as some have claimed. The law has increasingly accepted the acceptance of a duty of care to others to not injure them. This requires parties to be other-regarding and conscious of the effects of their behaviour on others. The ruthless pursuit of self-interest must be curbed, in light of the impact of the behaviour on others. It does not seem so far removed from imposing a good faith obligation on contracting parties to similarly be other-regarding. The requirement is to act reasonably. It is accepted and workable in one context; it is surely acceptable and workable in the other, when the parties are in a known, close relationship.

[184] *Esso Australia Resources Pty Ltd v Southern Pacific Petroleum NL* [2005] VSCA 228, [3]–[4] (emphasis added); J Freire, 'Implied Obligation of Good Faith in Contracts: Only "Vulnerable" Parties Need Apply' (2006) 25 *Australian Resources and Energy Law Journal* 99; see also M Ellis, 'Utmost Good Faith: The Scope and Application of s 13 of the *Insurance Contracts Act* in the Wake of *CGU v AMP*' (2009) 20 *Insurance Law Journal* 92, 92: 'the relationship between insurer and insured is one characterised by a particular vulnerability that each party has to the other. The insurer must trust that the insured has provided complete and accurate information about the nature of the risk insured while the insured must trust the insurer to protect the protection promised under the policy and when it is required'.

[185] [1908] 2 KB 863, 883–84; see also C Tay, 'The Duty of Disclosure and Materiality in Insurance Contracts – A True Descendant of the Duty of Utmost Good Faith?' (2002) 13 *Insurance Law Journal* 1, 3: 'the concept of the duty of utmost good faith is inextricably linked to the idea of "fair dealing". This sense of fair dealing is seen in tort law as requiring care and responsibility to neighbours'.

IX. Good Faith in the Insurance Context

Finally, given that this book argues for the recognition of good faith as a general organising principle of contract law, it is sensible to consider one particular contractual context where the principle has been accepted and applied for 250 years, that of insurance. This might provide some insight into the workability or otherwise of such a concept.

It is generally considered that the tale of the law of insurance in the common law begins in the Lloyd's coffee house in London.[186] Lombardy insurance brokers would meet with clients or their agents in relation to insuring vessels that were at sea. It was just not possible for insurers or their representatives to adequately assess the risk relating to the proposed insurance. Thus, it became practical to insist that the one seeking the insurance disclose to the would-be insurer everything that was relevant to the risk they were effectively being asked to carry. These were matters typically only within the knowledge of the insured. This was part of an obligation of good faith. This has obvious links with good faith in the Roman law of contract,[187] as discussed in chapter one. Good faith in Roman law frowned upon non-disclosure of material information in the contractual context. The disclosure obligation became part of the law merchant.[188]

It was this practice that was recognised by *Lord Mansfield in Carter v Boehm*.[189] Obviously known as the judge that sought to synthesise the law merchant into the common law, it is not surprising that Lord Mansfield would embrace the commercial reality of the negotiations leading up to the finalisation of a policy by insisting upon a duty of full disclosure, as part of a good faith obligation. As explained in chapter one, Lord Mansfield insisted this was a general contractual obligation. He did not confine it to the insurance context, as the common law would subsequently move to do.[190]

Carter involved an insured who managed a fort in Indonesia. He insured the property against the risk of invasion. It was said that the defensive structures of the fort were substandard, rendering it liable to invasion. The insured was apparently aware of this, but did not disclose it to the insurer. The fort was invaded, and the insured sought to enforce the policy. The insurer sought to evade the policy on the basis of the non-disclosure.

[186] J Herschaft, 'Not Your Average Coffee Shop: Lloyd's of London – A Twenty-First Century Primer on the History, Structure and Future of the Backbone of Marine Insurance' (2005) 29 *Tulane Maritime Law Journal* 169, 180.

[187] R Davis, 'The Origin of the Duty of Disclosure Under Insurance Law' (1994) 4(1) *Insurance Law Journal* 71, 76; R Ashton, 'Keeping the Faith – Good Faith in Insurance and the Emergence of General Contractual Good Faith' (2011) 22 *Insurance Law Journal* 81, 82.

[188] Howard Bennett, 'Mapping the Doctrine of Utmost Good Faith in the Insurance Contract Law' (1999) *Lloyd's Maritime and Commercial Law Quarterly* 165, 191 ('may' have been created by the law merchant).

[189] (1766) 3 Burr 1905; 97 ER 1162.

[190] 'The governing principle is applicable to all contracts and dealings': (1766) 3 Burr 1905, 1910; 97 ER 1162, 1164.

Lord Mansfield held that an insured had a duty of disclosure of material relevant to the risk the insurer was being asked to take on. This was because such matters were most commonly in the knowledge of the insured only. The insurer trusted, and should be able to trust, that the insured fully disclosed material matters. Although Lord Mansfield does use the word 'fraud' to describe non-disclosure of material matters, he also says the insured's duty of non-disclosure might also be breached through 'mistake' and not fraudulent intent. Still the policy would be void because 'the risk run is really different from the risk understood … at the time of the agreement'.[191] He said good faith prevented a party from concealing what they knew to draw the other party into a bargain with a mistaken belief.[192] He indicated the obligation applied to both parties.[193] The duty of disclosure did not extend to matters of which the insurer was aware or ought to have been aware.[194] The insurer lost on this basis, Lord Mansfield concluding the insurer was in a better position than the insured to judge the risk of invasion, given their knowledge of world events.[195]

The assumed asymmetry of information between the insured and the insurer on particular matters, and the difficulty or impossibility of the less informed party gaining this knowledge, has continued to be presented as the rationale for the duty of disclosure.[196] It continues to be accepted that the obligation applies to both parties.[197] The obligation is to disclose material information,[198] judged objectively.[199] It is material that a prudent insurer would take into account in determining whether and on what terms it would offer insurance.[200] It includes material of which the insured is aware and ought to be aware.[201] The obligation arises both in relation to pre-contractual disclosure and disclosure during the term of the contract.[202] However, the scope of the obligation with respect to pre-contractual matters is likely different to the scope of the obligation with

[191] (1766) 3 Burr 1905, 1909; 97 ER 1162, 1164.

[192] ibid.

[193] ibid.

[194] ibid, 1165.

[195] ibid, 1167.

[196] A Tarr and J Tarr, 'The Insured's Non-Disclosure in the Formation of Insurance Contracts: A Comparative Perspective' (2001) 50 *International and Comparative Law Quarterly* 577, 577; *Manifest Shipping Co Ltd v UniPolaris Insurance Co Ltd* [2003] 1 AC 469, 491 (Lord Hobhouse); Lords Steyn and Hoffmann agreed (480); *Pan Atlantic Insurance Co Ltd v Pine Top Insurance Co Ltd* [1995] 1 AC 501, 555 (Lord Lloyd).

[197] *Banque Financiere de la cite S.A. v Westgate Insurance Co Ltd* [1991] 2 AC 249.

[198] *Associated Oil Carriers Ltd v Union Insurance Society of Canton Ltd* [1917] 2 KB 184; *Lindenau v Desborough* (1828) 8 B & C 586, 592 (Bayley J); *Bates v Hewitt* (1867) LR 2 QB 595, 604–05; Insurance Act 2015 (UK) s 3(4) (in respect of non-consumer insurance contracts).

[199] *Joel v Law Union and Crown Insurance* [1908] 2 KB 863, 884 (Fletcher Moulton LJ).

[200] *Pan Atlantic Insurance Co Ltd v Pine Top Insurance Co Ltd* [1995] 1 AC 501. It was not necessary that the material be of a decisive character in this context. However, in order that the insurer be able to terminate the contract for non-disclosure of the material, it must have induced them to offer insurance on the terms they did.

[201] *Proudfoot v Montefiore* LR 2 QB 511, 521 (Cockburn CJ Blackburn and Shee JJ (CA)); Insurance Act 2015 (UK) s 3(4) (in respect of non-consumer insurance contracts).

[202] *Boulton v Houlder Bros & Co* [1904] 1 KB 784, 792 (Mathew LJ).

respect to matters subsequent to the execution of the contract.[203] Subsequently the duty of disclosure was broadened beyond material within the exclusive knowledge of the insured; at common law, it could also apply to material that the insurer might have discovered themselves.[204] While at one time it was considered the duty of good faith was an implied term,[205] the better view is that it is a rule of law developed by the courts.[206] It is based on 'a matter of business and fair dealing'.[207] Remedy for breach of the duty was typically limited in the common law to rescission, not damages,[208] though the Insurance Act 2015 (UK) has altered this position.[209] It is argued the word 'utmost' adds nothing of substance to good faith.[210] The rule that insurance contracts are contracts are of utmost good faith must now be read subject to the Insurance Act 2015 (UK) where applicable.[211] The legislation intends that good faith remain an interpretative principle.[212]

Section 3 of the Insurance Act 2015 (UK) requires an insured to make a fair presentation of risk to the insurer prior to contract, in respect of non-consumer insurance contracts. A fair presentation of risk requires:

Disclosure of all material facts of which the insured knows or ought to know, or at least disclosure such that the insurer is placed on notice to make further investigation;

Disclosure to be in a clear and accessible format; and

Disclosures of material fact are correct and disclosures of expectation or belief are in good faith.

[203] *Manifest Shipping Co Ltd v UniPolaris Insurance Co Ltd* [2003] 1 AC 469 (*The Star Sea*), 482 (Lord Clyde), 494 (Lord Hobhouse) and 511 (Lord Scott), Lords Steyn and Hoffmann agreeing (480).

[204] *Bates v Hewitt* (1867) LR 2 QB 595, 604–05 (Cockburn CJ), 611 (Shee J) (CA); cf *Friere v Woodhouse* (1817) 1 Holt NP 572, 573 which suggested the insured's duty of disclosure did not extend to facts of which the insurer might reasonably have been aware by making fair inquiry; see F Achampong, 'Uberrima Fides in English and American Law: A Comparative Analysis' (1987) 36 *International and Comparative Law Quarterly* 329, 332–33 and RA Hasson, 'The Doctrine of Uberrima Fides in Insurance Law – A Critical Evaluation' (1969) 32 *Modern Law Review* 615. In *Blackburn Low & Co v Vigors* (1886) 17 QBD 553 it was held the insured's obligation to disclose did not apply to matters of which the insurer ought to have been aware: 560 (Lord Esher MR). This is now reflected in the Insurance Act 2015 (UK) s 3(5) in respect of non-consumer insurance contracts.

[205] *Blackburn Low & Co v Vigors* (1886) 17 QBD 553, 562 (Lord Esher MR) (he referred to it as a 'condition precedent'); 578 (Lindley LJ) and 583 (Lopez LJ).

[206] *Manifest Shipping Co Ltd v UniPolaris Insurance Co Ltd* [2003] 1 AC 469, 493 (Lord Hobhouse) (with whom Lords Steyn and Hoffmann agreed: 480); *Khoury v Government Insurance Office* (NSW) (1984) 165 CLR 622, 636–37 (Mason Brennan Deane and Dawson JJ).

[207] *Blackburn Low & Co v Vigors* (1886) 17 QBD 553, 578 (Lindley LJ).

[208] *Banque Financiere de la Cite SA v Westgate Insurance Co Ltd* [1991] 2 AC 249, 280 (Lord Templeman) (with whom Lords Brandon (269), Ackner (281) and Jauncey (281) agreed).

[209] Section 14(1) states the general position that an insurer cannot void a policy because of non-compliance with an insured's duty of utmost good faith, subject to specific provision in Schedule 1 in respect of non-consumer insurance contracts.

[210] YQ Han, 'Good Faith in Insurance Law: General and Independent, Not a Duty But an Interpretive Principle' (2017) 28 *Insurance Law Journal* 95, 96; *Manifest Shipping Co Ltd v UniPolaris Insurance Co Ltd* [2003] 1 AC 469 (*The Star Sea*), 482 (Lord Clyde) and 511 (Lord Scott).

[211] S14(2).

[212] Insurance Act 2015 (UK) Explanatory Notes [116].

Of course, good faith extends beyond requirements of disclosure. It includes an obligation not to submit a fraudulent claim.[213] The insurer's duty of good faith was considered in Groom v Crocker.[214] There the court considered the exercise of an insurer's powers to take over proceedings involving the insured. It emphasised that, in such cases, the insurer must have due regard to the interests of both the insured and themselves. They could not exercise their power in such a way as to secure an advantage to themselves, at the expense of the insured.[215]

In *Distillers Co v Biochemicals (Australia) v Ajax Insurance Co Ltd*,[216] the High Court of Australia considered the obligations that an insurer owed to an insured in relation to the settlement of a claim. He stated:

> The implied obligation imposed on the insurer to have regard to more than its own interests when exercising its rights and powers under the contract of insurance, is perhaps most clearly seen in the well established doctrines of the United States courts … this duty of good faith and fair dealing must … not only control the actions of an insurer (exercising subrogation rights) but will equally apply to the insurer's exercise of its power of granting or withholding of consent to the making of admissions etc … It would … be improper for the insurer to refuse its consent to an otherwise proper and reasonable settlement.[217]

In *CGU Insurance Ltd v AMP Financial Planning Pty Ltd*,[218] Gleeson CJ and Crennan J rejected the view that good faith was limited to honesty. Rather

> We accept that utmost good faith may require an insurer to act with due regard to the legitimate interests of an insured, as well as to its own interests. The classic example of an insured's obligation of utmost good faith is a requirement of full disclosure to an insurer (in other words) … a requirement to pay regard to the legitimate interests of the insurer. Conversely, an insurer's statutory obligation to act with utmost good faith may require an insurer to act, consistently with commercial standards of decency and fairness, with due regard to the interests of the insured. Such an obligation may well affect the conduct of an insurer in making a timely response to a claim for indemnity.[219]

[213] *Orakpo v Barclays Insurance Services Company Ltd* [1995] LRLR 443; *Manifest Shipping Co Ltd v UniPolaris Insurance Co Ltd* [2003] 1 AC 469 (*The Star Sea*), 482 (Lord Clyde), 493 (Lord Hobhouse), 506 (Lord Scott) (Lord Steyn and Lord Hoffmann agreed).

[214] [1939] 1 KB 194.

[215] Sir Wilfred Greene MR (203) and MacKinnon LJ (226) (CA); O Gurses, 'What Does "Utmost" Good Faith Mean?' (2016) 27 *Insurance Law Journal* 124, 130 (insurer required to exercise indemnity rights in good faith, having due regard to the interests of the insured as well as themselves). They must also pay claims within a reasonable time: Insurance Act 2015 (UK) s 13A. Similarly, it would be a breach of good faith for an insured to interfere with an insurer's right of subrogation: *Horwood v Land of Leather Ltd* [2010] All ER (D) 177 (Mar).

[216] (1973) 130 CLR 1.

[217] ibid 31. In *Gan Insurance Co Ltd v Tai Ping Insurance Co Ltd* [2001] EWCA Civ 1047 the Court found that the reinsurer's approval rights regarding settlement were conditioned by a requirement of good faith: [76] (Mance LJ) to exercise it in the 'common interest' ([72]) and consistently with contractual purpose.

[218] (2007) 235 CLR 1.

[219] ibid 12.

Kirby J stated that in this context lack of good faith meant considering criteria such as dishonesty, caprice and unreasonableness.[220] In *Manifest Shipping Co Ltd v UniPolaris Insurance Co Ltd*, Lord Hobhouse equated good faith in this context with a requirement of 'fair dealing'.[221] Subsequently the Court of Appeal indicated this might mean, for example, that exercise of an insurer's right to rescind the contract for material non-disclosure by the insured might be conditioned upon a requirement of proportionality,[222] and/or a requirement to properly investigate the precise nature of the non-compliance before exercising contractual rights.[223]

It can be argued that, having been accepted for centuries in the context of insurance contracts, there is no reason why a good faith obligation should not be applicable to contracts more generally.[224] The duty of good faith in the insurance context is premised on the information asymmetry between the parties. Even though parties' ability to investigate matters has obviously substantially improved since the late eighteenth century,[225] in 2015 with the passage of the Insurance Act 2015 (UK) parliament has seen fit to maintain the good faith principle in some form. The argument is that the rationale of information asymmetry can also be applied to other contracts.[226] It will usually, if not almost always, be the case that in respect of a contract one party will have access to different information than the other party. This information can be pertinent to the risk that contracting parties are taking on. Almost all contracts involve parties taking on some risk. It would help to reduce the risk if both parties could rely on particular expectations regarding the other's performance and behaviour, thus reducing transaction costs.

Of course, good faith can mean different things in different contexts.[227] It is not argued here that, just as parties to an insurance contract have a duty of disclosure, parties to other contracts should have a duty of disclosure.[228] What is argued is that imposition of a good faith obligation in contracts generally would help to reduce transaction costs, by permitting both parties to make assumptions that the other party will act in a particular manner during the performance of the

[220] ibid 43.

[221] [2003] 1 AC 469, 493 (with whom Lords Steyn and Hoffmann agreed: 480).

[222] *Drake Insurance Plc v Provident Insurance Plc* [2004] QB 601, 629 (Rix LJ).

[223] 649 (Pill LJ).

[224] Han (n 210) 104: 'the duty of good faith performance is applicable to insurance contracts, the law for which is not and should not be fundamentally (different) from general contract law'.

[225] WJ Marwedel and SA Espinoza, 'Dagger, Shield or Double-Edged Sword: The Reciprocal Nature of the Doctrine of Uberrimae Fidei' (2009) 83 *Tulane Law Review* 1163, 1186; WP Yee, 'The Duty of Disclosure – Proposals for Reform' (2000) 21 *Singapore Law Review* 100, 102.

[226] J Lowry, 'Whither the Duty of Good Faith in UK Insurance Contracts' (2009) 16 *Connecticut Insurance Law Journal* 97, 103–04: 'although the disparity of knowledge between the parties has been proffered as the explanation, this is hardly a satisfactory rationale in itself given that in other common contracting situations, the parties similarly lack equality of information'.

[227] Bennett (n 188) 166.

[228] *Macquarie International Health Clinic Pty Ltd v Sydney South West Area Health Service* [2010] NSWCA 268, [18] (Allsop P).

contract. That one party will not seek to obtain an unfair advantage by exploiting information not known to the other party, for example that one party intends to act in a way that is unexpected given commercial norms, wishes to unreasonably enforce particular provisions of the contract, and so on.

Julie-Anne Tarr and Jeanette Van Akkeren also make this point:

> The imposition of a duty of good faith in insurance contracting imposes a form of 'commercial morality' upon the parties. The obligation to act towards one another with fairness, reasonableness and decency and to have regard to the other party's reasonable expectations goes far beyond traditional notions of 'let the buyer beware' and strict adherence to contractual terms.[229]

Of course, there is no logical reason to confine this sentiment to contracts relating to insurance only.[230] I must respectfully disagree with claims that there is a 'vulnerability' and 'special relationship' in the insurance context that it said not to apply to general commercial relationships:[231]

> Unlike most commercial arrangements, the relationship between insurer and insured is one characterised by a particular vulnerability that each party has to the other. The insurer must trust that the insured has provided complete and accurate information about the nature of the risk insured while the insured must trust the insurer to provide the protection promised under the policy if and when it is required.

With respect, it is not clear to me why other contracting parties are not 'vulnerable'. An employee may be particularly vulnerable – they typically rely on employment to pay their household bills, if an employee were dismissed, others may make judgment upon them and they may find securing other employment difficult. A person's career is often very important to a person's self-identity and worth. Other contracting parties may be vulnerable – a small business may have a contract with a large customer who purchases most of the output of the small business, such that if the small business lost that customer, it may be in financial jeopardy. The market for a particular product or service may be small, placing suppliers to it in a vulnerable situation. A purchaser of a product or service may be vulnerable, because there are few suppliers with the required expertise.

To an extent, all contracts make the parties vulnerable – they are likely to lose at least something from the other's non-performance or substandard performance – whether that be putting up with an inferior product or service, paying another to correct problems, engaging in dispute resolution with the non-performing party, time delays, loss of profit and so on. We all rely on the other

[229] J Tarr and J Van Akkeren, 'Accountability for Good Faith in Commercial Dealing: The *Carter v Boehm* Legacy 250 Years On' (2016) 27 *Insurance Law Journal* 275, 284.

[230] Yee (n 225) 107: 'it is unjustified for the insurer's business now to receive favoured legal treatment over other similarly vital commercial activities'; B Harnett, 'The Doctrine of Concealment: A Remnant in the Law of Insurance' (1950) 15 *Law and Contemporary Problems* 391, 409: 'the insurer comes forward with no good reason why his business should receive favoured legal treatment over other similarly vital commercial and social activities'.

[231] Ellis (n 184).

party to keep their promises – it is not just insureds who rely on the insurer to do so. Often general contracting parties will rely on the information and advice provided by the other – perhaps because the other has more expertise, or it is not time efficient to investigate claims made and so on. Thus, one should not too readily accept the argument that insurance contracts are, and should be, in a special category governed by special considerations. It can be reasonably argued they are no longer, if they ever were, special contracts subject to special rules. And this when the original architect of the rule, Lord Mansfield, himself did not think them only applicable to insurance contracts; on the contrary, asserting it was a rule applicable to all contracts. Ashton suggested good faith in insurance and non-insurance context should find 'mutual repose in congruent principle'.[232]

X. Conclusion

In sum, this discussion has demonstrated that good faith is quite workable in a commercial context. The requirement to be other-regarding, and to abide by ethical practice, has not proven to be anathema to commercial practice or impossible to apply legally. A requirement that parties act consistently with commercial standards of decency and fairness, as members of the High Court described good faith in the insurance context, is feasible. The law of insurance has reflected the parties' reasonable expectations in relation to disclosure. There is no reason to limit it to that context. The parliament has had opportunities to review the operation of the principle, yet did not see fit to abolish it. Just as vulnerability is said to underpin good faith obligations in the insurance context, it also underpins a duty of care obligation, and can underpin a general good faith obligation in contract. In short, experience of good faith in the insurance context has proven that Lord Mansfield's statement in *Carter* that good faith is applicable to all commercial dealings is realistic and workable. There is not acceptable rationale today for applying a requirement of good faith to the insurance context but not to other contracting contexts.

[232] Ashton (n 187) 95: 'good faith in insurance contracts and good faith in non-insurance contracts were born in the same stellar event, *Carter v Boehm*, but over the last 250 years they have traced quite different orbits. Now, there is some basis for a view that they are approaching reunion. My personal preference would be that they find mutual repose in congruent principle rather than pass each other by with perhaps no more than the hope of a Halley-like rendezvous in another 250 years'.

Conclusion

I hope to have demonstrated the very long history of good faith in our law. It was developed in Roman times as an expectation of those engaged in contracting, a way to evade the results from rigid rules. Roman law was transplanted to England, and for a long time it flourished. However, the supposed needs of a capitalist economy in the industrial revolution time precipitated a move away from good faith, because of its supposed uncertainty, in favour of fixed rules. These evidently produced much unfairness, and questionable certainty. Again, the law evolved, away from freedom of contract, to reflect the need for flexibility and the innate desire for justice.

In this context, it might have been thought that the law might re-embrace good faith. However, so far, the English courts have been very tentative and wary of doing so. Good faith has been held to condition the exercise of contractual discretion, and to apply to a small number of contract types. There has been little defence or explanation as to why good faith is only accepted in these contexts, but not others, apart from general assertions about uncertainty. Of course, good faith could potentially cause uncertainty in these contexts where it has been accepted. Good faith is simultaneously criticised as 'foreign' and 'alien' to the common law, but also superfluous because it already underlies existing doctrine. Respectfully, one cannot have it both ways. It is unsatisfactory that judges can sometimes feel forced to twist facts, or law, in order to get to results that would align with good faith, because it is considered too 'radical' to accept the doctrine as a general principle. As has been documented, the Canadian Supreme Court has done so, and the doctrine has applied in that leading capitalist economy the United States for many years, as well as throughout Europe. 'Brave' sub-national courts have also embraced it in Australia, though the highest court is yet to indicate its view. The law will probably continue to limp along in this fashion. However, it is argued the Canadian precedent of recognising a generalised duty of good faith has much to recommend it. It is likely that the content of such an obligation will include many principles that the common law already recognises, though in a piecemeal manner, such as the obligation to do all that is necessary to let the other contracting party to have the benefit of the bargain, not to hinder or obstruct the fulfilment of pre-conditions to the contract coming into existence etc.

The idea of the relational contract is probably best placed to provide the intellectual support for this suggested shift in the law. It would align commercial law with commercial practice, and give effect to the reasonable expectations of contracting parties. Surely, this is what commercial law should do. It should not be antagonistic to those expectations, or operate in a pretend world that does not reflect reality. What we regard today as the law of negligence, and its obligations to our legal neighbour, is considered to be highly pertinent to the argument about good faith. We accept and apply a law that requires us to have due regard to the interests of strangers who we can reasonably foresee will be affected by our actions. This generalised operating principle has worked well for 90 years. In this light, it does not seem radical or unreasonable for contracting parties, who by definition do know one another, to be expected to have due regard to the interests of the other. And this accords with parties' general expectations of the other.

When I embarked on this project, I intended one book on good faith. As it has turned out, the volume of material and the topics I wished to consider have meant that two books are required. Thus, at the time of writing, a sequel is in the works. That book will consider in more detail what acceptance of good faith would mean in relation to specific existing doctrines of contract law. As far as I am aware, this has not been done in the detail that I believe it warrants. Whether or not you agree my argument, I trust that this book (and the sequel) have given you an interesting perspective on the question of good faith in contracting. Of course, my hope is that one day English and Australian contract law will embrace good faith as a general organising concept of the common law, for the reasons explained in this book.

BIBLIOGRAPHY

Achampong, F, 'Uberrima Fides in English and American Law: A Comparative Analysis' (1987) 36 *International and Comparative Law Quarterly* 329

Allsop, J, 'Good Faith and Australian Contract Law: A Practical Issue and a Question of Theory and Principle' (2011) 85 *Australian Law Journal* 341

Aristotle, *Nichomachean Ethics*, Book 1

Arrighetti, A, Bachmann, R and Deakin, S, 'Contract Law, Social Norms and Inter-Firm Co-Operation' (1997) 21 *Cambridge Journal of Economics* 171

Arrow, K, 'Economic Development: The Present State of the Art', 6 *Collected Papers of Kenneth Arrow* (Cambridge, Harvard University Press, 1984)

—— 'The Economics of Moral Hazard: Further Comment' (1968) 58(2) *American Economic Review* 537

Ashton, R, 'Keeping the Faith – Good Faith in Insurance and the Emergence of General Contractual Good Faith' (2011) 22 *Insurance Law Journal* 81

Atiyah, PS, *The Rise and Fall of Freedom of Contract* (Oxford, Clarendon Press, 1979)

—— 'Contracts, Promises and the Law of Obligations' (1978) 94 *Law Quarterly Review* 193

Baildon, WP and Barbour, WT, 'The History of Contract in Early English Equity' 4 *Oxford Studies in Social and Legal History* (London, Clarendon Press, 1916)

Baker, JH, 'From Sanctity of Contract to Reasonable Expectation' (1979) 32(1) *Current Legal Problems* 17

—— *An Introduction to English Legal History* (Oxford, Oxford University Press, 2002)

Baker, JH and Milsom, SFC, *Sources of English Legal History: Private Law to 1750* (Oxford, Oxford University Press, 2009)

Barbour, W, *The History of Contract in Early English Equity* (4 Oxford Studies in Social and Legal History, Oxford, Clarendon Press, 1914)

Barker, K, Fairweather, K and Grantham, R (eds), *Private Law in the 21st Century* (Oxford, Hart Publishing, 2017)

Beale, H and Dugdale, T, 'Contracts Between Businessmen: Planning and the Use of Contractual Remedies' (1975) 2(1) *British Journal of Law and Society* 45

Beatson, J and Friedmann, D, 'Introduction: From "Classical" to Modern Contract Law' in Beatson, J and Friedmann, D (eds), *Good Faith and Fault in Contract Law* (Oxford, Clarendon Press, 2002)

Beatson, J and Friedmann, D (eds), *Good Faith and Fault in Contract Law* (Oxford, Clarendon Press, 2002)

Bede, *Historium Ecclesiastical Gentis Anglorum* (1735)

Bennett, H, 'Mapping the Doctrine of Utmost Good Faith in the Insurance Contract Law' (1999) *Lloyd's Maritime and Commercial Law Quarterly* 165

Bentham, J, *Jeremy Bentham's Economic Writings* (New York, Routledge, 2010)

Bernstein, L, 'The Questionable Empirical Basis of Article 2's Incorporation Strategy: A Preliminary Study' (1999) 66 *University of Chicago Law Review* 710

—— 'Opting out of the Legal System: Extra-Legal Contractual Relations in the Diamond Industry' (1992) 21 *Journal of Legal Studies* 115

—— 'Private Commercial Law in the Cotton Industry: Creating Cooperation Through Rules, Norms and Institutions' (2001) 99 *Michigan Law Review* 1724

—— 'Merchant Law in a Merchant Court: Rethinking the Code's Search for Immanent Business Norms' (1996) 144 *University of Pennsylvania Law Review* 1765

Bingham, T, 'A New Thing Under the Sun? The Interpretation of Contract and the ICS Decision' (2008) 12 *Edinburgh Law Review* 374

Blom, J, 'The Evolving Relationship Between Contract and Tort' (1985) 10(3) *Canadian Business Law Journal* 257

Bohnet, I, Frey, B and Huck, S, 'More Order With Less Law: On Contract Enforcement, Trust and Crowding' (2001) 95(1) *American Political Science Review* 131

Bomball, P, 'Statutory Norms and Common Law Concepts in the Characterisation of Contracts for the Performance of Work' (2019) 42 *Melbourne University Law Review* 370

—— 'Subsequent Conduct, Construction and Characterisation in Employment Contract Law' (2015) 32 *Journal of Contract Law* 149

Boyle, M, 'The Relational Principle of Trust and Confidence' (2007) 27 *Oxford Journal of Legal Studies* 633

Bridge, M, 'Does Anglo-Canadian Contract Law Need a Doctrine of Good Faith?' (1984) 9 *Canadian Business Law Journal* 385

—— 'The Overlap of Tort and Contract' (1982) 27 *McGill Law Journal* 872

—— 'Doubting Good Faith' (2005) 11 *New Zealand Business Law Quarterly* 430

Brodie, D, 'How Relational is the Employment Contract?' (2011) 40 *Industrial Law Journal* 232

Brownsword, R, 'Two Concepts of Good Faith' (1994) 7 *Journal of Contract Law* 197

—— 'Individualism, Co-operativism and an Ethic for European Contract Law' (2001) 64 *Modern Law Review* 628

Burdick, W, *The Principles of Roman Law and their Relation to Modern Law* (Rochester, Lawyers Cooperative Publishing, 1938)

Burrows, A, 'Construction and Rectification' in Burrows, A and Peel, E (eds), *Contract Terms* (Oxford, Oxford University Press, 2007)

—— *Understanding the Law of Obligations* (Oxford, Hart, 1998)

Burrows, A and Peel, E (eds), *Contract Terms* (Oxford, Oxford University Press, 2007)

Burton, S, 'Breach of Contract and the Common Law Duty to Perform in Good Faith' (1980) 94 *Harvard Law Review* 369

Byles, J, *Observations on the Usury Laws* (London, 1845)

Camerer, C and Thaler, R, 'Anomalies: Ultimatums, Dictators and Manners' (1995) 9 *Journal of Law and Economics Perspectives* 209

Campbell, D, 'Truth Claims and Value-Freedom in the Treatment of Legitimacy: The Case of Weber' (1986) 13 *Journal of Law and Society* 207

—— 'Adam Smith and the Social Foundation of Agreement: *Walford v Miles* as a Relational Contract' (2017) 21(3) *Edinburgh Law Review* 376

—— 'The Incompleteness of our Understanding of the Law and Economics of Relational Contract' [2004] *Wisconsin Law Review* 645

—— '*Arcos v Ronaasen* as a Relational Contract' in Campbell, D, Mulcahy, L and Wheeler, S (eds), *Changing Conceptions of Contract: Essays in Honour of Ian Macneil* (London, Palgrave Macmillan, 2013)

Campbell, D and Collins, H, 'Discovering the Implicit Dimensions of Contract' in Campbell, D, Collins, H and Wightman, J (eds), *Implicit Dimensions of Contract: Discrete Relational and Network Contracts* (Oxford, Hart Publishing, 2003)

Campbell, D and Harris, D, 'Flexibility in Long-Term Contractual Relationships' (1993) 20 *Journal of Law and Society* 166

Campbell, D, Collins, H and Wightman, J (eds), *Implicit Dimensions of Contract: Discrete Relational and Network Contracts* (Oxford, Hart Publishing, 2003)

Campbell, D, Mulcahy, L and Wheeler, S (eds), *Changing Conceptions of Contract: Essays in Honour of Ian Macneil* (London, Palgrave Macmillan, 2013)

Cannon, JP et al, 'Contracts, Norms and Plural Form Governance' (2000) 28 *Journal of Academic Marketing Science* 180

Carlin, T, 'The Rise (and Fall?) of Implied Duties of Good Faith in Contractual Performance in Australia' (2002) 25(1) *University of New South Wales Law Journal* 99

Carter, J, 'Commercial Construction and Contract Doctrine' (2009) 25 *Journal of Contract Law* 83

Carter, J and Stewart, A, 'Interpretation, Good Faith and the "True Meaning" of Contracts: The *Royal Botanic* Decision' (2002) 18 *Journal of Contract Law* 182

Catterwell, R, 'Co-Operation and Prevention in Contract Law' (2023) 47(1) *Melbourne University Law Review* 114

Charles, S, 'Interpretation of Ambiguous Contracts by Reference to Subsequent Conduct' (1991) 4 *Journal of Contract Law* 16

Charny, D, 'Illusions of Spontaneous Order: "Norms" in Contractual Relationships' (1996) 144 *University of Pennsylvania Law Review* 1841

Christie, D, Sainter, S and Viven-Wilksch, J, 'Industry-Led Standards, Relational Contracts and Good Faith' (2022) 43 *Liverpool Law Review* 287

Cicero, *On Obligations* (PG Walsh trans, Oxford, Oxford University Press, 2000) Book 3

Cimino, CF, 'The Relational Economics of Commercial Contract' (2015) 3 *Texas A & M Law Review* 91

Coase, R, *The Firm The Market and the Law* (Chicago, University of Chicago Press, 1987)

—— 'The Problem of Social Cost' (1960) 3 *Journal of Law and Economics* 1

Cohen, M, 'The Basis of Contract' (1933) 46 *Harvard Law Review* 553

Cole, T, 'The Parol Evidence Rule: A Comparative Analysis and Proposal' (2003) 26 *University of New South Wales Law Journal* 680

Collins, H, *Regulating Contracts* (Oxford, Oxford University Press, 1999)

—— 'Introduction: The Research Agenda of Implied Dimensions of Contracts' in Campbell, D, Collins, H and Wightman, J (eds), *Implicit Dimensions of Contract: Discrete Relational and Network Contracts* (Oxford, Hart Publishing, 2003)

—— 'The Sanctimony of Contract' in Rawlings, R (ed), *Law, Society and Economy: Centenary Essays for the London School of Economics and Political Science 1895–1995* (Oxford, Clarendon Press, 1997)

—— 'Implied Terms: The Foundation in Good Faith and Fair Dealing' (2014) 67 *Current Legal Problems* 297

—— 'Discretionary Powers in Contracts' in Campbell, D, Collins, H and Wightman, J (eds), *Implicit Dimensions in Contracts: Discrete, Relational and Network Contracts* (Oxford, Hart Publishing, 2003)

—— 'Employment as a Relational Contract' (2021) 137 *Law Quarterly Review* 426

—— 'Is a Relational Contract a Legal Concept?' in Degeling, S, Edelman, J and Goudkamp, J (eds), *Contract in Commercial Law* (Sydney, LawBook Co, 2016)

Cooke, R, 'Tort and Contract' in Finn, PD (ed), *Essays on Contract* (Sydney, Law Book Company Ltd, 1987)

Corcoran, S, 'Good Faith as a Principle of Interpretation: What is the Positive Content of Good Faith?' (2012) 36 *Australian Bar Review* 1

Courtney, W, 'Good Faith and Termination: The English and Australian Experience' (2019) 1 *Journal of Commonwealth Law* 185

Cowell, J, *The Institutes of English Law* (London, 1651)

Daintith, T, 'The Design and Performance of Long-Term Contracts' in Daintith, T and Teubner, G (eds), *Contract and Organisation: Legal Analysis in the Light of Social and Economic Theory* (Berlin, De Gruyter, 1986)

Daintith, T and Teubner, G (eds), *Contract and Organisation: Legal Analysis in the Light of Social and Economic Theory* (Berlin, De Gruyter, 1986)

Davis, R, 'The Origin of the Duty of Disclosure Under Insurance Law' (1994) 4(1) *Insurance Law Journal* 71

Dawson, J, 'Economic Duress and the Fair Exchange in French and German Law' (1973) 11 *Tulane Law Review* 345

Degeling, S, Edelman, J and Goudkamp, J, *Contract in Commercial Law* (Sydney, LawBook Co, 2016)

Devlin, P, 'The Relation Between Commercial Law and Commercial Practice' (1951) 14 *Modern Law Review* 249

—— *The Enforcement of Morals* (Oxford, Oxford University Press, 1965)

Diamond, T, 'The Tort of Bad Faith Breach of Contract: When, If At All, Should it be Extended Beyond Insurance Transactions?' (1981) 64 *Marquette Law Review* 425

Diamond, T and Foss, H, 'Proposed Standards for Evaluating When the Covenant of Good Faith and Fair Dealing Have Been Violated: A Framework for Resolving the Mystery' (1996) 47 *Hastings Law Journal* 585

Dicey, AV, *Lectures on Law and Public Opinion in England During the Nineteenth Century* 2nd edn (London, Macmilllan and Co, 1914)

Dixon, B, 'Common Law Obligations of Good Faith in Australian Commercial Contracts – A Relational Recipe' (2005) 33 *Australian Business Law Review* 87

Donahue, C Jr, 'The Modern Laws of Both Tort and Contract: Fourteenth Century Beginnings' (2017) 40 *Manitoba Law Journal* 9

Dubroff, H, 'The Implied Covenant of Good Faith in Contract Interpretation and Gap Filling: Reviling a Revered Relic' (2006) 80 *St John's Law Review* 559

Duke, A, 'A Universal Duty of Good Faith: An Economic Perspective' (2007) 33 *Monash University Law Review* 182

Eisenberg, M, 'Relational Contracts' in Beatson, J and Friedmann, D (eds), *Good Faith and Fault in Contract Law* (Oxford, Clarendon Press, 2002)

—— 'The Responsive Model of Contract Law' (1984) 36 *Stanford Law Review* 1107

—— 'Why There is No Law of Relational Contracts' (2000) 94 *Northwestern University Law Review* 805

Eldridge, J and Pilkington, T (eds), *Australian Contract Law in the 21st Century* (Sydney, Federation Press, 2021)

Ellis, M, 'Utmost Good Faith: The Scope and Application of Section 13 of the Insurance Contracts Act in the Wake of *CGU v AMP*' (2009) 20 *Insurance Law Journal* 92

Falconer, C, *Opening Speech for the European Contract Law Conference* (London, 2005)

Farnsworth, A, 'Good Faith Performance and Commercial Reasonableness under the Uniform Commercial Code' (1962–63) 30 *University of Chicago Law Review* 666

Feinman, JM, 'Relational Contract Theory in Context' (2000) 94 *Northwestern University Law Review* 737

—— 'The Last Promissory Estoppel Article' (1992) 61 *Fordham Law Review* 303

—— 'Critical Approaches to Contract Law' (1983) 30 *UCLA Law Review* 829

Field, I, 'Good Faith Defences in Tort Law' (2016) 38 *Sydney Law Review* 147

—— 'Good Faith Protections and Public Sector Liability' (2016) 23 *Torts Law Journal* 210

Fifoot, CHS, *History and Sources of the Common Law Tort and Contract* (London, Steven & Sons, Limited, 1949)

Finn, PD (ed), *Essays on Contract* (Sydney, Law Book Company Ltd, 1987)

—— 'Equity and Contract' in Finn, PD (ed), *Essays on Contract* (Sydney, Law Book Co, 1987)

—— 'Commerce, the Common Law and Morality' (1989) 17 *Melbourne University Law Review* 87

Fleming, J, 'Tort in a Contractual Matrix' (1995) 33 *Osgoode Hall Law Journal* 661

Freire, J, 'Implied Obligation of Good Faith in Contracts: Only "Vulnerable" Parties Need Apply' (2006) 25 *Australian Resources and Energy Law Journal* 99

Fridman, GHL, 'The Interaction of Tort and Contract' (1977) 93 *Law Quarterly Review* 422

Fuller, LL and Purdue, WR, 'The Reliance Interest in Contract Damages' (1937) 46 *Yale Law Journal* 52

Gardner, J and J Murphy, J, 'Concurrent Liability in Contract and Tort: A Separation Thesis' (2021) 137 *Law Quarterly Review* 77

Gava, J, 'Do We Need a Hybrid Law of Contract? Why Hugh Collins is Wrong and Why it Matters' (2004) 63 *Cambridge Law Journal* 605

Getzler, J, 'Interpretation, Evidence and the Discovery of Contractual Intention' in Degeling, S, Edelman, J and Goudkamp, J (eds), *Contract in Commercial Law* (Sydney, LawBook Co, 2016)

Giancaspro, M, 'Renegotiation in the Real World: A Study of Australian Small to Medium-Sized Enterprises, Contract Variation and the Law' (2022) 41(3) *University of Queensland Law Journal* 299

Gillette, C, 'Limitations on the Obligation of Good Faith' (1981) 4 *Duke Law Journal* 619

Gilmore, G, *The Death of Contract* (Columbus, Ohio State University Press, 1974)

Glanville, R, *Tractatus de Legibus et Consuetudinibus Regni Angliae* (estimated to be published between 1180–90)

Gleeson, M, 'Individualised Justice – The Holy Grail' (1995) 69 *Australian Law Journal* 421

Gleeson, JT, Watson, JA and Peden, E (eds), *Historical Foundations of Australian Law – Volume II Commercial Common Law* (Sydney, Federation Press, 2013)
Godolphin, FRB (ed) and George Rawlinson (trans), 1 *The Greek Historians* (New York, Random House, 1942)
Goetz, C and Scott, R, 'Principles of Relational Contracts' (1981) 67(6) *Virginia Law Review* 1089
Goff, R, 'Commercial Contracts and the Commercial Court' [1984] *Lloyd's Maritime and Commercial Law Quarterly* 382
Golding, G, 'Employment as a Relational Contract and the Impact on Remedies for Breach' (2021) 30(2) *Griffith Law Review* 270
Gordon, R, 'Macaulay, Macneil and the Discovery of Solidarity and Power in Contract Law' [1985] *Wisconsin Law Review* 565
Gottlieb, G, 'Relationism: Legal Theory for a Relational Society' (1983) 50 *University of Chicago Law Review* 567
Gounari, Z, 'Developing a Relational Law of Contracts: Striking a Balance Between Abstraction and Contextualism' (2021) 41 *Legal Studies* 177
Gray, A, *Criminal Due Process and Chapter III of the Australian Constitution* (Sydney, Federation Press, 2016)
—— 'Relational Contract Theory, The Relevance of Actual Performance in Contractual Interpretation and its Application to Employment Contracts in the United Kingdom and Australia' (2023) 52 *Common Law World Review* 45
—— 'Recent Developments in Good Faith in Good Faith in Canada, the United Kingdom and Australia' (2015) 55(3) *Canadian Business Law Journal* 84
—— 'Good Faith in Australian Contract Law After Barker' (2015) 43 *Australian Business Law Review* 358
Grosman, B and Marcus, S, 'New Developments in Wrongful Dismissal Litigation' (1982) 60 *Canadian Bar Review* 656
Grotius, H, *De Jure Belli ac* Pacis (1625)
Gudel, P, 'Relational Contract Theory and the Concept of Exchange' (1998) 46 *Buffalo Law Review* 763
Guest, AC, 'Tort or Contract' (1961) 3 *University of Malaya Law Review* 191
Gurvitch, G, *Sociology of Law* (New York, Routledge, 1974)
Hale, M, *History of the Common Law of England* (Chicago, University of Chicago Press, 1971)
Han, YQ, 'Good Faith in Insurance Law: General and Independent, Not a Duty But an Interpretive Principle' (2017) 28 *Insurance Law Journal* 95
Harnett, B, 'The Doctrine of Concealment: A Remnant in the Law of Insurance' (1950) 15 *Law and Contemporary Problems* 391
Harrison, R, *Good Faith in Sales* (London, Sweet & Maxwell, 1997)
Hasson, RA, 'The Doctrine of Uberrima Fides in Insurance Law – A Critical Evaluation' (1969) 32 *Modern Law Review* 615
Havighurst, H and Berman, S, 'Requirement and Output Contracts' (1932) 27 *Illinois Law Review* 1
Herschaft, J, 'Not Your Average Coffee Shop: Lloyd's of London – A Twenty-First Century Primer on the History, Structure and Future of the Backbone of Marine Insurance' (2005) 29 *Tulane Maritime Law Journal* 169
Hiscock, M, 'The Keeper of the Flame: Good Faith and Fair Dealing in International Trade' (1996) 29 *Loyola Los Angeles Law Review* 1059
Hoffman, E and Spitzer, ML, 'The Coase Theorem: Some Experimental Tests' (1982) 25 *Journal of Law and Economics* 73
Holdsworth, W, *A History of English Law* 3rd edn (London, Sweet and Maxwell, 1945)
Holmes, E, 'A Contextual Study of Commercial Good Faith: Good-Faith Disclosure in Contract Formation' (1978) 39(3) *University of Pittsburgh Law Review* 381
Horwitz, MJ, 'The Historical Foundations of Modern Contract Law' (1974) 87(5) *Harvard Law Review* 917
Ibbetson, DJ, *A Historical Introduction to the Law of Obligations* (Oxford, Oxford University Press, 1999)

—— '*Coggs v Barnard*' in Mitchell, C and Mitchell, P (eds), *Landmark Cases in the Law of Contract* (Oxford, Hart, 2008)

Irvine, A, 'The Law: An Engine for Trade' (2001) 64 *Modern Law Review* 333

Jackman, A, 'Vulnerability, Autonomy and Protection: The Role of Actual and Hypothetical Contracts in the Duty of Care to Protect Against Pure Economic Loss' (2020) 49 *Australian Bar Review* 82

Jackman, I, 'Why the History of Restitution Matters' in Gleeson, JT, Watson, JA and Peden, E (eds), *Historical Foundations of Australian Law – Volume II Commercial Common Law* (Sydney, Federation Press, 2013)

Jackson, Sir R, *Does Good Faith Have any Role in Construction Contracts?*, Pinsent Mason Lecture, November 2017

Jennejohn, M, 'Contract Adjudication in a Collaborative Economy' (2010) 5(2) *Virginia Law and Business Review* 173

Jolis, C, Sunstein, C and Thaler, R, 'A Behavioural Approach to Law and Economics' (1998) 50 *Stanford Law Review* 1471

Jowell, J and Lester, A, 'Beyond Wednesbury: Substantive Principles of Administrative Law' [1987] *Public Law* 368

Justinian, *Digest*

Keynes, JM, *The End of Laissez-Faire* (London, Hogarth Press, 1926)

Kimel, D, 'The Choice of Paradigm for Theory of Contract: Reflections on the Relational Model' (2007) 27 *Oxford Journal of Legal Studies* 233

King, D, 'Reshaping Contract Theory and Law: Death of Contracts Part I' (1994) 7 *Journal of Contract Law* 245

—— 'Reshaping Contract Theory and Law: Death of Contracts Part II' (1995) 8 *Journal of Contract Law* 16

Kostritsky, J, 'Taxonomy for Justifying Legal Intervention in an Imperfect World: What to do When Parties Have Not Achieved Bargains or Have Drafted Incomplete Contracts' [2004] *Wisconsin Law Review* 323

Kreitner, R, 'Fault at the Contract-Tort Interface' (2009) 107 *Michigan Law Review* 1533

Kronman, AT, *Max Weber* (California, Stanford University Press, 1983)

Kuehne, G, 'Implied Obligations of Good Faith and Reasonableness in the Performance of Contracts: Old Wine in New Bottles' (2006) 33 *University of Western Australia Law Review* 63

Langille, B and Davidov, B, 'Beyond Employees and Independent Contractors: A View from Canada' (1991) 21 *Comparative Labor Law and Policy Journal* 7

Larkin, L, 'Uberrima Fides – Quo Vadis? Where to From Here? (1995) 7(2) *Bond Law Review* Article 2

Leggatt, LJ, *Lecture to the Commercial Bar Association*, 18 October 2016

Lidbetter, J, '"Third Time's a Charm": The Historical Development of Contract Law Through the English Forms of Action' (2022) 51 *Australian Bar Review* 357

Litvinoff, S, 'Good Faith' (1997) 71 *Tulane Law Review* 1645

Lowry, J, 'Redrawing the Parameters of Good Faith in Insurance Contracts' (2007) 60(1) *Current Legal Problems* 338

—— 'Whither the Duty of Good Faith in UK Insurance Contracts' (2009) 16 *Connecticut Insurance Law Journal* 97

Lucke, HK, 'Good Faith and Contractual Performance' in Finn, PD (eds), *Essays on Contract* (Sydney, Law Book Co, 1987)

McCamus, J, 'The New General Principles of Good Faith Performance and the New Rule of Honesty in Performance in Canadian Contract Law' (2015) 32 *Journal of Contract Law* 103

—— *The Law of Contracts* 2nd edn (Toronto, Irwin Law, 2012)

McGivern, B, 'A Tale of Two Duties: Utmost Good Faith and Reasonable Care' (2016) *27 Insurance Law Journal* 261

—— Coming to the Party: The Evolution of Post-Contractual Duties of Utmost Good Faith under the ICA' (2013) 24 *Insurance Law Journal* 159

McInnis, A, 'The New Engineering Contract: Relational Contracting, Good Faith and Co-Operation: Parts I and II' (2003) *International Construction Law Review* 128, 289
McLachlin, B, 'The Evolution of the Law of Private Obligation: The Influence of Justice La Forest' in Johnson, R et al, *Gerard V La Forest on the Supreme Court of Canada 1985–1997* (Winnipeg, Canadian Legal History Project, 2000)
McLaren, J, 'The Convergence of Tort and Contract: A Return to More Venerable Wisdom?' (1989) 68 *Canadian Bar Review* 30
McLaughlan, D, 'Contract Formation, Contract Interpretation and Subsequent Conduct' (2006) 25 *University of Queensland Law Journal* 77
—— 'The Continuing Confusion and Uncertainty Over the Relevance of Actual Mutual Intention in Contract Interpretation' (2021) 37 *Journal of Contract Law* 25
—— 'Contract Interpretation: What is it About?' (2009) 31 *Sydney Law Review* 5
—— 'The Contract That Neither Party Intends' (2012) 29 *Journal of Contract Law* 26
—— 'Common Assumptions and Contract Interpretation' (1997) 113 *Law Quarterly Review* 237
McMeel, G, 'Foucault's Pendulum: Text, Context and Good Faith in Contract Law' (2017) 70(1) *Current Legal Problems* 365
Macaulay, S, 'Non-Contractual Relations in Business: A Preliminary Study' (1963) 28(1) *American Sociological Review* 55
—— 'The Real and the Paper Deal: Empirical Pictures of Relationships, Complexity and the Urge for Transparent Simple Rules' (2003) 66 *Modern Law Review* 44
—— 'Relational Contracts: Floating on a Sea of Custom? Thoughts About the Ideas of Ian Macneil and Lisa Bernstein' (2000) 94(3) *Northwestern University Law Review* 775
—— 'An Empirical View of Contract' [1985] *Wisconsin Law Review* 465
Macdonnell, Sir J and Manson, E (eds), 2 *Great Jurists of the World* (Boston, Little, Brown and Co, Association of American Law Schools, 1914)
Macneil, I, 'Efficient Breach: Circles in the Sky' (1982) 68 *Virginia Law Review* 947
—— 'Values in Contract: Internal and External' (1983) 78(2) *Northwestern University Law Review* 340
—— 'The Many Futures of Contracts' (1974) 47 *Southern California Law Review* 691
—— 'Contracts: Adjustment of Long-Term Economic Relations Under Classical, Neoclassical and Relational Contract Law' (1978) 72(6) *Northwestern University Law Review* 854
—— 'Economic Analysis of Contractual Relations: Its Shortfalls and the Need for a "Rich Classificatory Apparatus"' (1981) 75(6) *Northwestern University Law Review* 1018
—— 'Relational Contract: What We Do and Do Not Know' (1985) *Wisconsin Law Review* 483
—— 'Restatement (Second) of Contracts and Presentiation' (1974) 60 *Virginia Law Review* 589
—— 'Relational Contract Theory: Challenges and Queries' (2000) 94(3) *Northwestern University Law Review* 877
—— 'Exchange Revisited: Individual Utility and Social Solidarity' (1986) 96(3) *Northwestern University Law Review* 567
—— *The New Social Contract: An Inquiry Into Modern Contractual Relations* (New Haven, Yale University Press, 1980)
Marwedel, WJ and Espinoza, SA, 'Dagger, Shield or Double-Edged Sword: The Reciprocal Nature of the Doctrine of Uberrimae Fidei' (2009) 83 *Tulane Law Review* 1163
Mason, A, 'Contract, Good Faith and Equitable Standards in Fair Dealing' (2000) 116 *Law Quarterly Review* 66
—— 'The Impact of Equitable Doctrine on the Law of Contract' (1998) 27 *Anglo-American Law Review* 1
Mason, K, 'Contract and Tort: Looking Across the Boundary form the Side of Contract' (1987) 61 *Australian Law Journal* 228
Mill, JS, O*n Liberty* (London, Longman, 1859)
Miller, A and Perry, R, 'Good Faith Performance' (2013) 98 *Iowa Law Review* 689
Millett, PJ, 'Equity's Place in the Law of Commerce' (1998) 114 *Law Quarterly Review* 214
Milsom, SFC, *Historical Foundations of the Common Law* 2nd edn (London, Butterworths, 1981)

Mitchell, C, *Contract Law and Contract Practice: Bridging the Gap Between Legal Reasoning and Commercial Expectation* (Oxford, Hart Publishing Ltd, 2013)
—— 'Contracts and Contract Law: Challenging the Distinction Between the "Real" and "Paper" Deal' (2009) 29(4) *Oxford Journal of Legal Studies* 675
Mitchell, C and Mitchell, P (eds), *Landmark Cases in the Law of Contract* (Oxford, Hart, 2008)
Morgan, J, *Contract Law Minimalism: A Formalist Restatement of Commercial Contract Law* (Cambridge, Cambridge University Press, 2013)
—— 'Liability for Independent Contractors in Contract and Tort: Duties to Ensure That Care is Taken' (2015) 74(1) *Cambridge Law Journal* 109
Mosey, D and Jackson, S, 'Good Faith and Relational Contracting – Do Enterprise Contracts Offer a Way Through the Woods?' (Society of Construction Law Paper, 2020)
Murphy, J, 'Hybrid Torts and Explanatory Tort Theory' (2018) 64 *McGill Law Journal* 1
Nicholas, B, *An Introduction to Roman Law* (Oxford, Clarendon Press, 1962)
Nicholls, D, 'My Kingdom for a Horse: The Meaning of Words' (2005) 121 *Law Quarterly Review* 577
O'Byrne, S and Cohen, R, 'The Conceptual Principle of Good Faith and the Duty of Honesty in Bhasin v Hrynew' (2015) 53 *Alberta Law Review* 1
O'Connor, JF, *Good Faith in English Law* (Aldershot, Dartmouth, 1991)
Oldham, J, 'Reinterpretations of 18th-Century English Contract Theory: The View from Lord Mansfield's Trial Notes' (1952) 76 *Georgetown Law Journal* 1949
O'Sullivan, J, 'Implied Terms in Fact and Evidence of Prior Negotiations: An Exploration' (2022) 138 *Law Quarterly Review* 558
Palay, T, 'Comparative Institutional Economics: The Governance of Rail Freight Contracting' (1984) 13 *Journal of Legal Studies* 265
Palmieri, N, 'Good Faith Disclosures Required During Precontractual Negotiations' (1993) 24 *Seton Hall Law Review* 70
Pastori, F, *Gli Istituti Romanistici Come Storia E Vita Del Diritto* 3rd edn (Milan, Cisalpino, 1992)
Patterson, E, 'Constructive Conditions in Contract' (1942) 42(6) *Columbia Law Review* 903
Peden, E, *Good Faith in the Performance of Contracts* (Sydney, LexisNexis Butterworths, 2003)
—— '"Cooperation" in English Contract Law – To Construe or Imply?' (2000) 16 *Journal of Contract Law* 56
—— 'Contractual Good Faith: Can Australia Benefit from the American Experience?' (2003) 15(2) *Bond Law Review* 186
—— 'When Common Law Trumps Equity: The Rise of Good Faith and Reasonableness and the Demise of Unconscionability' (2005) 21 *Journal of Contract Law* 226
Percy, A, 'The Emergence of Good Faith as a Principle of Contract Performance' in Degeling, S, Edelman, S and Goudkamp, J (eds), *Contract in Commercial Law* (Sydney, Law Book Co, 2016)
Phang, A, 'Tenders, Implied Terms and Fairness in the Law of Contract' (1998) 13 *Journal of Contract Law* 126
Plunkett, J, 'The Historical Foundations of the Duty of Care' (2015) 41 *Monash University Law Review* 716
Pollock, F and Maitland, F, *The History of English Law Vol 2 Before the Time of Edward I* (Cambridge, Cambridge University Press, 1895)
Pound, R, *Jurisprudence Volume 1* (St Paul, West Publishing, 1959)
Powell, R, 'Good Faith in Contracts' (1956) 9(1) *Current Legal Problems* 16
Prosser, WL, *Selected Topics on the Law of Torts* (Ann Arbor, University of Michigan, 1953)
Ramsay, I, 'Consumer Redress Mechanisms for Poor-Quality and Defective Products' (1981) 31 *University of Toronto Law Journal* 117
Razzolini, O, 'The Need to go Beyond the Contract: Economic and Bureaucratic Independence in Personal Work Relations' (2010) 31 *Comparative Labour Law and Policy Journal* 267
Reiter, BJ, 'Good Faith in Contracts' (1983) 17 *Valparaiso University Law Review* 705
Robertson, A, 'On the Distinction Between Contract and Tort' in Robertson, A, *The Law of Obligations: Connections and Boundaries* (London, UCL Press, 2004)
—— *The Law of Obligations: Connections and Boundaries* (London, UCL Press, 2004)

Robertson, JT, 'Good Faith as an Organising Principle in Contract Law: *Bhasin v Hrynew* – Two Steps Forward and One Look Back' (2015) 93 *Canadian Bar Review* 809
Rommen, HA, *The Natural Law: A Study in Legal and Social History and Philosophy* (St Louis, B Herder Book Co., 1947)
Sales, P, 'Use of Powers for Proper Purposes in Private Law' (2020) 136 *Law Quarterly Review* 384
Sayles, GO (ed), *Select Cases in the Court of Kings Bench* Under Edward III Vol 3 (London, Selden Society, 1939)
Schermaier, MJ, 'Bona Fides in Roman Contract Law' in Zimmermann, R and Whittaker, S (eds), *Good Faith in European Contract Law* (Cambridge, Cambridge University Press, 2000)
Schultz, F, 'The Firm Offer Puzzle: A Study of Business Practice in the Construction Industry' (1952) 19 *University of Chicago Law Review* 237
Scott, R, 'Conflict and Co-operation in Long-Term Contracts' (1987) 75 *California Law Review* 2005
—— 'The Death of Contract Law' (2004) 54 *University of Toronto Law Journal* 369
—— 'A Relational Theory of Default Rules for Commercial Contracts' (1990) 19 *Journal of Legal Studies* 597
—— 'The Case for Formalism in Relational Contract' (2000) 94(3) *Northwestern University Law Review* 847
Silverstein, J, 'The Contract Interpretation Policy Debate: A Primer' (2021) 26 *Stanford Journal of Law, Business and Finance* 222
Simon, H, 'A Behavioural Model of Rational Choice' (1955) 69 *Quarterly Journal of Economics* 99
Simpson, AWB, 'The Horwitz Thesis and the History of Contracts' (1979) 46(3) *University of Chicago Law Review* 533
—— *A History of the Common Law of Contract: The Rise of the Action of Assumpsit* (Oxford, Clarendon Press, 1987)
Smith, A, *The Wealth of Nations* (New York, Bantam Classic, 2003)
—— *The Theory of Moral Sentiments* (Raphael and Macfie ed, Oxford, University Press, 1976)
Smith, M, 'Rectification of Contracts for Common Mistake, Joscelyne v Nissen, and Subjective States of Mind' (2007) 123 *Law Quarterly Review* 116
Spelman, Sir H, *Of the Law Terms* (1684)
Spigelman, J, 'From Text to Context: Contemporary Contractual Interpretation' (2007) 81 *Australian Law Journal* 322
Stapleton, J, 'Good Faith in Private Law' (1999) 52(1) *Current Legal Problems* 1
—— 'Comparative Economic Loss: Lessons from Case-Law Focussed "Middle Theory"' (2002) 50(2) *University of California Los Angeles Law Review* 531
Stevens, R, 'Objectivity, Mistake and the Parol Evidence Rule' in Burrows, A and Peel, E (eds), *Contract Terms* (Oxford, Oxford University Press, 2007)
Stewart, A, 'Redefining Employment? Meeting the Challenge of Contract and Agency Labour' (2002) 15 *Australian Journal of Labour Law* 1
Stewart, A and McCrystal, S, 'Labour Regulation and the Great Divide: Does the Gig Economy Require a New Category of Worker?' (2019) 32 *Australian Journal of Labour Law* 4
Steyn, J, 'Interpretation, Legal Texts and their Landscape' in Markesinis, BS (ed), *The Clifford Chance Millennium Lectures* (Oxford, Hart, 2000)
—— 'The Role of Good Faith and Fair Dealing in English Contract Law: A Hairshirt Philosophy?' (1991) 6 *Denning Law Journal* 131
—— 'Contract Law: Fulfilling the Reasonable Expectations of Honest Men' (1997) 113 *Law Quarterly Review* 433
—— 'The Intractable Problem of the Interpretation of Legal Texts' (2003) 25 *Sydney Law Review* 5
—— *Democracy Through Law: Select Speeches and Judgments* (Ashgate, Routledge, 2004)
Stratton, H, 'The Uncertain Boundary Between Contract and Tort' (2021) 137 *Law Quarterly Review* 222
Stoljar, S, 'Prevention and Co-Operation in the Law of Contract' (1953) 31(3) *Canadian Bar Review* 231
Summers, R, '"Good Faith" in General Contract Law and the Sales Provisions of the Uniform Commercial Code' (1968) 54(2) *Virginia Law Review* 195

—— 'The General Duty of Good Faith – Its Recognition and Conceptualization' (1982) 67 *Cornell Law Review* 810
Tay, C, 'The Duty of Disclosure and Materiality in Insurance Contracts – A True Descendant of the Duty of Utmost Good Faith?' (2002) 13 *Insurance Law Journal* 1
Trebilcock, MJ, *The Limits of Freedom of Contract* (Cambridge, Harvard University Press, 1993)
Swain, W, 'Reshaping Contractual Unfairness in England 1670–1900' (2014) 35 *Journal of Legal History* 120
—— 'Equitable Doctrine, Fairness and the Law of Contract in Australia' in Eldridge, J and Pilkington, T (eds), *Australian Contract Law in the 21st Century* (Sydney, Federation Press, 2021)
—— '"The Steaming Lungs of a Pigeon": Predicting the Direction of Australian Contract Law I the Next 25 Years' in Barker, K, Fairweather, K and Grantham, R (eds), *Private Law in the 21st Century* (Oxford, Hart Publishing, 2017)
Swan, A, 'The Obligation to Perform in Good Faith: Comment on *Bhasin v Hrynew*' (2015) 56 *Canadian Business Law Journal* 395
Swanton, J, 'The Convergence of Tort and Contract' (1989) 12 *Sydney Law Review* 40
Tan, ZX, 'Disrupting Doctrine: Revisiting the Doctrine Impact of Relational Contract Theory' (2019) 39 *Legal Studies* 98
Tarr, A and Tarr, J, 'The Insured's Non-Disclosure in the Formation of Insurance Contracts: A Comparative Perspective' (2001) 50 *International and Comparative Law Quarterly* 577
Tarr, J and Van Akkeren, J, 'Accountability for Good Faith in Commercial Dealing: The *Carter v Boehm* Legacy 250 Years On' (2016) 27 *Insurance Law Journal* 275
Tete, WT, 'Tort Roots and Ramifications of the Obligations Revision' (1986) 32 *Loyola Law Review* 47
Tetley, W, 'Good Faith in Contract: Particularly in the Contracts of Arbitration and Chartering' (2004) 35 *Journal of Maritime Law and Commerce* 561
Teubner, G, 'Legal Irritants: Good Faith in British Law or How Unifying Law Ends Up in New Divergences' (1998) 61 *Modern Law Review* 11
Thomas, P, 'Late Republican (R)evolutions in Roman Law' (2020) 65 *SUBBiur*
Tipping, A, 'Obligations in Contract, Tort and Equity: Reliance, Responsibility, and the Moral Dimension: Essay in Honour of Sir John McGrath' (2021) 52 *Victoria University of Wellington Law Review* 643
Trebilcock, MJ, *The Limits of Freedom of Contract* (Cambridge, Harvard University Press, 1994)
Triggiano, A, *Holistic Analysis of Law, Connecting Theory and Practice: Universal Solutions to Global Problems* (Newcastle, Cambridge Scholars Publishing, 2023)
Trubek, DM, 'Reconstructing Max Weber's Sociology of Law' (1985) 37 *Stanford Law Review* 919
—— 'Max Weber's Tragic Modernism and the Study of Law in Society' (1986) 20 *Law and Society Review* 573
Unger, RM, 'The Critical Legal Studies Movement' (1983) 96 *Harvard Law Review* 561
Varuhas, J, 'The Socialisation of Private Law: Balancing Private Right and Public Good' (2021) 137 *Law Quarterly Review* 141
Wallwork, A, 'A Requirement of Good Faith in Construction Contracts' (2004) 20 *Building and Construction Law Journal* 257
Warren, M, 'Good Faith: Where Are We At?' (2010) 34 *Melbourne University Law Review* 344
Weber, M, *Economy and Society: An Outline of Interpretive Sociology* (Berkeley, University of California Press, G Roth and C Wittich ed, reprinted 1978)
Weintraub, R, 'A Survey of Contract Practice and Policy' [1992] *Wisconsin Law Review* 1
Williston, S, 'Freedom of Contract' (1921) 6 *Cornell Law Quarterly* 365
Winfield, P, *Province of the Law of Tort* (Cambridge, Cambridge University Press, 1931)
Yee, WP, 'The Duty of Disclosure – Proposals for Reform' (2000) 21 *Singapore Law Review* 100
Yihan, G and Yip, M, 'Concurrent Liability in Tort and Contract: An Analysis of Interplay, Intersection and Independence (2017) 24 *Torts Law Journal* 148
Zimmermann, R, *The Law of Obligations Roman Foundations of the Civilian Tradition* (Oxford, Oxford University Press, 1990)

INDEX

www.ingramcontent.com/pod-product-compliance
Ingram Content Group UK Ltd.
Pitfield, Milton Keynes, MK11 3LW, UK
UKHW020245290926
15470UKWH00002B/747